GW00674469

WATERLOO

THE DECISIVE VICTORY

OSPREY
PUBLISHING

WATERLOO

THE DECISIVE VICTORY

EDITED BY COLONEL NICK LIPSCOMBE

WATERLOO 200

1815 - 2015

A DEFINING MOMENT IN EUROPEAN HISTORY

CONTENTS

LIST OF CONTRIBUTORS

Peter Snow CBE is a highly respected journalist, author and broadcaster. Educated at Wellington College and Balliol College, Oxford, he joined ITN as a reporter in 1962, where he was the Diplomatic and Defence Correspondent. In 1980 he became the first presenter of *Newsnight* and went on to cover elections and live political events for the BBC. In 2002, in order to mark the 60th anniversary of the Battle of Alamein, Peter and his son Dan, also a historian, made a programme for BBC 2, which led to them presenting two further series – *Battlefield Britain* and *The World's 20th Century Battlefields*; both of which are accompanied by books of the same title. Peter is the author of a number of books, including *To War With Wellington: From the Peninsula to Waterloo* (2010) and *When Britain Burned the White House: The 1814 Invasion of Washington* (2013).

Jeremy Black MBE is Professor of History at the University of Exeter. Graduating from Cambridge with a starred first, he did post-graduate work at Oxford, and then taught at Durham, eventually as professor, before moving to Exeter in 1996. He has lectured extensively in Australia, Canada, Denmark, France, Germany, Italy, New Zealand and the USA, where he has held visiting chairs at West Point, Texas Christian University and Stillman College. A past Council member of the Royal Historical Society, Black is a Senior Fellow of the Foreign Policy Research Institute. He was appointed to the Order of Membership of the British Empire for services to stamp design. He is or has been on a number of editorial boards including the Journal of Military History, and he is the author of over 100 books, with particular focus on 18th century British politics and international relations. Publications include *The Power of Knowledge: How Information and Technology Made the Modern World* (2014) and *War in the Nineteenth Century: 1800–1914* (2009).

Julian Spilsbury is an ex-regular soldier, and is the author of several books including major works on both the Crimean War and the Indian Mutiny. A TV scriptwriter, he writes many of the military obituaries that appear in the *Daily Telegraph*. Julian has written scripts for popular television programmes, and is a very popular tour guide as well as being extremely knowledgeable and entertaining, as anyone who has been on any of the tours following Napoleon's campaigns will tell you.

Philip Haythornthwaite is an internationally respected author and historical consultant specialising in the military history, uniforms and equipment of the 18th and 19th centuries. His main area of research covers the Napoleonic Wars. He has written some 40 books, including more than 20 titles for Osprey Publishing, and numerous articles and papers on military history – but still finds time to indulge in his other great passion, cricket.

Mark Adkin was educated at Bedford School and served in the British Army for 14 years, which included active service in Malaya and Aden. On leaving the army he joined the Overseas Civil Service and was posted to the British Solomon Islands, and spent many years based in Tarawa. His final posting was as a contract officer with the Barbados Defence Force, and it was as Caribbean operations staff officer that he participated in the American invasion of Grenada in 1983. It was this experience that led him to write his first book, *Urgent Fury*, which described the Grenada operation as he saw it. Since returning to the UK he has lived in Bedford, devoting much of his time to writing military history books. He has had 14 books published, including the popular *Waterloo, Trafalgar, Gettysburg* and *Western Front Companions*. Major Adkin is married and a fellow of the International Napoleonic Society.

Natalia Griffon de Pleineville was born in 1977 in Petrozavodsk, Russia. She is Editor-in-Chief of the history magazines *Prétorien, Tradition* and *Gloire & Empire*, as well as a lecturer and translator. She is the author of numerous articles and books on military history of the First Empire. A specialist on the Peninsular War, in 2009 she published a detailed study of Napoleon's campaign against Sir John Moore's British Army in 1808–09 entitled *La Corogne, les Aigles en Galice*, and in 2012 another Peninsular War book, *Chiclana-Barrosa 5 March 1811: the Eagles in Andalusia*. She lives near Paris, France.

Nick Lipscombe has always had a passionate interest in the Napoleonic Wars. After a 34-year career in the British Army, during which time he saw considerable operational service and was awarded the US Bronze Star, he now concentrates on writing and running tours to the Napoleonic battlefields. His first book, *The*

Peninsular War Atlas (2010), was selected as the *Daily Telegraph* (History) Book of the Year. He is Chairman of Peninsular War 200, the UK official organisation for the commemoration of the bicentenary of the war, a member of the Waterloo 200 Committee and a Trustee of the British Cemetery at Elvas, Portugal. He speaks German and Spanish and lives in Spain with his wife: they have three daughters.

Ian Fletcher is one of the leading authorities on the Peninsular War and Wellington's Army. Born in London in 1957, his first book, *In Hell Before Daylight*, was published in 1984, and since then he has written or edited almost 30 others. Ian first visited the battlefield of Waterloo in 1978 and travelled to the Iberian Peninsula for the first time in 1983. He now runs his own battlefield tour company (www.ifbt.co.uk), but still manages to continue writing, as well as work on other projects. He worked on the BBC's *Decisive Weapons* series, The History Channel's *Line of Fire* and *Sharpe's War* series and Channel 4's series on *Revolutionary Armies*. He is a Fellow of the International Napoleonic Society.

Charles Esdaile currently holds a Personal Chair in the Department of History in the University of Liverpool and is the Academic Vice-President of Peninsular War 200. Best known for his numerous works on the Peninsular War of 1808–14, he has also written extensively on the Napoleonic period in general, contributing numerous articles on the subject. His publications include *Outpost of Empire: The Napoleonic Occupation of Andalucia, 1810–1812* (2012) and *The Peninsular War: A New History* (2003).

Andrew Field MBE has recently retired after an army career that stretched over 36 years. He has been a student of the Napoleonic Wars for even longer, with a particular interest in Napoleon's *Grande Armée*, his campaign in Northern France in 1814 and Waterloo. His publications include *Waterloo: The French Perspective* (2012) and *Prelude to Waterloo: Quatre Bras – the French Perspective* (2014) exploring the Waterloo campaign from a French viewpoint, drawing on many accounts of French participants previously unpublished in English.

Huw Davies has been a lecturer in Defence Studies since March 2005. He gained his PhD from the University of Exeter in 2006, and, in addition to numerous articles on Napoleonic military history, his first book, *Wellington's Wars: The Making of a Military Genius*, was published by Yale University Press in 2012. He is also contracted to write a history of the First Anglo-Afghan War for Harvard University Press, and is currently researching the rise of British military power between 1754 and 1815.

FOREWORD

HIS GRACE, THE DUKE OF WELLINGTON

K.G., L.V.O., O.B.E., M.C., D.L.

My heart is broken by the terrible loss I have sustained in my old friends and companions and my poor soldiers. I always say that next to a battle lost the greatest misery is a battle gained.

Wellington's grief on the evening after one of the most decisive battles in the history of the world was indisputable. In the immediate aftermath of the gargantuan struggle, the magnitude and repercussions of the Allied victory were too premature to grasp. In the battlefields just south of Wellington's small headquarters in the village of Waterloo, 48,000 men and 40,000 horses lay dead or wounded.

In the two hundred years since that defining battle there have been thousands of books which have considered the campaign, the battle and the aftermath in exquisite detail. This book is no exception. Ten international experts have focused on certain key and specific aspects of this extraordinary clash of arms and have drawn some new and interesting conclusions as a result.

This work is part of the bicentenary commemorations of what was arguably Britain's greatest land battle but, as with the other aspects of Waterloo commemoration, it has not been approached in the context of triumphalism. It is, like the battle itself, a representation of alliance and cooperation and is warmly applauded.

Wellington

INTRODUCTION

PETER SNOW

PREVIOUS
The turning point in the battle, when the Duke of Wellington hears that Prussian help is on the way. Victory and the end of 20 years of war are in sight. (Rijksmuseum)

A depiction of the storming of the Tuileries Palace on 10 August 1792 by Jean Duplessis-Bertaux. The French Revolution of 1789 had led to a mobilisation of people behind a national cause as never before, and Europe's nations found themselves fighting for their survival. (Public domain)

Few events in human memory have had the impact of Waterloo. The titanic struggle that took place on a small ridge near Brussels on 18 June 1815 is implanted as one of history's unforgettable landmarks. No image captivated me as a schoolboy more forcibly than the moment when Wellington, at the climax of the battle, called out to the commander of his 1st Brigade of Guards, 'Now Maitland, now's your time!' The next few minutes decided the future of Europe. Napoleon's advancing Imperial Guards, undefeated in 20 years of conflict, saw long lines of redcoats suddenly rise to their feet only metres ahead of them. The devastating volley from British muskets that followed was the turning point that Andrew Field vividly recalls in this book with his chapter, *La Garde Recule*. It was the most dramatic moment in the first and only clash between two of the world's greatest commanders, the Duke of Wellington and the French Emperor Napoleon. And it was decisive. Waterloo finally shattered the dreams of the man who sought to dominate Europe, and secured a lasting peace.

Post-war negotiations established a broad balance of national interests which postponed another continent-wide upheaval for a century. For the hundred years of comparative calm that followed people remembered Waterloo as the

battle that ended what for them was the 'great war'. Even after the far more catastrophic wars of the 20th century people saw Waterloo as an ultimate moment, a single conclusive clash that ended at a stroke two decades of conflict.

And European culture was deeply affected too. The horror of the battlefield that saw 45,000 dead and wounded, the passionate eyewitness accounts, the unique grandeur of the commanders inspired writers and poets like Victor Hugo, Walter Scott, Tennyson and Byron. The battle has lent its name to streets, monuments, whole precincts, to Britain's busiest railway station and even to popular songs like Abba's 1974 triumph in the Eurovision song contest. The very word Waterloo evokes that moment in life when each of us faces an ultimate challenge.

This book illuminates Waterloo's bicentenary. It is a collaborative project: Waterloo 200, the committee established to commemorate the battle's 200th anniversary, and Osprey, Britain's leading military publisher, have combined to invite those who know the story best to re-examine it. Every student of military history relishes the controversy that surrounds a great battle, and none has provoked it in such abundance as Waterloo. Was it a battle more lost by Napoleon Bonaparte or won by the Allies? Would the Allied commander the Duke of Wellington have won if Prussia's Marshal Blücher had not turned up until later? How far did Wellington risk losing by delaying in Brussels and failing to help Blücher on 16 June? Was it fair of Napoleon to blame Grouchy and other French commanders for his defeat? What mistakes were made by the cavalry on either side?

All of these and many other issues are tackled in this book by an array of military historians who have already made striking contributions to the study of the Napoleonic Wars.

Warfare in 1815 had changed little from a century earlier but it was utterly different from the massive industrial wars of machine guns, tanks, aircraft and telecommunication that followed a hundred years later. It was far more primitive. The horse was the fastest means of travel and the musket was still the primary infantry weapon – with an effective range of little more than 50 metres. This meant that battlefields were little larger than they had been in the middle ages.

What was different from earlier wars was that the French Revolution of 1789 had led to a mobilisation of people behind a national cause as never before, and Europe's nations found themselves fighting for their survival. Millions died as French armies and their opponents marched and counter-marched across the continent from Lisbon to Moscow. Until 1812 Napoleon, who had risen from artillery commander during the Revolution to Emperor of France in 1805, had looked unstoppable. He controlled just about all of Europe except Britain and Russia. But then, like Hitler more than a century later, he took a step too far. He led an army of half a million into Russia and emerged with only 25,000 men. With Britain's financial help the countries of Eastern Europe mustered an army that defeated Napoleon at Leipzig in 1813 and he was forced into abdication and exile in the spring of 1814. But the Allies made the mistake of banishing him only to the island of Elba, 160 kilometres from the south of France. In March 1815, as the victors haggled over the future shape of Europe in Vienna, Napoleon landed in France and found enough support there to seize back power from the king and whip up enthusiasm for a new campaign against the Allies.

Surprised and horrified, the Allies, Britain, Russia, Prussia and Austria, appointed Wellington the commander of the frontline army in Brussels. He was to be in action within 100 days of Napoleon's return. Napoleon set himself the task of destroying the Allies piecemeal before they could put together an army so strong that he would have no chance. Wellington in Brussels had not yet joined up with Marshal Blücher's Prussian Army advancing from the east. Napoleon seized his opportunity and crossed the border into what is now Belgium on 15 June 1815.

Jeremy Black – in our first chapter – analyses the strategic background to the three days of fighting that followed. By bursting back to power in France with the obvious intention of renewing the war against the rest of Europe that he had fought for two decades, Napoleon swept away any differences and tensions between the Allies. The speed and audacity of his military thrust towards Brussels confirmed their conviction that peace with him was impossible. They had been working on what would have been a generous settlement for France but Napoleon's return united them in forthright opposition and provoked massive mobilisation. War was inevitable and Black highlights what he calls the strategic asymmetry between Napoleon and his opponents. Napoleon had to win, and win dramatically, while Wellington only needed to avoid serious defeat. Wellington and the approaching Prussians were not the only military counter to Napoleon's offensive. There were at least 300,000 Russians and Austrians mustering to confront Napoleon if he crushed Wellington and Blücher.

Julian Spilsbury picks up the story of Napoleon's first encounter with the Prussians inside Belgium. The French success in foiling any attempt by Britain and Prussia to link up their two armies on 16 June prompts Spilsbury to pronounce that first day of fighting an 'overall' success for Napoleon. But Blücher was able to limp off the battlefield of Ligny where his army had been crippled but not decisively defeated. Poor communication between Napoleon and Marshal Ney, who was tasked with stopping Wellington at Quatre Bras, robbed the French of outright victory over the Prussians. The misunderstanding resulted in a whole corps of more than 20,000 men under Count d'Erlon marching and counter-marching between the two battlefronts without having the opportunity to fight on either. This failure allowed Blücher to make what Spilsbury calls a 'clean break' on the night of the 16th. Furthermore Napoleon failed to follow up his success at Ligny by pursuing Blücher and pressing hard on the heels of Wellington's withdrawal from Quatre Bras on the 17th.

Spilsbury – as well as other contributors – also tackles the issue of the Prussians' decision to retire not from the field altogether but to an area – around the town of Wavre – from which they could assist Wellington if he chose to do battle a day or two later. He did just that – at Waterloo on the 18th – and he did so for the very reason that he felt he could rely on the Prussians. Blücher promised him generous reinforcement, which did,

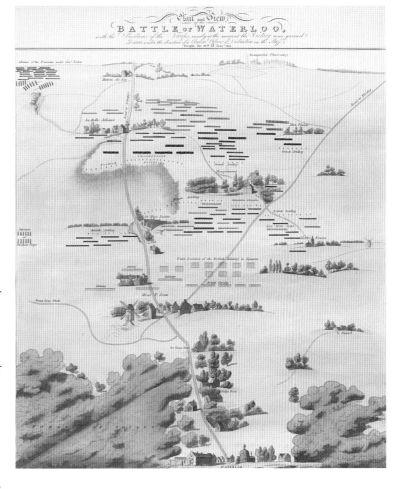

The plan for the Battle of Waterloo, looking south, depicting the positions of all the troops before battle was commenced. (Rijksmuseum)

eventually, arrive in time to intervene before the end of the day. Wellington later thanked Blücher for his 'timely assistance'. But how was that key Prussian decision made? Did Blücher's chief of staff General Gneisenau make the essential commitment to stay within reach of Wellington or was it Blücher himself in spite of Gneisenau declaring his reluctance? Spilsbury indicates that while Blücher was out of action after being crushed by his horse at Ligny, Gneisenau ordered a retreat to Wavre but kept open the option of a further retreat to the north-east. Esdaile writes that Gneisenau plumped for Wavre for a number of reasons and that the order was 'vigorously confirmed by Blücher'. Haythornthwaite is unequivocal: Blücher's 'iron will was crucial' in the decision to keep within reach of Wellington. Whoever it was who played the critical role in the decision, Wellington was in no doubt of his debt to the Prussians when he said later that their action was the decisive moment of the century.

In their analysis of the decisive battle on the ridge of Mont Saint Jean near Waterloo on 18 June, few of our contributors see any fault in Wellington's leadership. He certainly overstated his dismay at being saddled with what he described as an 'infamous army'. It was only one third British and of those only a few were units which had helped him win the Peninsular War between 1808 and 1814. Mark Adkin says Wellington's concerns about the likely performance of the Dutch, Belgian and German units which formed the majority of his command were 'largely unjustified'. The duke went to great lengths to stiffen the fibre of his foreign troops by mixing them with British formations right along his front. And he was in the end well served by the men who were not British. The King's German Legion, who exclusively provided the garrison of the vital farmhouse at La Haye Sainte, in the centre of the British line, fought valiantly throughout the day and were only forced to withdraw under massive French pressure when Wellington's staff failed to replenish the Legion's ammunition supply.

But the duke wins praise from all contributors for his determination always to be where he was most needed in the action at great personal risk. His overall strategy derived from his string of successes in the defensive battles he had fought in the Peninsula – Vimeiro, Talavera, Bussaco and Fuentes D'Onoro. He would place his main forces just behind the brow of the ridge and his skirmishers would command the view forward and alert him of any attack. Most of his men would thus be out of sight of French artillery gunners and ready to leap up with bayonets fixed at any enemy advance that exposed itself as it reached the top of the incline.

To protect his flanks and his centre he stationed men in some strength in two farmhouses which were on the forward – downward – slope in front of his position. The key one – Hougoumont on his right flank – he considered of ultimate importance in foiling any attempt by Napoleon to outmanoeuvre him to the right. He was less concerned about his left flank where he expected the Prussians to come to his assistance. Nick Lipscombe describes the desperate and bloody fighting that took place in each of these outposts and how the loss of La Haye Sainte in the late afternoon nearly cost Wellington the battle.

All contributors reckon Napoleon did much to bring about his own defeat. His health, which he could do little about, did much to weaken him. He was not the man who had displayed such energy and visible leadership as in his great victories at Marengo and Austerlitz. Haythornthwaite mentions cystitis and haemorrhoids, but Napoleon never alluded to his health as a weakness. Nor did he blame his own leadership for his defeat. In a particularly mean-minded memoir which he wrote in final exile on the island of St Helena, he singled out two of his subordinates, Marshal Michel Ney and Marshal Emmanuel de Grouchy.

They were indeed responsible for many of the mistakes, but they were, after all, his own appointments, as was Marshal Nicolas Soult,★ who Spilsbury, Haythornthwaite and Adkin agree was a poor substitute for the exemplary Louis-Alexandre Berthier as his chief of staff. If Ney's co-ordination of the great infantry and cavalry charges was at fault – as Fletcher and Lipscombe suggest and as Captain Lemonnier-Delafosse attests in Natalia Griffon de Pleineville's chapter – and if Grouchy's shadowing of the Prussians was incompetent, the mistake was Napoleon's in giving them their jobs. Napoleon noticeably did not directly blame his brother Jérôme who failed to capture the farm at Hougoumont and then persisted in throwing battalion after battalion into the fight without effect. The result was an insupportable number of casualties.

But there are more reasons for criticising Napoleon's conduct of his army, which are analysed in detail in this book. For those who have studied the agility of Napoleon's tactics in his previous campaigns, his readiness to manoeuvre and combine attacks by infantry and cavalry and his emphasis on gunnery, the surprise is how little he deployed these skills at Waterloo. It surprised Wellington too. The battle, he famously remarked, was fought in the old style and he won it in the old style.

Broadly we can divide the Battle of Waterloo into five phases: the opening French attack on Wellington's right at Hougoumont, the massed infantry assault on Wellington's left centre that prompted the charge of the British heavy cavalry, the French cavalry assaults on Wellington's centre right, the Prussian attacks on Napoleon's right, and the final assault by the French Imperial Guard that ended in defeat.

Nick Lipscombe assesses the value to both sides of Hougoumont where the French lost thousands of men in a struggle that failed to break Wellington's grip on the farm. Wellington thought Hougoumont was vital, and when its British defenders slammed shut the northern gate, which had been briefly forced open by a French assault, Wellington was later to remark that 'the success of the battle of Waterloo' depended 'upon the closing of the gates at Hougoumont'.[1] Lipscombe recognises the importance of Hougoumont but believes that the farm at La Haye Sainte in the centre of Wellington's position was more critical to Wellington's defence. The French capture of the farm was largely the result of what Lipscombe calls the 'indefensible blunder' of allowing its ammunition supply to dry up. The farm fell, exposing Wellington's centre to possible fracture from the French artillery that promptly moved forward. However, the opportunity this offered for a decisive attack on Wellington's centre was missed

★   Although many sources give Soult's first name as Nicolas it does not appear on his birth certificate. He is also known as Jean de Dieu.

A small example of two big men: a post-Waterloo illustration depicting Wellington and Blücher playing badminton with 'shuttlecock Napoleon'. (Rijksmuseum)

when Napoleon rejected Ney's appeal for more troops – a moment that Andrew Field discusses in his chapter on the final phase of Waterloo.

Ian Fletcher takes up the story of the next episode in the battle in the early afternoon when the British faced an overwhelming attack by d'Erlon's infantry. Fletcher says that this assault was almost successful. It reached the brow of the hill just behind which Wellington had stationed his line of defending infantry. It was the timely action by Lord Uxbridge's heavy cavalry that effectively rescued the British infantry. As few as 2,300 sabre-armed horsemen of the Union and Household Brigades ploughed into d'Erlon's 15,000 attackers and scattered them. And this action meant that Wellington suffered no other attack on his left centre for the rest of the day. Fletcher points out that other historians have frowned on this heavy cavalry attack condemning its cost in British lives, but, he suggests, they have misinterpreted the casualty figures. They represent the whole day's total not just the toll of this one single episode. Fletcher concludes that far from deserving the label 'little short of disastrous', the British cavalry charges were 'largely successful'.

But he agrees with most historians in describing the next great phase in the battle – the massed charges of the French cavalry on Wellington's centre right – as 'an unmitigated disaster'. Marshal Ney sent a series of waves of French cavalry against Wellington's infantry which rapidly formed squares on the ridge and in the area behind it. They failed to break a single square.

Wellington's guns and the relentless musket fire of the foot-soldiers directed at the French horsemen swirling around them took a toll of Napoleon's cavalry that in the end became insupportable. Remarkably neither Ney nor Napoleon ordered any French infantry or artillery support for the thousands of cuirassiers and other riders who threw themselves again and again into the maelstrom on the ridge. The fruitless cavalry assaults went on for two hours and gave Wellington an immensely valuable breathing space. Every minute that passed brought more and more of Blücher's Prussians into the battle.

Charles Esdaile reviews the assessments historians have made of the role of the Prussians at Waterloo. He recounts how the weather and ground conditions delayed the Prussian advance and points out that Count Bülow, who led the spearhead corps of the Prussian Army against Napoleon's right at Plancenoit, was inclined to be cautious: a reluctance that had Blücher angrily urging him on. No one doubts that Blücher's single-minded determination to throw in as many of his men as soon as he could was a valuable contributor to the Allies' victory. But was it decisive? On one side of the argument are the experts whom Esdaile describes as 'Anglo-centric'. They say Blücher made only a marginal difference to Wellington who was set to win anyway. At the other extreme are those like the respected annalist of the campaign David Chandler who believe that Wellington would have lost Waterloo if the Prussians had not arrived. Esdaile plants himself somewhere in between. He says that while we can never know what would have happened if the Prussians had not shown up when they did, it would be wrong to pretend that they did not play 'an important role' at Waterloo. Wellington himself was generous in his praise of Blücher at the time but later, as Peter Hofshröer has detailed in his controversial book *Wellington's Smallest Victory*, he was seen as attempting to downgrade the Prussian contribution. It remains the most hotly argued issue about Waterloo.

Andrew Field addresses the critical last two hours of the battle from the moment La Haye Sainte was captured by the French at around 6 p.m. to the final rout of the Imperial Guard. With Napoleon facing increasing pressure from the Prussians, the capture of La Haye Sainte presented him with a major opportunity. Field argues there is no doubt that if the French emperor had launched 'a final desperate attack' at that stage, Wellington could have faced defeat. But when Ney asked him for the troops to make the move, Napoleon shook his head and asked where were the troops? Napoleon judged he could not spare the men; part of his Imperial Guard had to be shifted to Plancenoit to stop the Prussians. In his desperation he sent one of his generals off to spread the word that the advancing army on his right flank was not the Prussians but

Grouchy speeding to the rescue. It was a stratagem that may have briefly heartened the troops on his other flank but it clearly ran the risk of utterly disheartening them when they discovered the truth. Within an hour they did indeed learn the truth and it had the disastrous effect on morale that Natalia Griffon de Pleineville describes in her chapter.

It wasn't until around 7 p.m. when the fight with the Prussians had stabilised somewhat that Napoleon felt able to spare the men. Field tells us that Napoleon sent nine battalions, six from the Middle Guard and three from the Old Guard into this final assault. The Middle Guard were to attack first with the Old Guard held back in reserve. The Middle Guard battalions then advanced in five squares each side three men deep. Field calculates that this formation meant that the frontage of each of the battalions was a mere 45 men. Such tight-packed units might have had a powerful impact and were easier to control in the awkward and muddy terrain, but only a few dozen muskets could be levelled at the British enemy ahead. However, Field says, the superb discipline and experience of the Guard allowed their commander to accept the risk of attacking in this formation: they could always fan out into line if they wanted to achieve maximum firepower.

The clashes that followed between Napoleon's veterans and Wellington's men on the ridgeline marked the decisive phase of the battle. At times, Field tells us, the Guards seemed close to breaking through. But without the assistance of skirmishes and supporting cavalry and with unrelenting fire from the massed Allied artillery deployed along the ridge, the Middle Guard's advance was halted and then reversed. Further along the line the French squares approaching Major General Maitland's British Guards were surprised by the sudden appearance of what Field describes as a 'wall of red soldiers'. Wellington himself gave Maitland the order to fire. Field has eyewitnesses on both sides describing the final savage struggle that followed. The French attack wavered and the coup de grace was delivered by Colonel John Colborne's 52nd Regiment which loosed off a withering fire at the flank of the 4th Chasseurs – on the French left. The French retreat turned into a rout. But Charles Esdaile reminds us that there is still a debate as to whether the British or the Prussians can claim responsibility for the knockout blow. The Prussians claim that it was the added punch of the arrival of Lieutenant General von Zieten's Corps that sent the French flying. Esdaile reckons it was probably a 'coincidence' that the Prussian breakthrough on Wellington's left matched the breakthrough that the duke himself initiated on his right.

It is the abundance of primary source material, the unprecedented number of eyewitnesses – more than in any other previous campaign in history – that brings Wellington's campaigns so vividly alive. It is the candour and spontaneity of their evidence that draws so many enthusiasts for history to study Waterloo and that prompted me to write *To War with Wellington – from the Peninsula to Waterloo* (published by John Murray in 2010). And Natalia Griffon de Pleineville in her chapter in this book analyses the rewards – and the pitfalls – of relying on these eyewitness accounts. She emphasises that those who write in the immediate aftermath of an action are likely to be closer to the truth than those who write months or years afterwards. Even a few days can dull the memory. And while private soldiers and non-commissioned officers are more prone to write accurately and with sincerity, they lack the broader overview of people of a higher rank. However, de Pleineville does point out that senior commanders often embroider what they write with their eye on their place in history. But all in all the savagery and suffering of the field of Waterloo are captured as well as any other battle in history by the compelling accounts of those who were there. Their words bring the battle alive as nothing else can – from the description by French Sergeant Anton of 'horses' hooves sinking in men's breasts' as the British heavy cavalry scattered d'Erlon's retreating infantry, to British Ensign Rees Gronow's image of the French massed cavalry charge as 'advancing like a stormy wave of the sea when it catches the sunlight'. And we are left at the end with the pitiable picture of the collapse of Napoleon's Army by Captain Duthilt: 'these miserable victims of war were crushed without pity and expired under the wheels of wagons and cannons... The soldiers ... fled in disorder without their chiefs, and the chiefs fled in despair without their soldiers.' De Pleineville reminds us – amongst other things – that the abundance of eyewitness accounts of Waterloo from British and Allied sources is matched by a wealth of material from the French side as well.

Finally, Huw Davies digs deep into the aftermath of the battle and its legacy. He leaves us in no doubt as to its importance in influencing the century that followed. The contrast between Prussia's harsh treatment of defeated France and Britain's more sensitive attitude set the pattern for the peace negotiations that followed. With Blücher rampaging about Paris threatening to blow up the Pont d'Jena, Wellington and Britain's foreign secretary Lord Castlereagh set about trying to persuade him and the other Allies that reconciliation rather than vengeance should be the watchwords in their dealings with France. Wellington's victory at Waterloo gave Britain a strong say in this and in persuading the Allies that the best chance of containing France was to restore the monarchy of Louis XVIII. Davies describes how Wellington and Castlereagh then set themselves the task of convincing the

Allies that a strong rather than a weak and resentful France would best guarantee peace. And here they faced opposition, not just from their more vengeful Allies, but from the British cabinet including the Prime Minister Lord Liverpool himself. The most difficult ally to persuade would be Prussia, smarting at its failure to secure the whole of Saxony at the Congress of Vienna and eager to deprive France of Alsace and Lorraine.

Castlereagh and Wellington had an uphill battle. The foreign secretary argued that the Allies should blame not France but *Revolutionary* France and the ambition of Napoleon Bonaparte for the two decades of war Europe had just endured. To hold France down and to 'pare her nails' – as Castlereagh put it – would only risk further conflict in Europe as France sought to reclaim her past strength. These arguments, Davies tells us, won Russia's support and in the end the approval of the other powers and of the rest of Whitehall including the Prime Minister. The peace treaty was finally signed on 20 November 1815.

But Castlereagh's clear-sighted vision for Europe went further: he was the prime mover in the creation of the Concert of Europe, a European system which would provide for the great powers to solve problems from then on by discussion and compromise. It was a settlement that allowed France – unlike Germany in the aftermath of the treaty of Versailles a century later, to play an equal part in such discussions. And Davies says this 'helped maintain peace in Europe for the next century'. The Crimean War in the 1850s and other conflicts later in the century gravely wounded the Concert and Europe finally collapsed into total war in 1914. But, Davies says, 'arguably' the Concert of Europe

The magnificent painting of the Battle of Waterloo by William Sadler captures the small area within which the battle took place. (Public domain)

established in the aftermath of Waterloo was the 'blueprint upon which later attempts with the same aim were based'.

We are left with Davies' reminder that Waterloo was a battle that Wellington himself described as a battle fought 'in the old style'. It appeared to be the triumph of 18th-century tactics in an age when the army needed to accept change. And yet, as Britain embarked on new military adventures in its bid to expand its empire, the army remained largely unreformed, due mainly to the continuing influence of the man who became an unassailable national hero.

So the aura – or the shadow, depending on which way you look at it – of Waterloo leaves an indelible mark on subsequent history. 18 June 1815 was the final decisive end of a war that had brought tragedy and suffering to all the nations of Europe. And although it ended with the military victory of Britain, Prussia and their Allies over a defeated France, perhaps it is fair to conclude, as Davies does, with the generous view that in the peace that followed and endured France was as big a winner as the others. She was not humiliated but allowed to maintain her power. Indeed if you visit the battlefield of Waterloo in this bicentenary year, and count the busts and pictures of Napoleon that seem to be everywhere, you might be forgiven for believing that he must have won the battle as well.

CHRONOLOGY

26 FEBRUARY Napoleon escapes from exile on the island of Elba with about 1,000 men.

1 MARCH Napoleon lands at Golfe-Juan near Antibes, around 5 p.m. They spend the first night on the beach at Cannes.

7 MARCH In six days the soldiers have marched 300 kilometres. The 5th Regiment is ordered to intercept Napoleon and does so south of Grenoble. Napoleon approaches the regiment alone and shouts, 'Here I am. Kill your Emperor, if you wish!' The soldiers rally to him and march towards Paris.

13 MARCH At the Congress of Vienna the Allies declare Napoleon an outlaw. The Congress is a conference of ambassadors of European states chaired by the Austrian, Prince Klemens von Metternich, and held between November 1814 and June 1815: its objective being the redrawing of the continent's physical map, and establishing the boundaries of France and its erstwhile satellites or conquests, after Napoleon's defeat at Leipzig (16–19 October 1813) and the first invasion of France. Wellington was Britain's representative.

14 MARCH Marshal Ney, who had been ordered to arrest Napoleon at Auxerre by King Louis XVIII, and who had said that Napoleon ought to be brought to Paris in an iron cage, joins him with 6,000 men – an ultimately fatal act of treason against the restored Bourbon monarchy.

15 MARCH Hearing of Napoleon's escape, Joachim Murat, King of Naples and Napoleon's brother-in-law, declares war on Austria (breaking an earlier treaty with Austria he had signed to preserve his crown).

17 MARCH Britain, Russia, Austria and Prussia, members of the Seventh Coalition, agree to mobilise 150,000 men each to defeat Napoleon.

20 MARCH Napoleon enters Paris, the official start of the Hundred Days.

8–9 APRIL	Murat is defeated at the Battle of Occhiobello. In Lombardy (Austrian-ruled since Napoleon's defeat in 1814) there were 40,000 Italian partisans, veterans of Napoleon's Army, waiting to join Murat if he reached Milan. But Austrian troops, assembled for an invasion of southern France following Napoleon's return, move south to block Murat, who is forced eastwards towards Ferrara. During the two-day battle, on 8 April Murat tries to cross the border via a lightly-held bridge on the Po at Occhiobello, but the Austrian artillery defeats repeated charges, causing 2,000 casualties and prompting mass desertions in Murat's 25,000-strong army. Most of his artillery has been diverted to besieging Ferrara. He is forced to retreat to his original headquarters at Ancona.
3 MAY	General Frederick Bianchi's Austrian I Corps crushes Murat at the Battle of Tolentino (2–3 May). At the climax, Murat orders an infantry attack in squares, normally a defensive formation, anticipating a cavalry counter-attack which does not come; instead his troops are devastated by musket fire. Murat suffers 4,120 casualties, and his army is unable to halt the Austrian advance through Italy.
20 MAY	Murat flees to Corsica, and the pro-Napoleon Neapolitans, now commanded by General Michele Caracosa after Murat's flight, sign the Treaty of Casalanza with the Austrians (and British), agreeing to the restoration of King Ferdinand IV.
23 MAY	Ferdinand IV is restored to the Neapolitan throne.
25 MAY	The Allies declare war; mobilisation and recruitment begin; rebellion commences in the Vendeé region.
15 JUNE	With available forces of 200,000, Napoleon decides to go on the offensive to drive a wedge between the advancing British and Prussian armies, and defeat them separately before enforcing a favourable armistice. The French Army of the North crosses the frontier into the United Netherlands (now Belgium).
3 p.m.	Armée du Nord commences crossing of the River Sambre.

3.30 p.m.	Marshal Ney arrives at Charleroi to join the campaign; Napoleon gives him command of the left wing of the army.
5.30 p.m.	Napoleon engages the Prussian rearguard at Gilly; Wellington receives news from Gneisenau of a 'major attack by the French'.
6.30 p.m.	Ney takes Frasnes.
8 p.m.	Napoleon returns to Charleroi; Wellington and his staff attend the Duchess of Richmond's ball in Brussels.

16 JUNE

4 a.m.	Napoleon back in the saddle.
6 a.m.	The Prussians seen moving towards Brye and St Amand.
9.30 a.m.	Wellington arrives at Quatre Bras having ordered reinforcements to the area; Ney does not attack as he is awaiting orders; Marshal Blücher is at Brye with the Prussian Army.
11 a.m.	Napoleon arrives at Fleurus with the Guard.
12 p.m.	Wellington rides to meet Blücher at Brye.
2 p.m.	The Battles of Ligny and Quatre Bras commence.

THE BATTLE OF QUATRE BRAS:

3 p.m.	French main advance checked by arrival of Picton's Division.
4 p.m.	Ney's all-out assault; d'Erlon acting as Ney's reserve receives orders to march to Ligny.
5 p.m.	Kellermann's cavalry charge.
5.30 p.m.	Alten's attack.
7 p.m.	British Guards retake Bossu Wood; Wellington orders a counter-attack in the centre.
9 p.m.	Battle ends with opposing forces at their original positions; d'Erlon returns to Fleurus.

THE BATTLE OF LIGNY:

3 p.m.	Attacks commence on Prussian-held villages/dwellings.

5 p.m.	Wagnele, St Amand and La Haye fall to the French.
5.30 p.m.	Tongrinelle falls to the French; Ligny still bitterly contested.
6 p.m.	Napoleon orders up the Guard; d'Erlon arrives behind the French flank; Blücher retakes St Amand.
7 p.m.	D'Erlon marches off to rejoin Ney; the Guard begins attack on Ligny; St Amand retaken.
9 p.m.	Napoleon returns to Fleurus, exhausted, possibly ill; he refuses to receive Grouchy later that night.

17 JUNE

2 a.m.	Sombreffe finally evacuated by last of the Prussians.
5 a.m.	Wellington dispatches an ADC (Colonel Gordon) to determine outcome of Ligny.
8 a.m.	Napoleon appears for breakfast and orders troops to prepare for inspection.
9.30 a.m.	Blücher confirms Wavre as destination of retreat to Gneisenau and Gordon; Napoleon tours the battlefield of Ligny.
10.30 a.m.	Wellington begins withdrawal from Quatre Bras.
11 a.m.	Napoleon receives a report from Ney and orders him to attack Wellington; Grouchy is to pursue Blücher.
12 p.m.	Last of Wellington's infantry leave Quatre Bras.
1 p.m.	Grouchy starts pursuit of the Prussians.
2.30 p.m.	Napoleon arrives at Quatre Bras to find only British cavalry rearguard remaining and Ney's troops in position preparing lunch; the weather turns and heavy rain begins to fall.
3 p.m.	Grouchy arrives at Point du Jour, a mile east of Ligny; he orders Vandamme to Gembloux.
6.30 p.m.	Napoleon's vanguard from the main body reaches La Belle Alliance.
8 p.m.	The lead elements of Vandamme's Corps reach Gembloux; with no sign of the Prussians the order is given to bivouac.

18 JUNE

3.30 a.m.	Wellington receives confirmation from Blücher that the Prussians will march to the field at Waterloo.
6 a.m.	Allied Army in position; French Army begins to move to La Belle Alliance from bivouacs around Genappe; Bülow's IV Corps starts to move from Wavre towards Waterloo.
7 a.m.	Wellington inspects the troops; Napoleon commences breakfast at La Caillou with his generals; the Prussian advance is delayed due to a fire at Wavre.
8 a.m.	Allied Army in final deployment positions; Napoleon rides forward from La Belle Alliance to conduct a reconnaissance of Wellington's deployment; lead elements of Bülow's IV Corps clear Wavre and are on the march.
9 a.m.	Wellington orders some readjustments to the defence of Hougoumont; Napoleon sends his Chief Engineer to conduct a reconnaissance of the Allied (physical) defences; Blücher sends a message to Wellington's Headquarters that he is en route.
10 a.m.	Readjustments taking place at Hougoumont and Wellington receives confirmation (via the 10th Hussars) that Blücher is marching towards Waterloo; Napoleon takes up his position at Rossomme and having heard nothing from Grouchy sends out 7th Hussars to the east. He also gives Soult the time of 11 a.m. for the attack to commence; Pirch's II Corps and Zieten's I Corps are following, in that order.
11 a.m.	Napoleon rides to La Belle Alliance and inspects his troops and makes a decision to commence the attack on the French left opposite Hougoumont. The first shots of the battle from Reille's artillery commence at (about) 11.20 a.m.
11.20 a.m.	The battle commences.
11.20 a.m.–12.20 p.m	The Allies are driven from the woods and orchard at Hougoumont by Prince Jérôme's 6th Division. The Allies conduct a counter-attack. The French bring more guns up to form the Grand Battery opposite the Allied centre.

12.20–1.15 p.m.	The French Grand Battery opens at about 1 p.m.; Bijlandt's Dutch Brigade is withdrawn from forward slope position in the Allied centre; fighting for Hougoumont continues and intensifies; Lieutenant Legros and 30 men succeed in forcing entry; leading elements of Bülow's vanguard reach Chapelle St Lambert.
1.15–2.15 p.m.	Napoleon received confirmation that the Prussian IV Corps is closing from the east; the cavalry divisions of Domon and Subervie are sent east to delay/block the Prussians and the balance of Lobau's VI Corps are sent east in their wake; Napoleon orders d'Erlon's Corps to attack the Allied centre at 1.30 p.m., after the Grand Battery bombardment; the Allied line is pushed back, La Haye Sainte is surrounded and Lord Uxbridge launches the Household and Union brigades against d'Erlon's Corps. Napoleon moves back to La Belle Alliance.
2.15–3 p.m.	The struggle for Hougoumont continues, more than 12,000 men are embroiled in the task in taking the chateau, which is being defended by 2,600 men; Union and Household brigade charges run out of steam and control; d'Erlon's divisions are driven back and the Grand Battery is (temporarily) out of action; Napoleon launches his heavy cavalry and lancers to counter the Allied cavalry and they inflict heavy losses; the leading Prussian brigades are negotiating the Lasne defile but progress is slow.
3–4 p.m.	The buildings at Hougoumont are set on fire and La Haye Sainte is reinforced but in bad need of ammunition resupply; a second concerted assault is made on La Haye Sainte by Quiot's battalions but they fail to capture the structure; d'Erlon's troops reorganise and the Grand Battery re-opens fire; to the east, at the Bois de Paris, the first clashes between Bülow's vanguard cavalry and the French cavalry screen take place.
4–5 p.m.	Ney misinterprets Wellington's troop readjustments as a sign of Allied withdrawal and orders a massed cavalry charge; all the Allied infantry west of the Brussels road forms square to meet the cavalry

charges; Lobau's Corps engages the Prussians as they debouch from the Bois de Paris; attacks continue on Hougoumont and La Haye Sainte.

5–6 p.m.	The French cavalry attacks continue despite making no progress; the 13e *Légere* deliver a concerted attack on La Haye Sainte where the defenders are now desperately short of ammunition; Hougoumont is still in Allied hands; Lobau's Corps is pushed back towards Plancenoit; Zieten's leading brigade reaches Ohain.
6–6.30 p.m.	La Haye Sainte falls at 6.30 p.m.; at much the same time, after a fierce fight, Plancenoit falls to the Prussians; Napoleon is compelled to deploy the Young Guard to recapture the village.
6.30–7 p.m.	The Young Guard succeed in driving the Prussians back out of Plancenoit; the Prussians counter-attack and regain most of the dwellings only to be countered again by the Old Guard who hold the village.
7–8.30 p.m.	Wellington energetically reorganises his central defence following the loss of La Haye Sainte; at 7.30 p.m. Plancenoit is once again in Prussian hands at much the same time that Napoleon gives the order for the Guard to advance north; the Guard suffers badly from the Allied artillery and are then taken in the flank by Halkett's, Maitland's and Adam's brigades; it triggers the French collapse and the commencement of the French rout.
8.30–10.30 p.m.	Wellington signals a general advance and rides to La Belle Alliance where he meets Blücher; the French recoil across the frontage and the Prussians take the lead in the pursuit.
21 JUNE	Napoleon arrives back in Paris.
22 JUNE	Napoleon abdicates in favour of his son.
29 JUNE	Napoleon quits Paris for the west of France.
7 JULY	Graf von Zieten's Prussian I Corps enters Paris.
8 JULY	Louis XVIII is restored and the Hundred Days ends.
15 JULY	Napoleon, thwarted in his desire to sail to America by the Royal Navy, surrenders with his entourage to

Captain Maitland of HMS *Bellerophon*. His plea to live in England like a country gentleman is refused, and he is exiled to St Helena in the South Atlantic, where he dies, almost certainly from stomach cancer, in 1821, aged 51.

13 OCTOBER Joachim Murat is executed (a fate also suffered by Ney on 7 December in Paris) by order of Ferdinand IV, in Pizzo, Calabria, having landed there five days earlier hoping to regain his kingdom by fomenting an insurrection.

20 NOVEMBER Treaty of Paris signed by France, Britain, Russia, Austria and Prussia. The Allies repudiate 'the revolutionary system reproduced in France' and impose substantial reparations on her.

CHAPTER 1

THE WATERLOO CAMPAIGN

The Strategic Background

Jeremy Black

The strategic dimension of the Waterloo campaign is the one that receives far too little attention. The operational dynamics and interactions of the campaign, and the tactics of the day itself, have been extensively, sometimes exhaustively, covered, but, as so often, the strategic dimension has been relatively neglected. This neglect reflects a number of factors. There is a tendency to believe that the strategic situation and issues are obvious, there are the serious limitations in the source base, there is the more general interest with the tactical dimension, and there is the widespread popular tendency to treat the operational level as if it was the strategic one.

The last links back to the first of the factors cited, namely the conviction that the broader parameters were set by the drive for victory, and that therefore 'strategy' should focus on the means adopted. That approach, however, fails to capture the key strategic element of the campaign, the strategic asymmetry between Napoleon and his opponents. This asymmetry will be the topic of this piece. It set the essential parameters of the campaign and also should provide the guide for judging the vexed issues of success and the respective role of the armies of Arthur Wellesley, 1st Duke of Wellington, and Field Marshal Gebhard Leberecht von Blücher in this success. Put simply, and these points will be fleshed out, Napoleon had to win, and win dramatically, while Wellington only needed to avoid serious defeat. In doing so, he would thwart Napoleon and thus overcome his strategy. As a consequence, Wellington won a defensive victory in successfully resisting successive attacks.

This victory was then transformed into a very different victory as a result of Blücher's advance and success against the French right. The second victory, however, was not 'necessary' in strategic terms as the advance of Austrian and Russian forces placed Napoleon in a very difficult position if he could not dissolve the Allied coalition. The strategic asymmetry rested on the legacy of the Napoleonic Wars hitherto. They had left a deep distrust of Napoleon, and this distrust took precedence over the tensions between the Allies. These tensions were as longstanding: Prussia's rise under Frederick the Great (r. 1740–86) had been achieved on the basis of Austrian failure, while Britain and Russia had come close to war on several occasions from the Ochakov Crisis of 1791.

More recently, tensions between Britain and Austria had been to the fore in 1813–14 as the latter continued to negotiate with Napoleon and the British feared a settlement that would leave France with a frontier on the Rhine and, notably, control of Belgium and its threatening naval facilities and harbour at Antwerp. In the winter of 1814–15, these serious differences received fresh direction and energy as a result of a dispute over the fate of Napoleon's former ally, Saxony. Russia supported Prussia's drive for crippling territorial gains, which Austria, backed by Britain and France, opposed.

These tensions suggested possibilities for the revisionism that Napoleon's return from exile in Elba represented. Ironically, this return overthrew a better-grounded revisionism that Louis XVIII and Talleyrand had sought to pursue at Vienna in 1814–15. Russia had sought co-operation with France against Britain, but Louis preferred an informal relationship with the British, which was designed to ensure that France played a role in the negotiations over the German and Italian questions. Talleyrand's co-operation with Austria and Britain over Saxony was designed to replace the alliance that had defeated Napoleon in 1814, the continuation of which would have left France with only a limited role, by a new diplomatic order in which France could have greater influence in Europe, as well as specific benefits on her frontiers. Count Blacas, the personal representative of Louis XVIII, advocated a league against Russia that initially would unite Britain, and her protégé the United Netherlands, with the Bourbon powers, and then be widened to include Austria and Prussia. Good relations were sought with the Ottoman Sultan Mahmud II. A politics of interest was

The Congress of Vienna, September 1814 to June 1815, was set up to provide a lasting peace for Europe. The Congress of Vienna was not a 'congress' in the literal sense, with most of the business conducted during face-to-face informal sessions among the Great Powers of Austria, Britain, France, Russia and sometimes Prussia. (Anne S. K. Brown)

linked to a sense that France was rightfully the arbiter of Europe and an accompanying suspicion of aggrandisement by others. Louis and Talleyrand disliked Russian predominance in Eastern Europe and tried to limit Austrian power and influence in Italy. In addition, Louis sought to recreate a Bourbon Family Compact with Spain and to restore the Bourbons to Naples.

Combining policy and strategy, this was diplomacy for a re-integration of France into the European diplomatic order, and such a re-integration was eventually to be achieved. Napoleon's return from Elba overthrew Louis XVIII's strategy and delayed this re-integration. The return also reset the international order as it had been in the spring of 1814, and thus set the context for the military strategies that were to be pursued during the 'Hundred Days'.

Napoleon had found his control of the principality of Elba, a small island, a frustrating lesson in impotence and one that mocked his greatly inflated sense of his own destiny, and he was only too happy to launch an attempt to regain France. On the evening of 26 February 1815, Napoleon took advantage of the absence of his British escort, Colonel Sir Neil Campbell, who was on a visit to Florence, to leave with a small flotilla and about 1,100 troops.

Louis XVIII, an out of touch and unpopular king, was unable to compromise to the will of the French people and as such found himself easily overthrown.
(Anne S. K. Brown)

The departure of Louis XVIII in March 1815 at the start of Napoleon's Hundred Days.
(Anne S. K. Brown)

Evading two frigates patrolling on the orders of Louis XVIII, as well as a British brigantine, Napoleon arrived near Antibes on the French Provençal coast on 1 March. The garrison was not welcoming, but soon surrendered in the face of Napoleon's force.

Napoleon offered both policy and strategy of his own for France's re-integration into the European diplomatic order. They were to be proven redundant by events, but their practicality also requires consideration. Advancing from south to north against no resistance, Napoleon was welcomed at the Tuileries Palace in Paris on the evening of 20 March. The unpopularity and lack of grip of Louis XVIII were important factors as was the uncertain response of the French military, but so also was Napoleon's drive, his ability to grasp the initiative, and his rapid advance.

This equation of relative advantage could not be repeated when Napoleon advanced into Belgium in June 1815. In a marked reversal of the situation the French encountered in Spain in 1808, Napoleon was to find the suppression of popular opposition easier in France in 1815 than engaging regular forces. Opposition in southern and western France was overcome in April and June 1815 respectively. The Army of the West which crushed the rising in the Vendée at the Battle of Rocheservière included part of the Young Guard of the Imperial Guard, which would otherwise have been at Waterloo.

Vive l'Empereur! Having travelled 300 miles north without opposition, Napoleon enters Paris in triumph on 20 March 1815. (Anne S. K. Brown)

Napoleon's return, a key instance of the use of force to overthrow a government, was unacceptable to the Allied powers. In his letters to the Allied sovereigns, Napoleon promised to observe existing treaties, in other words the Vienna agreement, and affirmed peace with the rest of Europe. Armand de Caulaincourt, Napoleon's last foreign minister, now returned to office, wrote to his British counterpart, Viscount Castlereagh, on 4 April, to inform him of the return of Napoleon and that Napoleon hoped for peace.

In theory, therefore, Napoleon offered re-integration on the basis of accepting the situation agreed by Louis XVIII. In theory, moreover, this should have proved possible. Napoleon had experience of bringing down successive coalitions organised against him and of fighting them into an acceptance of his position. The same had been the achievement of the domestically more radical French Revolutionaries. Despite the 'we will/should never negotiate' position of Edmund Burke and others, the powers of the First Coalition had all eventually negotiated with the Revolutionaries, some had signed treaties, and Spain had allied.

Royalists denounced the returned Napoleon as a Jacobin, and he courted support in France by populist measures, such as the abolition of feudal titles and the commissioning of public works, but these were not unacceptably radical on the model of those of 1792–94. Instead, the promises of constitutional and liberal government that were offered, which included freedom of the press and the maintenance of Louis XVIII's constitutional assemblies, would not have worried a British commentator. These steps and promises are emphasised in some recent French works, but not in those produced by non-French writers.

At the same time, Napoleon found little enthusiasm in France for a new struggle, and conscription was particularly unwelcome. Conscription had been abolished, and the Legislative Chamber was unwilling to recall the class of 1815. Napoleon responded by seeking to circumvent the situation and the Chamber, which he correctly identified as a source of élite opposition. To do so, Napoleon classified the class of 1815 as discharged soldiers who had to serve, and he was able to raise about 46,000 men, but none reached his army in the field.

However, Napoleon could call on veterans whose experience was essentially one of war and most of whom saw few opportunities under Louis XVIII. Many of the veterans served among the 200,000 troops in the Royal army. Moreover, repatriated prisoners, discharged veterans, soldiers recalled from half-pay, as well as sailors from the navy, all served to build up the Napoleonic army. The pool of French troops was not limited, as it had been in 1814, by the deployment of many in besieged garrisons.

The possibility apparently offered by Napoleon for those of a counter-factual disposition is therefore of a France akin to that under the July Monarchy

(1830–48), a France with which Britain was able to co-operate and that was easily re-integrated into the European diplomatic order and, indeed, into that of the expanding Western world. Taking this argument further, it can be pointed out that the British ministries during the July Monarchy were Whig or Peelite Tory, and that a ministry of either type might have been able to work with Napoleon, whereas the more conservative Tories of the Liverpool and Wellington ministries found the reformed Bourbons more conducive.

There is also a military dimension to such counter-factualism. The latter tends to focus on the events of the day of Waterloo, or on the campaign as a whole. Yet, there is also a more profound counter-factualism in strategic terms. This looks at strategy in terms of prioritisation, and points out that in 1815 France did not benefit, as it had repeatedly, from the diversion of its opponents' attentions and energies, let alone from divisions between them. In 1770, during the Falkland Islands Crisis; in 1778–83, during the War of American Independence; and in 1790, during the Nootka Sound Crisis, France had been able to focus on Britain without the distraction of opposition from Austria, Prussia and/or Russia. The French Revolutionaries had benefited from the focus of the three last on the Polish question in 1793–95, while Napoleon had sought to profit from the rivalry between Turkey and Russia and from that between Britain and the United States.

Armand de Caulaincourt, Napoleon's foreign minister, saw a rise in fortunes upon Napoleon's return. (Topfoto)

1815 represented a strategically flawed moment in this scenario for France. Although Britain was engaged in war with Kandy and Nepal, these were small-scale and localised conflicts, and not as serious as earlier wars with Mysore and the Marathas. Moreover, the war with the United States had ended earlier in the year. Russia had no diversions.

Not only were these powers able to focus on Napoleon in 1815, but, in addition, he suffered from their earlier successes and, in particular, from their ability to overcome their geopolitical and strategic problems. Russia's victory over France in 1812–13 was simply the culmination of a triumphant overcoming of the *barrière de l'est* also seen in successes at the expense of Sweden (1808–09) and Turkey (1806–12), with victories resulting in treaties in which Russia's position was accepted.

So also for Britain. A structural or systemic account of British empire building can make war, naval power, imperial expansion and maritime hegemony appear not only as obviously linked, but also as inevitably leading to a synergy of success. This approach is misleading and, in particular, underrates the multiple difficulties posed to Britain's domestic and international situations. Even if the

This split view shows how quickly the French officials, previously loyal to Louis, switched allegiance to Bonaparte. (Anne S. K. Brown)

Viscount Castlereagh, Caulaincourt's British counterpart and good friend of the Duke of Wellington. (Topfoto)

synergy appeared clear-cut overseas after the major victory over the French and Spanish fleets at Trafalgar in 1805, there was still the danger that defeat on the European Continent or simply the collapse of Britain's alliance system would lead to a return of colonial gains in order to obtain peace, as had occurred in 1748 and 1802. The possibility that Austria might settle with Napoleon as late as early 1814 had made this a continuing danger. Trade and empire had to be fought for, by Britain, both on their own and as part of an often complex and difficult foreign policy. The latter was to the fore in 1815 but a united Allied approach against Napoleon made this issue less threatening for Britain.

For Britain by 1815, the geopolitical challenge by the combination of French, Spanish and Dutch naval power had been overcome, as had the economic threats of exclusion both from French-dominated Europe and from the United States. Moreover, the American attempt to conquer Canada had been driven back. Napoleon had seen the War of 1812 as a threat to Britain. In late January 1815, a British visitor who saw him on Elba recorded his host as saying that: 'peace with America should have been made sooner, as it would have given us [Britain] greater influence in the Congress'.

THE PROPOSED ALLIED INVASION OF FRANCE

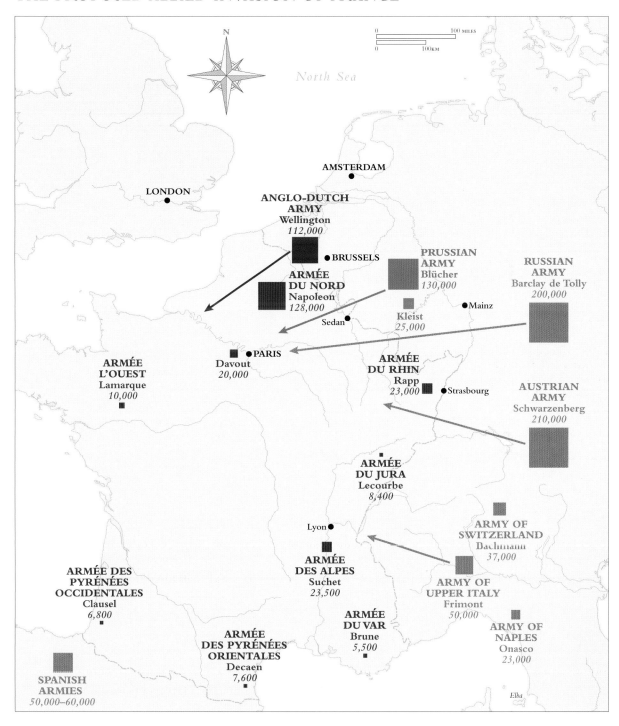

In 1815, there was no French attempt at *revanche* at sea comparable to that mounted by Napoleon in Belgium. Like those of 1814, 1870, 1914 and 1940, the conflict of that year was to be decided on land; although sea-power was to prove of much greater relevance in all of these wars bar the Franco-Prussian of 1870–71. At the same time, in 1815 British naval power posed a major danger for Napoleon as it permitted British action in support of Royalists within France and also supported a blockade that ensured that France would not be able to trade with neutral powers or maintain links with its colonies. The former meant that the Anglo-American peace at Ghent would not be able to provide a basis for a *rapprochement* between the United States and France that could help Napoleon. The United States would only be able to trade with Britain.

Thus, Britain had emerged triumphant in the Atlantic world, as Russia had in Eastern Europe. These successes reflected a range of factors, not least the superiority of *Ancien Régime* military systems over the French Revolutionary/ Napoleonic model that attracts so much attention in a misleading teleological account of the development of modern war.

The War of 1812 against the United States of America had provided some naval respite to the French as many ships of the Royal Navy were diverted to the east coast of America from the Atlantic and Mediterranean fleets. This print depicts the attack on Fort Oswego, on Lake Ontario, 6 May 1814. (Anne S. K. Brown)

The geopolitical context made it difficult for Napoleon unless he could avoid war by negotiations or, once begun, end it by dividing his opponents, as he had repeatedly done hitherto. However, Napoleon's return united the powers, which had been divided over the future of Saxony. On 13 March 1815, the powers assembled at Vienna declared Napoleon's invasion an illegal act and offered help to Louis XVIII. The presence of Alexander I of Russia and Frederick William III of Prussia in Vienna eased tensions among the Allies and speeded deliberations. Across Europe, Napoleon's envoys were promptly sent back by the Coalition powers. On 21 March, 'Boney's Return from Elba, or the Devil among the Tailors', a caricature by George Cruikshank, appeared in London. It captured the change that Napoleon's return appeared to usher in, but also the response. Looking far younger than he really was, Napoleon, sword in hand, pushes Louis XVIII of France onto the floor and throws the gathering of European potentates into confusion. Yet, there are also signs of resistance. John Bull promises help to Louis and to sew up Napoleon, Blücher challenges the latter with a large pair of tailors' scissors, and an unperturbed Tsar Alexander I declares 'I'll take a few Cossack *measures* to him'.

On 25 March, the powers at Vienna renewed their alliance in order to overthrow Napoleon. Austria, Britain, Prussia and Russia each promised to provide forces of 150,000 men, with Britain being permitted to provide some of its contribution with money to be used to subsidise the forces of Allies or to hire troops from rulers lacking the necessary funds. An agreement was reached over Saxony in May.

Napoleon had no real alternative to war. Indeed, at the same time that he had approached the Allies, his rhetoric within France towards the other powers was hostile and bellicose. Caulaincourt was also ordered to create a new league with the lesser powers, including Spain, Portugal, Switzerland, and the minor German and Italian states. This proposal was a testimony to Napoleon's lack of realism, as well as to the flawed basis for the revisionism he represented and sought to foster. So also was his confidence that the people elsewhere who had known his rule would reject war against France whatever their rulers thought. This diplomacy to peoples led Napoleon to order the publication of appeals to foreigners who had served in his forces to rejoin them.

Ordered back from being a delegate at Vienna to take command of the British forces in Belgium, Wellington sought a repetition of the campaign of 1814: one in which overwhelming pressure was brought to bear on Napoleon. He argued that the Coalition should begin operations 'when we shall have 450,000 men', including Prussians and Russians, and he was confident that Napoleon could bring no more than 150,000 troops to strike at any one point.

The Battle of New Orleans on 8 January 1815 was the final major battle of the War of 1812 and a victory for Major General Andrew Jackson against the attacking British force under the command of Wellington's brother-in-law, Edward Pakenham.
(Anne S. K. Brown)

Napoleon, therefore, had to prevent the impact of this capability gap by disrupting the operations of the Coalition forces, using location and interior lines to even the odds and win successive victories. Moreover, such success would disrupt the Coalition, provide supplies from conquered territory, and secure support within France. In short, Napoleon was offering a reprise of the policy and strategy he had followed since 1799. Moreover, he appeared to have a chance for quick success given the proximity of vulnerable Allied forces in Belgium. Their exposed character provided an opportunity for sequential success, both military and diplomatic. The combined strength of the Allied forces in Belgium was considerably greater than that of the French, but they were not well prepared for operations. Moreover, Napoleon aimed to drive apart Wellington's and Blücher's armies by attacking along the axis of the division between their spheres of responsibility; then he planned to defeat them separately.

Napoleon depicted in the finery of an emperor on 1 June 1815, just days before the Battle of Waterloo. (Anne S. K. Brown)

Napoleon's key force was the Army of the North, comprising 123,000 troops and 358 cannon, as other units had to be deployed to protect France's other frontiers and to resist possible rebellion. In combination, these other units were a considerable force of about 105,000 men, and more troops could have been taken from them to bolster the Army of the North, but other frontiers could not be left completely bare, while only so many troops could have been redeployed. Numbers were not the only difficulty in fielding the Army of the North, as there was also a serious problem in providing the necessary equipment. This problem reflected the degree to which the army had been neglected under Louis XVIII, with a particular failure to maintain the necessary *matériel*. As a result, once back in Paris, Napoleon had to devote a major effort to secure sufficient weaponry and horses.

At the same time, war is a matter of relative risk, advantages and capabilities. The poor state of Wellington's Army was a reflection of the rapidity with which Britain and the Netherlands had rushed to take a peace dividend. The British Army had been cut with large-scale discharges, while other units had been sent to North America in 1814 in order to take the offensive in the War of 1812, or were deployed to deal with disaffection in Britain, notably from the Luddites, who violently opposed new industrial technology, or to garrison Ireland. Wellington's British units initially were essentially based on those that had operated in the Low Countries in 1814, operations that had not proved especially successful. The army as a whole was a very mixed one, in background, experience and competence. There were concerns about the experience and trustworthiness of the Belgian and Dutch units.

Napoleon on horseback, resplendent in gold. Napoleon used over 150 horses during his military life. At Waterloo he rode an Arab Grey named Marengo. (Anne S. K. Brown)

Boney's Return from Elba –
or the *Devil among the Sailors,*
a caricature by Cruikshank.
It captured the change that
Napoleon's return appeared to
usher in, but also the response.
(Rijksmuseum)

Wellington made an urgent attempt to mould his army by reorganising it, notably by adopting a method he had employed in the Peninsular War that entailed mixing formations in order to put the impressive alongside the less impressive down to divisional level. This method was seen as a way to stiffen the less impressive units and thus to improve the defensive strength of the entire army. Wellington's system was opposed by William I of the Netherlands, who wanted the Belgian and Dutch forces concentrated in one corps, but, benefiting from his own notable reputation and from the crisis environment, Wellington got his way. This decision was to be very important to the strength of his army at Waterloo. With time, Wellington was also more successful in obtaining the staff officers he wanted.

The strategy for both sides was therefore clear. In the event, it was an element that does not tend to receive attention that was one of the most significant in the strategic mix, namely the consequences of French defeat in the field. The counterfactuals tend to focus on French victory, but the defeat could have taken a different course. More particularly, Napoleon not only coped far worse militarily with failure than Louis XIV or Louis V had done, but also faced very different political consequences. This point underlines the importance of a grounding of rulership in legitimacy as well as success. The fall of his regime in 1814 both established a pattern and also left a legacy of weakness that played a role in 1815. Napoleon had fallen in 1814 when he conducted an active defence of France against invading Allied forces. Although he fought a number of successful defensive battles, France was demoralised and the state was collapsing. A combination of heavy taxes, unwelcome demands for conscripts shooting up, the heavy casualties of 1813, and a sense of failure destroyed Napoleonic rule even while the fighting went on. Ready to pile up the bodies, Napoleon refused to face reality; but the Senate deposed him on 2 April 1814, and his remaining generals then insisted on his abdicating.

This context was also to determine the outcome of Waterloo, and thus set the strategic parameters. France in 1815 fell the same way Prussia had in 1806: there was no lengthy struggle. The situation would have been different had Napoleon won; for the Allies, most of whose armies were not yet engaged, would have kept on fighting. Napoleon's regime, however, was dependent on his main battle army and on his prestige. Resting on these fragile and now weakened foundations, it rapidly collapsed.

Despite his claims, Napoleon's lack of political legitimacy and support helped ensure that his opponents were able to make defeat in the field decisive. To revisit the famous military commentator Carl von Clausewitz, the varied nature of politics gave differing results to the events of war.

The Duke of Wellington. Ordered back from being a delegate at Vienna to take command of the British forces in Belgium, Wellington sought a repetition of the campaign of 1814. (Anne S. K. Brown)

The Tsar Alexander I of Russia with some of his staff officers in 1815. (Anne S. K. Brown)

That it was Wellington who defeated Napoleon, by denying him, in a defensive battle, the success he needed, highlighted the contrast between France's failure and the contemporaneous success of Britain and Russia, a success that set the context for Waterloo. This success was given concrete form in 1815, when Napoleon surrendered to a British warship and Alexander I reviewed 150,000 Russian troops east of Paris, on the third anniversary of Borodino. Britain and Russia indeed dominated the geopolitics of the West during the subsequent decades.

The revolutionary ethos and purposes of the French Army in the 1790s had transformed the political context of military activity, freeing greater resources for warfare. The end result, however, of this warfare was to enhance British maritime and Russian land power. Both states were outside Europe, more able

Frederick William III of Prussia had steered a difficult course between France and her enemies following major military defeats in 1806. He was King of Prussia during the Congress of Vienna having turned against France in 1813. (Anne S. K. Brown)

Plans of the Battles of Waterloo, Ligny and Quatre Bras. (Courtesy of the Council of the National Army Museum)

to protect their home base than other European countries, yet also able to play a major role in European politics.

As a result, they saw off Napoleon, exploiting his inability to provide lasting stability in Western and Central Europe, and thus thwarted the last attempt before the age of nationalism to remodel Europe. In 1814–15, Europe was returned by Napoleon's victorious opponents to the multiple statehood that distinguished it from so many of the other heavily populated regions of the world. This was as much a consequence of Napoleon's political failure as of the absence of a lasting military capability gap in favour of France.

CHAPTER 2

THE BATTLES OF LIGNY AND QUATRE BRAS

Napoleon's Lost Opportunities

JULIAN SPILSBURY

For this campaign I have adopted the following general principle – to divide my army into two wings and a reserve… The Guard will form the reserve, and I shall bring it into action on either wing as circumstances dictate… Also, according to circumstances I shall draw troops from one wing to strengthen my reserve.

Thus, in his orders to Marshal Michel Ney written at 6 a.m. on 16 June, Napoleon summarised his plan of operations.

The emperor had spent the night at Charleroi. Ney had joined him at midnight and there they had discussed the situation until 2 a.m. when Ney had returned to Gosselies. Napoleon was working on the reasonable assumption that the two Allied commanders would withdraw in order to concentrate their forces. His plan for the 16th, therefore, was to operate against Wellington with Ney's wing of the *Grande Armée* and the reserve and either destroy the Allied Army or at least drive it in the direction of Antwerp, away from Field Marshal Gebhard Leberecht von Blücher's Prussian Army. In order to ensure that Blücher could not move to assist Wellington it would be necessary to sever the communications between them by driving Lieutenant General Hans Ernst Carl von Zieten's I Prussian Corps beyond Gembloux and Sombreffe and the Namur–Wavre–Brussels road.

Accordingly at 6 a.m. on the morning of the 16th Napoleon prepared two important despatches. Marshal Emmanuel de Grouchy – commanding the right wing of the Army of the North – he ordered to advance against Gembloux–Sombreffe and engage any Prussians he encountered there – Napoleon estimated them to be 40,000 strong. 'My intention,' the order stated, 'is to operate with my left wing, which is commanded by Marshal Ney, against the English.'[1] Later in the day – at some unspecified time – Grouchy was to dispatch part of his force along the lateral Namur–Nivelles road to operate against Wellington's left and rear. The despatch to Ney re-iterated this plan – thus making it clear to both commanders that Ney's advance would be the main axis for the Army of the North that day. Ney's instructions also told him to hold himself in readiness to advance on Brussels once the reserve reached him.

Napoleon and his staff survey the field of Ligny, 16 June 1815. (Painting by G. Weiss)

In the meantime he was to place one division 8 kilometres north-west of Quatre Bras, retain six on the crossroads itself, and send one to Marbais to maintain contact with Grouchy.

It may be that a certain vagueness in these orders caused Ney to waste six crucial hours that morning before moving on Quatre Bras. The masterful Marshal Nicolas Soult was ill-equipped, in many ways, for the role of chief of staff and the bad blood between him and Ney – dating back to Spain – did not encourage discussion and explanation. Here, the absence of Marshal Louis-Alexandre Berthier, Napoleon's previous very competent chief of staff, made itself felt.[2]

Napoleon's orders to Ney and Grouchy had hardly been dispatched when a message arrived from Grouchy at about 8 a.m., reporting large numbers of Prussian troops approaching Sombreffe from the direction of Namur. At first it seemed inconceivable that Blücher – even given what Napoleon called his 'hussar habits' – could be thinking of making a stand at St Amand and Ligny, while Wellington surely intended to withdraw towards Brussels. Believing the report to be false, he rode forward to Fleurus – which had always been his intention – intending to see for himself.

By 11 a.m. Napoleon and his forward Headquarters were with Lieutenant General Vandamme's III Corps looking towards Zieten's positions around St Amand. From there Napoleon saw enough to convince him that – far from being a rearguard as he had at first assumed – Zieten's Corps was in fact an *advance* guard covering a general deployment in the area Gembloux–Sombreffe,

THE SITUATION ON THE EVENING, 14 JUNE 1815

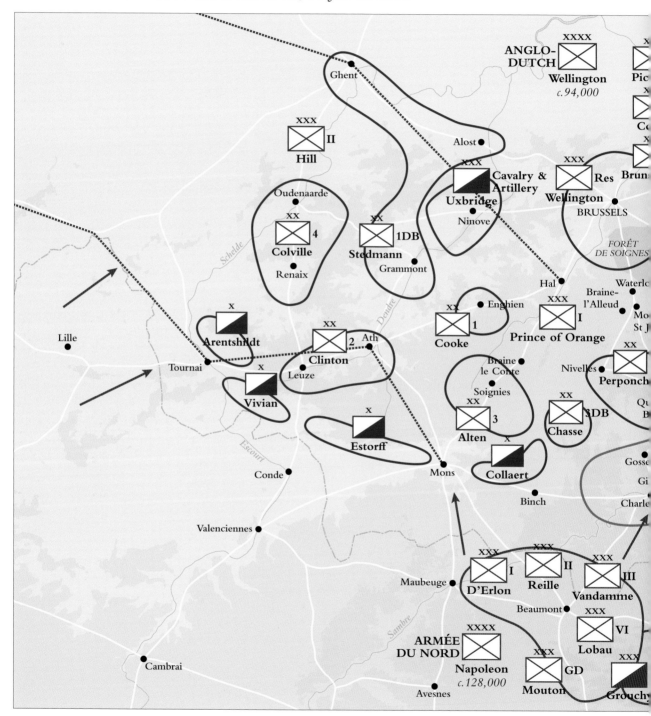

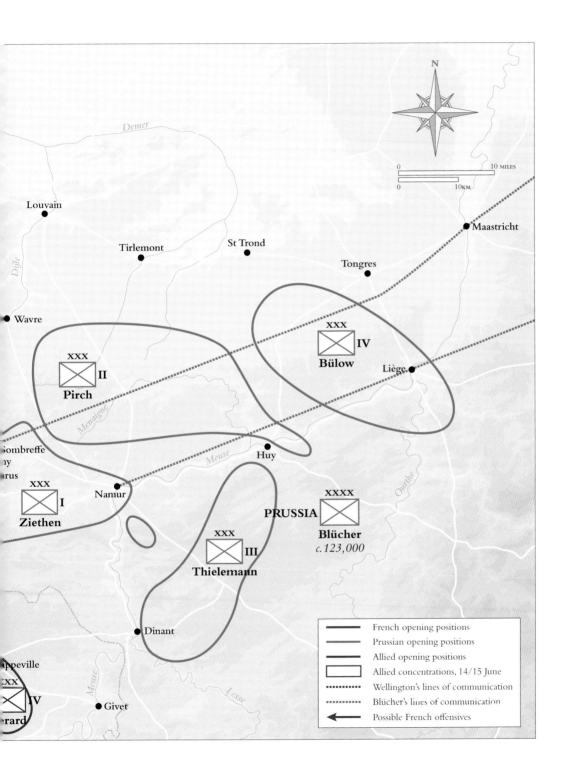

Louvain

Tirlemont

St Trond

Tongres

Maastricht

Wavre

XXX
II
Pirch

XXX
IV
Bülow

Liège

Demer

Dijle

Menaigne

Meuse

Huy

Ourthe

Sombreffe
ny
rus

XXX
I
Ziethen

Namur

XXXX
PRUSSIA
Blücher
c.123,000

XXX
III
Thielemann

Dinant

Meuse

Lesse

ppeville

XXX
IV

rard

Givet

————	French opening positions
————	Prussian opening positions
————	Allied opening positions
▭	Allied concentrations, 14/15 June
··········	Wellington's lines of communication
··········	Blücher's lines of communication
◄——	Possible French offensives

Lieutenant General Pajol, commander of I Cavalry Corps at Ligny. (Anne S. K. Brown)

as well as guarding the Namur–Nivelles road, the main road by which Wellington could approach. So it was that the whole French plan was now reversed – Grouchy's would be the main operation of the day and Ney – when the time was right – would swing part of *his* force *down* the lateral road to envelop Blücher's right and rear. The ability to switch axes like this shows the beautiful simplicity of Napoleon's 'two wings and a reserve' system – but it depended on good staff work, good communications and good understanding between commanders and staff. All of these were to prove wanting as the day progressed.

It was not possible for Napoleon to launch an immediate attack. Lieutenant General Gerard's IV Corps had not yet arrived, largely due to poor staff work, and although the Imperial Guard – having been on the march since 4 a.m. – were now approaching Fleurus, Count Lobau's VI Corps was still in Charleroi, awaiting orders. Three hours were passed in concentrating the force that was to attack Blücher: Vandamme's III Corps, Gerard's IV Corps and the I and II Cavalry Corps of Lieutenant Generals Pajol and Exelmanns – a total of 68,000 infantry, 12,500 cavalry and 210 guns.

Blücher's position at Ligny was, at first sight, a strong one, well suited for defence. Zieten's I Corps occupied a salient along the line of the Ligne Brook, with Wagnelée at its right, St Amand at its centre and the village of Ligny at its left. To his left, between Sombreffe and Mazy, was Lieutenant General Johann von Thielmann's III Corps (numbering 29,500). The hill behind the Ligny salient – a good artillery platform – was occupied by Major General von Pirch's II Corps (32,000 men). In total, by 3 p.m. Blücher had in place 84,000 men, of whom 8,000 were cavalry, and 224 guns, arrayed along an 11-kilometre front, to which the Ligne Brook acted as a moat.

This front contained ten hamlets and villages – each one a strong point – and the Ligne Brook was crossed by only four bridges, each in turn covered by a village. The villages were in hollows and surrounded by marshy ground, hedges and ditches which the Prussians had spent the morning fortifying. The one flaw in this deployment was that the Ligny position was – like all salients – vulnerable to crossfire from enemy artillery. This was exacerbated by the Prussian tendency to mass infantry on forward slopes. In the fighting Blücher's reserves would take severe punishment from French artillery without being able to aid – by musketry – the efforts of Zieten's men in the front line.

If the Prussians were a little thinly spread – by the standards of the time – for a front of 11 kilometres, Blücher had reason to hope for reinforcement both from General Friedrich Wilhelm Count von Bülow with his IV Corps and from Wellington proceeding down the Namur–Nivelles road. Blücher's plan, if attacked, was for two corps (Zieten's I Corps and Pirch's II Corps) to hold the French, while two others (Thielmann's III Corps and Bülow's IV Corps), together with Wellington, would attack their flanks.

At 1 p.m. Wellington joined Blücher and his staff at the windmill at Bussy from which – according to Zieten's chief of staff – both commanders could see Napoleon making a tour of the front-line units. For his part, Wellington had his reservations about the Prussian position, observing that the Prussian infantry could not attack the French but could themselves be exposed to a severe

This view of Ligny provides an idea of the topography that the French and Prussians had to contend with. (akg-images)

THE BATTLES OF QUATRE BRAS AND LIGNY

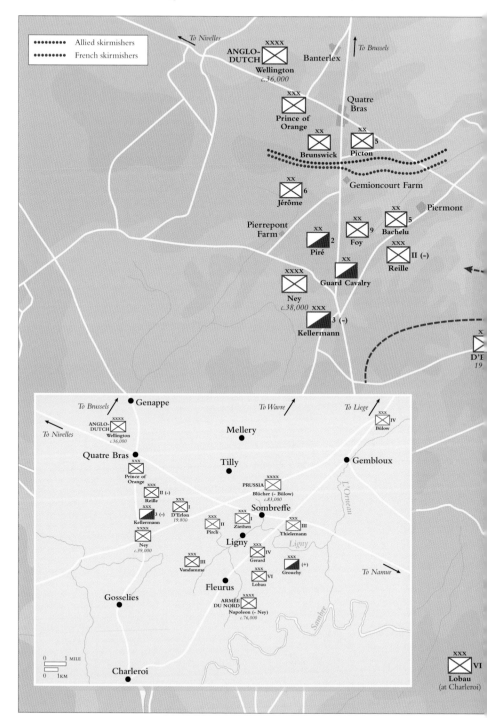

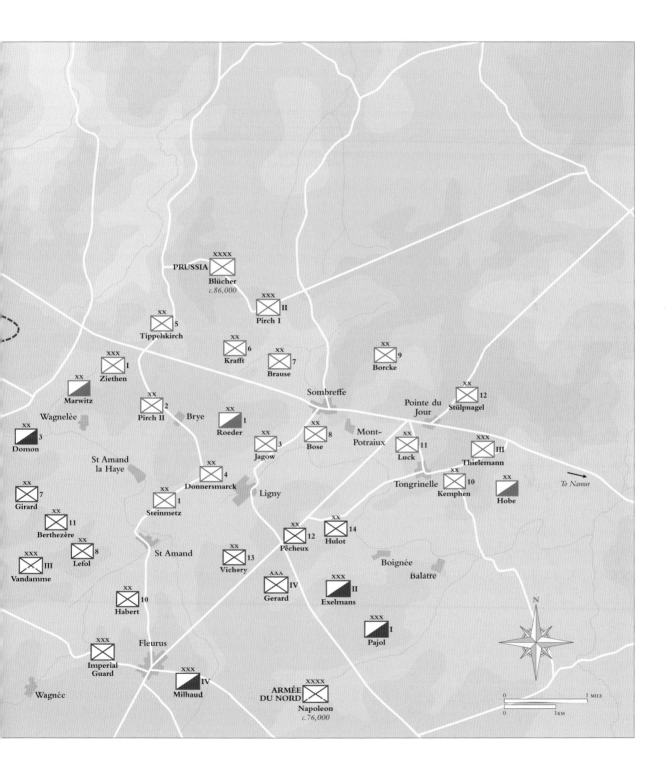

PRUSSIA

XXXX Blücher c.86,000

XXX II Pirch I

XX 5 Tippelskirch

XX 6 Krafft

XX 7 Brause

XX 9 Borcke

XXX I Ziethen

XX Marwitz 3

Sombreffe

XX 12 Stülpnagel

Pointe du Jour

XX Pirch II 2

Brye

XX Roeder 1

XX 8 Bose

Mont-Potraixu

XX 11 Luck

XXX III Thielemann

Wagnelèe

XX 3 Domon

XX 3 Jagow

Tongrinelle

XX 10 Kemphen

XX Hobe

To Namur

St Amand la Haye

XX 4 Donnersmarck

Ligny

XX 7 Girard

XX 1 Steinmetz

St Amand

XX 11 Berthezère

XX 8 Lefol

XX 13 Vichery

XX 12 Pêcheux

XX 14 Hulot

Boignée

Balatré

XXX III Vandamme

XX 10 Habert

XXX IV Gerard

AAA II Exelmans

XXX I Pajol

XXX Imperial Guard

Fleurus

XXX IV Milhaud

ARMÉE DU NORD

XXXX Napoleon c.76,000

Wagnèe

N

0   1 MILE

0   1 KM

cannonade, after which the French could attack them over the bridges. It was Wellington's opinion that the Prussians would do better to deploy their reserves behind the shelter of the rising ground. 'Our troops like to see the enemy,' was the curt response of Lieutenant General August Neithardt von Gneisenau, Blücher's Anglophobe chief of staff. Commenting to Lieutenant Colonel Sir Henry Hardinge, the British liaison officer with Blücher, that if the Prussians fought here they would be 'damnably mauled', Wellington rode off in the direction of Quatre Bras telling Blücher that 'I will come; provided I am not attacked myself.'

While this conference was taking place Lieutenant General Gerard's IV Corps had been arriving on the battlefield and forming up in front of Ligny, with one detached division – Lieutenant General Girard's 7th, from Lieutenant General Honoré Reille's Corps – on its left. Gerard himself detached one of his divisions – Hulot's – to join Exelmanns' cavalry on his right. By 2 p.m. the French deployment was complete. Napoleon's plan was for Pajol's and Exelmanns' cavalry to contain Thielmann's Corps on the right, while Vandamme's and Gerard's infantry attacked St Amand and Ligny respectively. Once Blücher had been compelled to commit all his reserves to the fighting on his centre and right – at about 6 p.m. by his calculation – Napoleon would summon Ney from Quatre Bras to fall on Blücher's right and rear, while the Guard delivered the *coup de grace* in the centre. Thus, two thirds of the Prussian Army – Zieten's and Pirch's Corps – would be destroyed and the remaining third – Thielmann's – driven off in the direction of Liège and away from Wellington. As Napoleon remarked to Gerard, 'It is possible that three hours hence the fate of the war may be decided. If Ney carries out his orders thoroughly, not a gun of the Prussian army will get away.'[3]

At 2 p.m. Napoleon told Soult to inform Ney that Grouchy's wing would attack the enemy between Sombreffe and Brye at 2.30 p.m. The order continues:

> His Majesty's intention is that you also will attack whatever force is in front of you, and after having vigorously pushed it back, you will turn in our direction, so as to bring about the envelopment of that body of the enemy's troops whom I have just mentioned to you. If the latter is overthrown first, then His Majesty will manoeuvre in your direction, so as to assist your operation in a similar way.[4]

At 2.30 p.m. three cannon shots from the Imperial Guard artillery heralded the French assault. Grouchy's cavalry advanced to engage the Prussian left, while Vandamme attacked St Amand with his 8th, 10th and 11th Divisions – with Girard's detached division in reserve while Gerard's Corps simultaneously advanced on Ligny.

The fighting for the villages along the line of the Ligne was bitter and bloody – a succession of attacks and counter-attacks with no quarter given. After a brief resistance at St Amand, the Prussians fell back but held onto the farm there and the village of St Amand la Haye, while their artillery on the heights subjected the French in the village to a hail of canister. At the same time Prussian reserves – as Wellington had foreseen – suffered heavy casualties from French artillery fire without being able to support their comrades in the front line with musket fire. Unable to advance beyond St Amand, Vandamme brought up more artillery and pushed Girard's Division towards St Amand la Haye. Slowly but surely – despite Prussians from Pirch's Corps being fed into the fight – French numbers began to tell; Steinmetz's Brigade (equivalent to a French division) were engaged with a full four French divisions.

Meanwhile at Ligny the men of Gerard's Corps – attacking in three columns – had to battle through hedges, felled trees and man-made obstacles under intense artillery fire and musketry from hordes of skirmishers. When they fought their way into the village they found every building loopholed and every wall and rooftop defended. As at St Amand, the Prussian plan was to retire slowly towards a main position further back, inflicting casualties all the way. Captain Charles François, attached to a brigade of Gerard's Corps, described the casualties suffered by his regiment – the 30th Line – as they fought their way into Ligny:

> In a moment, Major Hervieux, commanding the Regiment, and two battalion commanders, Richard and Lafolie had been killed; another battalion commander, Blain by name, was slightly wounded and had his horse killed under him; five captains were killed, and three wounded, two adjutants and nine lieutenants and sub-lieutenants were killed, seven wounded, and close on seven hundred rank and file killed and wounded.[5]

As at St Amand, however, despite heavy losses, French numbers slowly started to tell.

Although the Prussians outnumbered the French overall, Napoleon's tactic of attacking all along the Prussian line – preventing Blücher from redeploying troops in his front line, and forcing him to make good casualties there from his reserves – as well as Grouchy's highly economic pinning of Thielmann's Corps with a force only one third as strong (Hulot's Division and 3,390 cavalry), had enabled the French to deploy superior numbers at the 'critical point'. By 3.15 p.m., having pinned Blücher's 84,000 men with 58,000 of his own, Napoleon still had 10,000 fresh, uncommitted troops – Clausewitz, present at the battle as a staff officer with Thielmann's Corps, would have been impressed.

As Vandamme's and Gerard's men battled their way into St Amand and Ligny, at 3.15 p.m. Napoleon ordered Soult to send a message to Ney:

> Marshal, I wrote to you an hour ago to inform you that, at 2.30 p.m. the Emperor would attack the position taken up by the enemy between the villages of St. Amand and Brye. At this moment the action is in full swing. His Majesty desires me to tell you that you are to manoeuvre immediately in such a manner as to envelop the enemy's right and fall upon his rear; the fate of France is in your hands.

Almost as soon as this message had been dispatched, a message arrived from Ney informing the emperor that he was heavily engaged at Quatre Bras against 20,000 men under Wellington. Clearly Ney could not now be expected to come down the Nivelles road and attack Blücher's right. It was at this point that Napoleon took a pencil and scribbled the controversial 'Third Directive' instructing Ney to send General Jean-Baptiste Drouet, Count d'Erlon's Corps to perform the same task. The controversy arose when certain historians asserted that the Third Directive – which has not survived – was not in fact written by Napoleon at all, but improvised, even forged, by his aide, General Charles de La Bédoyère, when he arrived near Quatre Bras. This is a minority view; most historians ascribe the confusion this directive caused to Napoleon's notoriously illegible handwriting. Either way this directive began a process which saw d'Erlon's Corps marching and counter-marching between both battlefields and intervening in neither. Having written – or not – the Third Directive, Napoleon seems suddenly to have remembered Lobau's VI Corps still waiting at Charleroi (Clausewitz would have been less impressed) and sent a messenger to call that force forward too.

The fighting in St Amand and Ligny had degenerated into a series of brutal close-quarter fights for every house, barn, building and garden with both sides bringing up artillery and feeding in reinforcements. Both villages – or parts of them – changed hands several times. By 5 p.m., however, Vandamme's Corps had captured Wagnelée, St Amand and St Amand la Haye with General Girard himself being killed during a Prussian counter-attack. In Ligny only the chateau and a corner of the village remained in Prussian hands.

Calculating that by 6 p.m. d'Erlon would be approaching Blücher's right from the direction of Quatre Bras, Napoleon now ordered up the Guard to deliver the final assault against the Prussians at Ligny.

As the Guard began to deploy, however, at about 5.30 p.m. Vandamme rode up to the emperor to report that an unidentified column – some

French I Corps commander, d'Erlon. His men spent 16 June marching between Ligny and Quatre Bras without participating in either attack. (akg-images)

20,000 or 30,000 strong – was approaching his left flank at Wangenies. Initial reports that this was a hostile column had already caused near panic among Vandamme's men and seemingly unnerved even the general himself. Deciding that this was no time to take risks, Napoleon at once sent his own scouts to investigate, moved Duhesme's Division of the Young Guard to support Vandamme's wavering troops, and postponed the Guard's planned attack. It was 6.30 p.m. before the true situation was made clear. The unknown column was d'Erlon's Corps – the scrappily written Third Directive seemed to him to order him to take his corps to 'Wangenies', rather than the intended Wagnelée. As he had neglected to send orderlies forward to warn Vandamme's Corps of his approach, d'Erlon's arrival had unsettled them to the extent that one of Vandamme's divisional commanders, Lieutenant General Lefol, had been forced to turn his artillery on some of his own men, who were quitting the line of battle.

Having dispatched an orderly to direct d'Erlon onto his correct line of march – on Wagnelée, to outflank Blücher – Napoleon was astonished to learn

Napoleon gives the order for the final advance at Ligny. (akg-images)

Charles Vanen 1818.

In the closing stages of the battle, Blücher is trapped beneath his horse. (Anne S. K. Brown)

on the orderly's return that d'Erlon had already marched off in the direction of Quatre Bras, leaving only Durutte's Division behind. Napoleon's final assault had already been delayed by an hour, darkness was falling and his outflanking corps had inexplicably left the battlefield (d'Erlon had in fact been summoned back to Quatre Bras by Ney, though the emperor had no way of knowing this). Worst of all Blücher chose this moment to launch a counter-attack.

Blücher had spent most of the day riding along the heights to the rear of the battlefront feeding in reserves wherever his line looked threatened. Since about 4 p.m. he had been aware that Wellington was heavily engaged at Quatre Bras, and would not be able to come to his assistance. This news confirmed all Gneisenau's suspicions: 'The Duke of Wellington had promised to attack the enemy in the rear…' he was to write later, 'but he did not come, because his army, Heaven knows why, could not concentrate.'[6] Blücher's aim now was to hold his position on the Ligne until nightfall and hope that Bülow and Wellington would be able to join him on the 17th. The confusion caused on the French left by d'Erlon's Corps' arrival had granted him a respite and he had not wasted it.

Gathering together six battalions and some stragglers, he led them forward personally – under a darkening, smoke-filled sky – against St Amand and Ligny.

'Forward! Forward my children!' Blücher leads the counter-attack at Ligny. (akg-images)

The initial onslaught took the French by surprise and hustled Vandamme's still-shaken men almost out of St Amand. However, the French forces rallied outside the village and the Young Guard advanced to retake it. With no further reserves the Prussians fell back once more.

Blücher's last effort had fatally weakened his centre – by 7.30 p.m. all was ready for Napoleon's *coup de grace*. Lead elements of Lobau's VI Corps were beginning to arrive on the scene as – in thunder and heavy rain – the Guard began its advance, half to the east of Ligny and half to the west, supported by 60 guns, with Milhaud's heavy cavalry and the cavalry of the Guard in support. General Roguet's command to his Old Guard – 'Warn the grenadiers that the first man who brings me a prisoner will be shot!' – was superfluous; for both sides this was a fight to the death.

The Guard columns swept into Ligny – driving before them the remaining Prussian defenders. As the emperor entered the village from the west and took up his position on a low mound, the Guard pressed on through the carnage and debris and onto the open ground beyond. The Battle of Ligny was all but won – but Blücher wasn't finished yet. To buy time for his infantry to get clear of the field, Blücher, reverting to his old hussar habits, rode over to where Major General von Roeder's 32 cavalry squadrons – Zieten's last cavalry reserve – were forming into line. Placing himself at their head and with a cry of 'Forward! Forward, my children!' he led them headlong at the Guard.

Forming square, the Guard met the Prussian cavalry with a succession of disciplined volleys at close range. Blücher's own horse – a splendid grey given to him by the British Prince Regent – was hit and collapsed, pinning the field marshal, unconscious, beneath it. His aide de camp, Major Count Nostitz, dismounted to protect his chief as French cuirassiers – oblivious to the prize that lay at their feet – galloped past. A Prussian counter-charge soon brought *Uhlans* (Prussian lancers) to the scene, with whose help Nostitz was able to drag the old man clear, throw him over a saddle and carry him from the field.

As the Prussians streamed away from the battlefield, the expected pursuit did not materialise. The French who had fought all day – first in sweltering heat and later in violent thunderstorms – bivouacked among their own dead and dying on the left bank of the Ligne Brook. To Napoleon it must have seemed that the Prussians were finished as a fighting force. To launch a pursuit in darkness with the whereabouts of Bülow's Corps still unknown was risky and besides he had heard nothing from Ney. Ordering Grouchy to begin the pursuit in the morning, he retired to Fleurus for the night – the Prussians were to be allowed a clean break.

While the French and Prussian armies had been engaged in a life-or-death struggle at Ligny, a very different kind of battle – smaller in scale but every bit as crucial to the outcome of the campaign and no less epic, had been going on all through the afternoon and evening, just 13 kilometres away at Quatre Bras.

Ney had returned from his late-night visit to Napoleon at Charleroi and spent the night at Gosselies. He issued no orders. There is no record of what had passed between Napoleon and Ney during their two-hour conference. Most historians agree, however, that Napoleon must have stressed to Ney the importance of the crossroads at Quatre Bras, standing as it did astride Ney's axis of advance towards Brussels *and* the lateral road connecting his wing of the *Grand Armée* with Grouchy's (or Wellington's Army with Blücher's, depending who held it). Ney has been much blamed for failing to take Quatre Bras early on the 16th, not least by Napoleon, talking of the battle when on St Helena. On the other hand Marshal Soult told Ney's son in 1829 that the 'Emperor had not

The Prince of Orange surveys the battlefield. (Anne S. K. Brown)

the slightest idea of occupying Quatre Bras on the evening of the 15th, and gave no orders to that effect.'[7]

Wherever the truth lies, Ney is surely open to criticism for his actions on the morning of the 16th – for not starting to concentrate his force, which was bivouacked along the line of march, for not sending Reille forward to seize Quatre Bras, and for not calling up d'Erlon in support. Whether he was waiting for written confirmation of the previous night's instructions or whether – as some historians have suggested – he was suffering from some form of 'shell-shock' from his exertions in 1812, there can be no doubt that Ney's failure to seize the all-important crossroads early in the day was in great measure responsible for the failure of the Ligny–Quatre Bras operation. Ney's lack of initiative in this instance is in sharp contrast to that of his opponent, Lieutenant General Perponcher, commanding the 2nd Netherlands Division in the Prince of Orange's I Corps; for without Perponcher's display of initiative Quatre Bras – now only thinly held by the Netherlanders – would not have been defended at all.

Perponcher had been joined at 6 a.m. by his corps commander, the Prince of Orange, and at 10 a.m. by Wellington himself. Wellington had approved the prince's dispositions and, finding all quiet in front of him, Wellington rode off towards Ligny to confer with Blücher. By now reinforcements were on their way to Quatre Bras; the Brunswickers from Genappe, the 1st and 3rd Divisions from Nivelles; and the reserve – set in motion by Wellington – from Mont Saint Jean. Even so, the odds at this point were greatly in favour of Ney – with 19,000 infantry, supported by 3,000 cavalry and 60 guns (and d'Erlon's 20,000 coming on behind them) against just 7,800 infantry, 50 cavalry and 16 guns.

Ney's seeming lethargy that morning was matched by Napoleon's, whose orders to Ney were only dispatched from Charleroi at 8 a.m. instead of the more usual 2 a.m. These orders which Ney received at 10 a.m. told Ney to 'hold yourself in readiness for an immediate advance on Brussels once the reserve reaches you'.[8] It was not until 11 a.m. that Ney issued his own orders – commanding Reille's II Corps to concentrate on Quatre Bras, which was at this stage held only by Perponcher's 8,000. By then of course Napoleon was with Vandamme in front of Ligny – changing Grouchy's pinning action against Blücher into the main French effort of the day. Of this, Ney was unaware – and would remain so until 6.30 p.m. Much of what was to follow – including his recall of d'Erlon from what would surely have been a decisive intervention at Ligny – would stem from Ney's mistaken belief that *his* was still the main operation.

Reille's subordinate, Foy. Another Peninsular veteran, he was a divisional commander in the Waterloo campaign. (Anne S. K. Brown)

Lieutenant General Honoré Reille. A Peninsular veteran, he was of aware of Wellington's tactics and advanced cautiously. (akg-images)

At 11.45 a.m. Reille began moving his troops through Frasnes towards Quatre Bras, with General Piré's cavalry leading – followed by General Foy's 9th and General Bachelu's 5th Divisions, with Prince Jérôme Bonaparte's 6th Division bringing up the rear. At 2 p.m. a French battery of 14 guns opening fire on an Allied battery heralded the opening of Reille's assault. His advance was over a landscape of undulating ground with farms, woods and fields of head-high rye. To his left Bossu Wood offered an enemy an excellent position from which to deliver flanking fire. Moreover, like his commander Ney, and his subordinate Foy, Reille was an old Peninsula hand and knew from experience Wellington's tactic of concealing his men until almost the last moment before delivering a devastating volley and charge. Unwilling to be drawn into another 'Spanish battle', Reille proceeded with caution.

The French advance was steady and relentless, driving before it Perponcher's skirmishers – Major General Willem Bylandt's 27th Jägers. Bachelu's 5th Division took Piraumont, on Perponcher's left; shortly afterwards Foy's 9th Division captured Gemioncourt, in the centre, after a hard fight with Nassauers and Netherlands militia. Pierrepoint Farm, to the left of Bossu Wood, proved a harder nut to crack and Foy's second brigade was checked there, until joined by Jérôme's 8,000 men and a further eight guns. With Pierrepoint in French hands, Jérôme began clearing the Nassauers out of Bossu Wood.

For the best part of an hour Bylandt's 2.5-kilometre-long skirmish line had been retiring in good order, but a charge by Piré's cavalry now broke the 27th Jägers and pushed on towards the Allied centre sweeping aside some Dutch light cavalry as they did so. It was at this moment – about 3 p.m. – that Wellington returned from his meeting with Blücher, to find the Allied line, which had fought well against superior numbers, about to crumple under the combined attacks of three French divisions. Ney with 17,500 infantry, 4,700 cavalry and 62 guns was now in a position to advance on the farm of Quatre Bras itself.

It was fortunate for the Allied cause that at almost the same moment the first reinforcements arrived: General Van Merlen's 2nd Netherlands Light Cavalry Brigade from Nivelles, and the eight battalions of General Thomas Picton's 5th Division from Brussels. Van Merlen's cavalry – exhausted as they were, having not unsaddled in 24 hours – were deployed south of the lateral road to plug the gap created by Piré's charge. Picton's Division was placed to the Allies' left rear. These troops – some 8,000 infantry and 1,000 cavalry – reduced the odds to 2–1 in Ney's favour. More than that, they put new heart into the wavering Allied line.

In order to give his newly arrived troops time to deploy Wellington now ordered a counter-attack. Pushing Picton's leading battalion, the 1st/95th, to Thyle to secure his left flank, he ordered the Dutch-Belgians to retake Gemioncourt, supported by the newly arrived 1st/28th, and Prince Bernhard of Saxe-Weimar to retake Bossu Wood on his left.

At first all went well. The French were driven out of that part of Bossu Wood that they had recently taken, Gemioncourt was re-occupied and two French cavalry charges were driven off. When the Prince of Orange tried to advance south of the farm, however, his

'Black Brunswickers'. Hussar and infantry of the Duke of Brunswick's Corps. (Courtesy of the Council of the National Army Museum)

entire force was overthrown by a regiment of French chasseurs, who scattered his cavalry, sabred his gunners and drove his infantry helter-skelter before them. With more of Piré's squadrons in support they pursued the Netherlanders almost to the Namur road before being halted by the fire of a battalion of Nassauers. Piré's cavalry were halted in their turn by Highlanders of Major General Sir Denis Pack's Brigade, lining the ditches at the roadside.

It was a critical moment for Wellington – who had almost been caught up in the rout himself – but by now Picton's Division was deploying in line of battle from Quatre Bras south-eastwards along the Namur road. At almost the same time further reinforcements arrived for Wellington – in the form of five battalions of Brunswickers, led by their duke. These took up a position between Quatre Bras and Bossu Wood. They were just in time, as Ney made another attempt to seize the crossroads – ordering Bachelu's Division forward against the Allied left, Foy's Division along and to the east of the Brussels road, supported by one of Jérôme's brigades, and Jérôme's remaining brigade back into Bossu Wood.

On the Allied right Ney had some success driving the Netherlanders out of Bossu Wood and forcing the Brunswickers back in some confusion. While trying to rally one of his battalions the Duke of Brunswick was mortally wounded – dying, like his father before him, in action against the French. On the Allied left it was a different story. Bachelu's Division, disordered by the broken ground, were first halted by volley fire from Picton's Division, then

The Duke of Brunswick leads
his 'avant-guard' forward.
(Anne S. K. Brown)

driven back by a bayonet charge. Only the intervention of Piré's lancers and chasseurs halted the British pursuit, before the fire of Bachelu's 42 guns drove them back. As they withdrew Piré's cavalry followed up and, after bloody clashes with the half-formed squares of the 42nd Highlanders and the 44th Foot, rode down a Hanoverian battalion before racing towards the Namur road. Here, once again, they were driven back by the fire of two British battalions that had taken cover in the ditches.

By now it was 4 p.m. For Wellington the latest crisis had been averted – and the arrival of the Brunswickers had brought his force up to 21,000 men, further tilting the balance of numbers in his favour. It was at this moment that Ney received Napoleon's message of 2 p.m. In this, the enemy facing Napoleon at Ligny is described as '*un corps de troupes*' and there is nothing to suggest that his (Ney's) battle is now a secondary action. The 2 p.m. order even suggests that Napoleon – apparently facing one Prussian corps with two French corps, the entire Guard and three corps of reserve cavalry – might well manoeuvre so as to attack Wellington's rear. It was clear to Ney at this point that he could not take the crossroads with Reille's Corps alone. Accordingly he sent an aide galloping back down the Charleroi road to hurry d'Erlon up to the front.

Since approximately midday d'Erlon had been marching his I Corps towards Frasnes – following up Ney's advance. By 4 p.m. his column was just crossing the Roman road to the south of Frasnes – d'Erlon himself had ridden forward to examine the Quatre Bras position before deploying. It was at this point that there arrived on the scene one of Napoleon's aides – General de La Bédoyère – bearing the infamous 'Third Directive'. Whether this note was actually scribbled in Napoleon's notoriously illegible handwriting or was written by La Bédoyère himself, acting on his own initiative, its effect was the same. D'Erlon's column was first halted, and then dispatched in the direction of Ligny. La Bédoyère rode forward to inform d'Erlon of his new mission; d'Erlon then rode off to join his corps on the march towards Ligny – sending his chief of staff – General Delacambre – to show the note to Ney.

On hearing that his much-needed reinforcement had been diverted, and was now marching *away* from his battlefield to join Napoleon at Ligny, Ney characteristically lost his temper. His state of mind was not improved by the arrival, a few minutes later, of Colonel Forbin-Janson, bearing Napoleon's 3.15 p.m. dispatch ordering him to 'manoeuvre immediately so as to envelop the enemy's [i.e. the Prussians'] right' informing him that 'the fate of France is now in your hands'. It must have seemed to Ney that the quickest way to achieve Napoleon's aim was to seize the crossroads, drive Wellington off towards Nivelles and Genappe and *then* send d'Erlon down the Namur road. Ney had no way of knowing that the battle at Ligny was at a crucial stage, and that the arrival

The death of Brunswick at the Battle of Quatre Bras. (Anne S. K. Brown)

of d'Erlon – as directed by La Bédoyère – would clinch victory there and bring about the destruction of Blücher's Army. Deciding to ignore the emperor's order, Ney immediately sent a series of aides galloping after d'Erlon to recall him. D'Erlon was almost in sight of the battlefield of Ligny – having, as we have seen, caused near panic in Vandamme's Corps, and delayed the Guard's attack by an hour – before he received Ney's orders. At once he turned his corps about and began marching back towards Quatre Bras. Thus d'Erlon's 20,000 men spent the entire afternoon and evening marching and counter-marching between two battlefields – on either of which their intervention would have been decisive – without actually participating in either. This crucial failure of communication and understanding between Ney and Napoleon was to rob Napoleon of decisive victory on 16 June.

At Quatre Bras, Ney now set-to to capture the crossroads with the troops he had. In fact the arrival, on Wellington's side, of Lieutenant General Alten's Division had brought his strength up to 24,000 infantry, 1,900 cavalry and 42 guns. By 5 p.m. Ney's only fresh reserve consisted of Lieutenant General François-Étienne Kellermann's heavy cavalry. 'General, a supreme effort is necessary', Ney told him. 'That mass of hostile infantry must be overthrown. The fate of France is in your hands' – an unconscious echo of Napoleon's words

The Prince of Orange on the battlefield of Quatre Bras. (Anne S. K. Brown)

in the 3.15 p.m. order. When Kellermann pointed out to Ney that he only had one brigade present (out of four) Ney replied to him in terms which Kellermann felt questioned his courage.

At a gallop – in order that his men might not have time to see the dangers that faced them, and in order to achieve a measure of surprise – Kellermann led his two regiments forward. The 69th Foot, caught in line owing to a mistaken order by the Prince of Orange, was cut to pieces, losing the King's Colour. A square of the 30th Foot – mostly new recruits – held firm but the 33rd, also composed of young soldiers, was driven in confusion into the nearby woods. For a few moments the triumphant cuirassiers were actually in possession of the crossroads, but cavalry alone cannot hold ground, and Ney's supporting infantry – battling up through Bossu Wood once more – could not support them. The fire of the King's German Legion battery and volleys from the British 30th and 73rd Foot soon had the cuirassiers fleeing in disorder. Kellermann, unhorsed himself, only escaped by clinging to the bridles of two of his men.

At 6.30 p.m. another of Napoleon's aides arrived at Ney's Headquarters. This time Major Baudas brought another copy of the 3.15 p.m. order and a verbal order to send d'Erlon immediately to Ligny. Now at last it was made clear to Ney that his assault on Quatre Bras was only of secondary importance to the dispatching of d'Erlon against Blücher at Ligny – but by now it was too late. With another outburst of rage, Ney stormed off to re-organise his infantry for yet another attempt. In fact the situation was worse than he knew. All day this battle had been a race against time – for Ney, to capture the crossroads while it was still weakly held; for Wellington, to hold it until reinforcements could arrive and shift the odds in his favour. The Allied troops now arriving on the field – which included the leading elements of 1st Division, Major General Sir Peregrine Maitland's Guards Brigade and two horse batteries – brought Wellington's numbers up to 36,000 men and 70 guns. With the advantage of numbers at last, Wellington ordered a counter-attack at 6.30 p.m.

By now both sides were equally exhausted, but a great part of the Allied troops, though fatigued from force-marching, were fresh to the battle. On the Allied right, Maitland's Guards drove Jérôme's troops southwards back through Bossu Wood – until they were halted by the fire of Ney's guns and the threat of his cavalry. In the centre Pack's and General Sir Colin Halkett's Brigades, together with the Netherlanders, Nassauers and Brunswickers, drove the French – who retired, according to one witness, 'with parade ground precision' – back towards Gemioncourt, and on the right Picton forced Bachelu back toward Piraumont. By nightfall the Allies were occupying most of the ground held by Perponcher that morning.

Overall, though – and considering the two battles as one – the day had gone well for Napoleon. The Allied armies had been kept apart and Blücher had been beaten, with the loss of some 16,000 killed and wounded, as well as some 10,000 deserters, and 21 guns. The French had lost between 11 and 12,000 but Lobau's and d'Erlon's Corps were still untouched; so – apart from 1,000 casualties in Ligny village – were the Guard. At Quatre Bras, Ney had lost 4,000 to the Allies' 4,800 (2,400 of the casualties British) and had prevented Wellington from coming to Blücher's assistance – further souring relations between him and Gneisenau, now in command of the Prussian Army. Yet Ligny was an incomplete victory. The Prussian centre was shattered but the wings were intact and had been allowed to break contact and disappear into the night. If Ney had held Wellington in check, the reverse was also true. Intervention by Ney, or d'Erlon, or even Lobau would have turned the Prussian reverse into a catastrophe – but a combination of bad staff work, poor communications and errors on the part of both Napoleon and Ney (amongst others) prevented this.

Napoleon's ill-health, compounded by exhaustion, was surely a factor in the seeming lethargy that overtook him at times. Whether or not Ney was suffering from what we would now recognise as combat stress is debatable but there can be no doubt that having betrayed both Napoleon and later the Bourbons, he was a troubled man – hence, perhaps, his volcanic outburst of rage which prevented a crucial instruction from being delivered at 3.15 p.m. What we can say with certainty is that he was not the man he had been ten years earlier.

If, as chief of staff, Soult was no Berthier, that was hardly his fault, but that of the man who appointed him; similarly, both Ney and Grouchy – both destined to be scapegoats – were also Napoleon's choices. It is fruitless, but almost irresistible, to imagine the outcome of the campaign with, say, Marshal Louis-Gabriel Suchet as chief of staff and Soult and Marshal Louis-Nicolas Davout, currently minister of war, commanding the wings of the Army of the North.

The battles of Ligny and Quatre Bras had offered Napoleon the opportunity to effectively end the campaign on 16 June, with the destruction of the Prussian Army. Although this opportunity had slipped away – or been squandered – there was still reason to believe that the following day Napoleon would be able to join Ney with the whole reserve and destroy Wellington, while Grouchy kept Blücher out of play. With Blücher currently missing – lying unconscious at a field hospital at Mellery, where Nostitz

Marshal Michel Ney.
(Anne S. K. Brown)

had taken him – much would now depend on what his chief of staff, the Anglophobe Gneisenau, would now decide.

By 9 p.m. Gneisenau – himself shaken by a fall from a horse – stood beside the Roman road at the inn of Aux Trois Burrettes, together with Zieten and Pirch and their staffs. Along the road a disorderly mob of soldiers – infantry, cavalry and guns – streamed away to the north-east. Thielmann had made a stand with the remains of his corps along the heights at Brye; Blücher was still unaccounted for. Gneisenau was now nominal as well as actual commander of the Prussian Army. He had a decision to make on which would depend the outcome of the campaign – possibly of the war – and he had to make it quickly. Which way should the Prussian Army retreat?

The logical line of retreat was towards Liège and Bülow's IV Corps – which was already *en route* to Baudaset, north of Gembloux. Bülow could then cover the army's retreat to Liège and on towards the Rhine, beyond which Field Marshal Schwarzenberg was approaching with an Austrian Army. However, the Prussians had already been driven off the Nivelles–Namur road – the shortest route to Liège – so an initial move north towards Louvain, to regroup, seemed in order. Moreover, to retreat to Liège and on to the Rhine would involve abandoning Wellington and his Anglo-Dutch Army. Distrustful of the British and still seething over what he saw as Wellington's failure to support the Prussians earlier in the day, Gneisenau nevertheless realised that uniting the two Allied armies offered the only chance of victory. A retreat north offered the perfect compromise; if the British – as he half-suspected they would – ran for their ships, he could still take his re-ordered army towards Liège. If – as he knew Blücher believed – Wellington intended to stand and fight, the Prussians would be near enough to go to his aid. North it would be then, but crowding round their maps in the half-light none of the Prussian generals could agree on a destination that they could all identify – until someone mentioned Wavre. Almost by accident, then, in what Wellington was later to designate 'the decisive moment of the century', Wavre was settled on as the destination for the night's retreat and at once staff officers were dispatched to block the road to Gembloux and start herding fugitives towards Tilly and Mellery. In this they were only partially successful – some 8,000 men were already heading towards Namur. Although these men took no further part in any fighting, their flight towards Liège – observed by French scouts – was to have a crucial impact on Napoleon's decision-making the following day.

At about 10 p.m. Gneisenau received news that Blücher was alive, and hurried to join him. The field marshal was conscious and lying on a camp-bed, his injuries having been treated with his preferred remedy – applications of gin,

Lieutenant General August Neithardt von Gneisenau, Blücher's chief of staff, orders the retreat to Wavre during the Battle of Ligny. (akg-images)

rhubarb and garlic (external) and a magnum of champagne (internal). Blücher ordered beer to be brought in stable buckets and a debate ensued which lasted most of the night. Gneisenau was still in favour of a retreat towards Liège; Blücher – supported by General Carl von Grolmann, the Prussian quartermaster general – was insistent that the Prussian Army should march so as to support Wellington. Lieutenant Colonel Sir Henry Hardinge, the British commissioner at Prussian Headquarters – who had spent the night in Blücher's ante-room recovering from the amputation of his left hand – was summoned by Blücher early the next morning. Blücher, still reeking from the treatment of his bruises, embraced Hardinge with the words, 'Ich stinke etwas!' and went on to tell him that '... he should be glad if in conjunction with the Duke of Wellington he was able now to defeat his old enemy'.[9] His aides told Hardinge that Blücher would have had himself tied in the saddle rather than resign his command through injury and that 'a thirst for bloody vengeance had taken possession of his will and of his intelligence'.

The Prussian withdrawal began at dawn. Covered by Thielmann's Corps, Zieten and Pirch managed to extract their corps unobserved by the enemy. To inspire a beaten, disorganised army on a rainy night retreat requires leadership of the highest order, and Blücher was the very man to provide it. 'He had had his bruised limbs bathed in brandy…' wrote a Westphalian officer, 'and had helped himself to a large *schnapps*, and now, although riding must have been very painful, he rode alongside the troops, exchanging jokes and banter with many of them, and his good humour spread like wildfire down the columns.'

Once they were clear, Thielmann withdrew towards Gembloux, met up with Bülow's Corps and placed himself under his command. As soon as Zieten's and Pirch's Corps were established in positions around Wavre, Bülow and Thielmann marched to join them. The march was exhausting, conducted for the most part in torrential rain, which at least discouraged the French cavalry – who were slowly following the rearguard – from attacking. By 8 p.m. Thielmann was safely across the River Dyle, and deploying north of Wavre – two hours later Bülow's last elements had joined them. The Prussian Army had regrouped and its commanders were rapidly restoring order.

Napoleon spent the night of the 17th at the Chateau of Fleurus. As far as he was aware everything was going according to plan – Blücher was retreating

The 1st Life Guards charging French lancers near Genappe on 17 June. (Courtesy of the Council of the National Army Museum)

down the Namur road towards Liège, while Wellington was presumably retreating towards Brussels. While he breakfasted a report came in from Count Pajol – whom Grouchy had sent out at 2.30 a.m. – of masses of Prussians on the move down the Namur road. What Pajol had actually seen was the mass of deserters who had escaped the Prussian staff officers before Gembloux and were fleeing in confusion towards Liège, but their presence on the Namur road – combined with a touch of wishful thinking – convinced Napoleon that Blücher was retreating away from the British. Next came Count Flahaut, from Quatre Bras, with the news that Ney had in front of him a large force of British, Dutch and German troops.

Accordingly he wrote to Ney instructing him to take up a position at Quatre Bras, driving off what must surely be Wellington's rearguard. If this should prove impossible – if in other words, Wellington was foolish enough to be holding Quatre Bras with his entire army – then the emperor would operate up the Nivelles road to attack Wellington's left and complete the destruction of his army. Soult's dispatch ended, 'Today it is necessary to end this operation, and complete the military stores, to rally scattered soldiers and summon back all detachments.'

It is clear from this dispatch that Napoleon was still unsure whether Wellington was at Quatre Bras with his whole army or not. With the Prussian Army in retreat – whichever way they were retreating – now was surely the time to move rapidly against Wellington. However, instead of sending Lobau with his VI Corps and General Antoine Drouot with the Guard in the direction of Quatre Bras to support any attack by Ney, Napoleon contented himself with sending a reconnaissance patrol towards Quatre Bras before visiting Grouchy's Headquarters and dragging that officer on a tour of the Ligny battlefield. When Grouchy finally asked him 'What are my orders, Sire?' Napoleon replied brusquely, 'I will give you your orders when it suits me.' It seems that Napoleon's main concern at this point was to rest his army and sort out some of the administrative chaos that had set in since the Army of the North had crossed the River Sambre into Belgium.

During his tour of inspection news came in from Exelmanns that his leading brigade had encountered a large force of Prussians at Gembloux. At about the same time an entire Prussian battery arrived under escort, which had been captured by Pajol on the Namur road – but this battery seemed to have lost its way and the road beyond it – in the direction of Namur – was reported to be empty. General Lutzow, captured in the final charges of the previous evening, had been heard lamenting the destruction of the Prussian Army, but was this in fact true? Was it possible that the Prussian Army had split, with part of it falling back towards Liège, and another part marching so as to join Wellington?

With the situation still not clear, Napoleon considered his options. He could launch a vigorous pursuit towards Liège – to which he was still inclined to believe the Prussians were retreating – but that would divert him from his main objective, Brussels, as well as robbing him of the chance to destroy Wellington. He could send Grouchy with a small force to keep his 'sword in Blücher's back', and attack Wellington in overwhelming force with the rest of the army, or he could play safe and detach Grouchy with a substantial force so as to guard against any possibility of Blücher – or any part of his army – joining Wellington. This would still leave him enough men to deal with Wellington. He took the third option, sending a written order to Grouchy:

> Proceed to Gembloux with the cavalry … and the III and IV Corps of infantry… You will explore in the directions of Namur and Maastricht and you will pursue the enemy… It is important to penetrate what the enemy is intending to do; whether they are separating themselves from the English, or whether they are intending still to unite, to cover Brussels or Liège, in trying the fate of another battle.[10]

By ordering Grouchy to explore to the south-east and the north-east of Sombreffe, Napoleon was looking for the Prussians in the wrong direction; the area between Tilly and Wavre was not scouted.

Grouchy rode off to meet Vandamme (with whom he had quarrelled on the 15th) and Gerard (who believed he should have been created marshal for the previous day's work) and ordered them to advance on Gembloux, III Corps leading. As Vandamme's lead elements passed through Pont du Jour – on the Namur road – the heavens opened.

Having previously dispatched Lobau and Drouot with VI Corps and the Guard to Marbais, Napoleon had, at about midday, written to Ney instructing him to '… attack the enemy at Quatre Bras and drive him from his position … the force which is at Marbais will second your operation. His Majesty is about to proceed to Marbais, and awaits your reports with impatience.'

It was 1 p.m. before Napoleon reached Marbais – perturbed at having heard no cannonading as he

An accomplished cavalry commander, Marshal Emmanuel de Grouchy was less well suited to the role of corps commander. (Topfoto)

approached. Finding Ney's troops still eating their midday meal he ordered all troops to fall in, but it was another hour before the leading elements – of d'Erlon's Corps – were ready to move. Seeing this priceless opportunity to destroy Wellington slipping from his grasp, Napoleon said to d'Erlon, 'France has been ruined. Go, my dear general, and place yourself at the head of the cavalry and pursue the rear guard vigorously.' Thus – in torrential rain, which confined the cavalry to the roads – began the French pursuit.

Wellington had spent the night of the 16th at Genappe, but was at Quatre Bras early on the 17th. There appeared to be no French activity to his front, and he had had no word from Blücher. Still unaware of the result of the fighting at Ligny he sent his senior aide de camp, Lieutenant Colonel Sir Alexander Gordon, with a squadron of the 10th Hussars out towards the east. By 7.30 a.m. Gordon was back bearing news: he had contacted Zieten; the Prussians had sustained a defeat and were now retiring on Wavre. At 9 a.m. a Prussian staff officer arrived confirming the news – the first communication Wellington had received from Prussian Headquarters since 2 p.m. the previous day. In fact Gneisenau had dispatched a messenger informing him of the Prussian defeat and withdrawal almost as soon as he had assumed command, at 9 p.m. the previous evening, but that messenger had been captured.

Wellington had with him at Quatre Bras two Dutch-Belgian divisions, four Anglo-Hanoverian divisions, the Brunswickers, Van Merlen's cavalry and Lord Henry Uxbridge's Cavalry Corps (who had arrived the evening before, too late to participate in the battle): 50,000 men in all, with more on the way. Exposed as he now was, he was in danger of being attacked by almost the entire Army of the North. His first instinct was to order an immediate withdrawal – but Baron Carl von Müffling, the Prussian commissioner on Wellington's staff, knew from his own experience in Germany that Napoleon liked to let his men rest and cook a meal on the day after a battle. He suggested that Wellington's exhausted troops would benefit from the same.

With Uxbridge's cavalry available to cover his withdrawal it was worth a slight delay to allow his men to start their march in better condition. After ordering the infantry to start 'thinning out' and be clear of Quatre Bras by 10 a.m. Wellington sent a messenger to Blücher informing him that he was falling back on Quatre Bras to a position at Mont Saint Jean, where he would stand and fight, provided Blücher could assist him with one or two corps.

At Mont Saint Jean, where the Nivelles–Brussels road and the Charleroi–Brussels road met, a series of ridges ran east to west and Wellington, who had ridden over the ground some months earlier, was confident he could fight there with the Forest of Soignes at his back. His only other option – to retire north of Brussels – would mean abandoning his line of communication to Ostend. The road around his right flank – from Mons to Brussels – still represented a threat, so he ordered General Rowland Hill, with two brigades of 4th Division, Prince Frederick's Dutch-Belgian Division and Anthing's Brigade to block that road at Halle.

Covering his rear with a strong screen of Lord Uxbridge's cavalry, as well as guns and Congreve rockets, Wellington waited until the last of his infantry were through Genappe (about 2 p.m.) before remarking to Uxbridge, 'No use waiting. The sooner you get away the better. No time to be lost.' Only moments later French cavalry – lancers and cuirassiers – could be discerned advancing up the Namur road; the French pursuit had begun.

Observing the French with his horse-artillery troop, Captain Alexander Cavalié Mercer suddenly recognised Napoleon – who, irritated at Ney's delay, had placed himself at the head of some light cavalry. 'I had often longed to see Napoleon, that mighty man of war – that astonishing genius who had filled the world with his renown. Now I saw him – and there was a degree of sublimity in the interview rarely equalled.'[11] Mercer is referring to the fact that heavy dark clouds now hung over the heads of the British while the French – and Napoleon – were still momentarily standing in brilliant sunshine. With the opening salvo from the British guns the clouds burst – turning the ground on either side of the road into a girth-deep quagmire.

Despite the British fire the French cavalry were coming on fast. Crying to Mercer 'Make haste, make haste! For God's sake gallop, or you will be taken!'[12] Uxbridge followed his own advice. Minutes later he, the 7th Hussars and Mercer's guns – confined, like their pursuers to the road – were galloping pell-mell in the

Lady Butler's picture of the 28th (North Gloucestershire) Regiment at the Battle of Quatre Bras, 16 June 1815. (Soldiers of Gloucestershire Museum www. glosters.org.uk)

lashing rain, over the bridge and through the main street of Genappe. 'We lost sight of our pursuers altogether…,' wrote Mercer, 'and the shouts and halloos, and even laughter, they had at first sent forth were either silenced or drowned in the uproar of the elements and the noise of our too rapid retreat.'[13] Once through Genappe the 7th Hussars turned, reformed and charged the French lancers, who were already emerging from the village. The Hussars – unable to make headway against the levelled lances – fell back. After a salvo of canister from a British battery, the Blues and Life Guards charged the lancers – Captain Kelly of the Life Guards killing their colonel – and drove them back into the village, where in the confined streets their lances were an encumbrance.

After that bloody encounter in the slippery streets of Genappe – where the French were in Mercer's phrase 'taught a little modesty'[14] – the pursuit was hardly pressed at all. The remainder of the retreat was conducted at a walk, with the French content to follow up and observe. At a cost of 93 killed, wounded and missing, Wellington had extricated his army and established himself on the ridge of Mont Saint Jean. It had been a well-conducted retreat, if a close-run thing, and the weather had been on Wellington's side. 'What would I not have given to have had Joshua's power to slow down the sun's movement by two hours,' mused Napoleon later on St Helena.[15]

As the emperor approached the inn of La Belle Alliance, still in driving rain, his advance guard came under fire from guns deployed across the Charleroi road where it crossed the ridge of Mont Saint Jean – about 60 of them by Napoleon's calculation. Clearly this was no rearguard – Wellington was going to stand and fight here. Later that evening at his Headquarters at the farmhouse of Le Caillou, as his army attempted to find shelter from the rain in the sodden fields all around, Napoleon received a dispatch from Grouchy. After a muddy and wearisome march Grouchy's two corps were settled for the night around Gembloux. Grouchy reported that his dragoons had encountered a Prussian rearguard at Tourinnes 8 kilometres north of Gembloux and 13 kilometres short of Wavre. A second column had been seen further east at Perwez. He wrote:

> We may perhaps infer that one column is going to join Wellington and that the centre which is Blücher's arm is retiring towards Liège … if I find the mass of Prussians is retiring on Wavre I shall follow them, so as to prevent them gaining Brussels, and to separate them from Wellington.

Napoleon was content. Even if the bulk of Blücher's Army *had* gone to Wavre they would surely be in no condition to fight for several days yet – and Grouchy had more than enough men to keep them occupied *and* away from Wellington.

The following day with the rest of the *Armée* he would decide the issue of the whole campaign by the destruction of Wellington's Army. It does not seem to have occurred to Napoleon – who considered Wellington a cautious commander – to wonder why he had been so bold as to make a stand at Mont Saint Jean.

Since early that day Wellington had been relying on Blücher's verbal assurance – transmitted by Baron Müffling – that if he stood before Brussels the Prussians would come to his aid with at least one corps. By 11 p.m., as Wellington was conferring with Uxbridge in a cottage in the village of Waterloo, the Prussian high command had reached a final decision. Blücher emerged from the room where the meeting had been held and declared to Hardinge, 'Gneisenau has given in. We are going to join the Duke.' (The phrase 'given in' is significant; it indicates Gneisenau's mindset at the time.) He then showed Hardinge the draft of his dispatch to Wellington: 'Bülow's (IVth) Corps will set off marching tomorrow at daybreak in your direction. It will be immediately followed by the (IInd) Corps of Pirch. The Ist and IIIrd Corps will also hold themselves in readiness to proceed towards you.'

At whatever time – and it is still uncertain – Wellington received this dispatch, it merely confirmed the faith he had already placed in Blücher. Tomorrow, for the first time in this campaign, the Allied armies would combine against Napoleon. As Blücher – refusing to allow fresh ointment to be applied to his bruises – commented to his doctor early the next morning, 'If things go well today, we shall soon be washing and bathing in Paris!'

Lieutenant Colonel Sir Henry Hardinge, the British liaison officer with Blücher, was wounded at Ligny. (Courtesy of the Council of the National Army Museum)

ANALYSIS

By the evening of 17 June everything was still in place for a French victory – but the odds had lengthened. Wellington, having been initially wrong-footed by Napoleon, had fought a masterly battle at Quatre Bras, feeding in reserves at the right moments until the balance tipped in his favour and getting his army away on the 17th to a previously reconnoitred position at Mont Saint Jean. Perponcher's 'intelligent disobedience', in taking his division to Quatre Bras, and the performance of the much-maligned (in some British accounts) Dutch-Belgian troops were crucial to the outcome of the campaign. It was Blücher's 'hussar habits' (Napoleon's phrase, describing the Prussian commander) that had induced him to concentrate at Ligny – too far forward

Napoleon, the night before the
Battle of Waterloo. (akg–images)

Marshal Nicolas Soult,
Napoleon's chief of staff and an
accomplished field commander.
(Anne S. K. Brown)

for a concentration of the two Allied armies. Prussian tactics – exposing troops on the hillside behind the Ligne – led to their army being (as Wellington had predicted) 'damnably mauled'. If their centre had been broken, however, the wings had made a clean break from contact, for which credit must go to Gneisenau, as well as for his decision to concentrate at Wavre, thus keeping his army's options open. The rapid recovery and regrouping of the Prussian forces was another major factor in the campaign's outcome. Nor should we discount another element – one on which Napoleon himself famously laid great emphasis – luck. Blücher's survival, revival and return to command was near-miraculous, and it was his 'hussar' mindset that would send the Prussian Army marching to support Wellington on the 18th. Napoleon's apologists over the years have placed the blame for the campaign's ultimate failure on his subordinates. These subordinates, however, were men he had appointed. Ney was a political choice – a prominent defector from the Bourbons and popular with the army. If he failed to act with speed on the morning of the 16th and seize the crossroads at Quatre Bras, he subsequently neutralised Wellington's Army with only one understrength corps and a heavy cavalry brigade.

'Order, counter-order – disorder!' is a well-known military maxim. Much has been made of the march and counter-march of d'Erlon – with Ney generally getting the blame. These things, however, happen in war (for example at Leipzig in 1813) and less has been made of Napoleon's failure – earlier in the day – to bring Lobau's Corps forward at least to a point where it could have intervened in either battle. If Lobau – whom Napoleon seems to have almost forgotten – had been at hand at the crucial moment at Ligny, he could have intervened just as effectively as d'Erlon. It is clear that after the initial concentration at Beaumont – a considerable feat – there were failures in staff work. Much of this can be attributed to what Clausewitz called the 'friction' of war – messengers get lost or killed, hastily scribbled orders are misread (luck again) – and to the poor communications of the time. It is difficult to resist the conclusion, however, that things would have gone more smoothly had Berthier been present as chief of staff. Soult (nicknamed 'King Nicolas' in Spain), an accomplished field commander, would have been arguably better suited to commanding one of the army's wings than to the 'chief clerk's' job of issuing another man's orders. Indeed, he had never done the job, even at corps level. Marshal Davout – left behind in Paris because of his political reliability – could have brought his considerable battlefield skills to the other wing. A better choice for chief of staff might have been Marshal Suchet, a formidable administrator, who was guarding the admittedly important eastern frontier. A gallant and spirited leader of cavalry, Grouchy had never before commanded even a corps, let alone a wing of the army, though he performed well at Ligny, keeping Thielmann's Corps out of play. That he failed to pursue the Prussians as vigorously as Marshal Murat (refused a command because of his double-dealing with the Allies) might have done, was as much Napoleon's fault as his own. Uncertain of Ney's fate (or Bülow's whereabouts) on the night of the 16th, Napoleon was reluctant to send Grouchy on the kind of helter-skelter pursuit that might have destroyed the Prussian Army. The following morning we see Grouchy impatiently asking Napoleon for orders only to be angrily rebuffed. Nor can Grouchy be blamed for the foul weather that hampered his operations later in the day. From the French point of view the story of the Battle of Ligny–Quatre Bras is one of lost opportunities. Waterloo was the battle that need never have happened.

CHAPTER 3

THE COMMANDERS

Philip Haythornthwaite

At least two of the three principal commanders in the Waterloo campaign were regarded in their own time as the greatest generals of their age, reputations which still endure, and whose influence on the campaign could not have been more profound: Napoleon Bonaparte, Emperor of the French, and Arthur Wellesley, 1st Duke of Wellington. They were almost the same age, born in 1769 only about 106 days apart: Wellington on or about 1 May[1] and Napoleon on 15 August. Both had attained their respective positions on merit, but the paths that led to their first and only confrontation on the field of Waterloo had been considerably different.

Napoleon Bonaparte, the dominant figure of the entire age that was to be named after him, was born at Ajaccio, Corsica, the son of a lawyer of minor

aristocratic background and little fortune. He was commissioned into the French Army as an officer of artillery, a branch of the service that under the *Ancien Régime* had held little attraction for the aristocracy and was thus more the preserve of the dedicated professional. Napoleon always held that luck played an important part in a general's success, and some evidence of this may be seen in his own career. He was possessed of prodigious military talents, but had the fortune to exercise them in the era of the French Revolution, a time of political upheaval and ferment, conditions conducive to rapid progress in his military and political career, despite his original lowly rank. From his first notable military success at Toulon in 1793, at the age of only 24, he displayed not only his immense military talents but also a high degree of political acumen, not to say ruthlessness and cunning, and an aptitude for unremitting toil.

A stunningly successful campaign in Italy forged Napoleon's military reputation; and in a very few years he had attained the highest political office, initially as one of the three Consuls appointed after the coup of Brumaire (November 1799), subsequently as First Consul for life and in December 1804 as Emperor of the French, with all power concentrated in his own hands. For almost a decade thereafter he was the dominant political and military personality in Europe; he defeated his main continental rivals (Austria, Prussia and Russia) and much of the continent fell under his sway. It did not endure: he over-reached himself with his invasion of Russia in 1812 and never recovered from his losses; his allies deserted as his enemies took their opportunity for revenge, and he was compelled to abdicate in April 1814. His ambition exerted a terrible price: as Sir John Seeley commented, 'he had stooped to pick up a crown but having held it in his hands, he dropped it'.[2] Napoleon had been consigned to the tiny Mediterranean island of Elba by his enemies, but with the restored Bourbon monarchy in France proving highly unpopular, he found widespread support among his old followers when he returned in the spring of 1815, and in an attempt to forestall his enemies, he marched against their nearest military forces in the Netherlands.

The most celebrated of those who opposed Napoleon's advance was Arthur Wellesley, a product of the Anglo-Irish aristocracy. His rise to high command had been less stellar than Napoleon's, and while the latter owed his initial success almost entirely to his own talents, Wellesley's family connections were of assistance in the early part of his career. Service in the Netherlands as a battalion commander in 1794 showed him, as he said, 'what one ought not to do'[3] and the lesson was taken to heart: successful campaigns in India led to his appointment to the chief command in the Peninsular War, the successful conclusion of which depended heavily upon his prodigious military (and indeed diplomatic) talents. Awards followed: successive steps in the peerage to the highest rank, a dukedom, using the title 'Wellington' chosen for him by his brother, and promotion to field marshal, the highest honours that could be bestowed by his sovereign and country. He was sent to the Congress of Vienna to exercise his diplomatic talents, but upon Napoleon's return was directed to command the Anglo–Allied force in the Netherlands.

Certain aspects of the style of command of the two generals were similar, including the confidence that their abilities imbued in their followers; but in many respects they were very different.

Although one of the greatest generals of all history, Napoleon was not really an innovator in the field of minor tactics, but rather built upon a system that was already in use. Tactical developments often depended upon circumstances and on the quantity of resources available, and Napoleon had the capacity to assemble large quantities of artillery and cavalry that were denied to some other armies. He tended to use both as offensive tools rather than as support elements, hence

Wellington in India, 1803.
(Print after Robert Home)

the deployment of huge quantities of artillery to soften an enemy line in preparation for an infantry or cavalry attack, while massed charges of heavy cavalry became a primary striking-force to the extent that Wellington commented that Napoleon:

gained some of his battles by the use of his cuirassiers as a kind of accelerated infantry, with which, supported by masses of cannon, he was in the habit of seizing important parts in the centre or flanks of his enemy's position, and of occupying such points till his infantry could arrive to relieve them. He tried this manoeuvre at the battle of Waterloo, but failed because we were not to be frightened away.[4]

At a more strategic level, Napoleon devised or adapted a number of manoeuvres which he used to considerable effect, including one utilised in the Waterloo campaign, which has been described as the 'strategy of the central position'. This was used when Napoleon was opposed by two enemy armies, or wings, which together might outnumber him. As in the case of the Anglo-Allied and Prussian Armies he confronted in the Waterloo campaign, he would attempt to interpose himself between them, and allocate a minority portion of his own army to contain one of the enemy formations. The greater part of his own army he would then throw at the second enemy, achieving 'local superiority' in numbers and overwhelming it; and having put it to flight, would use a small force to pursue and with the remainder switch his attention to the first enemy, and defeat that in the same way. The effectiveness of this manoeuvre was facilitated by the organisation of his army into semi-autonomous *corps d'armée*, self-contained miniature armies including infantry, cavalry and artillery, able to sustain a fight unaided for some time. Because

Napoleon could not be present on both battlefields involved in such a strategy, it demanded an able subordinate to conduct one action, freeing Napoleon to lead at the other. Such a dual battle had been most decisive at Jena-Auerstädt in 1806, when Napoleon had utilised the very considerable talents of Marshal Louis-Nicolas Davout; but as in 1815 it worked less well with subordinate commanders of more limited ability. In this case, Napoleon used Marshal Michel Ney to occupy Wellington's attention at Quatre Bras, while he engaged the Prussians at Ligny; and then, having detached Marshal Emmanuel de Grouchy to follow the retreating Prussians, he switched the remainder of his army onto a major drive against Wellington.

A crucial factor in Napoleon's system of command was his relationship with his troops, of all ranks. A master of psychology when dealing with his army, he had fostered a culture of personality, in which he was the fount of all. His name was carried upon the flags of his army; all rewards and promotions were in his gift, and the cry taken up with such enthusiasm by his troops did not relate to their nation but was '*Vive l'Empereur!*' One of his great skills was in relating to the ordinary soldiers; he had a phenomenal memory but there was a degree of artifice in his apparent ability to recollect individual private soldiers, to some extent the result of careful preparation by his aides. A typical example was recorded in which a sergeant approached him and asked to be awarded the *Légion d'Honneur*, a decoration that Napoleon had instituted and was in his personal gift, and thus regarded as the most precious award in the eyes of his troops. The sergeant was notably ugly which perhaps helped fix him in Napoleon's memory, but he told the man that he remembered him precisely and that he had promised him the decoration ten months before at the bakery at Vilna. The recounting of such anecdotes reinforced the aura of Napoleon's infallibility and the belief that he cared for, and remembered, every one of his men, which bound them to him ever closer. A few words spoken to a regiment before battle could take on the aspect of a near-divine pronouncement and elevate morale. Although not all were susceptible, the cult of personality had electrifying effects, as Napoleon himself described:

Napoleon in his customary undress coat of the *Chasseurs à Cheval* of the Imperial Guard; the breast-star, ribbon and first medal are those of the *Légion d'Honneur*, the second medal that of the Italian Order of the Iron Crown. (Print after Horace Vernet)

Napoleon on campaign: a classic image. (Print after Jean-Louis Meissonier)

> When, in the heat of battle, passing along the line, I used to exclaim, 'Soldiers, unfurl your banners, the moment is come', our Frenchmen absolutely leaped for joy. I saw them multiply a hundred-fold. I then thought nothing [is] impossible.[5]

Unlike the commanders he faced in the Waterloo campaign, Napoleon possessed a considerable advantage in that he alone was the master of his course of action, a supreme commander responsible to no other. He had complete freedom of command in every aspect of his strategy, in his selection of subordinates and in the positions they occupied. He had lost a number of his most trusted deputies, and in 1815 it could be argued that perhaps he did not make best use of those he had left. A most grievous loss was that of his invaluable chief of staff, Marshal

Louis-Alexandre Berthier, who having accepted the Bourbon restoration in 1814 had remained loyal to them, and who had fallen to his death from a window on 1 June 1815, conceivably suicide (he had been watching Russian troops marching past on the way to enter France). In his place Napoleon appointed Marshal Nicolas Soult, one of the best of his generals who might have been employed more effectively in a field command. Two of his remaining most capable subordinates were not even with his Army of the North: Marshal Louis-Nicolas Davout had been appointed minister of war and governor of Paris, important duties but a waste of his battlefield abilities; and Marshal Louis-Gabriel Suchet, who had enjoyed success in virtually independent command in Spain, had been appointed to lead the Army of the Alps in 1815. Instead, Napoleon put great reliance on two generals of lesser talent: Marshal Emmanuel de Grouchy, who was to attract much criticism (some probably unjustified) by his handling of Napoleon's right wing in the pursuit of the Prussians in their withdrawal after Ligny, and for not marching to Napoleon's assistance on the day of Waterloo; and Marshal Michel Ney.

Napoleon in his usual campaign uniform, protected by sentinels of the *Grenadiers à Pied* of the Imperial Guard. (Print after Jean-Louis Meissonier)

Ney was renowned for courage, notably in Russia in 1812 – Napoleon had termed him 'bravest of the brave' – and he had joined Napoleon in 1815 under unusual circumstances. Having pledged his allegiance to the restored Bourbon monarchy, Ney had declared his intention to take the field against Napoleon, but then relented and joined his old chief. Napoleon was conciliatory, declaring that:

> he had behaved very ill to me; but how could I forget his brilliant courage, and the many acts of heroism that had distinguished his past life! I rushed forward to embrace him, calling him the 'bravest of the brave' – and from that moment we were reconciled.[6]

For all his bravery, however, Ney was not a great tactician, and was criticised for his conduct of the Battle at Quatre Bras; yet

Napoleon was content to allow him to conduct much of the Battle of Waterloo as well, within the emperor's broad tactical plan. Like Napoleon himself, he displayed little subtlety in his handling of the battle.

Other factors were significant in Napoleon's conduct of the campaign, including his health. At times in the previous few years he had exhibited periods of uncharacteristic lethargy, even though in the 1814 campaign he had displayed much of his old skill and vigour. In the Waterloo campaign it has been stated that he was suffering from attacks of haemorrhoids and cystitis, though these painful conditions were not made known until many years later, and then not with great certainty. If he were unwell, Napoleon concealed any malady from those around him, though it may have been a factor in his conduct of the campaign. Certainly he never made illness an excuse for what occurred, but then he never seems to have acknowledged that he had made any mistakes in his direction of the campaign.

This would seem to exemplify another factor in the campaign: Napoleon's self-confidence. On the morning of the battle Napoleon breakfasted at the farm of Le Caillou, and then held a conference with some of his commanders, who urged caution or perhaps just expressed a realistic appreciation of the situation. Soult advocated that at least part of the force allocated to Grouchy on the right

Napoleon wearing his usual undress coat of the *Chasseurs à Cheval* of the Imperial Guard. (Engraving by H. Meyer after Jean-Baptiste Isabey)

A characteristic pose: Napoleon reviews the *Grenadiers à Pied* of the Imperial Guard. (Print after Auguste Raffet)

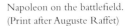

Napoleon on the battlefield.
(Print after Auguste Raffet)

Napoleon on the battlefield.
(Print after Auguste Raffet)

be used instead to bolster that part of the army in direct opposition to Wellington. Napoleon was dismissive: 'You think,' he declared, 'because Wellington defeated you, that he must be a great general. I tell you that he is a bad general, that the English are poor troops, and that this will be the affair of a *déjeuner*.' Soult replied, 'I hope so!'[7]

Lieutenant General Honoré Reille, who had fought Wellington in the Peninsular War and now commanded II Corps, also advocated caution; he stated, from experience, that the British infantry, posted as Wellington knew how to post them, were usually impregnable when attacked because of their calm tenacity and firepower; but that he considered the French superior in terms of manoeuvre, and that manoeuvring might be the way to success. Napoleon liked this no better than Soult's opinion, which recalls his reported dismissal of a similar plan proposed by Davout in 1812, that might have avoided the butchery of the frontal assault at Borodino: 'Ah! You are always for turning the enemy: it is too dangerous a manoeuvre!'[8] Napoleon was equally dismissive of the belief of his brother Jérôme Bonaparte, who commanded a division under Reille, that Field Marshal Gebhard Leberecht von Blücher and Wellington intended to unite in front of the Forest of Soignies, i.e. around Wellington's position (although this was founded on nothing more than a conversation between British officers overheard by a waiter in the inn at Genappe). Napoleon rejected this idea, believing that after their mauling at Ligny the Prussians would not be able to execute such a union with Wellington. (With the benefit of hindsight, during his exile at St Helena Napoleon declared that if he *had* manoeuvred to

Napoleon and his staff (1813).
(Print after Auguste Raffet)

turn Wellington's right, he would have succeeded, but that he had preferred to pierce the centre and attempt to separate the two enemy armies.)

Napoleon's refusal to consider the advice of those who knew the enemy and his declaration that it would be a *déjeuner* could be seen as an attempt to hearten nervous subordinates; but both Soult and Reille were battle-hardened and talented generals not likely to exhibit trepidation. Instead, it may have been an example of Napoleon's over-confidence, as described by Armand de Caulaincourt, an experienced soldier, Napoleon's chief diplomatic advisor and his foreign minister in 1815. He observed that Napoleon always had antipathy to any opinions he disliked, and that, 'Once he had an idea implanted in his head, the Emperor was carried away by his own illusion. He cherished it, caressed it, became obsessed with it.'[9] Indeed, on his return to Paris after Waterloo, Napoleon remarked to Caulaincourt that the day had been won and that the enemy had been defeated at every point save Wellington's centre, when his own army had inexplicably been seized with panic and all was lost.

Caulaincourt's opinion seems to be reinforced by subsequent remarks. Comte de Las Cases, Napoleon's companion on St Helena, recorded how

Napoleon disliked to speak of Wellington, until on one occasion he burst out with a tirade that Las Cases found astonishing: 'His gestures, his features, his tone of voice, were all expressive of the utmost indignation.' He declared that 'Wellington's troops were admirable, but his plans were despicable; or, I should rather say, that he formed none at all… His glory is wholly negative. His faults were enormous … he has no ingenuity; fortune has done more for him than he has done for her', so that it was inconceivable that he and Blücher should have defeated 'an enemy so prompt and daring as myself'. Napoleon claimed that in the three days fighting he had had victory snatched from his grasp on three occasions: by a general who deserted and revealed his plans to the Allies (presumably Lieutenant-General Louis Bourmont, who had commanded Napoleon's 14th Division until his defection on 15 June, and whose information was probably actually of little value); by Ney's mishandling of the action at Quatre Bras; and by Grouchy's conduct on 18 June which 'instead of securing victory, completed my ruin, and hurled France into the abyss'.[10] Napoleon seems to have accepted no personal responsibility for the crushing defeat, exhibiting self-confidence taken to a dangerous level.

Napoleon's rapport with his ordinary soldiers is exemplified in this scene in which he is greeted by members of the Young Guard. (Print after Auguste Raffet)

Contrary to Napoleon's somewhat uncharitable view of his opponent, Wellington had no doubts about Napoleon's abilities as a general: 'There was nothing like him. He suited a French army so exactly! Depend upon it, at the head of a French army there was never anything like him … I used to say of him that his presence on the field made the difference of forty thousand men';[11] and 'Napoleon was the first man of his day on a field of battle, and with French troops'. He added, 'I confine myself to that. His policy was mere bullying, and, military matters apart, he was a Jonathan Wild',[12] referring to the notorious organiser of robberies hanged at Tyburn in 1725. Nevertheless, Wellington expressed some disappointment at Napoleon's apparent absence of imagination at Waterloo. Sir Andrew Barnard recalled that during the battle the duke had remarked of Napoleon, 'Damn the fellow, he is a mere pounder after all'.[13] He also commented on Napoleon's failure to manoeuvre in a letter to William Beresford a couple of weeks after the battle:

> Never did I see such a pounding match. Both were what the boxers call gluttons. Napoleon did not manoeuvre at all. He just moved forward in the old style, in columns, and was driven off in the old style. The only difference was, that he mixed cavalry with his infantry, and supported both with an enormous quantity of artillery. I had the infantry for some time in squares, and we had the French cavalry walking about us as if they had been our own. I never saw the British infantry behave so well.[14]

However, in fairness it is conceivable that Napoleon did intend something more sophisticated than a simple frontal assault: the attack on Hougoumont was probably pressed so strongly in an attempt to draw in Wellington's reserves, leaving his centre weakened and more vulnerable to the French attack.

In contrast to Wellington's great activity during the battle, once his tactics had been decided Napoleon seems to have been largely content to allow his senior commanders, mainly Ney, to conduct the minutiae of the fight, instead of exercising total personal direction himself. An account of Napoleon's conduct during the battle was given by a Belgian civilian, Jean-Baptiste de Coster, who was picked up by Napoleon's staff and kept at Headquarters as a guide to the local terrain. This allowed him to observe Napoleon throughout the action at Waterloo:[15]

> At noon, Buonaparte[16] went out with his staff, and placed himself on an eminence by the side of the causeway, at a very little distance in rear of the farm [Rossomme], from whence he had a view of the whole field of battle. Persons very soon came

Napoleon reconnoitring on campaign, wearing his characteristic grey greatcoat; his horse is held by a member of his escort of the *Chasseurs à Cheval* of the Imperial Guard. (Print after Auguste Raffet)

to tell him, that the attack on the farm and chateau of Hougoumont, which he had ordered to commence at eleven o'clock, had not succeeded.

At one o'clock the battle became general. Buonaparte remained in his first station, with all his staff, till five o'clock. He was on foot, and walked constantly backwards and forwards, sometimes with his arms crossed, but more frequently with his hands behind his back, and with his thumbs in the pockets of his slate-coloured great-coat. He had his eyes fixed on the battle, and took out alternately his watch and snuff-box. De Coster, who was on horseback near him, frequently remarked his watch [sic]. Buonaparte, perceiving that he also took snuff, and that he had no more, frequently gave him some.

When he saw that his attempts to carry the position of the chateau of Hougoumont had been vainly reiterated, he took a horse, quitted the farm of Rossum [sic] at five o'clock, and, moving forward, placed himself opposite to the house of De Coster, at the distance of a gun-shot from La Belle Alliance. He remained in this second station till seven o'clock. It was at that moment that he first perceived, by means of his glass, the arrival of the Prussians... Some fifteen minutes afterwards [he] gave orders that his guards should make a movement on the centre of the English army. He himself, again moving forward at the gallop, went and placed himself, with his staff, in a ravine formed by the causeway, half way between La Belle Alliance and La Haye Sainte. This was his third and last position. Buonaparte and his suite had been in great danger before arriving at this ravine: a ball even carried away the pommel of the saddle of one of his officers, without either touching him or his horse. Buonaparte merely told him coldly, that he ought to keep within the ravine.

De Coster recalled one incident in which Napoleon's old training as an artillery officer impelled him to action:

Perceiving that one of the guns of the battery on the left was not making good fire, he alighted from his horse, mounted on the height at the side of the road, and advanced to the third gun, the firing of which he rectified, while cannon and musket-balls were whistling around him. He returned with tranquillity, with his hands in the pockets of his great-coat, and took his place among his officers.

Having witnessed the defeat of the last attack, de Coster heard Napoleon say to General Henri-Gatien Bertrand, 'All is now over – let us save ourselves.' Passing with difficulty through Genappe, the streets of which were choked with vehicles, at Charleroi Napoleon rested and took a glass of wine before mounting again and continuing his ride. De Coster was released there and left to make his own way home on foot, with just a gold Napoleon for his trouble.

Protected by the *Grenadiers à Pied* of the Imperial Guard, Napoleon surveys the wreck of his army towards the end of the Battle of Waterloo. (Print after Auguste Raffet)

Wellington's temporary Headquarters at the time of the battle. (Print by and after James Rouse)

De Coster observed that Napoleon 'did not appear at all moved by the dangers of the battle', unlike de Coster himself who often crouched over his horse's neck as balls flew overhead, while Napoleon:

> repeatedly expressed his dissatisfaction at this, telling him, that these movements made the officers believe he was hit; and added, that he would not shun the balls any better by stooping down than by keeping upright … during the whole action [Napoleon] displayed the same calmness and *sang-froid*, that he never manifested any ill humour, and spoke always with great gentleness to his officers.

The Duke of Wellington, wearing the 'state' coatee of a field marshal. (Print by W. Say after Thomas Phillips)

When he arrived to take command of the Anglo-Allied Army in the Netherlands in April 1815, the Duke of Wellington was acknowledged as the most successful British general since Marlborough, a judgement that is arguably still valid. He had earned that position by the scale of his success in the Peninsular War, founded not only upon his military talents but an ability, like Napoleon, for prodigious labour and a desire to oversee everything himself. This he clearly regarded as a necessity, as his subordinates in general had not proved especially adept in independent command, conversely, it might be argued that his constant superintendence may have inhibited the development of their abilities. There was, however, probably truth in his complaint of January 1813 concerning officers 'incapable of performing service in the field… It is impossible to prevent incapable men from being sent to the army; and, when I complain that they are sent, I am to be responsible.'[17]

A number of significant factors characterised Wellington's conduct of a campaign. Unlike some of his contemporaries, he was acutely aware of the necessity of feeding his troops, with not only an adequate ration but also one that was delivered regularly, despite the difficulties that this often entailed on campaign, and with hardly any militarised transport service. Wellington frequently made reference to the importance of logistics; for example, when recommending William Beresford as his successor should he be incapacitated in the Peninsula, despite Beresford's limited tactical ability, he remarked that 'what we need now is some one to feed our troops, and I know of no one fitter for the purpose'.[18] Similarly, when praising the great improvement that had been effected among his Portuguese troops, he stated that, 'I believe we owe their merits more to the care we have taken of their pockets and bellies than to the instruction we have given them.'[19] That this concern was appreciated by his troops is evident in Captain John Kincaid's comments that follow.

One of Wellington's characteristic organisational methods was to integrate veteran troops with novice or less reliable elements, so that the latter could gain confidence from the former. This was evident in the Peninsular War, when the British and Portuguese military were almost entirely integrated at divisional level,

The Duke of Wellington c.1820. (Print after Sir Thomas Lawrence)

Before the Battle of Quatre Bras: Wellington (right) with the Duke of Brunswick. (Print by S. Mitan after Captain George Jones)

with British and Portuguese brigades serving within the same division. The same method he applied in the Waterloo campaign; although for political reasons the Dutch-Belgian troops had to serve in their own divisions, the novice Hanoverian troops he united with British brigades in his divisions, so that the less experienced troops usually had veterans alongside them from whom to derive inspiration.

Like Napoleon, Wellington introduced no radical tactical theories but adapted those already in place. His most notable practice was probably that of the 'reverse slope', in which, when the terrain permitted, his troops were positioned on the rear of rising ground, with only skirmishers thrown forward and visible to the enemy. This deployment had a dual advantage: being hidden from the enemy's view, the troops were less likely to suffer from long-range fire; and as the French customarily attacked in column, deploying into line as they came within musket-range, when their target was hidden behind a hill crest they were unable to gauge the moment for deployment. As they ascended the rising ground, Wellington's 'hidden' troops would ascend to the crest and use all their muskets against French troops still in column and thus only able to fire from their first two or three ranks; this unequal contest usually led to the rapid repulse of the attacking French column as the British seconded their fire with a limited counter-charge.

Wellington in the costume he wore at Waterloo. (Print by R. G. Tietze after Sir Thomas Lawrence)

Wellington's own assessment of his method of operation was to emphasise its flexibility; he stated that his French opponents:

> planned their campaigns just as you might make a splendid set of harness. It looks very well; until it gets broken; and then you are done for. Now I made my campaigns of ropes. If anything went wrong, I tied a knot; and went on.[20]

In the event, whatever plans he had formulated for facing Napoleon in 1815 were disrupted severely by the speed of Napoleon's advance, which caught the Allied armies completely

The Duke of Wellington wearing the uniform of a field marshal, with the cloak he wore at Waterloo. (Print by Ryall after Sir Thomas Lawrence)

off-balance. Wellington is supposed to have remarked, 'Napoleon has humbugged me, by God! He has gained twenty-four hours' march on me.'[21] Doubts have been placed upon the veracity of this remark, but it was true: Napoleon had seized the initiative, taken his opponents by surprise, and the situation was only stabilised by good fortune and the sterling resistance of the Dutch-Belgian troops at Quatre Bras prior to the hurried arrival of Wellington's leading British elements.

Unlike Napoleon, Wellington did not have a free choice of his subordinates, though he did have many reliable officers from the Peninsula Army. Before his forces were assembled fully he made his famous statement that, 'I have got an infamous army, very weak and ill equipped, and a very inexperienced staff.'[22] He complained that:

I might have expected that the Generals and Staff formed by me in the last war would have been allowed to come to me again; but instead of that, I am overloaded with people I have never seen before; and it appears to be purposely intended to keep those out of my way whom I wished to have.[23]

He was able to make some changes, rejecting, for example, the services of Sir Hudson Lowe (subsequently Napoleon's gaoler at St Helena) and replacing him with Colonel Sir William Howe De Lancey as deputy quartermaster general, in effect his chief of staff. Most awkwardly, the Earl of Uxbridge was appointed to lead his cavalry, with whom Wellington had not served previously because of family enmity, Uxbridge having eloped with Wellington's sister-in-law.

An exchange on the night before Waterloo reveals the duke's style of leadership. Knowing that he might have to take command on the morrow should Wellington be incapacitated, with some trepidation Uxbridge plucked up courage to ask about the duke's plans. Wellington replied calmly, 'Who will attack first tomorrow, I or Bonaparte?' 'Bonaparte,' said Uxbridge.

Wellington and his staff at Waterloo. The officer in hussar uniform on the left is presumably the Earl of Uxbridge, colonel of the 7th Hussars, who wore cavalry uniform at Waterloo. (Print by S. Mitan after Captain George Jones)

'Well,' continued the duke, 'Bonaparte has not given me any idea of his projects: and as my plans will depend upon his, how can you expect me to tell you what mine are?' Then, patting Uxbridge on the shoulder, he added, 'There is one thing certain, Uxbridge, that is, that whatever happens, you and I will do our duty.'[24]

It has been said that Wellington was primarily a defensive general, and during the Peninsular War it is true that circumstances compelled him to act on the defensive until he had the resources to initiate offensive operations; but on the battlefield his mode of defence was never purely static. As in other cases, he was forced to fight in a defensive role at Waterloo, and indeed he acknowledged his own mastery of it. Lieutenant Colonel Daniel Mackinnon, a distinguished officer who fought at Hougoumont, recounted 'a truly characteristic trait' from the morning of the battle, involving the Spanish representative at Allied Headquarters, Wellington's friend General Miguel Alava:

> General Alava went from Brussels to join his Grace, and found him in a tree observing the movements of the French army. On the Duke turning round and seeing General Alava, he called out, 'How are you, Alava? Buonaparte shall to-day how a General of Sepoys can defend a position!' – a remark which showed at once his contempt for an opinion given of him by Buonaparte, and a confidence in himself and in his troops, accompanied with a degree of cheerfulness almost amounting to an assurance of victory.[25]

Wellington and his staff at Waterloo. The Duke wears his cloak over his customary civilian frock-coat, and while most of his companions wear the staff uniform, the officer to the right of Wellington, wearing his light dragoon uniform with shako, is presumably his aide de camp Lieutenant Lord George Lennox of the 9th Light Dragoons. (Print by S. Mitan after Captain George Jones)

Although merited, Wellington's reputation for skill in defence should not conceal his wider skills. Colonel Sir Augustus Frazer, commander of the horse artillery in the Waterloo campaign, gave his assessment two days after the battle:

> Where, indeed, and what is not his forte? Cold and indifferent, nay, apparently careless in the beginning of battles, when the moment of difficulty comes intelligence flashes from the eyes of this wonderful man; and he rises superior to all that can be imagined.[26]

The description of 'cold and indifferent' represents another facet of Wellington's character and style of command that had a crucial effect: relations with his men. One of his best-known, and most misinterpreted statements, concerned his view that his troops were 'scum of the earth', which might be taken as the patrician disdain for those of the lower strata of society. In reality, this remark was made in relation to the British system of recruiting, which drew most of the ordinary soldiers from the labouring classes, in contrast to the French conscription that brought together men from all levels. Wellington certainly had no illusions about the private soldier in general: 'you can hardly conceive such a set brought together', but then added, 'it is really wonderful that we should have made them the fine fellows they are'.[27]

At least overtly, Wellington was undoubtedly aloof and unemotional, never courting the adulation of his troops, unlike Napoleon. A characteristic moment occurred at Waterloo as he passed the 33rd Foot, his old regiment, at a crucial stage of the battle. A veteran who had served with him in India called out, 'Let us have three cheers for our old Colonel'; Wellington just held up his telescope and said 'Hush, hush, hush', as if he feared that an outburst of emotion would cause disorder within the battalion.[28]

Nonetheless, the trust that the troops reposed in his abilities was a major factor in maintaining morale during the stress of combat. To the old Peninsula hands he seemed invincible, which bred the confidence demonstrated by the reception of the news that he was to take command of the Army in the Netherlands; Sergeant William Wheeler of the 51st stated that 'I never remember anything that caused such joy, our men were almost frantic', drinking his health and declaring that they gave not a damn for France even if every man were a Napoleon, so that the celebratory alcohol 'caused a general fuddle'.[29]

Captain John Kincaid of the 95th, who had served under Wellington in the Peninsula, provided a memorable assessment of his qualities as perceived by the soldiers:

> … he was not only the head of the army but obliged to descend to the responsibility of every department in it. In the different branches of their various duties, he received the officers in charge, as ignorant as schoolboys, and, by his energy and unwearied perseverence, he made them what they became – the most renowned army that Europe ever saw. Wherever he went at its head, glory followed its steps – wherever he was not – I will not say disgrace, but something near akin to it ensued… Lord Wellington appeared to us never to leave anything to chance. However desperate the undertaking – whether suffering under momentary defeat, or imprudently hurried on by partial success – we ever felt confident that a redeeming power was at hand, nor were we ever deceived. Those only, too, who have served under such a master-mind and one of inferior calibre can appreciate the difference in a physical as well as a moral point of view – for when in the presence of the enemy, under him, we were never deprived of our personal comforts until prudence rendered it necessary, and they were always restored to us again at the earliest possible moment … it is astonishing in what a degree the vacillation and want of confidence in a commander descends into the different ranks.

'Stand up, Guards!': Wellington prepares the Foot Guards to repel Napoleon's final attack at Waterloo. (Print by S. Mitan after Captain George Jones)

And, Kincaid added, 'we would rather see his long nose in the fight than a reinforcement of ten thousand men any day … and I'll venture to say that there was not a bosom in that army that did not beat more lightly, when we heard the joyful news of his arrival'.[30]

Writing of the time that Wellington ordered the final advance at Waterloo, another Peninsular veteran, Major Harry Ross-Lewin of the 32nd, recalled how he was cheered, and gave another reason for the army's trust:

Wellington encourages the final advance at Waterloo, with the 52nd Light Infantry and 95th Rifles. (Print by S. Mitan after Captain George Jones)

I am confident that there was not a man in the army who did not feel elated at the sight of their victorious chief, safe and unhurt after this perilous and bloody day. Never did any general share the dangers of a battle in a greater degree than did the Duke of Wellington on the field of Waterloo. He was frequently in the hottest of fire; almost every individual in his staff was either killed or wounded, and even he himself took refuge at one time in the midst of a square, when charged by the enemy's cavalry. One would have thought that, throughout this memorable conflict, the commander vied with his troops, and the troops with their commander, in giving evidence of their mutual confidence.[31]

Contrasting with Napoleon's conduct of the battle, Wellington was continually on the move, appearing wherever the situation was most critical, and intervening in person. Captain James Shaw, assistant quartermaster general attached to the 3rd Division, recalled an example, when he informed Wellington that a gap had opened in the line:

This very startling information he received with a degree of coolness, and replied to in an instant with such precision and energy, as to prove the most complete self-possession; and left on my mind the impressions that his Grace's mind remained

Wellington and his staff directing the final Allied advance at Waterloo. (Print published by R. Bowyer, 1816)

perfectly calm during every phase, however serious, of the action; that he felt confident of his own powers to being able to guide the storm which raged around him; and from the determined manner in which he spoke, it was evident that he had resolved to defend to the last extremity every inch of the position.

Wellington responded with typical calmness and clarity of vision: 'I shall order the Brunswick troops to the spot, and other troops besides; go you and get all the German troops of the division to the spot that you can get, and all the guns that you can find'; and then he personally led the Brunswickers to plug the gap. Shaw added:

> In no other part of the action was the Duke of Wellington exposed to so much personal risk as on this occasion, as he was necessarily under a close and most destructive infantry fire at a very short distance; at no other period of the day were his great qualities as a commander so strongly brought out, for it was the moment of his greatest peril as to the result of the action.[32]

Sir Augustus Frazer concurred:

> Several times were critical; but confidence in the Duke, I have no doubt, animated every breast. His Grace exposed his person, not unnecessarily but nobly: without his personal exertions, his continual presence wherever and whenever more than usual exertions were required, the day had been lost.[33]

Sir William Fraser, whose father had fought at Waterloo as aide de camp to Uxbridge, thought that Wellington had deliberately placed himself in danger:

> … to inspire confidence in his soldiers. His calmness of demeanour, his methodical way of dealing with the various Regiments during the day, all of which was visible to his men, gave them unbounded confidence in the success of his orders … he also felt that he would show to the brave men who fought under him that, however great were their risks, however much he exacted from their courage and endurance, he exacted the same qualities and conduct from himself… There was not one, from the chief of his staff to the last-joined recruit, who did not know [that he] was jeopardising his life to at least the same degree as the poorest outcast who had become a soldier from starvation.[34]

Towards the end of the battle one of Wellington's staff remonstrated with him for risking his life, which elicited an alarming response: let them fire away, reportedly replied the duke, for the battle was won and thus his life was no longer of consequence.

The famed Scottish novelist, Sir Walter Scott, visiting the army shortly after Waterloo, reported further evidence of Wellington's effect:

Wellington writing the Waterloo dispatch on the evening of the battle; his aide Sir Alexander Gordon lies dying in the room behind him. (Engraving after Lady Burghersh)

The meeting of Wellington (left) and Blücher on the evening of Waterloo, supposedly at La Belle Alliance, though it may actually have been nearer Genappe: one of the earliest depictions of the event. (Print published by Thomas Kelly, 1817)

There was scarcely a square but he visited in person, encouraging his men by his presence, and the officers by his directions. Many of his short phrases are repeated by them, as if they were possessed of talismanic effect … when many of the best and bravest men had fallen, and the event of the action seemed doubtful even to those who remained, he said, with the coolness of a spectator, who was beholding some well-contested sport, 'Never mind, we'll win this battle yet'. To another regiment, then closely engaged, he used a common sporting expression; 'Hard pounding, gentlemen; let's see who will pound the longest'. All who heard him issue orders took confidence from his quick and decisive intellect, all who saw him caught mettle from his undoubted composure.[35]

Another aspect of Wellington's command was the need to act in concert with his allies, for unlike Napoleon, who had complete control over his strategy, Wellington had to co-operate: the Prussian contribution in the campaign was to prove vital for its successful outcome. Wellington had been used to working with allies in the Peninsular War, but at a political level: militarily he had been in complete command of his own army and of the Portuguese and Spanish troops under his control. In 1815, relations with King William I of the Netherlands and his administration initially were somewhat strained, until on 4 May the king placed all his troops under Wellington's command and appointed the duke a field-marshal in Netherlands service. It was, however, a matter of political expediency that the young Prince of Orange, who had commanded the Allied troops in the region before Wellington's arrival, was given command of the army's I Corps. The young prince had served in the Peninsula and held the rank of lieutenant general in the British Army, but in terms of independent command he was entirely inexperienced, to the extent that the British Colonel Sir John Colborne stated that the British government had urged him 'to prevent the Prince from engaging in any affair of his own before the combined operations'.[36]

Although Wellington had control over his own forces, the Prussians were allies upon an equal footing. Their commander was one of the most celebrated Prussian soldiers of his generation, Field Marshal Gebhard Leberecht von Blücher, Prince of Wahlstadt, who had been one of Napoleon's most implacable opponents. Born in 1742, he had served in Frederick the Great's Army, had commanded a hussar regiment and to some extent retained the élan of the typical hussar mentality. He had fought on for as long as possible after Napoleon's defeat of Prussia at Jena-Auerstädt, and had been implacably opposed to any Prussian collaboration with the French. In the 'War of Liberation' in 1813–14 he commanded the Army of Silesia where he exhibited his tenacity and refusal to countenance defeat, and came to be idolised by his troops who gave him the appropriate nickname of '*Marschall Vorwärts*' ('Marshal Forward').

Unlike Napoleon and Wellington, Blücher was not greatly experienced in truly independent command. The Army of Silesia, while autonomous, had operated as part of a united strategy involving a number of Allied formations; and even within his own army, Blücher had been the head of a command partnership with his chief of staff, Lieutenant General August Neithardt von Gneisenau. They were ideally matched: Gneisenau's calculating intelligence combined with Blücher's fire and determination to produce a most effective collaboration. Gneisenau was clear-sighted in a strategic sense, Blücher the inspirational head who had a direct appeal to his men which served to maintain their morale. Wellington's opinion was that Gneisenau was 'not exactly a tactician, but he was very deep in strategy… In tactics Gneisenau was not so much skilled. But Blücher was just the reverse – he knew nothing of plans of campaign, but well understood a field of battle'; and, he added, Blücher 'was a very fine fellow, and whenever there was any question of fighting, always ready and eager – if anything too eager'.[37]

The two Allied commanders each posted an intelligence officer at the other's Headquarters to act as liaison; the Prussian officer with Wellington was Baron Carl von Müffling, who passed a somewhat harsh opinion on Blücher:

Lieutenant General August Wilhelm von Gneisenau, wearing the form of rank-marking introduced into the Prussian Army from mid-1814. (Print after F. Kruger)

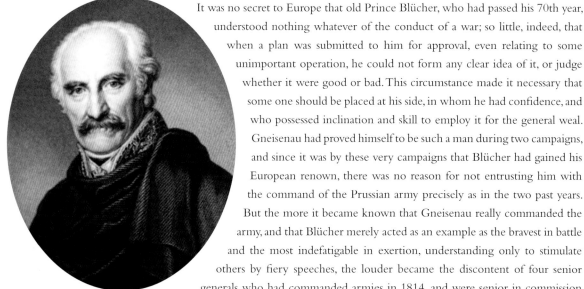

It was no secret to Europe that old Prince Blücher, who had passed his 70th year, understood nothing whatever of the conduct of a war; so little, indeed, that when a plan was submitted to him for approval, even relating to some unimportant operation, he could not form any clear idea of it, or judge whether it were good or bad. This circumstance made it necessary that some one should be placed at his side, in whom he had confidence, and who possessed inclination and skill to employ it for the general weal. Gneisenau had proved himself to be such a man during two campaigns, and since it was by these very campaigns that Blücher had gained his European renown, there was no reason for not entrusting him with the command of the Prussian army precisely as in the two past years. But the more it became known that Gneisenau really commanded the army, and that Blücher merely acted as an example as the bravest in battle and the most indefatigable in exertion, understanding only to stimulate others by fiery speeches, the louder became the discontent of four senior generals who had commanded armies in 1814, and were senior in commission to Gneisenau.[38]

Blücher. (Engraving by T. W. Harland after F. C. Gröger)

Although collaboration between the two Allied armies was to bring about the defeat of Napoleon, apparently there were some issues of trust. Müffling recalled that:

> On my departure General von Gneisenau warned me to be much on my guard with the Duke of Wellington, for that by his relations with India, and his transactions with the deceitful Nabobs, this distinguished general had so accustomed himself to duplicity, that he had at last become such a master in the art as even to outwit the Nabobs themselves.

Duplicity was probably not something that would have been recognised by those familiar with Wellington, and Müffling's relations with him were entirely cordial: 'The Duke soon perceived that, on every point discussed … I told him the simple truth, whether it concerned the Prussian army or relations between the two, and that he could meet me with perfect confidence.'[39]

Müffling recognised Wellington's position in the need to co-ordinate the actions of the two armies, explaining how:

> The Duke was accustomed to direct *alone* all the strategical operations of his army; and in defensive battles to indicate from his central point of operation the moment for assuming the offensive… The Duke, more than any one in Europe,

had reason to know the value of a command which, proceeding from one master-mind, directs great operations and battles. He was necessarily sensible that the manner of conducting business to which he had become accustomed could not now be continued.

In discussing the co-operation with Blücher, Müffling stated that he told Wellington:

> You may depend upon this: when the Prince has agreed to any operation in common, he will keep his word, should even the whole Prussian army be annihilated in the act; but do not expect from us *more* than we are able to perform; we will always assist you as far as we *can*; the Prince will be perfectly satisfied if you do the same.[40]

This determination was tested in the aftermath of the mauling of the Prussian Army at Ligny, especially as Blücher was temporarily incapacitated. During the

Blücher unhorsed at Ligny; his aide, Count August-Ludwig von Nostitz, prepares to rescue him. (Print published by Thomas Kelly, 1817)

battle he had reverted to the hussar of old and very unwisely had attempted to lead a cavalry charge; his horse fell heavily upon him and he was ridden over. His aide managed to get him up and away, but for some time Gneisenau had to take command. As the Prussians withdrew, perhaps suspicious because Wellington had not aided them in the fight, Gneisenau considered retiring to reorganise instead of supporting his ally directly. Wellington's liaison officer at Prussian Headquarters, Lieutenant Colonel Sir Henry Hardinge, not present in person but recovering from the amputation of a hand, stated that:

> I was told that there had been a great discussion that night in [Blücher's] rooms, and that Blücher and Grolmann[41] carried the day for remaining in communication with the English army, but that Gneisenau had great doubts as to whether they ought not to fall back to Liege and secure their own communication with Luxembourg. They thought that if the English should be defeated, they themselves would be utterly destroyed.[42]

Gneisenau's misgivings were reasonable under the circumstances; shortly after the battle he stated that their ammunition was low and that it had almost been impossible to march to Wellington's support, but the determination of the indomitable old Blücher convinced him that they had to keep their word. Despite his ordeal Blücher never considered surrendering command; with potions rubbed into his bruises and fortified by champagne, he visited the wounded Hardinge:

> … calling me *Lieber Freund*, &c., and embracing me. I perceived he smelt most strongly of gin and rhubarb. He said to me, *Ich stinke etwas*, that he had been obliged to take medicine, having been twice rode over by the cavalry, but that he should be quite satisfied if in conjunction with the Duke of Wellington he was able now to defeat the old enemy.[43]

The decision to aid Wellington was crucial, for despite the later opinion of some British survivors of the battle that it could have been won without the Prussians, their appearance on Napoleon's right flank had been vital, and indeed was acknowledged by Wellington in his first account of the battle:

> I should not do justice to my own feelings, or to Marshal Blücher and the Prussian army, if I did not attribute the successful result of this arduous day to the cordial and timely assistance I received from them. The operation of General Bülow upon the enemy's flank was a most decisive one; and, even if I had not found myself in a

situation to make the attack that produced the final result, it would have forced the enemy to retire if his attacks should have failed, and would have prevented him from taking advantage of them if they should unfortunately have succeeded.[44]

Blücher's role in the outcome of the campaign, and his iron will, had been crucial, and despite the tendency of some later Anglo-centric sources not to emphasise the Prussian contribution, many at the time had no doubt, like Sir Walter Scott, when at a ball in Paris he observed Wellington and Blücher shake hands: 'Look at that!', he declared; 'A few weeks ago these two men delivered Europe!'[45]

The experiences of the three leading commanders on the evening and night of the battle were very different. As the French retired, Wellington met Blücher, the duke recalling that the old Prussian had embraced him, exclaiming '*Meine lieber Kamerad*' and '*Quelle affaire!*' which, Wellington claimed, was almost the only French Blücher knew. (It is usually asserted that this meeting took place near the inn of La Belle Alliance, an apt name for their co-operation, though less than a year after the battle Wellington stated that it was actually near Genappe.)

A medal by Brandt commemorating Blücher and featuring the dates of his birth and death; on the reverse he is depicted as a Roman general, hurling thunderbolts from his chariot, an image that might have appealed to '*Marschall Vorwärts*', while the eagle of Prussia flies overhead.

Napoleon in defeat.
(Engraving by J. François after
Paul Delaroche)

Blücher being exhausted, Gneisenau began to pursue the defeated French, until darkness and fatigue called a temporary halt. Wellington retired to his temporary Headquarters at Waterloo to write his dispatch to the government in London. The cool facade slipped when he received news of the death of his aide de camp, Sir Alexander Gordon, and the first casualty returns; brushing away tears, he said that he had never known what it was to lose a battle, but that nothing could be more painful than to win one with the loss of so many friends. For Napoleon, the night saw the beginning of his road into exile at St Helena, as described in the account of Jean-Baptiste de Coster. It was said that his aide Auguste-Charles-Joseph Flahaut de La Billarderie remarked to him, 'Is your Majesty not surprised?' (by the defeat); Napoleon replied, 'No, it has been the same thing since Crecy.'[46]

Of the three generals, Blücher, the oldest, survived the shortest time after his victory. He was fêted throughout Europe, but the last time Wellington saw him he was labouring under a strange delusion, the recurrence of which Wellington attributed to a blow on the head sustained by falling from his horse while showing off before some ladies in Paris, that he was pregnant, expecting an elephant fathered by a French soldier. He died on 12 September 1819. Napoleon lasted less than two years longer; he ended his days on the isolated island of St Helena, consigned there by the Allied powers who dared not risk him returning again to France. He died there on 5 May 1821. Wellington, conversely, lived for some 37 years after Waterloo, in which period he became acknowledged as the greatest Englishman of his generation. He survived a period of political unpopularity, serving as prime minister, and became a national icon; but for all his success in the Peninsular War, it was for Waterloo that he was most celebrated, a measure of which was the fact that, uniquely, his name was carried with that of the Prince Regent on the Waterloo Medal, the first British campaign medal to be awarded universally to all participants, regardless of rank. By the time of his death on 14 September 1852 he was known universally as just 'the Duke', as if there had never been another holder of such a peerage. Many would have agreed with his friend and fellow Peninsular veteran Reverend George Gleig, who described him as 'the grandest, because the truest man, whom modern times have produced. He was the wisest and most loyal subject that ever served and supported the English throne.'[47]

CHAPTER 4

THE BATTLE

The Armies, their Weapons and Tactics

MARK ADKIN

THE ARMIES

Like modern armies the three that fought at Waterloo were composed of formations, units and sub-units. A unit was usually an infantry battalion of up to 1,000 men, normally commanded by a lieutenant colonel (in the French Army, a major), and cavalry or artillery regiments also commanded by lieutenant colonels. Sub-units formed the component parts of units such as infantry companies, cavalry squadrons or artillery companies (the term 'battery' was applied to an artillery position) commanded by captains. Formations were larger forces. Brigades consisted of two or three battalions commanded by major generals (in the French Army, general of division); divisions comprised two or three brigades also commanded by senior major generals, and a corps was an all arms force (infantry, cavalry and artillery) formed of several divisions normally commanded by lieutenant generals or equivalent. This simple system was more complex at Waterloo, although by and large it applied to the Anglo-Allied Army. A Prussian brigade equated to a British division, each consisting of three regiments divided into three or four battalions. Their cavalry also had brigades instead of divisions with regiments having four squadrons. A French infantry brigade had two regiments of three, sometimes four, battalions; the cavalry had brigades of two regiments, each with three or four squadrons. The Imperial Guard was really an army within an army although it acted as a corps at Waterloo under the personal direction of the emperor. Its tactical grouping for the battle was three infantry divisions – Old, Middle (unofficial title) and Young Guard, and the Guard Light and Heavy Cavalry Divisions with the Guard artillery batteries initially divided among them. The different types of infantry (guard, grenadier, line and light), of cavalry (heavy, medium or light) and of artillery (field and horse) are discussed below under army tactics.

Prince William of Orange.
(Anne S. K. Brown)

The Anglo-Allied Army was organised into three corps. I Corps, under the young William, Prince of Orange, consisted of the 1st and 3rd British Divisions, the 2nd and 3rd Netherlands (Dutch-Belgian) Divisions and the Netherlands Cavalry Division. The II Corps commanded by Lieutenant General Lord Rowland Hill had only the 2nd British Division and one British brigade as the bulk of the corps (17,000) were stationed at Hal over 7 kilometres to the west, guarding against Napoleon making an attempt to outflank Wellington's right. The Reserve (III) Corps under Wellington's direction consisted of the 5th British Division, and the Brunswick Division (contingent). The Cavalry Corps under the Earl of

Uxbridge had seven brigades that were deployed as separate formations with, in general terms, the heavy in reserve behind the front line and the light on the flanks.

Of the Prussians only the IV Corps (31,000) under General Friedrich Wilhelm Count von Bülow, with four infantry and three cavalry brigades arrived in its entirety in the late afternoon. It was followed two hours later by three infantry and one cavalry brigade from the II Corps (12,800) commanded by Major General George von Pirch I. Finally, at about 7.30 p.m. one infantry and one cavalry brigade from Lieutenant General Hans Ernst Carl von Zieten's I Corps (5,000) arrived – too late to be of much use as by then the French were on the verge of defeat.

Napoleon famously stated that God was on the side of the big battalions, and perhaps the most obvious factor among the many considered when assessing an army's strength and battle worthiness is the number of soldiers in it. The numbers discussed here are those available to the army commanders on the actual battlefield during 18 June. In round figures the Anglo–Allied Army (under the command of the Duke of Wellington) had 73,200; the Prussians (under the command of Field Marshal Gebhard Leberecht von Blücher) ultimately had some 49,000. Emperor Napoleon's French Army had about 77,500 available having sent Marshal Emmanuel de Grouchy off chasing the Prussians with 30,000. At the start of the battle Napoleon had a very slight advantage of about 4,500 men – certainly nowhere near enough to give him the 'big battalions', and by the end of the day, including casualties, he was hopelessly outnumbered. However, at 11.30 a.m. he had five hours in which to defeat Wellington before the first Prussians arrived on the battlefield – although at the start he was convinced he had Wellington to himself.

The overall numbers available to a general are by no means the only, or even the most important factor, in establishing an army's worth. The numbers become more relevant if the strengths or otherwise of the components of the army are also compared. At Waterloo Wellington had 53,800 infantrymen in

Bülow's entry into Arnhem in 1813. At Waterloo he commanded the IV Corps of Blücher's Army and headed the attack on the French right at Plancenoit. (Rijksmuseum)

84 battalions, 13,350 cavalry in 93 squadrons and 157 artillery pieces and one rocket troop in 24 batteries. The total eventual Prussian contribution amounted to 38,000 infantry in 62 battalions, 7,000 cavalry in 61 squadrons and 134 artillery pieces in 17 batteries. Napoleon deployed 53,400 infantry in 103 battalions, 15,600 cavalry in 113.5 squadrons and 246 artillery pieces in 34 companies (batteries). Wellington and Napoleon had virtually identical

Lieutenant General Rowland Lord Hill, one of the Duke of Wellington's most trusted commanders, commanded II Corps at Waterloo. He was to become commander-in-chief of the British Army in 1828. (Courtesy of the Council of the National Army Museum)

numbers of infantry, but in battalions the latter had 19 battalions more. The reason for this was that Wellington's battalions averaged about 640 all ranks but Napoleon's only 520 (the Prussians 615); thus Wellington and Blücher had the 'big battalions' in the literal sense. In comparison Napoleon's cavalry exceeded that of his main opponent, certainly at the start of the battle, by some 2,250, although it was in artillery that he had the obvious advantage. Napoleon was a gunner by training and always strove to have superiority in this arm. At Waterloo he achieved a superiority of 89 pieces with six batteries of heavy 12-pounders making up almost 40 per cent of the total. These pieces, in batteries of eight (six cannons and two howitzers), were the most powerful on the battlefield throughout the day.

Other key factors in comparing the armies and understanding their organisation (leaving aside the commanders in chief discussed in an earlier chapter) include training, experience and composition of the arms and support services. These last include staff officers, supply of ammunition and food and medical arrangements. Wellington complained bitterly some six weeks before the battle that his army was very weak, ill-equipped and with an inexperienced staff. He was primarily railing against the cosmopolitan nature of his army, and the shortage of funds with which to make the local purchases necessary to pay, feed and move his army. However, things had improved by early June.

Napoleon was a gunner by training and throughout his many campaigns he relied on massed artillery fire to prepare the way for his main attack. (Print after JOB, René Chartrand)

Wellington's command was an Anglo-Allied force in which the majority of the men spoke languages other than English – German predominating. The regular British Army element, making up around 49 per cent of the total, included eight battalions of the King's German Legion (KGL), recruited from the German State of Hanover, along with 16 cavalry squadrons and three artillery batteries. The remainder was made up of Allied contingents. The most numerous were the Hanoverians (excluding the KGL) who supplied 17 battalions, or 21 per cent of the infantry, four cavalry squadrons and two batteries. The Dutch Netherlands (Dutch and Belgian) provided 13 battalions, 14 squadrons and two batteries; Brunswick eight battalions, five squadrons and two batteries; Nassau (a German territory) eight and a half battalions; and the Belgian Netherlands four battalions, nine squadrons and just over two batteries.

This composition gave Wellington some misgivings and the realisation that he needed to group inexperienced formations with experienced ones. Generally he did this by placing formations of potentially uncertain reliability within larger British ones. With the four Hanoverian infantry brigades (1st, 3rd, 4th and 5th) a number of KGL officers and senior NCOs were transferred into the *Landwehr* (militia reserve) battalions to stiffen the leadership. The 1st Brigade, the strongest with five battalions, was part of the British 3rd Division and fought well at Quatre Bras and at Waterloo, where it was posted in the front line near the centre. It suffered severely, losing over 1,500 men and three battalion commanders in the course of the two battles. The 3rd Brigade (part of the 2nd Division) was deployed in reserve behind the right flank and was not involved in the fighting until the final advance on a retreating enemy. The 4th Brigade (part of the 6th Division), consisting of four *Landwehr* battalions, was placed on the left flank of the infantry line where it saw little action and suffered few casualties. The 5th Brigade (5th Division), another *Landwehr* formation, was placed in the front line on the left but was not heavily engaged and its losses were minimal. The Duke of Cumberland's Hussars were the only regiment of the Hanoverian Cavalry Brigade at Waterloo (the others were at Hal). It was a volunteer unit of doubtful value and posted well to the rear. Later the regiment was seen withdrawing from the battlefield without orders, and efforts to stop them proved unavailing. Their commander, Lieutenant Colonel von Hake, was later court-martialled.

In the Netherlands contingent the Dutch contribution was much stronger than the Belgian. This kingdom, under King William I, was only formalised three months before Waterloo from the former northern and southern states (Holland and Belgium respectively) that had previously been part of Napoleon's empire. The fact that many of the officers and men had previously fought for

Napoleon, along with the language differences (the 2nd Netherlands Division had French, Dutch and German speakers), gave Wellington cause for (largely unjustified) concern. The 2nd Netherlands Division (the 1st Division was at Hal) was part of I Corps and grouped with the 1st British (Guards) Division and the 3rd British Division. It played a crucial part in holding the crossroads at Quatre Bras where it lost 1,100 men. Another 2,000 were lost at Waterloo where it was posted in the front line and faced the 2nd French Infantry Division's attack at the start of Napoleon's first attempt to break Wellington's line. The duke also had his doubts about the loyalty of the 3rd Division commanded by the Dutchman Lieutenant General David Hendrik Baron Chassé, who had spent five years fighting for the French. It was posted well out on the west flank and not committed to the action until the Imperial Guard attacked at the end

Sketch of a typical soldier of Napoleon's Imperial Guard in the uniform of 1812. (akg-images)

of the battle, when Dutch commander Detmer's Brigade charged enthusiastically into the wavering guardsmen. Lieutenant General Jean Antoine de Baron Collaert, who along with his three brigade commanders had fought for Napoleon, commanded the Netherlands Cavalry Division. Wellington initially kept this division back in reserve. However, despite its recent history it participated successfully in several counter-charges against the French cavalry milling round the Allied squares in the afternoon.

Blücher had two main concerns regarding the reliability of his army. The first revolved around the officers and men recently recruited from new Prussian territories such as Westphalia and Saxony. These feelings were particularly prevalent among the Saxon contingents. Saxony had supported Napoleon and provided troops for him until their defection in the Leipzig campaign of 1813. Saxony had been split in two with the northern part taking half the army, and in 1815 many Saxon soldiers had no wish either to be part of Prussia or to fight for her. At Liège in May Saxon soldiers at Blücher's Headquarters mutinied shouting threats and

Dutch soldier Lieutenant General Baron Chassé had spent five years fighting with the French before deciding to fight on the side of the Allies. He commanded the 3rd Division at Waterloo. (Painting by Jan Willem Pienemann, Rijksmuseum)

throwing stones. Seven officers were executed and 14,000 soldiers sent home. Discipline remained fragile and this manifested itself again after the Battle of Ligny when some 6,000–8,000 disappeared during the army's retreat to Wavre after heavy losses in the fighting around the village. By 18 June the Army of the Lower Rhine had shrunk from 130,000 to 100,000 due to casualties and desertion.

Blücher's other potential problem was the high proportion of *Landwehr* units, many of which had recently been demobilised and whose soldiers had little desire to fight again. Of the Prussian units that reached the Waterloo battlefield a third of the infantry and a quarter of the cavalry were *Landwehr*. However, any misgivings Blücher may have had were dispelled by the *Landwehr* units' aggressiveness in the struggle for Plancenoit village.

When Napoleon crossed the frontier into Belgium with his Army of the North he commanded around 123,000 men of the 500,000 under arms that had been assembled, in great haste and despite daunting difficulties, to confront the armies that threatened France's borders. His return from Elba had largely been triumphal, with many units eagerly transferring their allegiance back to their beloved emperor. These included numerous veteran officers of middle and junior rank who had resented being put on half pay, while their places were filled with young and inexperienced non-entities who had secured royal patronage. A number of these Royalist officers refused to break their new oath of loyalty to the king and fled the country, while others 'sat on the fence' uncertain of what to do. However, Napoleon's main dilemma was in selecting his senior commanders, a number of whom had so recently transferred their allegiance to the king.

One of the two key marshals at Waterloo was Marshal Nicolas Soult, the chief of staff. A former corporal and drill instructor; he had always been an ardent supporter of his emperor, who later declared Soult to be 'an excellent "*état*-major" general (chief of staff)'. Nevertheless, Soult had little staff experience and there is some reason to doubt Soult's role in charge of what was a strong professional staff. An example from the battle was that he did not insist on the normal procedure of sending messages in triplicate – something that contributed to French communication difficulties at Waterloo. A far more experienced man for this role was Marshal Louis-Alexandre Berthier, who although remaining loyal to the king had refused to fight his former master, and died after a fall from a window on 1 June. Napoleon was initially doubtful about giving Marshal Michel Ney the critical command of the army's left wing, on account of the fact that Ney had sworn to the king that he would bring Napoleon to Paris in an iron cage. It was not until 12 June, when the army was already on the march, that the emperor finally overcame his misgivings and gave him his command – something that at Waterloo resulted in Ney becoming Napoleon's second in command responsible for co-ordinating all major attacks.

Other senior commanders such as Major Generals D'Hurbal, L'Heritier, Jacquinot and Kellerman had all hesitated to join the returning emperor, thus generating a question mark over their true commitment. That said, they all fought well at Waterloo. The exception to this was Lieutenant General Louis Bourmont, commanding the 14th Infantry Division (not at Waterloo), who had defected to Blücher on 15 June along with his staff. Blücher gave him a frosty reception, remarking to the effect that a cur will always be a cur.

One divisional commander who was notoriously incompetent was Napoleon's youngest brother, Prince Jérôme Bonaparte, commanding the 6th Infantry Division in Lieutenant General Honoré Reille's II Corps. He spent the day fruitlessly attacking Hougoumont, an error compounded by his corps commander who reinforced failure with yet another division.

Despite initial doubts as to the reliability of several senior commanders, the great bulk of the men Napoleon took to Waterloo were seasoned troops, and in that respect superior to most of his enemies. They were battle-hardened, confident

Prussian and French infantry cross bayonets at Ligny. (Anne S. K. Brown)

The high level of destruction and mounting casualties at Waterloo is clear to see; there simply was not the medical support on either side to cope with the enormity of the losses. (akg-images)

veterans whose overall morale at the return of their emperor was excellent. The same cannot be said for the pre-battle discipline of many units. Some soldiers doubted the loyalty of those officers who had been rewarded by promotion for rejoining the emperor while they had received nothing. The 12th Dragoons (in Grouchy's force) went so far as to petition for the removal of their colonel, and groans and jeers greeted the appearance of some officers. There were severe problems with shortages of equipment and uniforms – a high number of the Young Guard had a strange assortment of uniform or headgear. Horses had been hard to obtain, particularly ones capable of pulling heavy guns, as the stock of animals had never recovered from catastrophic losses in Russia in 1812.

The French supply train was not up to its task. French armies notoriously relied on foraging to supplement rations and on 17 and 18 June the supply wagons had dropped well to the rear as the long columns pressed further into Belgium. This meant soldiers went marauding for food and plundered during the day and night before the battle. Many were out of their officers' control and indeed a number of officers joined in. This dispersal of units was one of the reasons why several formations were late arriving on the battlefield on the morning of the battle, with the 4th Division still arriving at 11.30 a.m. The disciplinary situation had been sufficiently serious for the provost marshal, Major General Radet, to offer his resignation – it was declined.

As regards rations, things were not much better in the Anglo-Allied Army. After the battle Wellington denied his commissary officers the Waterloo Medal as supplies of food failed to get through to the troops on the 17th and 18th. Medical arrangements on both sides were rudimentary and unable to cope with the number of casualties the battle would cause. M. K. H. Crumplin in his book *The Bloody Fields of Waterloo* estimates there were around 55,000 casualties at the battle, of which 15,000 were dead and around 35,000 wounded. The burden on the Allied and Belgian civilian medical services was exacerbated as not only had the French spent much of the day attacking and so left dead and wounded strewn all over the battlefield, but so many were abandoned when the French retreated. With the casualties at Quatre Bras, Crumplin estimates the Anglo-Allied, Prussian and French armies had up to 40,000 wounded to deal with in the days and weeks after the battle. The situation on the battlefield was made even worse as French ambulance wagons had civilian drivers many of whom, on coming under fire, unhitched their horses, mounted up and fled. With the hard fighting at Quatre Bras most of Wellington's ambulance wagons had been used to take casualties to Brussels and when attempting to return many were unable to get through the clogged roads leading south. Assistant Surgeon John Haddy James attached to the 1st Life Guards (each unit had a regimental surgeon or assistant) was appalled at his helplessness; firstly due to the late arrival of his instruments and then the total inadequacy of the contents of his medical bag.

At dawn on 18 June the soldiers of both armies were suffering precisely the same hardships. They were soaking wet from torrential rain, hungry and exhausted both from lack of sleep and hard marching. All had the problem of keeping their powder dry so there was much cleaning of muskets and a continual popping of weapons being test fired. An anonymous French soldier described the situation thus:

Throughout the Napoleonic Wars supplies were always hard to obtain on campaign, as depicted here by this French supply train in Poland, 1806. Waterloo was no exception. (akg-images)

About 8 o'clock the wagons arrived with cartridges and hogsheads of brandy; each soldier received a double ration; with a crust of bread we might have done very well, but the bread was not there… This was all we had that day … marching all night without rations, sleeping in the water, forbidden to light a fire… We were glad to pull our shoes out of the holes in which they were buried at every step, and, chilled and drenched to our waists by the wet grain …

Most of Wellington's and Blücher's men would have echoed these comments.

THE WEAPONS

The weapons used at Waterloo can be divided into three basic categories – firearms, blade and artillery. Very few soldiers on any Napoleonic battlefield did not have a firearm of some sort, even if it was their secondary weapon. In each army the primary weapon of the infantryman was the musket (or rifle), of the cavalryman the sword/sabre and of the gunner his cannon (or howitzer). These were the weapons of the day upon which battle tactics were based. Although the size and weight of each type varied slightly from army to army, in practice there was little to choose, in terms of effectiveness, between a French, British or Prussian musket. Similarly the sword or sabre wielded by a French cavalryman was not a lot different from that held by a British or Prussian horseman. Of greater importance was the comparative skill and training of the holder and the tactical situation he was in.

Firearms

These included muskets, rifles, carbines (or equivalent) and pistols. The musket overwhelmingly predominated. Of the 145,000 infantrymen who participated in the battle only around 8,000 were not armed with one. All muskets were flintlock, smoothbore, black powder and muzzle-loading weapons with much the same characteristics in terms of range, accuracy and defects. The minor differences were in length of barrel, weight and size (diameter) of the bore. The British used the India (designed for the British East India Company) pattern 'Brown Bess' that had an 18.7-millimetre bore, meaning it fired a larger ball than the French Charleville year IX model with a bore of 17.2 millimetres. The Prussian 1809 Potsdam musket with a bore of 19.5 millimetres meant that in an emergency a Prussian infantryman could use the ammunition of any army on the battlefield, whereas a Frenchman could not, although if using the small French ball it would rattle down the barrel with the excess windage causing much less accuracy and stopping power. The Brown Bess could also fire French musket balls, and as with the Potsdam was therefore marginally easier to load, particularly as fouling increased after continual firing. Various versions of the Brown Bess were in service with the British Army for over 100 years (1722–1838). Although it was generally reliable, one officer at Waterloo considered the French weapon superior for skirmishing due to its comparative lightness and slightly longer barrel, and claimed that soldiers could sometimes be seen searching to find discarded weapons due to problems with the locks on their own muskets.

The inherent problems of all muskets were similar. Perhaps the most significant was their wild inaccuracy at anything over 80–100 metres. At that range an individual soldier might hope to hit a man in one out of 20 shots. However, at short ranges – the shorter the better – massed fire could be devastating as the large lead balls had massive stopping power. A hit on the arm would knock a man down, ripping through muscle and smashing bones. Another problem was the time taken to load – this applied to all muzzle-loading firearms. Thus a fundamental requirement for infantrymen was the ability to follow the lengthy loading drill. If this was not mastered in barracks then he would have little hope of coping in the confusion, excitement and adrenalin rush of battle. He had to follow the correct sequence of actions automatically without thinking, and as fast as possible.

The drill involved taking the cartridge (made up of powder and ball wrapped in greased paper), biting the end off and, while keeping the ball in his mouth, pulling back the cock (hammer) to the half cock position – firing of the musket at this stage gave us the expression 'going off at half cock'. A small amount of powder from the cartridge was poured into the pan and the frizzen moved to the vertical position to secure the powder. The butt was grounded and the remaining powder poured down the barrel and the ball spat down after it. Next the ramrod was taken from its slot under the barrel and the cartridge paper rammed down the barrel, which compacted the paper, ball and powder at the bottom. The ramrod

A dragoon carbine found on the field of Waterloo, 1815. (Courtesy of the Council of the National Army Museum)

was replaced (if lost or broken the musket could not be reloaded) and the cock pulled back to full cock. The musket was now ready to fire. To fire two shots a minute was a reasonable average, three exceptionally good. Invariably the first shot fired was the least likely to go wrong, as time had usually been spent getting everything correct. From then on firing rates tended to decline as barrels became fouled and mistakes were made, some of which took time to rectify. In emergencies the rate of fire could be speeded up by cutting corners, for example by banging the butt on the ground instead of ramming – a procedure that dramatically reduced effectiveness.

Several things could go wrong with muskets once firing started and clouds of smoke from the black powder developed. With little wind, smoke hung around and was continually reinforced by further firing (by artillery as well); this obscured targets, sometimes making it hard to tell friend from foe. Rain could ruin powder, or perhaps wash it from the pan. A good flint would last for up to 40 shots, but the setting required numerous adjustments and they were often dropped, so spares were essential. About one misfire could be expected every ten shots and it was not uncommon to have a hang fire. This meant the powder in the pan burnt more slowly than expected, resulting in a delay in firing of several seconds. This was most disconcerting for the firer, when, just as he lowered the weapon thinking he had a misfire, it fired. As more rounds were fired, so the fouling in the barrel accumulated, making ramming more difficult and eventually impossible until it was cleaned. At the same time the barrel was getting hotter and hotter – this could happen after ten minutes of continuous firing. The danger was not just the possibility of burnt hands as soldiers could avoid this by holding the sling, but the risk of the powder charge in the barrel exploding (called 'cooking-off'), possibly disabling the firer. Captain Coignet, Napoleon's wagon master at Waterloo, described how at the Battle of Marengo soldiers urinated down the barrels and dried them by pouring in loose powder and setting it alight!

Human errors made in the heat of battle with the enemy closing in could cause men to forget their drills.

The famous Brown Bess – the flintlock musket that became synonymous with the British during the 18th century. (Courtesy of the Council of the National Army Museum)

One was not removing the ramrod before firing, resulting in it being shot away and rendering the musket useless until another was found. Soldiers sometimes put the ball down the barrel first, which meant the musket would not fire. A similar result came from not closing the pan before loading the cartridge, which meant the powder could fall out or be blown away. Spiking their right hand while ramming a musket with fixed bayonet was not uncommon, as was forgetting the weapon was loaded and loading it again. The subsequent explosion was more likely to injure the firer than the enemy. Badly bruised shoulders from the kick of a loosely held musket, partial deafness, a bitter, gritty taste in the mouth, burnt cheeks and stinging eyes were the lot of soldiers involved in a prolonged firefight.

Some rifles were used at Waterloo, but only in Wellington's Army, as in 1807 Napoleon had ordered the withdrawal of those in use in the French Army. Rifles had grooved barrels that spun the ball, enabling greater range and accuracy than a smoothbore weapon. A trained marksman could hit a man at 200–300 yards. Around 4,000 Anglo-Allied soldiers were armed with rifles. The Baker rifle was carried by the 95th Rifles, 1st and 2nd Light Battalions KGL and three light companies in the KGL line battalions. The two *Jäger* companies of the Orange-Nassau Regiment; the Brunswick Advance Guard Battalion; two *Jäger* companies of the 1st Hanoverian Brigade and one light company in the Hanoverian Lüneburg and Grubenhagen Battalions were so armed, mostly with hunting rifles.

Rifles were primarily intended for use by sharpshooters and skirmishers, who were able to pick off enemy officers, gun detachments, horsemen or other worthwhile individual targets. This sharpshooter tactic was facilitated by the shorter (by 22cm) barrel permitting reloading in the prone position. The ball was 0.615 millimetres smaller than the musket ball but the same as carbines. However, at Waterloo Wellington used most of his rifle-armed troops as line infantry, relying on light companies of line battalions armed with muskets for most skirmishing. The grooving, while twisting the ball in flight, meant slower loading than with a musket as fouling built up more rapidly, resulting in increasing ramming difficulties. The loading drill was the same as with a musket but the rifleman carried a powder horn with fine powder and a bag of balls in addition to their supply of prepared cartridges in their cartridge box. Ramming the ball wrapped in a circular greased cloth followed a pinch of powder in the pan. A skilled rifleman could load and fire at around half the rate of his musket-armed comrade. The Baker rifle was to remain the British Army's rifle for 40 years.

Most cavalry carried muzzle-loading pistols, some French horsemen having two in a holster on either side of the saddle. Their range was exceedingly short, it was extraordinarily difficult to fire accurately from a horse, and to secure a hit the target had to be very large or so close that the enemy was only feet away. To load on

The Baker rifle, carried by the 95th Rifles and light battalions of the King's German Legion at Waterloo. (Courtesy of the Council of the National Army Museum)

horseback meant the cavalryman must be stationary. Even when loaded the chances were that the powder fell out of the pan in the holster, rendering it useless if needed immediately. Some infantry officers carried privately purchased pistols.

Various models of carbine included the short-barrelled cavalry firearm. It was carried, usually hooked to the shoulder belt, by all cavalry in Wellington's Army except for marksmen in the 10th Hussars, who had the shorter version of the Baker rifle. The Household troops and heavy dragoons carried the heavier 1796 pattern carbine with a 26-inch barrel, and the light cavalry the Paget carbine. They were all short-range weapons primarily for use for skirmishing.

Typical British riflemen in the uniforms of 1812. (Courtesy of the Council of the National Army Museum)

Their use at Waterloo was negligible. All Napoleon's cavalry, except for cuirassiers and lancers, carried a long firearm – dragoons had the musketoon that was extremely awkward to handle as it had a barrel of almost musket length.

Blade weapons

The sword and the sabre were the primary weapons of the cavalry, apart from the lancers. While there were exceptions, swords were generally straight or almost straight bladed, while sabres were usually more curved, some markedly so. There was considerable disagreement as to whether the thrust or the cut was the most effective way of disabling an opponent. The thrusters correctly maintained that a stab wound to the body had only to penetrate 6–8 centimetres to be fatal. However, if it penetrated too far the blade could become trapped in the rib cage and be difficult to withdraw. The slashers did not have that problem. A hard swipe with a well-balanced sabre would certainly inflict a fearful wound that would disable although not necessarily kill outright. There were numerous variations of length, curve or otherwise of blade, weight, balance and design of hilt as a weapon that could do both thrust and cut with equal facility was sought.

British heavy cavalry such as the Union Brigade carried a somewhat ineffective 1796 pattern sword that was 90 centimetres long and straight bladed apart from the 10 centimetres at the tip that curved on one side to make a point. Before Waterloo many had the tip of the blade ground into a spear point for easy penetration. However, it was a heavy, cumbersome weapon that was good for thrusting or hacking at an infantryman, but hard and tiring to wield when duelling with other cavalrymen. British light cavalry carried the 1776 pattern sabre with a slightly shorter blade that was markedly curved, and wider at the point than the hilt. This gave the point end more weight and resulted in it being capable of inflicting dreadful slashing wounds with deep long cuts. It was not unknown for a man's arm to be severed or skull split through a helmet. French heavy cavalry were armed with swords and sabres with the cuirassiers and dragoons carrying straight bladed weapons, and the carabineers, *grenadiers à cheval* and *gendarmes d'élite* heavy straight sabres. Light cavalry carried a lighter curved sabre, including the lancers. The Prussian dragoons, hussars, *Uhlans* (lancers) and *Landwehr* cavalry all had curved sabres.

French infantrymen were also armed with a short sword (*sabre-briquet*) in addition to their musket and bayonet, although it was rare for an infantryman to fight with a sword. Most French officers also carried swords with many preferring the robust sabre of the élite companies. British Highland Regiment officers were

This cavalry figure from 1815 is depicted holding his primary weapon of the era: the sabre. (Anne S. K. Brown)

armed with the heavy, basket-hilted broadsword or claymore, while the British 95th Rifles officers were ordered to carry pistols, as their curved sword was such a poor weapon.

Every infantryman had his bayonet, mostly used for defence against cavalry. The British bayonet had a 43-centimetre blade (rifle bayonets were slightly longer as the barrel was shorter). There was little bayonet fighting at Waterloo except in Plancenoit village, where the Imperial Guard clashed with the Prussians. Sergeants in British infantry units were unique in carrying 2-metre pikes as their primary weapon. The exceptions were the sergeants of rifle regiments, who had rifles, or of the light companies of battalions, who had muskets. Pikes had a crosspiece below the spike to prevent over-penetration. They were of limited value to a battalion compared with the loss of over 30 muskets.

The final blade, or rather spiked weapon, was the lance. It was about 2.7 metres long and weighed over 3 kilograms, with a steel point, blackened wooden staff, leather wrist strap and steel ferule. Its advantages lay in its long reach, and it was an intimidating sight to see a mass of lancers charging towards you with lowered lances. It could be a deadly killer when held by a moving horseman as the point was driven into the body with the weight of the horse behind it. It was eminently suited to spearing fleeing infantrymen. However, a swordsman in a mêlée could comparatively easily parry it, and thereafter the lancer was seriously disadvantaged unless he dropped his lance and drew his sword – as they often did. It is likely that French regiments at Waterloo only armed the front rank of lancer squadrons with lances. Over half the Prussian cavalry present were lancers.

Artillery

As noted above, at the start of the battle Wellington deployed 157 pieces of ordnance and Napoleon 247. In the late afternoon and evening Blücher brought another 134. All were smoothbore, muzzle-loading pieces. This ordnance was divided into cannons (guns) that fired at direct line of sight targets, and howitzers that could lob projectiles over low obstacles at long distances as well as fire canister (see below) at closer ranges. Ordnance was classified according to the weight of the projectile it fired or the diameter of the bore. The cannons were 6-pounders (Wellington had 67, Napoleon 142, Blücher 82), 9-pounders (Wellington 60) and 12-pounders (Napoleon 36, Blücher 18); those with the Imperial Guard were dubbed Napoleon's 'beautiful daughters'. Howitzers were 5½-inch (Wellington 30, Napoleon 56), 6-inch (Napoleon 6), 7-inch (Blücher 28) and 10-pounders (Blücher 6). Howitzers were distinguishable from cannons by their short stubby barrels.

Teams of horses working in pairs drew all artillery. The 12-pounders had teams of eight horses, the 9-pounders six and the 6-pounders six or four. The size of gun detachments varied according to the size of the piece but on average Wellington had 33 men to keep a gun in action, while Napoleon had 26, figures that include the officers, gunners, drivers for ammunition, forage and stores and wagons, and specialists such as farriers. Ordnance was divided into batteries (also called brigades and companies) for tactical purposes, having four, six or eight pieces; all except the four-gun batteries normally included two howitzers. All the artillery was divided between foot and horse artillery. The former was intended to support the army from static or semi-static positions, while horse artillery could manoeuvre on the battlefield in support of cavalry or infantry, whereas with foot batteries only the ordnance and accompanying caissons for ammunition and wagons were horse drawn.

Loading procedures were similar to those of muskets in that powder was placed in the vent at the base of the barrel and the charge and projectile were muzzle loaded and rammed home and the powder lit with a slow-burning match. The main difference was that after firing the barrel was swabbed with a wet sponge to remove any glowing embers. The rate of fire was slow as the piece recoiled backwards after firing and had to be re-aligned after every shot as well as reloaded. This was tiring work, particularly with the heavier pieces, and a good rate was two rounds a minute. This soon dropped to one or

A 6-inch howitzer of the Foot Artillery of the Imperial Guard, c.1808–15. (Print after Maurice Orange, René Chartrand)

Austrian horse artillery in 1815. (Anne S. K. Brown)

less with exhausted or depleted detachments – the French had to call in infantrymen for muscle power after the Grand Battery lost men to the Union Brigade's attack.

The ammunition held with the gun, in the axle box and limber, was usually dumped beside the piece for static firing. The limber then withdrew, undercover if possible, nearby. The bulk of the ammunition was kept further back on caissons (ammunition wagons), with more wagons in a third line behind that – there were slight variations between nationalities.

Cannons fired either round shot (an iron cannon ball) or canister, and howitzers shell or canister. Round shot accounted for about 75 per cent of all artillery ammunition carried at Waterloo, as it was dual-purpose ammunition equally capable of smashing walls, equipment or men's bodies, particularly if they were packed together in columns. Cannon balls would ricochet on hard ground bowling over any soldier in their path, although wet ground at Waterloo largely prevented this. However, they were line of sight projectiles, and as Wellington usually deployed his troops behind a ridge, or got them to lie down or dismount, losses were considerably reduced. Round shot was effective for ranges up to 1,100 metres, but best at around 500–600 metres. Canister (also called case shot) was an anti-personnel, anti-horse projectile normally fired at ranges up to 350 metres for the 'lighter' type, and out to 400 or 500 metres for 12-pounders. British light canister consisted of a tin canister filled with 85 42-gram balls and the heavy variety 41 100-gram balls. It was effectively a huge shotgun cartridge that could do enormous damage as the balls spread out in a cone.

Howitzers could fire canister in emergencies but normally relied on shells fired at a high angle to hit targets hidden from view. The common shell was a hollow iron sphere filled with gunpowder and lit by a fuse ignited by the flash of the propellant charge. The iron fragments flung out by the bursting charge were effective against men and horses, although with an airburst many were thrown upwards and thus were useless. The key to success was to cut the fuse to the right burning time for the range – a frequent cause of error. In wet ground shells would often bury themselves and limit the lethality of the explosion. The only howitzers to fire spherical case or shrapnel (invented by Henry Shrapnel in 1784) at Waterloo were the British,

Artillery train of the Imperial Guard under fire, c.1808–12. The gun (right background) has been unhooked from its limber and is in action. (Print after JOB, René Chartrand)

as it was unique to Britain. This was an iron sphere filled with a mix of gunpowder and musket balls ignited by a fuse. It was an effective projectile, very much the British 'secret weapon' at the battle, capable of flinging musket balls from an airburst out as far as 900 metres. At Waterloo French howitzers also successfully fired 'carcass' projectiles at the buildings in Hougoumont Farm. This was an incendiary projectile made from a bound canvas container in which was a solidified mixture of turpentine, resin, tallow, sulphur, saltpetre and antimony that was lit by the propellant charge. It burnt for around 12 minutes and was almost impossible to extinguish.

Another artillery weapon exclusive to the British was 'ammunition without ordnance' or rockets (called Congreve Rockets after their inventor Colonel William Congreve). They looked very similar to modern firework rockets. One troop was present at Waterloo firing 6-pound incendiary or canister rockets. They were cheap to make, did not need guns to fire them and had a range out to 2,700 metres. However, they were wildly inaccurate and could even turn back on the firers,

The Earl of Anglesey leads the heavy cavalry and dragoon guards in a charge at Waterloo. The range of weapons used by the cavalry are clear to see, including sabres and pistols. (Anne S. K. Brown)

although they could frighten both troops and horses. Wellington had little use for them and was only reluctantly persuaded to accept a few. At Waterloo the rockets were part of the 6-pounder battery of Captain Whinyates, Royal Horse Artillery (RHA). Normally a high-angle weapon, they could also be fired along the ground; they were employed in this way at the battle, where some 50 rockets were used.

TACTICS

For Wellington Waterloo was primarily a defensive and counter-attack battle fought against an opponent whose success depended on attacking. Napoleon was only forced onto the defensive on his eastern flank when the Prussians attacked in the evening. Throughout history the weapons used, their effectiveness and range have dictated tactics. Waterloo was no different. It was largely, though not exclusively, the characteristics of the infantry musket that shaped how armies fought.

The infantry had to learn to manoeuvre, change formation between column, line or square, retire and skirmish. During the battle the British 71st Regiment changed from column to square to column and then to line. To do this under battle conditions necessitated constant training in the drills required. Similarly, the cavalry had to master various formations and how and when best to charge, to retire or skirmish. The commanders in chief set the overall grand tactics at Waterloo. Napoleon decided he would defeat his enemy by smashing a hole in the Anglo-Allied line with frontal attacks, and then exploit that break with reserves. Wellington decided to hide virtually all his army, except for his artillery, behind the Mont Saint Jean ridge to give them cover from view and direct fire. He kept the bulk of his cavalry and less experienced infantry formations in reserve for counter-strokes. Additionally he manned three outposts some distance in front of his line – Hougoumont and La Haye Sainte farms and the cluster of farms Papelotte/La Haye/Smohain. Blücher's plan was to march to join Wellington on his left flank and then attack.

Tactical success is most easily achieved when all arms co-operate and support each other on the battlefield. Co-ordination, not just between different arms but also between fire and movement, combined with surprise and concentration of force, has invariably been the key to victory.

The basic infantry formations used during the battle were the column, line and square. Battalion columns were not marching columns, but rather companies in two (British) or three (French and Prussian) ranks formed one behind the other with distances between companies varying dependent on the tactical circumstances and need to change formation quickly. A British column of ten companies closed up would have a frontage of about 20 metres (one company in two ranks), and a depth of 50 metres with the grenadier (élite) company at the front and the light company at the rear. Its commander would lead each company with the other officers in the rear. The colour party was in the centre of the column. A battalion column in open order would be 20 metres wide but around 200 metres deep. Most of Wellington's battalions formed up in close order columns behind the Mont Saint Jean ridge at the start of the battle, as this formation was comparatively easy to control for movement. A battalion attack column, used mostly by the French and Prussians for advancing against the enemy such as those of Reille's divisions attacking Hougoumont, usually consisted of the six companies, each in three rank lines, three companies deep alongside each other. Again, this was easier to control, and from it to change formation to line to develop more firepower, or square to defend against cavalry. It was common to deploy light companies well in advance of the attackers to act as skirmishers (see below).

Dense columns (a French attack column could be nine ranks deep) were very vulnerable to fire. They were almost impossible to miss when within effective musket range, while cannonballs and canister could be devastating. An example of this was the 1st Nassau that remained in close column for most of the day and suffered accordingly. According to Captain Friedrich Weiz the battalion was 'at a serious disadvantage due to the depth of the column'.[1] Another serious drawback was a column's inability to develop much firepower at the front – only the first two ranks of the two leading companies could fire. Equally they were vulnerable to physical attacks on their flanks, particularly by cavalry. French drill manuals decreed that attack columns should deploy into line to maximise firepower as they neared the enemy. This was seldom achieved or attempted as the French normally relied on sheer weight of numbers and momentum to push home their assault. The difficulty for the column commander was when precisely to order the change to line, which could take several minutes – too soon and he was open to attack by cavalry and was out of musket range; too late and he was vulnerable to massed musket fire.

At Waterloo General Jean-Baptiste Drouet, Count d'Erlon's Corps, advanced against an enemy largely hidden behind a crest so commanders could not see the Allied formations until too late to change formation. This particular attack was made even more difficult to control and vulnerable by advancing in divisional battalion columns in an attempt to combine firepower to the front with weight in the assault. Two complete divisions plus two brigades – 25 battalions, some 12,500 infantry – formed up with each complete division of eight or nine battalions deployed in line in three ranks closed up one behind the other. For example, Marcognet's Division of eight battalions had its leading battalion in three ranks with a frontage of some 120 metres. The column thus had 24 ranks and a depth of only 80 metres – a gunner's dream.

When Wellington's front-line battalions deployed forward to meet the French infantry assault they formed into line – that is battalions drawn up in two ranks (with some Allied battalions in three). The objective was to get virtually all muskets available to fire. Firing was done by platoons, by files or by the front rank firing while the second 'made ready'. However, one massive volley by up to 500 muskets firing at short range into a dense target caused horrific loss. If followed by an immediate bayonet charge, as was British preference, it was invariably decisive.

For defence against cavalry attacks infantry relied upon a defensive square formation – if caught in line or column by charging cavalry they were lost. The

British infantry in 1812 pattern uniforms and equipment, equipped with muskets and bayonets. (Courtesy of the Council of the National Army Museum)

5th KGL was caught in line and destroyed when advancing to support La Haye Sainte. In some cases the formation was more rectangular than square. A British eight-company battalion, if not deploying skirmishers, would have two companies on each side facing outwards; six companies would have two companies at front and rear and one on each side. If casualties had been heavy two battalions could combine to form one square, examples at Waterloo being the British 2nd/30th and 2nd/73rd and 3rd and 4th Battalions, KGL. The square was usually formed with companies in two or more ranks, the front rank(s) kneeling. All had bayonets fixed so that in addition to the firepower the sides of the square became a 'hedgehog' of spikes that horses were reluctant to face despite the vicious use of spurs. This is what happened during Ney's massed cavalry assaults during the afternoon when his horsemen washed round the Allied squares like an incoming tide round rocks. The attacking cavalry mostly halted close to the squares, fired their pistols or carbines and retired, or were counter-attacked and driven off by Wellington's cavalry and devastating close-range volleys from the squares.

Battalion squares could be used for movement if there was a danger of cavalry attack. According to General of Brigade Baron Jean Martin Petit, commanding the 1st and 2nd Battalions of the 1st Regiment of Grenadiers of

British infantry repulse a French cavalry assault. Note the Congreve rocket being fired in the background. (Anne S. K. Brown)

the Old Guard, who watched them advance, this was the formation of the eight battalions of the Imperial Guard when they launched their final assault. Napoleon finally withdrew from the battlefield in a square of the 1st Regiment of Grenadiers of his Guard.

It was not impossible, if rare, for cavalry to break a square – for example, if the infantry was caught in the process of changing formation, or if it was manned by shaken, hesitant troops, or if a gap was created by artillery fire or a horse collapsed into the square. In these circumstances horsemen could break through, and the square was almost certainly doomed. Infantry would often be ordered to fire at the horses, as bringing down both animal and rider resulted in a tangled confusion of bodies that formed an obstacle to those coming behind. In the evening a Hanoverian square of the Bremen Field Battalion was compelled to form first a triangle and then 'an irregular mass' by devastating case shot and musketry to the extent that all order within the ranks was lost within half an hour, and whatever remained of the exhausted troops retired.[2]

Either infantry or cavalry could undertake skirmishing, although at Waterloo only the former did so. It normally involved light infantry companies trained as marksmen to deploy 200–250 metres forward of a defensive position or in front of advancing infantry. They operated in open order in pairs and in extended lines employing individual aimed fire to disrupt an enemy advance, or screen an advance from enemy skirmishers and drive them away. They could be particularly effective against artillery detachments or picking off mounted officers. Indeed, the 3rd Battalion, KGL, suffered severely from the heavy skirmish fire of French tirailleurs, who were several battalions strong.

Skirmishers were highly vulnerable to cavalry attacks so individuals unable to seek shelter or form square were trained to face attacking horsemen until the last minute and then fall down and sham death. If this was too risky each individual should at the last moment jump to the right onto the horseman's left ('blind') side and thrust his bayonet at the horse. Normally as the attackers closed in skirmishers would withdraw to their parent unit or round the flanks, or between the attacking units.

At Waterloo Wellington deployed skirmishers from the outset in an irregular line stretching almost 4,000 metres from Hougoumont Wood to La Haye Sainte, and then east of the Brussels road to south of Papelotte. It averaged about 200 metres forward from the crest of the ridge. The object was to protect the batteries

French Consular Guard form a square at Marengo, June 1800: the same formation was probably adopted to the Imperial Guard's final advance during the early evening. (Print after Raffet, Philip Haythornthwaite)

The 85th Regiment skirmish at Nivelle in November 1813: the men are in open order, operating in pairs. Skirmishers often played an important role on the battlefields of the era.
(Print after Richard Simkin, Philip Haythornthwaite)

behind and inflict losses on advancing infantry but to retire to the shelter of the squares if faced by cavalry or pressed by the main attack. This line was sparsely spread, but being down a forward slope the artillery behind was initially able to fire over their heads.

With the French this duty fell to the voltigeur companies in the line or light battalions. A strong skirmisher screen fronted d'Erlon's massive infantry advance at the start of the battle. If all the attacking battalions had contributed their voltigeur companies then up to 2,600 French skirmishers would have outnumbered the thin Allied skirmish line by well over two to one. As the main body closed in the French skirmishers were trained to either withdraw through the main line, or if this was impossible to lie flat and let the infantry walk over them. For some reason during the final major infantry assault by the Imperial Guard in the final stages of the battle no skirmishers were deployed.

Cavalry operated on the battlefield in squadrons and charged, if possible knee to knee, in a line of three or four squadrons each of two ranks, or with the squadrons in echelon, chequered or column formations. The massed French cavalry attacks in the afternoon were mostly in squadron columns as they were forced to attack on a narrow frontage. A theoretical sequence of a charge was walk, trot, canter, gallop and finally an all-out dash for the final 50 metres. It seldom happened this way. At Waterloo the gap between Hougoumont and La Haye Sainte was only 950 metres and Ney crammed 9,000 horsemen through it during the course of the afternoon so at best they approached the squares at a trot. When counter-attacked by Allied cavalry many were caught stationary or just milling around. Even the Union Brigade's counter-attack on d'Erlon's divisions as they crested the ridge and pushed through the hedges was mostly at a trot or canter. Captain Kennedy Clark, 1st (Royal) Dragoons, whose squadron confronted Donzelot's Division, stated:

> From the nature of the ground we did not see each other until we were very close, perhaps eighty or ninety yards … they [the enemy] had forced their way through our line – the heads of the columns were on the Brussels side of the double hedge… In fact the crest of the height had been gained… The charge of the cavalry took place on the crest, not on the slope of the ridge …

If cavalry charged other cavalry it was a tactical principle that those threatened should counter-charge, as being caught stationary was a serious disadvantage. This happened when the Household Brigade charged down onto the French cuirassiers that had advanced on d'Erlon's left flank west of La Haye Sainte. The resultant momentum against the slow-moving or stationary French horsemen soon drove the cuirassiers back. The classic example of a perfectly timed cavalry counter-attack was when the scattered and out of control Household and

British gunners undergoing artillery training at Woolwich Barracks prior to Waterloo. (Anne S. K. Brown)

WATERLOO, 18 JUNE 1815 – THE SITUATION AT 11 A.M.

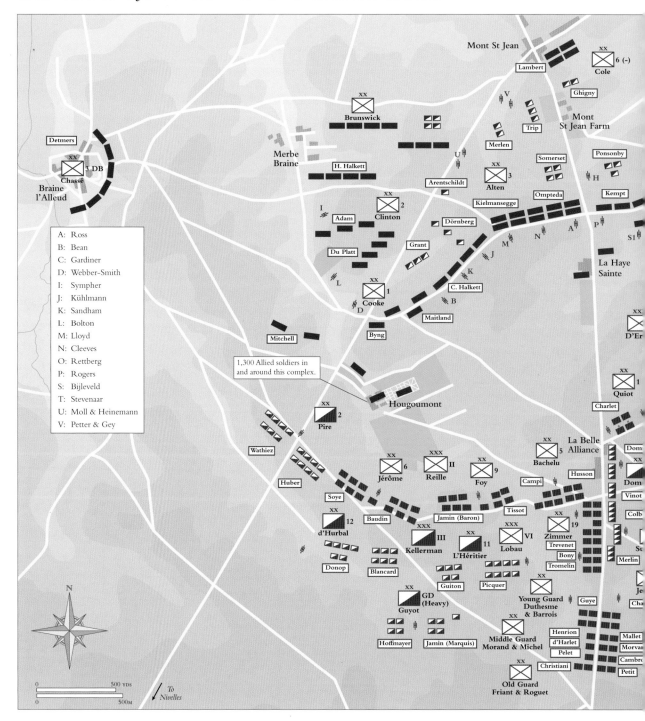

Mont St Jean

Lambert

Cole 6 (-)

Ghigny

V

Mont St Jean Farm

Trip

Brunswick

Merlen

Somerset

Ponsonby

Detmers

Chassé 3 DB

Braine l'Alleud

Merbe Braine

H. Halkett

U

Alten 3

Arentschildt

Kielmansegge

Ompteda

Kempt

I

Adam

Clinton 2

Dörnberg

M

N

A

P

S1

Du Platt

Grant

J

La Haye Sainte

A: Ross
B: Bean
C: Gardiner
D: Webber-Smith
I: Sympher
J: Kühlmann
K: Sandham
L: Bolton
M: Lloyd
N: Cleeves
O: Rettberg
P: Rogers
S: Bijleveld
T: Stevenaar
U: Moll & Heinemann
V: Petter & Gey

L

K

Cooke 1

C. Halkett

D

B

Maitland

D'Er

Mitchell

Byng

1,300 Allied soldiers in and around this complex.

Hougoumont

Quiot 1

Charlet

Pire 2

La Belle Alliance

Bachelu 5

Dom

Wathiez

Husson

Dom

Soye

Jérôme 6

Reille II

Foy 9

Campi

Vinot

Huber

Baudin

Jamin (Baron)

Tissot

Zimmer 19

Colb

d'Hurbal 12

Kellerman III

L'Héritier 11

Lobau VI

Trevenet

St

Donop

Blancard

Guiton

Picquer

Bony

Tromelin

Merlin

Guyot GD (Heavy)

Young Guard Duthesme & Barrois

Guye

Cha

Je

Hoffmayer

Jamin (Marquis)

Middle Guard Morand & Michel

Henrion d'Harlet

Pelet

Mallet

Morva

Christiani

Cambro

Petit

Old Guard Friant & Roguet

N

500 YDS

500M

To Nivelles

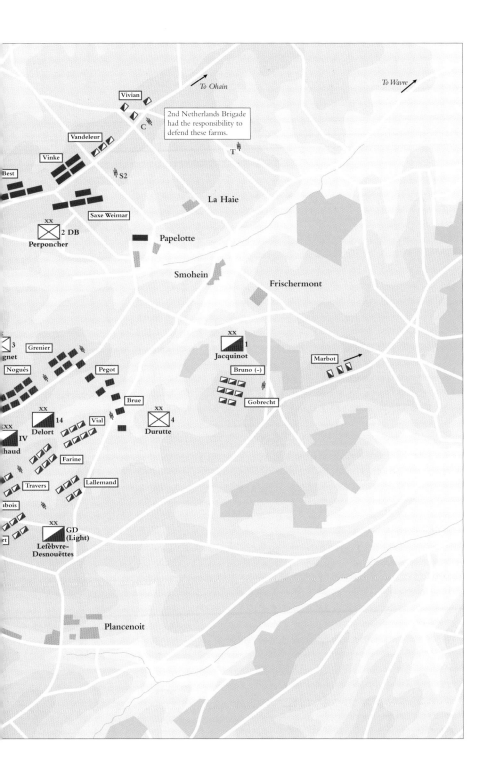

To Ohain

To Wavre

Vivian

C

2nd Netherlands Brigade
had the responsibility to
defend these farms.

T

Vandeleur

Vinke

Best

S2

La Haie

Saxe Weimar

XX
2 DB
Perponcher

Papelotte

Smohein

Frischermont

XX
Jacquinot 1

Marbot

Grenier

gnet 3

Nogués

Pegot

Bruno (-)

Gobrecht

Brue

XX
Delort 14

Vial

XX
Durutte 4

XXX
IV
haud

Farine

Travers

Lallemand

bois

XX
GD
(Light)
Lefèbvre-
Desnouëttes

Plancenoit

Union Brigades were caught on blown horses milling around the Grand Battery position. They were hit in front by cuirassiers and on their left by lancers and chasseurs (some 2,400 horsemen) and lost heavily, including the commander of the Union Brigade Major General Sir William Ponsonby. The French cavalry were in turn forced to retire by another well-executed counter-attack by the light cavalry brigades of both Major General John Vandeleur and Major General Charles Étienne Ghigny's Netherlanders.

ARTILLERY

As with musketry, artillery fire had to be concentrated to be effective. Napoleon made the point with his maxim, 'In battle like a siege, skill consists in converging a mass of fire on a single point.' He succeeded in grouping 80 pieces (60 cannons and 20 howitzers) in a 'Grand Battery' to bombard the centre and left of Wellington's line before launching the attack by d'Erlon's Corps. On this occasion results were disappointing as, except for the artillery batteries, the Allies were sheltered behind the ridge and spread over a large area out of sight of the gunners. Co-operation with, and support of, other arms was a key artillery tactical principle; something that Napoleon (and Ney) only belated achieved to a limited extent. When some French horse batteries came forward during Ney's massed cavalry attacks they were able to fire effectively into the Allied squares – it was virtually entirely cannon fire that inflicted serious losses on the squares. However, they were only able to fire in between the cavalry attacks and it was generally not well co-ordinated with their mounted comrades. When La Haye Sainte was taken and a French horse battery unlimbered close to Captain Alexander Cavalié Mercer's Battery's left flank, he felt sure that due to the rapidity and precision of fire, they would be annihilated. After the farm fell another French battery opened effective canister fire a mere 150 metres from Major General Sir James Kempt's Brigade but fortunately it was soon driven off by accurate rifle fire from the 1st/95th.

Wellington departed from the usual artillery tactics in two ways. First, apart from a small reserve of guns, he removed the horse batteries from his cavalry formations and placed them with the foot batteries, most initially in the front line along the ridge. In this way he achieved considerable concentration against his attackers as they advanced through the high-standing rye up the slope. However, these batteries were exposed to French guns, and during the day many suffered severely from losses of men and horses, and exhaustion. Secondly, Wellington ordered his gunners to abandon their pieces and seek shelter in the nearest infantry square if about to be overrun by cavalry. However, it could have been damaging to the infantry morale seeing the gunners running away, and for this reason the order was not universally obeyed. Abandoning the guns meant the enemy would capture them, and might either spike them (drive a tapered steel wedge into the vent) or drag them away. Fortunately the French were too disorganised or ill equipped to do either (the British Household and Union Brigades also failed to spike any Grand Battery guns), enabling the detachments to run back and resume firing as the French withdrew. Wellington also forbade his artillery from counter-battery fire – he wanted ammunition conserved for softer targets. Major H. J. Kuhlmann, KGL Horse Artillery, stated, 'the Duke of Wellington visited us several times and gave us the distinct order never to fire at the enemy artillery'.[3] On one occasion Captain Mercer RHA disobeyed this order and suffered severely in consequence.

Waterloo was the final deciding clash of the Revolutionary and Napoleonic Wars between the two great opposing commanders of the era. Wellington was usually at his best when defending, and Waterloo was a classic example of his infantry and artillery defensive tactics and the use of cavalry for counter-attacks. Napoleon on the other hand had secured most of his great victories as an attacking general, with the main assault preceded by a concentrated artillery bombardment. Being a gunner, whenever possible he endeavoured to assemble a 'grand battery' with which to open a battle. Waterloo is an obvious example of his use of guns in this manner at the start followed by an attempt by massed infantry attack in close columns against the enemy's centre. Also it demonstrated again his invariably keeping the Imperial Guard as a last reserve either to clinch a victory or to counter an unexpected threat, or a final fling to snatch a victory from impending defeat – at Waterloo it was the latter two.

This battle also featured most if not all the common features of Napoleonic battle tactics, the most obvious being the defeat of the heavy infantry column assault by the extended line. The side bringing the most muskets to bear at close range invariably destroyed a column attack. With cavalry attacks against the infantry in squares, Waterloo demonstrated again and again that horsemen could not break a steady square. At various stages of the battle there are examples of skirmishers, fighting in woods or for buildings, cavalry counter-attacks, the importance of disabling captured guns and of achieving co-operation between cavalry, horse artillery and infantry in an attack.

It would be 40 years before European armies fought again. During the Crimean War both the weapons and tactics of Waterloo had changed little and a number of the generals of that era had been subalterns four decades earlier.

CHAPTER 5

WATERLOO EYEWITNESSES

Different Perspectives

Natalia Griffon de Pleineville

The perception of a battle by its participants is influenced by a variety of factors. Dependent on rank, the position on the battlefield, political convictions or personal experience, the exact same event can be perceived in an entirely different manner. The number of the recollections often depends on the importance of the battle or campaign and is proportional to its long-lasting consequences. It is particularly true for the Napoleonic period; indeed the Battle of Borodino in 1812 generated more first-hand accounts than the Battle of Rivoli in 1797.

History has recorded a great number of eyewitness accounts of the Battle of Waterloo, which definitively ended Napoleon's rule, from the lowest ranks to the most senior commanders. These accounts can be divided into two main categories. The first – and the most precious for a historian – are diaries or letters written during the immediate hours or days after the fighting, which forcibly reflect the real impressions of the participants. However, even these are not perfect, because it was usually not until some days after the events that the participants could put down their recollections on paper, writing from a sometimes imperfect memory. Secondly, there are a great number of narratives written or dictated many years after the events; of these, numerous accounts contain few personal details but instead many excerpts from books published in the decades after the battle. For example, numerous British memoirs on the Peninsular War are largely compiled from William Francis Patrick Napier, the author of the acclaimed *History of the War in the Peninsula*. They are, therefore, less reliable than direct contemporary evidence, although some of them may be taken into account as there are short personal anecdotes incorporated throughout the text. Many French histories of the battle are based on Napoleon's not very credible accounts and may therefore twist the facts.

Differences can also be ascertained in the perception of the same event by the participants according to their national character. Accounts by British soldiers frequently evoke God's name, whereas their French counterparts generally reflect little or no religious feeling owing to the collapse of the influence of the church during the French Revolution and the anti-clerical ideas of the French philosophers of the Age of Reason. Rather than a judgement by God, an element of fatality is sometimes evoked: *Chef d'escadron* Jean-Baptiste Lemonnier-Delafosse of the II Corps wrote that '24 hours of a thunderstorm destroyed all the combinations of a military commander'.[1] Perhaps somewhat surprisingly for an English audience even the very name of the battle is recalled differently by those involved. For the British, the name of Waterloo is, of course, sacred. As for the French, Louis-Vivant Lagneau, a surgeon major of the 3rd Grenadiers of the Old Guard, calls it 'the battle of Waterloo or of Mont-Saint-Jean'.[2] *Adjudant commandant* Auguste Petiet, a member of the French General Headquarters under the orders of Marshal 'Nicolas' Jean de Dieu Soult, stated: 'I would have wished, like my comrades, to see this disastrous day of 18th June be called Mont-Saint-Jean, after the name of this miserable hamlet which is now so famous.'[3]

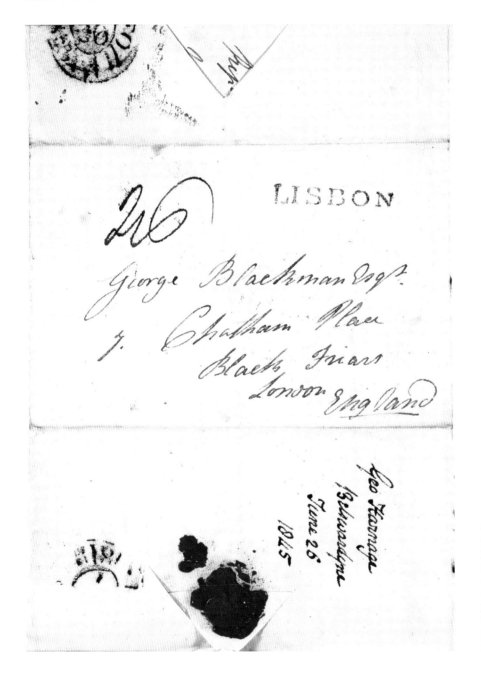

LISBON

26

George Blackman Esqr.
7. Chatham Place
Black Friars
London England

Geo Haomaa
Betesardene
June 26°
1845

Captain John Blackman of the Coldstream Guards wrote many letters to his parents describing the progress of Wellington's Army during the Napoleonic Wars, through Spain, France and into Belgium, before his death at Waterloo in June 1815. (Courtesy of the Council of the National Army Museum)

PART I.

CIRCUMSTANTIAL DETAIL

PREVIOUS, DURING, AND AFTER

THE BATTLE OF WATERLOO,

Containing also

FURTHER PARTICULARS COLLECTED FROM THE
COMMUNICATION AND CORRESPONDENCE OF
SEVERAL OFFICERS OF RANK
AND DISTINCTION,

Who were occupied in different Parts of the Field of Action,

INCLUDING

A FRENCH OFFICER'S DESCRIPTION,

WHO WAS AN EYE WITNESS, &c.

On the evening of Thursday the 15th of June, a Courier arrived at Brussels, from Marshal Blucher to announce, that hostilities had commenced. The Duke of Wellington was sitting after dinner, with a party of officers, over the desert and wine, when he received the dispatches containing this unexpected news. Marshal Blucher had been attacked that day by the French; but he seemed to consider it as a mere affair of outposts, which was not likely to proceed much further at present, though it might probably prove the prelude to a more important engagement.* It was the opinion of most military men in Brussels, that it was the plan of the Enemy by a false alarm to induce the Allies to concentrate their chief military force in that quarter, in order that he might more successfully make a serious attack upon some

* The first intelligence of the commencement of hostilities was known in London, at four o'clock on Tuesday afternoon, June 20, 1815. (*Vide Part* 3, p. 156.)

b

There were many accounts of Waterloo after the battle, including this one by 'a near observer' who collected communication and correspondence from a range of officers to depict the fighting. (Courtesy Osprey Publishing)

British memoirs, unless they are of an immediate nature (such as letters or diaries), usually glorify Wellington and the British Army, leaving aside the other nationalities present, especially the crucial and decisive participation of the Prussian Army. Another key aspect of British memoirs is that they tend to focus on the individual. On the other hand, French memoirs, usually written long after the events, tend to dwell at length on Marshal Emmanuel de Grouchy's alleged mistakes and Field Marshal Gebhard Leberecht von Blücher's unexpected arrival on the battlefield. Also, French memoirs tend to not be all that specific about personal details – a consequence both of the time elapsed when writing and also of the trauma of the defeat.

The degree of sincerity is generally not the same in the memoirs of private soldiers and superior officers. Soldiers and NCOs are usually more spontaneous and genuine, but they lack an overview. Senior commanders wrote for posterity's sake and their sincerity is calculated; some facts are simply omitted or distorted. Furthermore, some of them embroidered the facts to justify their own conduct, or avoided telling the truth in order to spare individual feelings and interests.

Undoubtedly, political changes sometimes also exerted influence on the accounts of the Battle of Waterloo. A good example of this is an account of the Waterloo campaign by Lieutenant General François-Étienne Kellermann who commanded the III Reserve Cavalry Corps at Waterloo; now in the Vincennes military archives, it is a veritable diatribe against Napoleon as Kellermann needed to gain favour with the Bourbon family in order to preserve his rank in the army and his titles. As Andrew Field wrote, 'the major failing of French accounts is their lack of objectivity. They are either unapologetically pro- or anti-Napoleon, and this seriously detracts from their value.'[4]

The accounts differ in their usefulness depending on the time of writing and the degree of the personal experience recorded. Some authors speak only about the events which happened to their unit or in the immediate vicinity. Others try to provide an overall review of military operations, but are valid only for the events that the diarist personally witnessed.

Globally, one finds many details in the memoirs of participants. The same event is often perceived in a different manner, depending on the rank, the personality and the situation of the diarist. Indeed, different phases of the battle, particularly the numerous cavalry charges which occurred throughout the course of the day, are frequently regarded entirely differently. Sometimes the facts are misrepresented because of memory lapses. Notwithstanding their

Lieutenant General Kellermann commanded the III Reserve Cavalry Corps during the battle, and wrote a detailed account of the action which is conserved in the French military archives. (akg-images)

imperfections, these primary sources are extremely precious for a historian and 200 years after the battle the richness of the sources, from the lowest ranks to the most senior commanders, is remarkable. By comparing the numerous accounts, it is possible to arrive at an overview of the Battle of Waterloo.

Undoubtedly rank played a huge part in how any battle was perceived and subsequently presented. Senior officers often try to justify themselves in their memoirs about their performance. Junior officers dwell on their own personal experience and sometimes discuss tactical considerations. NCOs and soldiers talk honestly about their feelings and remember their comrades killed in the battle. But it should be remembered that NCOs, soldiers and junior officers are simply unable to give a complete account of the battle as their position on the battlefield and on the front line means that their perspective is immediately limited. Alexander Cavalié Mercer, an artillery captain and famous British diarist of the Waterloo campaign, wrote lucidly:

> He who pretends to give a general account of a great battle from his own observation deceives you – believe him not. He can see no further (that is, if he be personally engaged in it) than the length of his nose; and how is he to tell what is passing two or three miles off, with hills and trees and buildings intervening, and all enveloped in smoke?[5]

With these considerations in mind let us now examine various eyewitness accounts of the Battle of Waterloo itself and attempt to draw out the relevant historical evidence from the multitude of surviving first-hand accounts.

THE NIGHT BEFORE THE BATTLE

Kellermann stated in his aforementioned account of the Waterloo campaign: 'Enough attention is never paid to the influence that excessive tiredness, bad weather, a lack of food and of rest, can exert on a human body. A physical weariness necessarily affects the morale, generating disgust and despondency.'[6]

The bad weather experienced the night before Waterloo is well known. Officers and soldiers had to sleep in the mud, without shelter, with their stomachs empty. Sergeant Major Louis-Marie-Sylvain-Pierre Larreguy de Civrieux of the 93rd *de ligne* recalled:

> The night of 17th–18th June was awful. Heavy rains had soddened the soil. It was impossible for us to light a fire, even to cook. Our bivouacs were strewn with beef

and mutton cut up by our sabres, but we were unable to cook them. The distribution of bread was still awaited; we lay in the water. Though we were so tired that we slept deeply under a torrential rain.[7]

In the words of Lemonnier-Delafosse:

> The night of 17th–18th seemed to be an omen of the misfortunes of the following day. A violent and continuous rain prevented the army from taking any moment of rest. To add to our trouble, the bad state of roads delayed the arrival of the provisions, so that the majority of the soldiers and officers were deprived of food.

Lieutenant Jacques-François Martin of the 45th *de ligne* subsequently recalled:

> The night was black like an oven, the water was continuously falling in torrents; to cap it all, our regiment was stationed in a wet ploughed field, where we had to take the pleasures of rest. No wood, no straw, no victuals and impossible to procure them.[8]

The British were no better provided for. Captain William Tomkinson of the 16th Light Dragoons recalled:

> The rain had fallen through the night without ceasing; the army had no tents; consequently there could not be a dry thread left to us. The fires were attempted to be kept up at the commencement of the night, but from the rain and want of fuel not many were continued through the night.[9]

Captain Joseph Thackwell of the 15th Light Dragoons wrote in his diary on 17 June:

> At three this afternoon the rain fell in torrents, which continued at intervals. The Thirteenth and Fifteenth bivouacked in a field of rye on the right of the village of Mont-Saint-Jean; fortunately there were some infantry huts standing, which afforded a little shelter from the torrents of rain which fell during the night. No rations or supplies of any description.[10]

In the words of Private William Wheeler of the 51st:

> It would be impossible for anyone to form any opinion of what we endured this night. Being close to the enemy we could not use our blankets, the ground was too

wet to lie down, we sat on our knapsacks until daylight without fires, there was no shelter against the weather: the water ran in streams from the cuffs of our jackets, in short we were as wet as if we had been plunged over head in a river. We had one consolation, we knew the enemy were in the same plight.[11]

Sergeant Major Thomas Playford, 2nd Life Guards, recalled:

We passed an uncomfortable night exposed to a cold wind and to heavy rain. There we stood on soaked ploughed ground, shivering, wet, and hungry; for there was neither food for man nor horse.[12]

Similarly Lieutenant James Hope of the 92nd recounted the miserable conditions:

When we took up our ground on the position of Waterloo, not one of us had a dry stitch on our backs, and our baggage was no one knew where. To add to our miseries, we were ordered to bivouac in a newly ploughed field, in no part of which could a person stand in one place, for many minutes, without sinking to the knees in water and clay; and where, notwithstanding the great quantity that had fallen, not one drop of good water could be procured to quench our thirst.[13]

Private Dixon Vallance of the 79th also remembered the terrible weather conditions on the eve of battle:

The rain continued to pour on us in torrents. We were exposed to the fury of the storm all night without any shelter. Our regiment was stationed in a field of rye. Some of us pulled bunches of it and lay on it to keep us out of the water that flooded the ground. We were all as wet as water could make us, and shivering with cold. We could not lie on the bunches of rye. We rose and tried to dance and leap about to warm ourselves with exercise. The ground was so flooded, soft and miry that, when we tried to leap and dance, we stuck in the mud and mire, and had to pull one another out. We had a miserable night and we were happy to see the first dawning of the morning light.[14]

Finally dawn arrived as Ensign and Quartermaster William Gavin of the 71st noted in his diary on the morning of 18 June:

Cows, bullocks, pigs, sheep and fowls were put into requisition and brought to camp. Butchers set to work, fires made by pulling down houses for the wood, camp

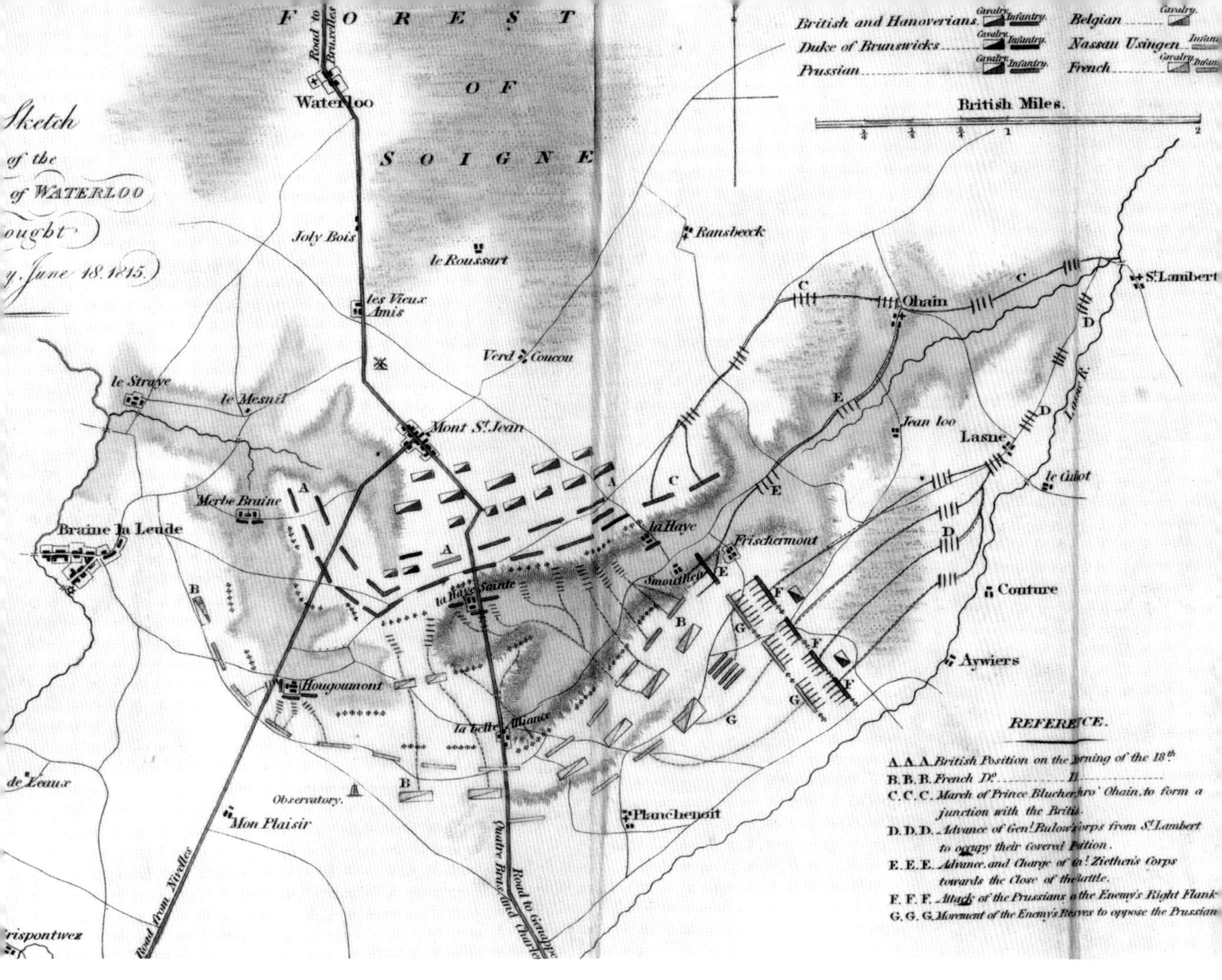

FOREST OF SOIGNE
Road to Bruxelles
Waterloo
Sketch of the … of WATERLOO … ought … y, June 18, 1815.
British and Hanoverians
Duke of Brunswicks
Prussian
Belgian
Nassau Usingen
French
Cavalry.
Infantry.
British Miles.
Joly Bois
le Roussart
Ransbeeck
les Vieux Amis
Verd Coucou
le Strayé
le Mesnil
Mont St. Jean
Ohain
St. Lambert
Jean loo
Lasne
le Gilot
Merbe Braine
Braine la Leude
la Haye
Frischermont
Smouhen
la Haye Sainte
Couture
Aywiers
Hougoumont
la Belle Alliance
Planchenoit
Observatory.
Mon Plaisir
Road from Nivelles
Quatre Bras and Charleroi
Road to Genappe
Lasne R.
REFERENCE.
A. A. A. British Position on the Morning of the 18th
B. B. B. French Do.
C. C. C. March of Prince Blucher thro' Ohain, to form a junction with the British.
D. D. D. Advance of Gen! Bulow's Corps from St. Lambert to occupy their Covered Position.
E. E. E. Advance, and Charge of Gen! Ziethen's Corps towards the Close of the Battle.
F. F. F. Attack of the Prussians on the Enemy's Right Flank
G. G. G. Movement of the Enemy's Reserves to oppose the Prussians

The plans for Waterloo, showing French and British positions at the outset. (Topfoto)

> kettles hung on, and everything in a fair way for cooking, when the word 'fall in' put everything to the route. Men accoutring, cannon roaring, bugles sounding and drums beating, which put a stop to our cooking for that day.[15]

It is easy to see that bad weather conditions and lack of food were common for both armies, and that most of the soldiers started the battle weary and hungry.

But the vast array of eyewitness accounts also clearly show that at the start of the battle both armies, despite the appalling weather conditions and logistical problems, were enthusiastic about the approaching engagement. Some of the British soldiers even regarded the bad weather as a good omen, as Wheeler explained:

> We had often experienced such weather in the Peninsula on the eve of a battle, for instance the nights before the battles of Fuentes de Oñoro, Salamanca and Vittoria were attended with thunder and lightning. It was always the prelude to a victory.

The morale of the French is sometimes described as rather low at the beginning of the campaign of 1815 because of the universal suspicion towards senior officers; nevertheless, the testimony of *Adjudant commandant* Toussaint-Jean Trefcon, chief of staff of General Bachelu's 5th Division, gives a different view:

> The enthusiasm of the soldiers was great, the music played, the drums beat and a shiver agitated all these men for many of whom this was to be their last day. They cheered the Emperor with all their might.[16]

A typical French foot chasseur of the Guard, 1815. (Anne S. K. Brown)

From the low ranks, Corporal Louis Canler of the 28th *de ligne* had the same impression:

> The Emperor passed along the front of all the corps, and by a spontaneous movement that resembled an electric shock, helmets, shakos, fur caps, were put onto sabres or bayonets with frenetic shouts of *Vive l'Empereur!!!*[17]

It clearly shows that the French firmly believed in victory.

On the British side, the enthusiasm was also palpable. Lieutenant Simmons of the 95th noted in his diary:

> Many old warriors who had fought for years in the Peninsula were proud of being pitted with our gallant chief against Buonaparte and the flower of France.[18]

He went further in a letter to his parents:

> If you could have seen the proud and fierce appearance of the British at that tremendous moment, there was not one eye but gleamed with joy.

Corporal John Douglas of the 1st Foot also eloquently summarised the mood as dawn broke and battle approached:

The morning of the 18th was ushered in, both armies drawn up in order of battle, and viewing each other with a determination not to yield up their former hard-earned labours. The French no doubt were confident of success, having the conqueror of Lodi, Marengo and Austerlitz to dwarf them, and their ranks filled up with old veterans from the hulks now turned to avenge the former defeat; whilst the British, equally confident of Wellington, stood cleaning out their pieces, preparing their ammunition, and getting all things in order for the conflict which was to decide the fate of Europe.[19]

Both armies cheered their commanders, the most famous military men during this period, and during the last hours before the contest recalled their previous victories. It was the first time that Napoleon and Wellington faced each other. The issue was still uncertain, although the universal glory of Napoleon played for him; indeed Wellington said that Napoleon was worth 40,000 men on the battlefield. But the British commander was confident and hoped to be supported in time by his Prussian ally.

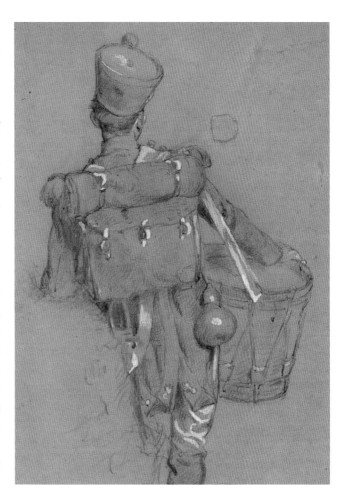

A French drummer on the morning of Waterloo. (Anne S. K. Brown)

HOUGOUMONT – 'A FATEFUL PLACE'

The feint attack on Hougoumont, which opened the battle, quickly descended into a bloody full-scale action. Trefcon underlines the fierceness of the fighting in this sector: 'The fighting was violent and lasted till the evening; the opponents were taking and losing alternately their positions. It was a battle of giants!' Lieutenant Philippe-Gustave Le Doulcet de Pontécoulant of the Guard artillery believed that the action there was badly handled:

The attack on the château of Hougoumont, behind the walls of which were entrenched the best shots of the English army, should have been an affair of artillery rather than a badly directed infantry battle that killed our bravest soldiers without

Wellington on the battlefield of
Waterloo. Many diarists expressed
their confidence in his leadership
during the battle.
(Anne S. K. Brown)

profit. This episode of the great battle would then have lasted half an hour instead of dragging on for several hours.[20]

Tomkinson considered that the defence of Hougoumont had been 'entrusted to too weak a force, and would have been carried but for the determined courage of the troops'. Lieutenant John Sperling, Royal Engineers, remarked in a letter to his father: 'Hougoumont was the scene of animated contest and great loss of life, but we kept possession of it or rather what remained of it.'[21]

Some units were not engaged but still suffered some loss by artillery fire. Larreguy de Civrieux noted:

> My regiment remained in a critical position for a long time. Though out of range of the musketry, it suffered from the enemy artillery. The cannonballs reached us after a ricochet provoked by a fold in the ground, that allowed us to see the curve the projectile made before decimating our ranks. Our devoted courage was put to a difficult test; and it was extremely distressing to wait for death in most complete inaction, surrounded by dying comrades and horribly mutilated bodies.

His regiment advanced shortly afterwards: 'Our feet bathed in blood. In less than half an hour, our ranks diminished to more than a half.'

Private Wheeler recalled his own impressions of the fighting at Hougoumont in a letter dated from 23 June 1815:

> A little to the front and to the left stood the farm of Hougoumont, on which the enemy was pouring a destructive fire of shot, shell and musketry. The house was soon on fire and the battle increased with double fury. Never was a place more fiercely assaulted, nor better defended, it will be a lasting honour and glory to the troops who defended it. So fierce was the combat that a spectator would imagine a mouse could not live near the spot, but the Guards, who had the honour to be posted there, not only kept possession but repulsed the enemy in every attack. The slaughter was dreadful.

D'ERLON'S ATTACK

The attack of the I Army Corps commanded by General Jean-Baptiste Drouet, Count d'Erlon was impressive. It was directed predominately against the farm of La Haye Sainte and the British centre. As recalled by Lieutenant Martin:

We were in column by battalions and *en masse* at the moment that the order arrived to climb the position and to seize *à la baïonnette* the English batteries and anything else that offered resistance. The ridgeline bristled with their cannons and was covered with their troops; it appeared impregnable. No matter, the order arrived, the charge was beaten, the cry of *Vive l'Empereur!* came from every mouth, and we marched ahead, closed ranks, aligned as on a parade.[22]

In the words of Corporal Canler:

The columns were formed, General Drouet d'Erlon took position in the middle of his army corps, and with a strong and clear voice pronounced these few words: 'Today it is necessary to vanquish or die!' The cry of *Vive l'Empereur!* came out of all the mouths in reply to this short speech, and carrying our arms at ease, to the sound of drums beating the charge, the columns moved off and directed themselves towards the English guns without firing a single musket-shot.

The sight was undoubtedly magnificent, as Captain John Kincaid of the 95th recalled:

The whole of the enemy's artillery opened, and their countless columns began to advance under cover of it. The scene at that moment was grand and imposing.[23]

The French advanced steadily under artillery fire, as Martin remembered:

Death crept up on us from every side; entire ranks disappeared under the grapeshot, but nothing was able to stop our march; it continued with the same order as before and the same precision. The dead were immediately replaced by those who followed; the ranks, although becoming fewer, remained in good order.[24]

Canler too recalled the devastating effect of the enemy artillery fire:

Then the enemy batteries, which until then had only fired balls and shells, turned against our columns and decimated them with grapeshot.

From the opposing ranks Kincaid witnessed the carnage wrought by the artillery fire, but the ceaseless advance of the French infantry continued nonetheless:

When the heads of their columns shewed over the knoll which we had just quitted, they received such a fire from our first line, that they wavered, and hung behind it a little; but, cheered and encouraged by the gallantry of their officers, who were

dancing and flourishing their swords in front, they at last boldly advanced to the opposite side of our hedge, and began to deploy.

Captain Pierre-Charles Duthilt, aide de camp to General Bourgeois, described the obstacles encountered by the French:

The 2nd brigade, which stationed in a hollow, formed a column of attack by battalions and set off at the *pas de charge*, preceded by skirmishers, and urged on by excited cries; but this haste and enthusiasm had disastrous consequences, because the soldier, who still had a long march before encountering the enemy, was soon tired by the difficulty of crossing the greasy and water-logged ground, in which he broke the straps of his gaiters and even lost his shoes, weighed down by the amount of dirt that attached itself to them and stuck to the soles and to the ground, and because commands could not be heard, lost in the thousands of repeated cries and drumming. There was soon some confusion inside the ranks.[25]

Canler was one of those who suffered from this misfortune:

French accounts of Waterloo tended to focus on the mistakes of officers, such as Grouchy, shown here, and the surprise arrival of Blücher. (akg-images)

After a course of about twenty minutes, we arrived near an earthwork where the English artillery was placed, and we began to climb it. The rain having fallen during all the night softened the soil already originally slimy, in such a way that in the course of my ascent, the strap of my right gaiter broke and the heel came off my shoe. I quickly bent down to sort this out; but at the same moment, I felt a violent shock that threw my shako back, it would probably had fallen without the chinstrap that held it on my head. It was a ball that had struck it.

The steadiness of the attack was highlighted by all the eyewitnesses, as well as the action of the artillery on the 'blue' ranks advancing to their death. But worse was still to come.

COUNTER-ATTACK BY THE BRITISH CAVALRY

D'Erlon's attack was followed by one of the most famous cavalry performances in the Napoleonic Wars. Indeed, the charges of the Household and Union Brigades were a tremendous feat. The shock of impact between Lord Edward Somerset's cavalry regiments and the French cuirassiers was terrific; swords clashed upon the helmets and cuirasses prompting Lord Somerset to observe: 'You might have fancied that it was so many tinkers at work.'[26] At the same time, the Union Brigade drove into the infantry.

Captain Tomkinson was another eyewitness:

> It was one of the finest charges ever seen. On going over the ground the following morning, I saw where two lines of infantry had laid down their arms; their position was accurately marked, from the regularity the muskets were placed in.

Sergeant Anton of the 42nd gave high praise to his fellow countrymen, the Scots Greys:

> What pen can describe the scene? Horses' hooves sinking in men's breasts, breaking bones and pressing out their bowels. Riders' swords streaming in blood, waving over their heads and descending in deadly vengeance. Stroke follows stroke, like the turning of a flail in the hand of a dexterous thresher; the living stream gushes red from the ghastly wound, spouts in the victor's face, and stains him with brains and blood. There the piercing shrieks and dying groans; here the loud cheering of an exulting army, animating the slayers to deeds of signal vengeance upon a daring foe. Such is the music of the field! Neither drum nor fife is here to mock us with useless din, but guns and muskets raise their dreadful voice, throw out the messengers of death to check a valiant foe, and bid him turn before the more revolting shock of steel to steel ensues. It was a scene of vehement destruction, yells and shrieks, wounds and death; and the bodies of the dead served as pillows for the dying.[27]

This graphic description of the slaughter is supported by another narrator, but in this case a French one, the aforementioned Corporal Canler:

> Hardly had we reached the summit of the plateau, than we were received by the Queen's Dragoons, who fell on us with savage cries. The first division did not have time to form square, could not meet this charge and was broken. Then started a veritable carnage; each found himself separated from his comrades and fought only

for his own sake. The sabre, the bayonet, opened a passage in the thrilling flesh, for we were too close to each other to use a firearm. But the position was unbearable for foot soldiers fighting individually in the midst of cavalrymen.

Adjudant Dominique Fleuret fought in the 1st Division of d'Erlon's Corps:

> We were charged by a mass of cavalry, and so far that we had jumped over the ditches, we had no time to rally properly. Some of us were sabred and others made prisoner.[28]

Martin too recalled the desperate situation of the French foot soldiers:

> In vain did our soldiers try to get to their feet and raise their muskets; they were unable to strike these cavalrymen mounted on powerful horses with their bayonets, and the few shots that were fired in this confused crowd were as likely to hit our own men as the English. We were thus defenceless against a fierce enemy, who, in the excitement of battle, sabred without pity even the drummers and fifers.[29]

Lieutenant John Hibbert of the 1st King's Dragoon Guards also recognised in a letter to his mother that in the heat of battle mistakes were made by the British cavalry units:

> Our brigade, never having been on service before, hardly knew how to act. They knew they were to charge, but never thought about stopping at a proper time, so that after entirely cutting to pieces a large body of cuirassiers double their number, they still continued to gallop on instead of forming up and getting into line; the consequence was that they got among the French infantry and artillery, and were miserably cut up… The Greys, I believe, acted in the same manner and of course got off as badly as we did.[30]

Major George de Lacy Evans, aide de camp to Major General Sir William Ponsonby, commander of the Union Brigade, remembered in his letter written on 1 September 1839:

> The remainder of the enemy fled as a flock of sheep across the valley – quite at the mercy of the Dragoons. In fact, our men were *out of hand*. The General of the Brigade, his staff & every officer within hearing, exerted themselves to the utmost to reform the men – but the helplessness of the enemy offered too great a temptation to the Dragoons, & our efforts were abortive.[31]

The charge of the 1st Life Guards against d'Erlon's infantry at Waterloo. (Courtesy of the Council of the National Army Museum)

It is easy to see that the British cavalry once again 'galloped at everything'. Lord Henry Uxbridge, commander of the Allied cavalry, himself later admitted:

> The pursuit had been continued without order and too far... I had in vain attempted to stop my people by sounding the Rally, but neither voice nor trumpet availed.[32]

Uxbridge recognised that:

> … the French were completely surprised by the first cavalry attack… These 19 squadrons pouncing downhill upon them so astonished them that no very great resistance was made, and surely such havoc was rarely made in so few minutes. When I was returning to our position I met the Duke of Wellington, surrounded by all the *Corps diplomatique militaire*, who had from the high ground witnessed the whole affair. The plain appeared to be swept clean, and I never saw so joyous a group as was this *Troupe dorée*. They thought the battle was over. It is certain that our squadrons went into and over several squares of infantry, and it is not possible to conceive greater confusion and panic that was exhibited at this moment. This forces from me the remark that I committed a great mistake in having myself led the attack. The *carrière* once begun, the leader is no better than any other man; whereas, if I had placed myself at the head of the 2nd line, there is no saying what great advantages might not have accrued from it.

His biographer says that 'for the rest of his life Uxbridge was haunted by this error'.[33]

The French cavalry attacked their British counterparts who had gone too far. Colonel Bro commanded the 4th *chevau-légers lanciers* and charged at its head:

> I took the head of the squadrons shouting: 'Come on, my children, we need to overturn this rabble!' The soldiers answered me: 'Forward! *Vive l'Empereur!*' Two minutes later, the shock took place. Three enemy ranks were overturned. We crashed into the others! The *mêlée* became terrible. Our horses crushed dead bodies, and the cries of the injured arose from all parts. For a moment I found myself lost in the smoke of the gunpowder.[34]

In the words of Canler:

> The French cavalrymen attacked the English dragoons with fury, sabring and playing the lance in all directions, in such a way that the latter were forced to retreat. They left a good number of their men on the battlefield.

Hibbert says that his brigade realised their mistake too late:

> A few (that is about half the regiment) turned and rode back again; no sooner had they got about five hundred yards from the French infantry than they were met by an immense body of lancers who were sent for the purpose of attacking them in the way. Our men were rendered desperate by their situation. They were resolved

BATTLE OF WATERLOO,

'The Duke of Wellington now ordered the whole line to move forward — nothing could be more beautiful : The Sun which had hitherto been veiled, at this instant shed upon us his departing rays, as if to smile upon the efforts we were making and bless them with Success.

Letter from a British Off

This illustration of the battle on 18 June includes details of an eyewitness account from a British officer: 'The Duke of Wellington now ordered the whole line to move forward – nothing could be more beautiful. The sun which had hitherto been veiled, at this instant shed upon us his defrosting rays, as if to smile upon the efforts we were making and bless them with success.' (Anne S. K. Brown)

either to get out of the scrape or die rather than be taken prisoners, so they attacked them, and three troops cut their way through them; about a troop were killed or taken prisoners.

His fellow officer Captain James Naylor wrote in his diary:

Our attack was most completely successful, but our men were too sanguine in the pursuit of the fugitive cuirassiers and at the moment our horses were blown we were attacked by a multitude of lancers who did us considerable injury.[35]

Adjudant Fleuret and his comrades had been rescued by the lancers, but they found themselves again amidst the British dragoons:

The majority of us threw themselves down in the cornfield. The English cavalrymen rode over us and did not fail to sound out our backs with their big swords, like doctors use to feel one's pulse to see if one is dead.

The priority for d'Erlon was then to rally as many soldiers as possible. *Chef d'escadron* Victor Dupuy of the 7th Hussars witnessed the rout of the I Corps and helped to rally the troops:

Panic seized several regiments of infantry of the 1st Army Corps and the *sauve-qui-peut* was uttered. They fled in the greatest disorder. I rushed over with a platoon of hussars to stop them. Seeing amongst them a standard-bearer with his Eagle, I asked him to give it to me; he was ready to do it, when the thought came to me: 'I do not wish to dishonour you, *Monsieur*', I said to him, 'display your flag and move ahead calling *Vive l'Empereur* with me.' He did it immediately, the brave man! Soon the soldiers stopped, and, in a short time, thanks to his efforts and ours, almost 3,000 had been collected and turned around.[36]

At this stage, the battle was fierce at every point. In the words of Trefcon:

At 3 p.m., the battlefield was like an oven. The thundering of cannon, the noise of musketry, the shouts of fighters, all this combined with a burning sun, resembled a damned hell!

Marshal Michel Ney commanded the left wing of the French Army during the 'Hundred Days' campaign. *Chef de bataillon* Octave-René-Louis Levavasseur was his aide de camp and could get an overview of the battlefield:

The battle was raging everywhere, but our army was not making progress. Our efforts to push through the English line were unsuccessful. However, the enemy's resistance seemed to diminish on numerous points.[37]

Tomkinson's account provides the same overall perspective:

The cannonade continued along the line through the day. Whenever the enemy made an attack, they covered it with all the artillery they could thunder at us, and we again worked their columns in advancing with every gun we could bring against them.

Mercer noted:

The roar of cannon and musketry in the main position never slackened; it was intense, as was the smoke arising from it. Amidst this, from time to time, were to be seen still more dense columns of smoke rising straight into the air like a great pillar, then spreading out a mushroom-head. These arose from the explosions of ammunition waggons [sic], which were continually taking place, although the noise which filled the whole atmosphere was too overpowering to allow them to be heard.

Vallance too vividly recalled the ferocity of the battle:

The battle now raged with awful fury, bombshells and balls of all sorts flying amongst us thick as hail. The noise was dreadful, a continued deafening roar of musketry. The earth shivered under our feet whilst three hundred pieces of artillery on each side were vomiting their death-dispensing charges. The work of death was making rapid progress.

Jean-Michel Chevalier, an NCO (*maréchal des logis-chef*) of the mounted chasseurs of the Imperial Guard, who took part in the counter-charge of the Guard cavalry against the British, recalled:

The *mêlée* became atrocious, it was a terrible slaughter; the ground was covered with dead or dying men and horses; the terror was at its height.[38]

Alexander Mercer, shown here on horseback, was a famous diarist of the campaign, having served as an artillery captain during the battle. (Officer RHA © MarkChurms.com 1998)

Sergeant Anton echoed his thoughts:

> Thus toiled both armies through the day, and the guns never ceased their dreadful roar, save amidst some slaughtering charge, when sword or bayonet did the work of destruction.

The horrific losses inflicted on both sides later caused Captain Kincaid to comment:

> I had never yet heard of a battle in which everybody was killed; but this seemed likely to be an exception, as all were going by turns.

Ensign Edmund Wheatley of the King's German Legion shared a similar view:

> I took a calm survey of the field around and felt shocked at the sight of broken armour, lifeless bodies, murdered horses, shattered wheels, caps, helmets, swords, muskets, pistols, still and silent. Here and there a frightened horse would rush across the plain trampling on the dying and the dead.[39]

This artwork by Denis Dighton depicts how the fighting at Waterloo descended into a mêlée as both sides clashed. Here, British infantry charge against French horse artillerymen. (Anne S. K. Brown)

The farm of La Haye Sainte in the centre of the battlefield was, in the words of Anton, just 'one pool of blood'. Lieutenant George Drummond Graeme of the King's German Legion recalled:

> The ground was literally covered with French killed and wounded, even to the astonishment of my oldest soldiers, who said they had never witnessed such a sight. The French wounded were calling out *Vive l'Empereur*, and I saw a poor fellow, lying with both his legs shattered, trying to destroy himself with his own sword, which I ordered my servant to take from him.[40]

The participants tend sometimes to amplify and exaggerate the atrocity of the contest, but one thing is sure: the Battle of Waterloo was one of the bloodiest in which they took part, and the use of emphatic terms to underline its bloody nature is understandable. The number of the losses, in killed and wounded, supports the eyewitnesses. Even people who remained some kilometres away from the battlefield on 18 June 1815 could make out the sound of battle: the French writer Chateaubriand was walking in the countryside near Ghent and remembered having heard 'a dull rumble' that he took firstly for an approaching storm.[41]

Amidst serious matters, we find in the recollections of simple soldiers and NCOs some trivial details which give a taste of the 'truth' to their narrative. Sergeant Anton remembered a particular circumstance caused by the Scottish national dress:

> We might have forced ourselves through as the Belgians had done, but our bare thighs had no protection from the piercing thorns; and doubtless those runaways had more wisdom in shunning death, though at the hazard of laceration, than we would have shown in rushing forward in disorder, with self-inflicted torture.

Another soldier, Private Friedrich Lindau of the King's German Legion, openly recognised his inclination for plundering:

> I saw not far from me the officer whom I had shot; I rushed up to him and took hold of his gold watch chain; I had scarcely got it in my hand when he raised his sabre by way of reprimand, I gave him a blow on the forehead with my rifle butt so that he fell back and dropped dead, when I noticed a gold ring on his finger. I first cut the little bag from his horse and was just about to take the ring off him when my comrades called out, 'Get a move on and come away, the cavalry are making a fresh charge.' I saw some thirty riders spring forward and I ran very quickly with my booty to my comrades.[42]

Lindau was made prisoner soon after, and the French plundered him in return:

> One of them snatched away my breadbag and found in it the purse of gold coins, whereupon another grabbed at it at once but the first held it fast and a violent quarrel instantly developed. Next my knapsack was torn from my shoulders. Others pulled at my equipment, feeling for the watches, and finding them – I had one gold and two silver watches.

Canler was crossing the battlefield to join his unit when he saw a British officer of dragoons killed in the charge, as he later recalled:

> A splendid gold chain was hanging from his waistcoat pocket. Notwithstanding the rapidity of my move, I stopped a moment to take this chain and a beautiful golden watch. The English having seized my bag and my arms, I just applied the law of retaliation.

Plunder was sorely suffered by the killed and wounded throughout the Napoleonic Wars, and Waterloo was no exception.

INFANTRY SQUARES *VERSUS* CAVALRY – 'A HURRICANE OF FLASHING SWORDS'

The first news of the arrival of the Prussians reached Napoleon, who committed his reserve against this new foe. For the French observers, Wellington's Army was seemingly shaken and ready to abandon the ground. Then came the moment of the great charges of the French cavalry, led by Ney. Waves of cavalrymen beat 'against the immovable squares, sweeping round their sides, and suffering appalling casualties to no purpose'.[43] Petiet recalled: 'We were watching anxiously this admirable charge. All our reserve of cavalry was being engaged, while the battle was far from being over!' Colonel Pierre-Agathe Heymès, aide de camp to Marshal Ney, explains this spontaneous movement of the French cavalry by the universal belief in Napoleon's Army that the British had begun their retreat.

Ensign Rees Howell Gronow, 1st Foot Guards, wrote in his recollections:

About 4 p.m., the enemy's artillery in front of us ceased firing all of a sudden, and we saw large masses of cavalry advance: not a man present who survived could have forgotten in after life the awful grandeur of that charge. You discovered at a distance what appeared to be an overwhelming, long moving line, which, ever advancing, glittered like a stormy wave of the sea when it catches the sunlight. On came the mounted host until they got near enough, whilst the very earth seemed to vibrate beneath their thundering tramp. One might suppose that nothing could have resisted the shock of this terrible moving mass. They were the famous cuirassiers, almost all old soldiers, who had distinguished themselves on most of the battlefields of Europe. In an almost incredibly short period they were within twenty yards of us, shouting *Vive l'Empereur!* The word of command, 'Prepare to receive cavalry,' had been given, every man in the front ranks knelt, and a wall bristling with steel, held together by steady hands, presented itself to the infuriated cuirassiers.[44]

Lord Uxbridge reported:

The cuirassiers attacked our squares of infantry with a desperation that surpasses all description, but no power of language can ever give an idea of the determined gallantry and real intrepidity of our infantry.

The casualty rates at Waterloo were high as all sides were engaged throughout the day. Here a wounded French soldier looks exhausted. (Anne S. K. Brown)

In the words of Trefcon:

The charges of our fine cavalry were certainly the most admirable thing I have ever seen. More than ten times they launched themselves on the English, and despite the fire, they reached their bayonets. They came back to reform near the small wood where we were and then charged again. I was more excited than I can express and despite the dangers that I ran myself, I had tears in my eyes and I cried out my admiration to them!

Tomkinson too was in awe of the ferocity of the French cavalry attacks although more inclined to regard them as a kind of 'suicide attack':

These attacks were made at intervals for nearly two hours; they were the most singularly daring attempts ever heard of, and in many instances appeared like an inclination to sacrifice themselves sooner than survive the loss of the day.

Corporal Douglas was in one of the infantry squares that faced the massed French cavalry:

Masses of cavalry rushing forward to force the adamantine squares fell in heaps beneath the British fire. Though their pigeon-breasted armour was of use if struck in a slanting position, where the well-rammed ball struck fair, through it went.

Private Thomas Morris of the 73rd was in another one:

A considerable number of the French cuirassiers made their appearance, on the rising ground just in our front, took the artillery we had placed there, and came at a gallop down upon us. Their appearance, as an enemy, was certainly enough to inspire a feeling of dread, – none of them under six feet; defended by steel helmets and breastplates, made pigeon-breasted to throw off the balls. Their appearance was of such a formidable nature, that I thought we could not have the slightest chance with them. They came up rapidly, until within about ten or twelve paces of the square, when our rear ranks poured into them a well-directed fire, which put them into confusion, and they retired; the two front ranks, kneeling, then discharged their pieces at them. Some of the cuirassiers fell wounded, and several were killed; those of them that were dismounted by the death of their horses, immediately unclasped their armour to facilitate their escape.[45]

The steadiness of the British infantry was exemplary. Lieutenant Colonel James Stanhope, 1st Foot Guards, wrote on 19 June to the Duke of York:

When the French cavalry attacked us in squares, which they did with the utmost persevering gallantry (never retiring above 100 or 150 paces, and charging again), our men behaved as though they were at a field day, firing by ranks & with the best possible aim. Under a most destructive cannonade & having several shells burst in the middle of us, not a man moved from his place.[46]

Sergeant William Lawrence, 40th Foot, confirmed:

British troops form a square to repel attack, bayonets at the ready. (akg-images)

Our numbers became terribly thinned by the successive charges, and by the enemy's cannon during the short intervals in between, yet we did not lose a single inch of ground the whole day. The men were very tired and did begin to despair, but the officers cheered them on.[47]

Other regiments of French cavalry joined in the charge although the charge itself seemed to be regarded as foolhardy by some French officers. In the words of Lemonnier-Delafosse: 'Marshal Ney's impetuosity made us lose everything; for his last charge, he had carried away even the Guard cavalry… It was not the Emperor's intention.' General Claude-Étienne Guyot commanded the heavy division of the Guard cavalry:

I received the order to put my division forward and to act under Marshal Ney's command. He immediately had me execute a charge on several squadrons that masked the artillery until on our approach they retired behind the squares. This retrograde movement exposed me to artillery fire and the fire from the squares that protected it and we suffered heavy losses. Our two divisions charged this line of artillery alternately, seizing it each time but always being obliged to retire quickly because we only had sabres to oppose to the musketry of the squares and to the volleys of grapeshot that we received as we approached.[48]

Chef d'escadron Georges-Nicolas-Marc L'Étang of the 7th Dragoons points out that the squares held their fire until point-blank range, which had a terrible effect on the morale of the French cavalry:

Realising that they would be exposed to a fire that would be much more murderous from being at point-blank range, fright seized them, and probably to escape such a fire, the first squadron wheeled to the right and caused a similar movement by all the following squadrons. The charge failed and all the squadrons rallied next to the fortified farm of La Belle-Alliance [most probably La Haye Sainte], that was still occupied by the English whose fire killed and wounded many in an instant.[49]

This last circumstance is confirmed by Kellermann, who deplored the ineffective coordination of the charges and the imbecility of one of his subordinates:

They all arrived mixed up, in disorder and out of breath, on the ridge that was occupied by the English artillery line. The guns were actually abandoned for a short time, but we did not have the horses to take them off. Besides, behind them was a double line of infantry formed in square. It was necessary to stop, to re-impose order, somehow, under enemy fire, but it was no more possible to force the cavalry, excellent as it was, into new charges: it found itself in the cruellest of positions, without infantry or artillery support.

According to Kellermann, his cavalry remained for several hours between the Hougoumont wood and La Haye Sainte, unable to retire or to charge, 'receiving death without being able to fight back, and, besides, exposed to the fire of our own batteries'. Is his account entirely fair? Kellermann possibly wanted to absolve himself of all responsibility. On the whole the French low-ranking participants naturally try to explain their failure by attributing it to bad handling, while the British emphasise the firmness of their infantry in face of the enraged cavalrymen.

Wheeler took a look at the battlefield after the charges had been concluded:

Drawing of a French field gun of the Gribeauval type, crewed by the Imperial Guard, 1815. (Topfoto)

> I went to see what effect our fire had, and never before beheld such a sight in as short a space, as about a hundred men and horses could be huddled together, there they lay. Those who were shot dead were fortunate for the wounded horses in their struggles by plunging and kicking soon finished what we had begun. In examining the men we could not find one that would be likely to recover, and as we had other business to attend to, we were obliged to leave them to their fate.

It is worth drawing attention to the fact that none of the first-hand accounts display contempt for the enemy. Remarkably, all diarists give praise to the opposing troops. However, in many instances this was undoubtedly in order to underline their own heroism, as stated honestly by Kellermann: 'In the very interest of one's own glory, the enemy's courage is usually exalted.' To quote Trefcon: 'Under a terrible impetus of our army, the English showed tenacity and remarkable courage.' Speaking about the fighting at Hougoumont, Tomkinson remarks: 'The defence, as well as the attack, was gallant.' Hibbert too praises the enemy but no doubt with a clear intention to exalt the success of the British Army: 'No men but the English could have fought better than the French.' The last word on this subject should go to the ever-eloquent Sergeant Anton:

That man who brands our foe with cowardice deserves the lie; he advances to our cannon's mouth, and seeks death from the destructive bayonet; but he meets with men inured to war, animated with an equal share of national pride, confident in the success of their leader, and thus rejoicing in the ambitious strife, protract the raging fight.

THE ARRIVAL OF THE PRUSSIANS – 'THE BATTLE CHANGED SOUL'

If we follow the eyewitnesses from the French side, in the late afternoon, the French firmly believed that they were at the point of winning the battle. Certainly this was a view shared by Chevalier, who expresses a general feeling in the French Army at this period of the battle about the state of the British Army, just before the great cavalry charges and even a mistaken belief that Wellington himself had fled the battlefield:

Blücher's march to Waterloo. (akg-images)

It was yet 4 p.m., and it looked like we had gained a decisive victory; the English army … terribly routed, was fleeing in all directions. It was jumbled in disorder on the Brussels road, tumbrils, artillery, baggage, cavalry, infantry, wounded, etc. Senior commanders, officers, soldiers, everybody was in full flight, the English army was nearly lost. Taken in the rout, Wellington fled like the others, and without the jam which formed on this road, we would have probably never seen again neither Wellington nor the English. Unfortunately, the Prussians under Bülow's orders arrived on the battlefield. These Prussians were supposed to be engaged by Marshal Grouchy, and here they fell on us, they were 30 thousand.

As such, and notwithstanding Ney's ineffectual cavalry attacks, the Prussian arrival came as a complete surprise to the majority of the French Army who were firmly under the impression that the Prussians were being driven east by Grouchy and that the battle was theirs for the taking.

Petiet also recalled the undoubted effect the arrival of the Prussians had on the battlefield and Napoleon's desperate attempts to counter it:

Wellington, in despair, had lost 10 thousand men; his army's baggage was fleeing towards Brussels. The commander of the Anglo-Belgian army was anxiously waiting for the arrival of the Prussians, and he thought that everything would be lost if Blücher had not come… But the Prussians gained some ground. At this moment, Napoleon, who knew without doubt that Blücher had escaped from Grouchy and had joined Wellington's left wing via the Ohain crossroad, committed the error to spread in the ranks that the cannonballs which crossed with those fired by the English over our heads were fired by Marshal Grouchy's army corps, whose arrival had caught the enemy in the middle. This news produced at once an immeasurable effect on our troops, who doubled their vigour and courage. But later, they remembered it and the retreat transformed itself into a rout, because the soldiers no more believed Napoleon's hitherto so sacred word!

In his recollections, *Chef d'escadron* Marie-Élie-Guillaume-Alzéar de Baudus, aide de camp to Marshal Soult, blames Napoleon for this lie, and states that this circumstance produced a very bad effect and destroyed the spirit of the army. To Ney it was subsequently clear that the emperor had been searching for a psychological impact to induce his army to make the last effort; the only thing he achieved was to enhance the demoralisation when the truth became known. As the day drew to a close, Lemonnier-Delafosse too regarded the arrival of the Prussians as the moment the battle was truly lost for the French:

It was 5.30 p.m., and all the advantage was for the French army, when the good fortune, which had abandoned Wellington only temporarily, came to his aid. The arriving Prussians announced their presence by the sound of cannon.

Surgeon Major Lagneau recalled:

> We fought with some advantage during the whole day, but after 3 or 4 p.m., the enemy attacked us in the flank; then, the Prussians, whom we believed to be still far away at Wavre bridge, fell on our rear and threatened our line of retreat. We were obliged to retreat in the evening, which was not done without disorder.

Captain Pierre Robinaux, from the II Corps, fought near the farm of Hougoumont. He wrote in his journal:

> About 6 p.m., Marshal Ney came to our position and shouted to us in a strong voice: 'Courage, the French army is victorious, the enemy is beaten on all points!' The Emperor, seeing a body that arrived in the plain, immediately announced the arrival of Grouchy, commander in chief of the cavalry; immediately he ordered to attack the position of the so-called Mont-Saint-Jean… The supposed body of Grouchy was none other than a strong Prussian body of fifteen thousand men commanded by Blücher that came to cut our army and to take it in flank; terror became general; the most sinister noises spilled in all ranks and soon the discomfiture was all about, in the whole army.[50]

It is clear that some in the French Army had desperately hoped until the last possible moment that Grouchy was indeed arriving, not the Prussians. *Chef de bataillon* Jean-Baptiste Jolyet of the 1st *léger*:

> It was about 7 p.m., when an ADC came to tell us, on behalf of the Prince [Jérôme Bonaparte], that Grouchy had debouched onto the English left wing, and that consequently the battle was won.[51]

Levavasseur was one of the aides de camp asked to announce Grouchy's arrival:

> Breaking into a gallop, raising my hat on the tip of my sabre, I passed along the front of the line and shouted: '*Vive l'Empereur!* soldiers, here is Grouchy!'. This sudden cry was repeated by a thousand voices; the excitement of the soldiers was indescribable; they all cried: '*En avant! En avant! Vive l'Empereur!*'

The soldiers' reaction was understandable when the truth became clear. In the words of Levavasseur:

> The greatest silence, the surprise, the anguish succeeded to this enthusiasm. The plain covered itself with our carriages and with this multitude of non-combatants who always follow the armies. The cannonade continued and approached. Officers and soldiers mingled with the non-combatants.

The context was especially dramatic for those elements of the French Army that firmly believed that Wellington's Army was by then exhausted and ready to retreat. Certainly, they were correct in the perception that the British Army was exhausted, as Kincaid recalled:

> I shall never forget the scene which the field of battle presented about seven in the evening. I felt weary and worn out, less from fatigue than anxiety. Our division, which had stood upwards of five thousand men at the commencement of the battle, had gradually dwindled down into a solitary line of skirmishers.

Numerous eyewitness accounts, mostly French, do indeed corroborate that the Battle of Waterloo was not only a 'near-run thing' but that the British came very close to defeat. Many French participants' accounts claim that the English were in full flight and ready to surrender, when the Prussians appeared on the battlefield. Their opponents are more reserved on this point, but somehow they recognise the extreme difficulty in which Wellington found himself at this stage. Gibney, Assistant Surgeon of the 15th Light Dragoons (Hussars), possibly expresses the general feeling in the British Army when he states that, having joined his regiment at approximately 7 p.m.:

> To me, coming fresh on this part of the field, it seemed as if the French were getting the best of it slowly but surely, and I was not singular in this view, for a goodly number of experienced officers thought the same, and that the battle would terminate in the enemy's favour.[52]

Significantly, however, the French Army (and indeed small elements of the Allied force) did not realise that the majority of the Anglo-Dutch Army was in the dead ground behind the ridge and out of the line of sight. Wellington's skilful use of terrain and his reverse-slope tactics proved once again their utility.

The vast majority of surviving French accounts blamed Marshal Grouchy for the defeat. Chevalier wrote:

Upon reaching the battlefield, Blücher's final attack formed the conclusion of Waterloo as he helped rout the French forces. (akg-images)

Marshal Grouchy was to arrive at Gembloux before the Prussians, in order to prevent them from joining Wellington; but, fatality or else, the marshal had marched so slowly that the Prussians arrived three hours before him and could open their communications with the English. Thus the army corps of 35,000 men commanded by Marshal Grouchy, which could certainly assure our victory, became totally useless, and it was the marshal's fault.

In an extract of the famous letter written by Colonel Jean-Baptiste-Antoine-Marcelin de Marbot of the 7th Hussars on 26 June, he gave his relatively fresh impressions on Waterloo:

> I cannot get over our defeat!… We were manoeuvred like so many pumpkins. I was with my regiment on the right flank of the army almost throughout the battle. They assured me that Marshal Grouchy would come up at that point; and it was guarded only by my regiment with three guns and a battalion of light infantry – not nearly enough. Instead of Grouchy, what arrived was Blücher's corps… You can imagine how we were served![53]

Some days later, Marbot visited Bro, another aforenamed diarist, in Paris and spoke indignantly about the battle:

> Waterloo, what a sad and deplorable affair! The Emperor should have won the battle. His plan was good, infallible, but Drouet engaged his infantry divisions with timidity and left them be sabred and forced to retreat, while he could take a formidable run-up and try to crush Lord Wellington's right… Our centre saw this retreat and was frightened. This fear communicated itself to the French right, and the divisions ran for their life, leaving the Imperial Guard to save at least the honour.

For the French, who had been assured by Napoleon himself that Grouchy was arriving, the apparition of the Prussians came as an emotional shock. Some of them believed that they had been betrayed. In contrast, their opponents congratulated themselves on the arrival of their allies, which changed the course of the battle. To quote Gibney once again:

> Whether we should have won the day without the aid of the Prussians I know not; but of this much I am certain, that if the French had retired, we were too much exhausted to follow them up.

The arrival of Blücher's troops was a surprise for the French, but not for their opponents. The British indeed had expected to see the Prussians arrive in time for the contest. Tomkinson: 'We were told very early in the day that a corps of Prussians were on their march to join us. Being on the left, we were constantly looking out for them.' When the Prussians did arrive, the relief was intense. Undoubtedly the British Army was grateful for their support as Tomkinson also recalled:

> Such a reinforcement during an action was an occurrence so different from former days in the Peninsula, where everything centred in the British army, that it appeared decisive of the fate of the day.

Sperling added:

> The Prussians had been expected all the afternoon to make an attack on the right of Bonaparte's position. They had, however, been delayed, and it was not till towards evening that the effect of their approach was made manifest on his flank and rear.

Colonel William Maynard Gomm, quartermaster general of Picton's Division, praised Blücher's determination to support his ally:

It deserves to be stated, to the honour of the Prussian leader, that on learning, at an advanced period of the day, that the enemy had pushed a column by Wavre, threatening his rear, he expressed little concern, and took no precautionary measures, judging well that the fate of the day depended upon the success of the operation he was conducting, and could be little influenced by the success of any detached corps.[54]

THE SACRIFICE OF THE IMPERIAL GUARD – NAPOLEON'S 'FINAL HOPE AND FINAL THOUGHT'

One of the most dramatic episodes of the battle was the participation of the Imperial Guard. All the British eyewitness accounts detail a sense of pride at having defeated these famous warriors. Lieutenant Colonel Stanhope wrote to the Duke of York:

The most gratifying event of the whole day was the desperate attack, made about seven o'clock by the Imperial Guard, headed by Bonaparte in person. The Grenadiers attacked the Guards and had soon cause to find that they would not sup in Brussels, as the Emperor had told them.

Napoleon shielded by the ranks of the Old Guard during the final stages of battle. (akg–images)

Lieutenant Colonel Alexander Fraser of the 1st Foot Guards wrote to his wife on 22 June:

> About ½ past six, Napoleon made his last desperate attack at the head of his Old Imperial Guard upon our brigade. It was a thing I always wished for and the result was exactly what I have often said it would be. To do them justice, they came on like men, but our boys went at them like Britons and drove them off the field in less than ten minutes. From that moment the day was our own and the French were completely routed and fled leaving their artillery, stores, baggage and an immense number of prisoners.[55]

It was an impression shared also by more lowly ranks. In the words of Private Thomas Jeremiah of the 23rd (Royal Welch):

> At this critical juncture the attention of our brave Wellington was directed to our right wing which was all but destroyed by those chosen cohorts of the French Imperial Guards and led on by their most distinguished generals whose names had been a terror to all Europe for more than 15 years, and whose ability and bravery in the field was inferior to none, their master, Napoleon, alone excepted. However, notwithstanding their invincibility, they found for the first time their victorious career put a stop to by the almost matchless and consummate ability of our commander and the able assistance of his brave officers famous in history.[56]

Of course French accounts also testify to the brave but ultimately futile efforts of the Imperial Guard. Levavasseur:

> Then 150 bandsmen marched off at the head of the Guard, playing the triumphant marches of the Carrousel.[57] Before long the road was covered by this Guard, marching by platoons behind the Emperor. The cannonballs and grapeshot struck them down, leaving the road scattered with killed and wounded. Another few paces and Napoleon would have been alone in front.

Sergeant Hippolyte de Mauduit of the 1st Regiment of Grenadiers of the Old Guard:

> This column suffered the fate of the formidable and victorious English column at Fontenoy, with the only difference that here a hundred of guns, instead of *three*, decimated our soldiers.[58]

For the French, the defeat of the Imperial Guard sounded the death knell. Chevalier later recalled the hour of defeat:

> Our eight battalions of the Old Guard were swept along by the mass of fugitives and crushed by numerous enemies. Nonetheless, these old warriors stayed united in battalions of iron, unconquerable and inaccessible. The rout was terrible.

THE END OF THE BATTLE – 'MOURNFUL PLAIN'

Then came the time for the general advance of the British line. Douglas was certainly one British infantryman who itched to close with the enemy:

> The British so long on the defensive were impatient for close quarters, longing and even calling out for the order to advance, eager to put an end to this glorious day of destruction, in which the patience, bravery and fortitude of the British soldier was put to the utmost trial. Four deep we advanced with 3 British cheers, while the sun, hitherto obscured, now shone forth, as if smiling on the last efforts of Britain for the liberties of Europe. We were supported by the cavalry, while the enemy gave way in the utmost confusion, abandoning their guns, and everything they possessed.

Anton also clearly remembered the moment of victory as the French forces were routed:

> The charge is given from right to left, and all Napoleon's columns and lines, foot and horse, in one mingled mass of confusion, fly over the field, while on our left the hardy Prussians come in to share the toils of the hard-fought day, and push the disorganised enemy over the face of the country, till midnight gives a respite to the pursuer and the pursued.

For the French, confusion reigned. In the words of Petiet:

> Several enemy squadrons appeared, and the rout became total. We marched with incredible speed until daylight, hoping to cross the Sambre and to stop there waiting for orders. But nobody commanded. Our generals, lost in the crowd, were swept along and separated from their troops. It was rumoured that the Emperor had been killed and that the Major General [Soult] had been taken. There was talk about treason, whereas nobody suggested a rallying place.

Larreguy de Civrieux too recalled the chaos that immediately followed the defeat:

> The army was struck with a sudden demoralisation. Cries of 'Sauve qui peut!', 'À la trahison!' were heard; the rout became general. All discipline disappeared; the regiments fell into an inexpressible disorder, forming shapeless masses of men that were ploughed in all senses by the enemy's cannon.

Kincaid remembered the British order in comparison to the French disorder:

> It was a fine summer's evening, just before sunset. The French were flying in one confused mass. British lines were seen in close pursuit, and in admirable order, as far as the eye could reach to the right, while the plain to the left was filled with Prussians.

A letter from William Serjeantson, Ensign in the 18th Gloucestershire Regiment, to his sister after the Battle of Waterloo. (Soldiers of Gloucestershire Museum www.glosters.org.uk)

However, Captain Duthilt later recalled that the Old Guard alone retained some sense of order:

> Except the Old Guard, everybody rushed through ammunition waggons, broken cannons and baggage of all kind. Carried along and insensitive, the men crossed over the heaps of dead bodies and trampled on the wounded without hearing their moans and groans; these miserable victims of the war were crushed without pity and expired under the wheels of waggons and cannons. The soldiers of all arms fled in disorder and without their chiefs, and the chiefs fled in despair without their soldiers. The last pushed the first; cannons, waggons, carriages, squashed up, unhorsed, blocked the roads; they became the prey of the greedy robbers.

But distressing scenes were not only the fate of the vanquished army, as follows from contemporary letters. Hibbert wrote to his mother on 13 July:

> The most melancholy thing is that no sooner were our poor men wounded than the Belgic troops, who were without exception the greatest set of cowards and rascals in the world, stripped them of everything but their shirts and left them in this miserable way all night. Our officers were only known by the name on the shirts; I daresay many died of cold in the night. Our brigade was so totally cut up that a party could not be mustered that night to go over the ground and consequently the wounded men and officers were left to shift for themselves. Such a scene of misery was never seen before; the action took place about eighteen miles from Brussels, and the road was strewed with dead men the whole way, who had been trying to crawl to the town from the field and had died on the road, some through cold, others through hunger and thirst.

Gibney recalled:

> Nothing could exceed the misery exhibited on this road, which, being the highpave [sic], or I might say the stone causeway leading to Brussels, was crowded to excess with our wounded and French prisoners, shot and shell meanwhile pouring into them. The hardest heart must have recoiled from this scene of horror; wounded men being re-wounded, many of whom had received previously the most frightful injuries.

The pursuit was mainly led by the Prussians. Gavin wrote:

> The enemy began to retreat about seven in the evening. We followed them to Nivelles and took a great number of cannon. The road was actually blocked up with cannon and waggons deserted by the French. We bivouacked this night outside the village, up to our knees in mud.

Kincaid remembered that

> After pursuing them until dark, we halted about two miles beyond the field of battle, leaving the Prussians to follow up the victory.

Hibbert, again in the letter to his mother, wrote:

> I fancied it was in the time of the Romans, for all the French were clad in complete armour of steel, and were lying in piles one on the other; this was two days after

Just one example of the battle reported in a newspaper. (Anne S. K. Brown)

the battle, for the French were not pursued by the English after the battle, but the Prussians who came up just as the battle was finished. The Prussians kept up a continual fire on the retreating French and consequently killed as many English prisoners as French.

The Battle of Waterloo was over.

CHAPTER 6

HOUGOUMONT AND LA HAYE SAINTE

Points d'appui or Pivotal Bastions?

NICK LIPSCOMBE

PREVIOUS
Defence of the Chateau de
Hougoumont by the flank
company, Coldstream Guards,
1815. Watercolour by Denis
Dighton, 1815. (Courtesy of the
Council of the National Army
Museum)

Wellington's decision to make a stand against Napoleon's forces south of the village of Waterloo is unchallenged but whether he personally selected the actual position at Mont Saint Jean is interestingly the subject of debate. Two modern histories both suggest that the Mont Saint Jean position was in fact selected by the quartermaster general, Colonel Sir William Howe de Lancey, when sent back by Wellington on 17 June to reconnoitre the exact position for the Allied defence.[1] This challenge to the theatrical tracing of the duke's thumbnail across the map 'behind Hougoumont and La Haye Sainte' in the Duke of Richmond's study in the early hours of 16 June is not, however, supported by other historical interpretations.[2] The suggestion that de Lancey had the latitude to reject the idea of deploying astride the ridge of La Belle Alliance should not be discounted but an examination of the advantages and disadvantages of both positions, from a defensive perspective, quickly reveals that Mont Saint Jean is the stronger of the two. Sergeant Major Edward Cotton of the 7th Hussars, a participant at the battle and a subsequent resident of Mont Saint Jean for 34 years until his death in 1849, perhaps knew the ground better than anyone.

> The juncture of the two high-roads immediately in rear of our centre ... added to
> the facility of communication, and enabled us to move ammunition, guns, troops,
> the wounded etc, to or from any part of our main front line as the circumstances
> demanded ... the continuous ridge from flank to flank towards which no hostile
> force could advance undiscovered, within range of our artillery upon the crest.
> Behind this ridge our troops could manoeuvre, or lie concealed from the enemy's
> view, while they were in great measure protected from the fire of hostile batteries...[3]

A perfunctory glance at a map, period or modern, of the Waterloo battlefield reveals three sets of farm buildings to the south of the Mont Saint Jean ridge, astride the main road running south to north from Charleroi to Brussels. To the east of the Nivelle–Mont Saint Jean road was the chateau and farm complex of Hougoumont; just to the west of the Brussels road was the smaller farm of La Haye Sainte; and on the left of the Allied positions were the farms of Papelotte, La Haye, Frischermont and the small hamlet of Smohain. These farms were of a typical Central European construction, designed to keep out thieves and intruders. Built with high brick or stone walls around an inner courtyard they provided a veritable strong point against attack by infantry but would not have lasted overly long if those infantry were supported by artillery. It was quite clear that these farm complexes would have to be held as part of the Allied static defences but until Napoleon revealed his hand, it was difficult for Wellington to determine the comparative importance of these strong points. Was their retention and/or capture essential for victory or, put another way, were they simply *points d'appui* or pivotal bastions?

Wellington's defensive position was undeniably strong but General Thomas Picton, commanding the Allied 5th Division, did not see it that way; commenting to the commanding officer of the 52nd Light Infantry that he 'never saw a worse position taken up by any army'.[4] Few Allied officers shared Picton's opinion but Napoleon was most certainly of the same mind. In the fading light on 17 June he made a reconnaissance of the Allied positions and concluded that 'if the English army remains there tomorrow, it is mine'.[5] This strident judgement was based entirely on the fact that Wellington's back, and therefore his line of retreat, was through the Forest of Soignes. By deploying forward of such an obstacle Wellington had reduced his tactical mobility and, following defeat, rendered any successful extraction a virtual impossibility. This was perhaps a rather hasty conclusion for there were several good roads through what was

A glance at a map of the Waterloo battlefield reveals three sets of farm buildings to the south of the Mont Saint Jean ridge, astride the main road running south to north from Charleroi to Brussels. (Topfoto)

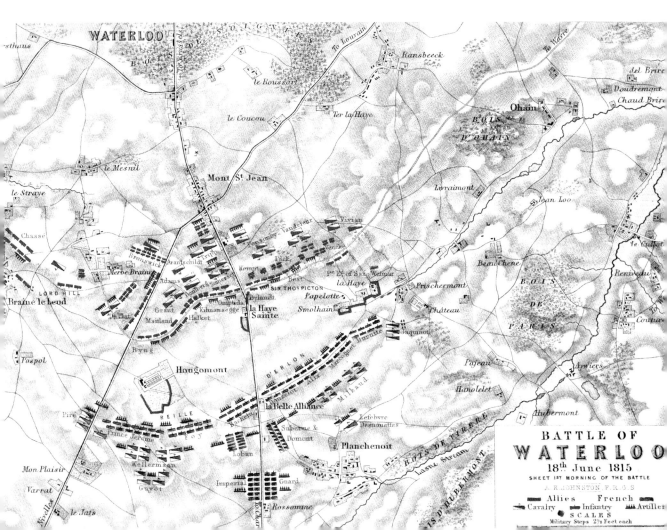

The exterior of Hougoumont at the commencement of battle. Coloured aquatint by Thomas Sutherland. (Courtesy of the Council of the National Army Museum)

essentially an 'open' forest; Baron Antoine-Henri de Jomini in his *Art of War* even considered the cover of the forest an asset not a liability.[6]

Following the battle at the crossroads around Quatre Bras on 16 June, Wellington spent the following day readjusting to a new defensive position from where he hoped to hold Napoleon and then defeat him with the arrival of Prussian support. Assisted by a particularly lethargic follow-up by Napoleon's Army, and by some appalling weather, Wellington was able to execute his defensive deployment virtually unhindered. Leaving aside the physical mix of his force, Wellington based the geographical dispersion on three factors: the difficult terrain on the left from which direction he was relying on Prussian reinforcement; the need to block the centre and the road to Brussels and hold this in depth from the Napoleonic sledgehammer; and finally the need to cover the more open right flank, protect his lines of communication (to Ostend) and counter the expected flanking manoeuvre. The likelihood of a Napoleonic manoeuvre on the Allied right was well-judged and Wellington retained 18,000 Dutch, Hanoverian and British troops at Hal and Tubize, and guarding the Mons–Brussels road, to counter such an eventuality.[7] As events transpired there was to be no such manoeuvre and Hougoumont which, to all intents and purposes started the day at the centre of the Allied position, became the Allied right.

Napoleon's decision not to manoeuvre resulted in a battlefield of 5,000 metres wide and 4,000 metres deep into which 200,000 men (including subsequently 40,000 Prussians), 60,000 horses and 537 guns were committed to action.[8] Between Hougoumont and Papelotte the balance of 73,000 Allied troops had been deployed, described by Clausewitz as follows:

In general the duke's deployment was such that the front was about 5,000 paces long, with 30 battalions of infantry in the first line, some 13 battalions in the second line, sixty squadrons of cavalry in the third and fourth lines. In addition another 38 battalions and 33 squadrons were placed at other points, either farther to the rear or on the flanks [not including Hal-Tubize], and could be considered as reserves. Thus one could say the deployment was exceptionally deep.

In front of the lines lay three strong points: the farmhouse of Hougoumont 1,000 paces in front of the right wing, La-Haye-Sainte 500 paces in front of the centre on the main road, and La Haye 1,000 paces in front of the left wing. All three were occupied by infantry and more or less prepared for defence.[9]

In 1815 Hougoumont was a small chateau and working farm. The complex of buildings was about 100 metres long and 50 metres wide onto which, on the east side, abutted the ornamental gardens laid out in Flemish style. It was

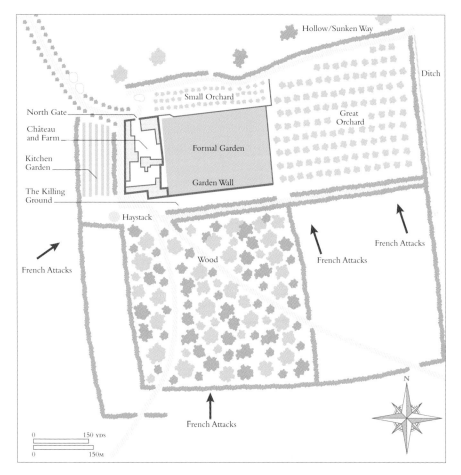

Diagram of Hougoumont chateau and farm in 1815. (© Osprey Publishing)

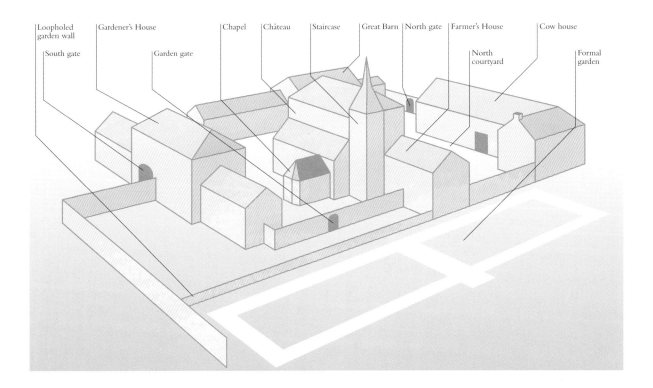

Loopholed
garden wall

Gardener's House

Chapel

Château

Staircase

Great Barn

North gate

Farmer's House

Cow house

South gate

Garden gate

North
courtyard

Formal
garden

Drawing of Hougoumont
chateau and farm in 1815.
(© Osprey Publishing)

enclosed to the south and east by a 2-metre-high brick wall and to the north by
a hedge. At the eastern end of the walled garden was the Great Orchard. To the
south of the buildings and the walled garden was a wood, which extended south
for about 400 metres. The tactical advantages of holding the farm and outlying
grounds were obvious enough and as darkness fell on the 17th Wellington
ordered four light companies of the 1st and 2nd Guards Brigades to take
possession of the farm.[10] They had a brief firefight with a French patrol before
occupying the position and preparing it for defence. The two light companies
of the 1st Guards, under the command of Lieutenant Colonel Lord Saltoun,
occupied the Great Orchard and part of the woods to the south of the farm,
while the other two light companies, under the command of Lieutenant
Colonel James Macdonell, occupied the buildings and walled garden. They
worked through the night barricading the numerous gates, loopholing the south
wall and constructing rudimentary firing platforms along the inner edge of the
wall. At some stage during the night Wellington ordered 200 (or 300) Hanoverian
Jägers (from Colonel Friedrich, Count von Kielmansegge's Brigade) to the area
and these green-jacketed infantry moved to the south end of the wood.[11] Soon
after first light on 18 June, following an inspection of the Hougoumont defences,
Wellington decided to further reinforce the defenders and ordered the Prince

of Weimar to dispatch one of his Nassau battalions from Papelotte to the area. The 1st/2nd Nassau deployed into the orchard and it appears that the two light companies under Lord Saltoun then withdrew back to the main position on Mont Saint Jean ridge. Consequently, by 11 a.m. there were 1,300 Allied soldiers in and around the Hougoumont complex and, contrary to popular perceptions, only 200 were British (1,600 British reinforcements arrived at varying times during the battle).[12]

La Haye Sainte was more of a typical Belgian farm, enclosed on four sides with an inner courtyard. Cotton described it as 'a post far from being so commodious as Hougoumont, but considerably nearer our position, consequently easier of access, although more exposed to the enemy's attacks and cannonade'.[13] On the south, or French side of the farm was an orchard about 250 metres long and 75 metres wide and on the north side was a garden adjoining the main farmhouse. There were two gates to the courtyard, the main gate off the Brussels road and another virtually opposite this structure opening out towards the fields. The 2nd Light Battalion of the King's German Legion (KGL) had been allocated the defence of the farm. When the 400 men arrived late on the 17th, wet, cold and exhausted, they broke down the inner gate and smashed it up to make firewood. Some time later they received orders to fortify the structure. Their endeavours were severely hampered by a lack of building materials and, to make matters worse, at some stage that evening their integral battalion pioneers were sent to Hougoumont leaving the hapless defenders 'without so much as a hatchet'. Lieutenant Graeme was with the 2nd Battalion and recalled:

> I saw no sapeurs [sic]. We had no loopholes excepting three great apertures, which we made with difficulty when we were told in the morning that we were to defend the farm. Our pioneers had been sent to Hougoumont the evening before. We had no scaffolding, nor means of making any, having burnt the carts etc. Our loopholes, if they may be thus termed, were on a level with the road on the outside…[14]

Major George Baring was in charge of the six KGL companies and he posted three in the orchard, two in the buildings and one in the rear garden. The loss of the large gate presented 'an insurmountable difficulty' and they could find nothing with which to barricade this opening.[15] An abattis was constructed on the main road at the south end of the boundary wall and Captain Kincaid of the 95th Rifles recalled that further along the road, towards the Allied positions, 'was a small knoll, with a sand-hole in its farthest side, which we occupied as an advanced post, with three companies'.[16]

The farm of La Haye Sainte after the battle; burial parties appear to be interring the dead in the sandpit adjacent to the complex. (Courtesy of the Council of the National Army Museum)

On the Allied far left were the two farms of Papelotte and La Haye, the small hamlet of Smohain and, furthest east, the farm and chateau of Frischermont.[17] Papelotte and La Haye were enclosed farms about the same size as La Haye Sainte; the former was a more substantial structure constructed of brick, while the latter had walls constructed of cob (clay, sand and straw) and was crowned with a thatched roof.[18] The small village of Smohain was further down the lane and consisted of 12 separate buildings, some quite substantial. On the far left was the chateau and farm of Frischermont, which was similar in size to Hougoumont and had been used by the Duke of Marlborough as his Headquarters in 1705. The remaining four battalions of Prince Saxe-Weimar's 2nd Netherlands Brigade had the responsibility to man and defend the three farms.[19] Skirmishers from these battalions were sent to the top of the hill to the south; while six companies of the 3rd/2nd Nassau defended Papelotte, one company was detached to La Haye and four companies of the 1st/28th Orange Nassau held Frischermont. The balance of the infantry was held to the north of the buildings on the forward slope.

On a two-dimensional map this cluster of farms and buildings seems as dominant and potentially significant as those of Hougoumont and La Haye Sainte. However, closer examination reveals this not to be the case. Due to the lie of the land on the Allied left the importance of these strong points is markedly different. The terrain falls off sharply in this area and a branch of the Ohain road runs east past Papelotte, La Haye and Smohain and then follows a stream towards Ohain. This sunken road, the defile, the stream and marshy banks, made worse by the very heavy rain, were considerable military obstacles to the movement of large formed bodies of infantry and cavalry. Jomini recognised this:

> We must endeavour in a defensive position not only to cover the flanks, but it often happens that there are obstacles on other points of the front, of such a character as to compel and attack upon the centre. Such a position will always be one of the advantageous for defence, – as was shown at Malplaquet and Waterloo. Great obstacles are not essential for this purpose, as the smallest accident of the ground is sometimes sufficient: thus, the insignificant rivulet of Papelotte forced Ney to attack Wellington's centre, instead of the left as he had been ordered.[20]

It would be wrong to disregard the tactical value of these buildings but it is clear from a detailed examination of the terrain and from the way this area was defended and attacked that these buildings were not vital to either side, or to the outcome of the battle. As such they cannot be considered in the same light as those of Hougoumont and La Haye Sainte.

From Wellington's orders to Macdonell to 'defend the post to the last extremity', his intentions to retain Hougoumont were clear. It was a determination which grew as the battle progressed; he took a considerable

La Haye Sainte farm complex (from the south) on the left of the Charleroi to Brussels road. From an engraving made a few months after the battle but depicting the farm prior to the conflict. (Courtesy of Nick Lipscombe)

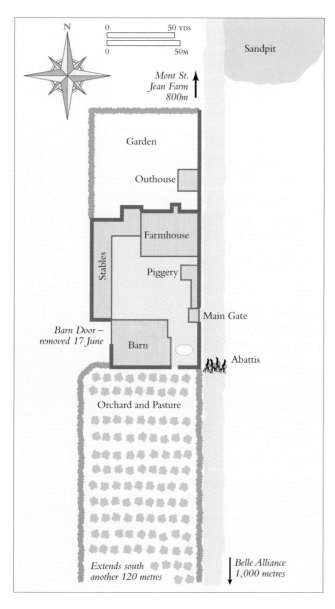

N

0   50 yds

0   50 m

Sandpit

Mont St.
Jean Farm
800m

Garden

Outhouse

Stables

Farmhouse

Piggery

Main Gate

Barn Door –
removed 17 June

Barn

Abattis

Orchard and Pasture

Extends south
another 120 metres

Belle Alliance
1,000 metres

Diagram of La Haye Sainte farm
in 1815. (© Osprey Publishing)

interest in the defence of the farm throughout the day. It is curious that he did not appear to have the same resolve with regard to La Haye Sainte, either at the start or during the battle itself. Yet the advantages in holding the farms individually were undeniably increased by the advantage of holding them both, for they funnelled the attacking forces into what General Foy described as 'a hail of death' and what is known in modern terms as a killing ground.[21] Nevertheless, of the two strong points, La Haye Sainte was evidently the more important; it was, to all intents and purposes (given Napoleon's plan of attack), the key to the battle. According to Professor Jeremy Black, La Haye Sainte was more important than Hougoumont 'with regard to the flow of the battle, and also in terms of a symbolism of success'.[22] Andrew Field notes that, 'if the French were able to seize it then it could be fairly said that they held a dagger to the heart of Wellington's line'.[23] Both observations encapsulate why Wellington had to retain and Napoleon had to capture this small farm complex located centre stage.

Napoleon's decision-making ability appears to have been curtailed by his ill health. He was almost certainly tormented by a bad bout of prolapsed haemorrhoids, may also have been afflicted by an attack of cystitis and, it has also been suggested, was suffering from acromegaly, a glandular disorder.[24] These maladies surely affected his physical performance but it is unclear as to whether and to what extent they may also have affected his mental ability. His lack of urgency on 17 June betrayed his maxim that 'when once the offensive has been assumed, it must be sustained to the last extremity'.[25] There is some mitigation for this tardiness but a similar lack of urgency on the morning of the battle is less easily dismissed. Napoleon was certainly aware, late on the 17th or early on the 18th, that elements of Field Marshal Gebhard Leberecht von Blücher's Prussian Army might elude Marshal Emmanuel de Grouchy and move west in support of Wellington's force. Many of Napoleon's lieutenants, in particular his chief of staff Marshal Nicolas Soult, had urged concentration of force and the recalling of all or a large part of Grouchy's 30,000 troops (and 96 guns). That Napoleon failed to do this betrayed a second of his maxims, 'when you have resolved to fight a battle, collect your whole force. Dispense with nothing. A single battalion sometimes decides the day.'[26]

It was, however, Napoleon's failure to comply with one of his principal maxims on the day of the battle which is most difficult to understand. 'It is an approved maxim in war, never to do what the enemy wishes you to do … never attack a position in front which you can gain by turning.'[27] Napoleon's actual plan and tactical intentions are unclear; Clausewitz summed it up as follows:

> Whether Bonaparte was intending to attack all along the line, break through the centre, or push in one of the wings, is something that cannot be clearly discerned, either from the measures that were actually taken or from the direction that the fighting took, and even less from what Bonaparte himself says regarding his plan.
>
> Judging by the distribution of forces and the initial advance, it was purely an attack all along the line; judging by the main efforts made during the latter course of the action, the intent was to break through the centre. But the latter seems to have been inspired more by the needs of the moment than by a clear plan…[28]

It certainly appears that Napoleon's plan was to break Wellington's centre by a heavy preliminary artillery bombardment followed by a concentrated and sustained infantry assault, which would then be exploited by massed cavalry. Everything else seems secondary to this intention and Clausewitz goes on to conclude that:

> it seems that the attacks on the advance post of Hougoumont and the village of La Haye had so little energy, and the attack in the centre was so large, that Bonaparte's intention must have been to break through the Allied centre, while merely keeping it occupied on the flanks.[29]

While there are some inaccuracies with this statement it does seem strange that Napoleon, having decided to break through the centre in strength, does not seem to have paid sufficient attention to the capture or masking of the strong points of Hougoumont and La Haye Sainte.

Napoleon was certainly concerned about fortifications; perhaps with his experience from Borodino in mind, very early on the 18th he had sent his chief engineer General François Haxo to reconnoitre the Allied centre.

The assault on Hougoumont by the French infantry of the 6th Division. (Hougoumont © MarkChurms.com, 1991)

I mounted my horse at once and went to the skirmishers opposite la Haie-Sainte; reconnoitred the enemy line again; and told the engineer General Haxo, a reliable officer, to get nearer to it, in order to satisfy himself as to whether they had erected some redoubts or entrenchments. This general returned promptly to report that he had seen no trace of fortifications.[30]

Leaving aside the rather flimsy abattis on the road adjacent to La Haye Sainte – which Kincaid described as little more than scattered branches – it seems strange that Haxo did not report on the defendable qualities of Hougoumont and La Haye Sainte as part of his engineer assessment. Andrew Field advocates that Haxo did not want to insult Napoleon's intelligence for after all Napoleon could see both Hougoumont and La Haye Sainte for himself. It is worth pointing out, however, that La Haye Sainte sits in a small depression while Hougoumont was (it is no longer the case) shielded by a large wood, so the full extent of these complexes on that dull and cloudy Sunday morning may not have been easily discernible. Once battle had commenced visibility would have decreased to a few yards; so thick would have been the dense white clouds of smoke from the concentration of infantry and artillery weapons in such a small field.[31] Consequently it would have been extremely difficult for Napoleon to have seen for himself the impact these strong points were having as the battle unfolded and he would have relied entirely on reports from his field commanders.

Napoleon's decision not to manoeuvre was, with the benefit of hindsight, a mistake. He had, in principle, four flanking options: a wide manoeuvre left or right and a shallow manoeuvre left or right. However, manoeuvre operations take time and that was one factor that Napoleon did not have in his favour. Furthermore, a wide flanking manoeuvre to the French right would have exposed a flank to the Prussians; although Napoleon was not aware that Grouchy had failed to fix Blücher's Army until a little while later. A similar manoeuvre on the French left would have become embroiled in the town of Braine-l'Alleud, which was covered by the 3rd Netherlands Infantry Division and vulnerable to a flank attack by the large force at Tubize and Hal under Prince Frederick of Orange. A shallow manoeuvre on the French right was constrained, as already examined, by the ground around the Papelotte, La Haye and Frischermont farms. That, in effect, left a shallow manoeuvre on the French left between Hougoumont and Braine-l'Alleud as the only viable option and Napoleon seems to have discounted this for fear of driving the Allies east towards the Prussians. Be that as it may, Napoleon's line of battle did not constrain him to any particular course of action; the

The French infantry assault the north gate of the Hougoumont complex. (Chris Collingwood)

whereabouts of the Prussians, and for that matter Grouchy, coupled with Wellington's rather 'confounding' reverse slope deployment, necessitated symmetrical deployment and resolute flexibility. 'Execution was everything' to Napoleon but on 18 June his execution was anything but.

Napoleon's explanation for a slow start to proceedings was that he allowed the troops to leave their bivouacs slightly later to allow the rain-soaked ground to dry out but then he lost another two hours forming his men up along the ridge at Belle Alliance. Clausewitz commented that:

> There was something strange about this parade formation, the image of which seems to be one of Bonaparte's most pleasing memories. It was extremely uncharacteristic, and nothing like it happens in any of Bonaparte's other battles. It was also completely unnecessary, for afterwards the corps had to form into columns again in order to attack.[32]

It is apparent that Napoleon was in no hurry and his initial orders, when they were finally disseminated at 11 a.m., appear to confirm his intention to bludgeon and disregard manoeuvre.

> Directly the army has formed up, and soon after 1 p.m., the Emperor will give the order to Marshal Ney and the attack will be delivered on Mt. S. Jean village in order to seize the crossroads at that place. To this end the 12-pdr. Batteries of the II and VI Corps will mass with that of the I Corps. These 24 guns will bombard the troops holding Mont S. Jean, and Count d'Erlon will commence the attack first by launching the left division [Quiot's], and, when necessary, supporting it by the other divisions of the I Corps [d'Erlon's]. The II Corps [Reille's] will advance keeping abreast of the I Corps.[33]

There is no mention of Hougoumont or, more surprisingly, of La Haye Sainte, although there has been a suggestion that Napoleon was confused and dictated Mont Saint Jean when he meant La Haye Sainte.[34] However, we know from his memoirs that in fact Napoleon's intentions for this first attack were to support General Joachim-Jérôme Quiot's attack on La Haye Sainte with the artillery fire from the Great Battery and to use the other two divisions of the I Corps to move on La Haye and get around the Allied left flank.

> They [the guns] were intended to support the attack on la Haie-Sainte, which two divisions of the I Corps and two divisions of the VI were to make, at the same time as the two other divisions of the I Corps were moving on La Haye... I had

preferred to turn the enemy's left, rather than his right, first, in order to cut it off from the Prussians who were at Wavre … secondly, because the left appeared to be much weaker; thirdly and finally, because I was expecting every moment the arrival of a detachment from Marshal Grouchy.[35]

This is wholly unsatisfactory for Napoleon's intent is certainly not implied in the orders issued at 11 a.m. and it is complicated further by the fact that, at some stage soon after issuing the order, Napoleon gave a verbal order (no written record exists) for proceedings to open earlier and not on the left or centre but on the Allied right at the Hougoumont complex. Marshal Michel Ney, who had been given a written copy of the (11 a.m.) orders, had written on the back in pencil, 'Count d'Erlon is to understand that it is by the left [i.e. Reille], instead of the right, that the attack is to start. You are to communicate this new disposition to General Reille.'[36]

No real explanation has ever been provided for this radical deviation. It has been suggested that having issued his orders, Napoleon received reports of a large Prussian force only 5 kilometres to the north-east, which convinced him to commence with proceedings at Hougoumont and then dispense with a shallow right flanking manoeuvre and concentrate everything on a frontal assault against Mont Saint Jean ridge. As no written orders detailing this major adjustment have surfaced it is difficult to be certain of Napoleon's intent.[37] Ney's rather unsatisfactory scribbled note was the only confirmation of an attack being initiated by Lieutenant General Honoré Reille and even this does not specify Hougoumont as the principal or sole objective.

Of the five generally accepted phases of the battle covering the attacks on the ridge at Mont Saint Jean (leaving aside the attacks by and against the Prussians), Hougoumont and La Haye Sainte are central to events, individually or collectively, in every phase.[38] The exact start time of the first of these phases, the attack on Hougoumont and therefore the start of the battle, is surprisingly uncertain although it is generally accepted to have been between 11.30 a.m. and noon. It ended at about 1.30 p.m. with the opening of the main attack in the centre. There is little, if any, contention that Napoleon's intentions with regard to Hougoumont were diversionary in nature. He intended to deny the wood to the Allied infantry, but not necessarily the farm complex; his intention was that this diversion would encourage Wellington to weaken his centre by moving reserves to reinforce Hougoumont. This succeeded to a lesser degree. Perhaps he was also buying time. Some historians have suggested that this attack was in fact linked, by way of pre-cursor, to the main attack by the I and II Corps, but there is more evidence to disprove than prove this hypothesis.[39]

PREVIOUS
French *Sous Lieutenant* Legros, nicknamed '*l'Enfonceur*', gained entry to the courtyard via the north gate. (Keith Rocco)

Prince Jérôme Bonaparte, Napoleon's youngest brother, led the diversionary attack on the complex at Hougoumont with his (6th) Division. (Topfoto)

Reille, having received his verbal orders, selected Prince Jérôme Bonaparte, Napoleon's youngest brother, to lead the diversionary attack with his (6th) Division. It signalled the start of a struggle that was to ensue for the next seven hours with huge loss of life and immense bravery on both sides. As such it was a diversionary attack which ran out of control. It elevated the struggle for Hougoumont to embody, with justification, British military courage and resolve, while, with far less justification, it promoted Hougoumont to a level of tactical significance which it simply did not merit. Fortescue summed it up succinctly:

A fortified post, when strenuously defended, frequently assumes in the eyes of the assailants an importance out of all proportion to its true tactical value. If the centre of the Allied line were pierced, pursuant to Napoleon's design, Hougoumont would become untenable on the spot.[40]

There is little contention on this point from participants and/or historians but it is worth adding Andrew Roberts' enlightening observation that many of the more sophisticated war-gaming techniques 'regularly demonstrate that it was nigh on impossible for Napoleon to have won Waterloo without first capturing Hougoumont'.[41] This extraordinary conclusion perhaps says more about the value of war-gaming than it does about Hougoumont and the outcome of the battle. Adding to the confusion, there remains disagreement over the number of attacks the French actually executed and which French troops were actually committed and when during the seven-hour 'battle within a battle'. Julian Paget in his excellent small book records seven separate attacks, three of which occurred in this first phase of the battle between 11.30 a.m. and 12.45 p.m.[42] However, Andrew Field has conducted a detailed assessment in his comprehensive work and can only dovetail five of these assaults but, more significantly perhaps, decidedly less involvement in these latter attacks by Reille's other two divisions.[43]

Prince Jérôme selected Baron Pierre-François Bauduin's Brigade to lead the assault on Hougoumont. Adolphe Thiers, although not a participant, provides confirmation of the artillery support to this opening phase.

> On our left general Reille had united the batteries of his divisions, those of the cavalry of Piré, and they fired on the wood and the chateau of Gomont [original name of Hougoumont]; Napoleon, to sustain the fire of this wing, had ordered [the timing is unclear] the artillery of Kellermann to join these batteries, which was moved behind the main body of Reille's troops, providing at least 40 guns to engage the right of the duke of Wellington. A lot of cannonballs were ineffective, but others carried the death to the thickest of the hostile masses, and produced deep openings there in spite of the care that the enemy had taken to deploy on the reverse side of the hill.[44]

This rather confusing observation does at least confirm that elements of the Grand Battery, which was still forming up at this stage and was one of the principal reasons for delay, opened at much the same time as Reille's divisional batteries. The artillery fire continued for about 15 minutes before Bauduin's Brigade began their advance to the (southern) edge of Hougoumont wood, preceded by a strong line of tirailleurs, and was immediately engaged by three Allied batteries firing from the ridge north of Hougoumont. In the wood the Nassauers and Hanoverians made best use of their cover, and the extended range of their hunting fusils, to inflict heavy casualties on the advancing French infantry. Bauduin was among the early casualties and command now fell to Lieutenant Colonel Amédée-Louis Despans, the commander of the *1e Léger* (1st Light Infantry) who had been leading the assault. After about an hour Jérôme's infantry had control of most of the woodland and had come up against a thick hedge running along the northern edge of the wood, which was 'formed of very big trees and greatly intertwined, presenting a kind of impenetrable wall … which they cut their way through with axes'.[45] On the far side was a strip of open ground and then the walled garden prepared for defence and manned by a company of the Coldstream Guards. Their heavy, sustained and accurate fire brought an immediate halt to the French advance. According to Reille, Jérôme had achieved his mission and should have been content with holding the wood; an order which, according to his corps commander, had been given (verbally) a number of times but which the headstrong young prince of the blood chose to ignore.[46]

Wellington sent a steady trickle of reinforcements to the garrison from the two British guards brigades positioned immediately to the north. He also ordered Major Robert Bull's horse artillery troop to the forward slope position

The interior of the courtyard during the height of the fighting; a captured French soldier in the foreground. (Print after Robert Hillingford)

in front of the Guards. This troop, equipped with six heavy 5½-inch howitzers, began to fire shrapnel shells into the wood with devastating effect. This anti-personnel artillery round was unique to the British artillery and it provided a force multiplication effect, the significance of which has never been fully recognised or properly recorded. Bull could not actually see if the shells were air-bursting at the right height and had to be assisted with indirect fire orders by the commander of the adjacent battery who had a better view. However, the effect of these shells, each containing well in excess of a hundred musket balls, which the French dubbed 'black rain', was devastating. Colonel George Wood, commanding the Allied artillery, wrote to Major Henry Shrapnel after the battle:

> Then the Duke ordered your (shrapnel) shells to be fired in and about the farm house, and this succeeded in dislodging them from this formidable position, to which, if Buonaparte had once been able to bring his artillery, the Duke must have lost the battle; that had it not been for these shells, it is very doubtful whether any effort of the British could have recovered the farm house, and hence on this simple circumstance hinges entirely the turn of the battle.[47]

This letter highlights the often-overlooked contribution made by Shrapnel's shell during the war in the Peninsula and at Waterloo. It also makes a very valid general observation about Hougoumont and the use of artillery in its defence but most significantly it provides another vital clue as to why the attacks at Hougoumont may have continued. Most of Bauduin's infantry were driven back as a result of this 'black rain' and then driven out of the woods by a spirited Allied counter-attack by the Guards and Germans. Jérôme, his reputation at stake, was under increasing pressure from his subordinates to support his first brigade. Having effectively failed in his mission to *capture and hold* the wood, he deployed his second brigade to the fight; thereby elevating the contest beyond the original diversion. Soye's Brigade wasted little time in driving back the few Allied infantrymen and were soon back at the hedge facing the walls of the farm complex. Bull was called upon for a repeat performance but the woods still contained some friendly forces that had not yet been extracted from the area; Bull would have been forced to fire at the southern end of the wood to avoid friendly casualties.[48] Soye's and (the remnants of) Bauduin's Brigades caught these exposed retreating infantry in the open, at the south-west corner of the complex, and a fierce firefight ensued. At the same time, French infantry began to make their way around the west side of the farm and it was at this point that French *Sous-Lieutenant* Legros, nicknamed '*l'Enfonceur*' (literally 'the Smasher'),

An inaccurate depiction of the infantry struggle for Hougoumont. The chateau was set on fire with incendiary carcasses at about 3 p.m. (Anne S. K. Brown)

gained entry to the courtyard via the north gate only to be denied by the courage and inspired leadership of Macdonell and his guardsmen. This gallant action prompted Wellington to declare some while later that 'the success of the Battle of Waterloo turned on the closing of the gates'. As significant as this action certainly was, there is, nevertheless, some evidence that this was not the only time the perimeter of the complex was penetrated by the attackers.[49]

During this period French higher command had been completely focused on preparations for the main attack in the centre and appears to have been unaware that events at Hougoumont were already running out of control. This command and control failure within the French II Corps is puzzling. Reille, as we have seen, was adamant that he had ordered his subordinates not to concern themselves with taking the buildings and Thiers supports that claim but adds that Reille did not stay close enough to the action and 'allowed his generals of division and brigade, driven by their ardour and that of their troops, to persist in trying [to] capture the farm and chateau'.[50] In fact Captain Pierre Robinaux of the 2nd *de ligne* (Soye's Brigade) states quite clearly that it was Reille who ordered the attack and stipulated the need to capture the strong point:

> Count Reille, who commanded the 2nd Corps, came to give us the order to take the position held by the English and to take the farm as a *point d'appui* and to maintain ourselves in this position during the battle, without losing or seizing terrain.[51]

This in itself is far from conclusive but what of the balance of the II Corps and their commitment to the struggle? It is inconceivable that Colonel Tissot, commanding Gauthier's Brigade (the latter officer having been killed at Quatre Bras), part of General Foy's Division, would have been committed without the corps commander's awareness and accord. Unfortunately Foy's account provides no clue as to who ordered what, but he is meticulously clear as to who supported the attacks and when. It is here that there appears to be a major discrepancy with British accounts. Foy plainly states that only Tissot's Brigade attacked Hougoumont and that the first attack by this brigade took place at 2 p.m. (not shortly before 1 p.m. as is widely recorded).[52] Furthermore, the commitment of Bachelu's Division is also challenged, with the brigade chief of staff stating that the brigade was committed only at 6 p.m. and not at 2.30 p.m. and 4 p.m. as indicated in many British accounts.[53] An examination of the relative strengths of this contest using the often cited '13,500 Frenchmen were occupied by 2,000 British' is of little help, and somewhat myopic. These figures assume that the whole of the II Corps was embroiled, which was not the case, and do not take into account the large numbers of Germans who were integral to the defending force. Nevertheless, this finer detail does not detract from the fact that the greater part of the II Corps was locked in a struggle for Hougoumont for most of the day. It was a struggle which evolved from a minor irritant into a major aggravation and consequently elevated the importance of Hougoumont from a *point d'appui* to a pivotal bastion.

The first attack on La Haye Sainte commenced a few minutes before 2 p.m. Within a few minutes the farm was surrounded by Quiot's infantry and Baring, who had directed his men to lie down and hold their fire until the French had closed, was soon forced to abandon the orchard and fall back to the courtyard and buildings.[54] Baring's men were armed with the Baker rifle, a longer range and more accurate weapon than the Brown Bess musket but with a correspondingly slower rate of fire: one round per minute in contrast to two to three rounds for the musket. When attacked in overwhelming force this reduced weight of fire was a serious disadvantage to the defenders. In an attempt to redress this disadvantage, and capitalise on the longer range of the Baker rifle, some companies were pushed out to the right (west) of the farm into the open ground.

> The companies of captain Christian Wynecken and captain von Goeben … as well as a company of Hanoverian riflemen under major von Sporken – the whole of whom had been placed in skirmishing order to the right of the farm, poured a severe fire upon the assailants as they advanced; suddenly however, some squadrons of cavalry appeared on their right flank, and the detached troops hastily attempted to collect together.[55]

Count Kielmansegge, commanding the 1st Hanoverian Brigade positioned immediately to the north of the farm, detached one of his light battalions to move forward and support the isolated riflemen in the open. At the same time Baring seized the opportunity to

The attack through the orchard at Hougoumont, led by Foy. (Courtesy of Patrice Courcelle)

counter-attack and recapture the orchard. Brigade General Étienne Jacques Travers had been ordered to cover General Jean-Baptiste Drouet, Count d'Erlon's far left, with his brigade of heavy cuirassiers and had been toying with the idea of engaging the few riflemen in the open. The enticement of an unsupported light infantry battalion moving to join them was too great a temptation and Baron Travers wasted no time in ordering the charge; throwing the exposed troops into confusion and breaking the counter-attack on the orchard. The cuirassiers swept around the farm, captured the gardens to the north and drove out Kincaid's three companies of Rifles positioned in the sandpit to the east of the road. La Haye Sainte was completely isolated. The French infantry were quick to exploit this success but they had not come forward with ladders and therefore concentrated their efforts on breaking down the gate; like Legros at Hougoumont, Lieutenant Vieux, a sapper 'of great stature, [and] of Herculean strength … could be seen, armed with an axe striking the gate ever harder'.[56] He gave up when he received a second wound and the gates and the garrison stood firm.

Less resilient, however, were Bijlandt's Netherlanders, who broke leaving a gap in the Allied lines to the rear left of the farm. General Thomas Picton manoeuvred his division and plugged the breach but was killed in the process. The arrival of Major General Sir James Kempt's and Major General Sir Denis Pack's Brigades was enough to stem the French tide and Lord Uxbridge, commanding the Allied cavalry, sensed d'Erlon's infantry wavering and ordered a mass cavalry attack with the Union and Household Brigades. The French were driven back across the frontage and the noose around La Haye Sainte was loosened. Precious time had been gained and the Prussians were drawing closer. Wellington took the opportunity of a lull to, *inter alia*, reinforce the garrison at La Haye Sainte with two light companies (1st Battalion KGL) and part of the Nassau battalion, while the 95th reoccupied the sandpit. Baring had decided not to hold the orchard and ordered the reinforcements to hold the garden while the balance of his defensive force concentrated on holding the buildings.

Cavalry and infantry of the King's German Legion. The defence of La Haye Sainte was undertaken by the green-jacketed, rifle-armed, infantry of the 2nd Battalion KGL under the command of Major George Baring. (Courtesy of the Council of the National Army Museum)

The centre of the British Army at La Haye Sainte. This engraving depicts the importance of the small farm complex right in the centre of the Allied line. (Courtesy of the Council of the National Army Museum)

During the lull the Grand Battery continued to ply trade in round shot and shell but surprisingly no concerted effort was made to batter the walls of the farm with the heavier 12-pounder guns. Nevertheless, Baring's men did not have to wait long for the second attack. Weighing up the reasons for d'Erlon's failure, Napoleon appears to have grasped the vital importance of La Haye Sainte and ordered Ney to capture the farm without delay. At about 3 p.m. the remnants of Quiot's Division, about 3,000 men (preceded by engineers), surrounded the farm and attacked the walls and gates with great determination. Baring takes up the story:

About half an hour's respite was now given us by the enemy, and we employed the time in preparing ourselves against a new attack; this followed in the same force as before, namely, from two sides by two close columns, which, with the greatest rapidity, nearly surrounded us, and, despising danger, fought with a degree of courage which I had never before witnessed in Frenchmen. Favoured by their advancing in masses, every bullet of ours hurt, and seldom were the effects limited to one assailant; this did not, however, prevent them from throwing themselves against the walls, and endeavouring to wrest the arms from the hands of my men, through the loop-holes; many lives were sacrificed to the defence of the doors and gates; the most obstinate contest was carried on where the gate was wanting, and where the enemy seemed determined to enter. On this spot seventeen Frenchmen already lay dead, and their bodies served as protection to those who pressed after them to the same spot.[57]

While this second attack was being executed the massed French artillery continued to engage the Allied right and left centre, prompting Wellington to order the front line to fall back behind the slope to afford them some protection. Ney misread the manoeuvre, believing it to be the prelude to a general retreat, and in the confusion nearly 5,000 French cavalry began to advance through the gap between Hougoumont and La Haye Sainte. The British infantry quickly transformed their lines into 20 squares, in front of which stood 60 Allied guns, many of which could enfilade the magnificent lines of advancing horsemen, creating the perfect killing ground against unsupported cavalry. Debate still rages as to the basis and detail of the order which set the French cavalry in motion a few minutes before 4 p.m. but as David Chandler wrote, 'the cavalry should not have been launched prior to the capture of La Haie Sainte' and I doubt there is anyone who would disagree with this statement.[58] John Keegan added that the ratio of men to space in the 'funnel', created by Hougoumont and La Haye Sainte, denied the French artillery room to accompany the cavalry. That is almost certainly the case but it does not explain why the opportunity was not taken to move artillery up in support of the attacks on La Haye Sainte during the time that the flower of the French cavalry was wasted engaging the Allied squares.

This second attack on La Haye Sainte abated sometime after 5 p.m. when the Prussians began to arrive on the field and the French cavalry had exhausted themselves, although their attacks on the Allied squares were to continue for another hour. Baring used the respite to care for the wounded but his greatest anxiety was his lack of ammunition and he immediately dispatched an officer to request urgent resupply. Meanwhile Napoleon, incredulous at the spectacle of the uncoordinated and unsupported French cavalry attacks and deeply preoccupied with the fight for Plancenoit against General Friedrich Wilhelm Count von Bülow's and Major General George von Pirch's Corps, rode up and down the line examining Wellington's positions and considering his options. Breaking Wellington's centre was still his best opportunity and capturing La Haye Sainte remained the key. He ordered Ney to renew the attack upon it. For the first time that day preparations were made for co-ordinated all-arms attacks upon both Hougoumont and La Haye Sainte by way of preliminary operations to puncturing the Allied centre. Against La Haye Sainte Ney directed part of Major General François Donzelot's Division, some cavalry and a battery of guns. Prior to the commencement of this attack, Baring had received reinforcement in the form of three additional companies of the Nassau battalion but crucially no rifle ammunition. Donzelot's infantry made a desperate attempt to force entry but having failed set the barn on fire. Baring recalled that:

> Luckily the Nassau troops carried large field cooking kettles; I tore a kettle from the back of one of these men; several officers followed my example, and filled the kettles with water, they carried them, facing almost certain death to the fire. The men did the same, and soon not one of the Nassauers was left with his kettle, and the fire was thus luckily extinguished – but alas with the blood of many brave men.[59]

Baring recalled that this attack lasted an hour and a half, although in reality it was probably a much shorter duration. He also recalled a distinct break before the next assault was delivered with the same fury. With the rifle ammunition almost exhausted he sent out, for the third time, an urgent appeal for immediate resupply. However, a short time after the attack was renewed the last of the rifle ammunition was expended and the loss of the farm was inevitable. The Prince of Orange, sensing defeat, had somewhat rashly ordered Colonel Christian von Ompteda to take the balance of his brigade and advance in support of the farm. Ompteda was killed and the 8th Line KGL virtually destroyed. Shortly after 6 p.m. Baring and 42 men managed to extract themselves through the garden under the cover of fire from the riflemen in the sandpit.[60] La Haye Sainte was in French hands and Wellington's position had been dangerously weakened.

This magnificent painting by Adolf Northern depicts the epic struggle for the defence of the small farm of La Haye Sainte by the King's German Legion. (akg-images)

The French tried to exploit their first major success of the day by launching a large body of French infantry against the British centre. They made some headway and Ney requested support. There was none forthcoming for Napoleon was now preoccupied with his right flank, the arrival of the Prussians and the almost unthinkable possibility of having to protect his lines of retreat. The opportunity passed and with it the most dangerous moment of the battle for Wellington and his men. Wellington was, according to Colonel George Cathcart, one of his aide de camps, 'much vexed' at the loss of La Haye Sainte.[61] He had every reason to be, for La Haye Sainte was much more than a *point d'appui*, it was without doubt a pivotal bastion and the key to the Allied defensive line along the Mont Saint Jean ridge. It is curious that Wellington, an undoubted master of the importance of ground particularly in defence, should have failed to grasp the importance of retaining La Haye Sainte at all costs. Only 800 men, a strong battalion, had been allocated or trickle-fed to its direct defence. Only three-quarters were armed with rifles and abandoned to their inevitable fate when their ammunition was expended, Baring's repeated requests for resupply apparently ignored.[62] It is a subject of

Quiot's Brigade (54th and 55th *de ligne*), having captured the orchard, fail to capitalise on their success and penetrate the La Haye Sainte farm complex. (akg-images)

Chateau de Hougoumont after the Battle of Waterloo. (Courtesy of Mick Crumplin)

considerable controversy. Regardless of the reasons the fact that Wellington's staff allowed the garrison to run out of ammunition was an indefensible blunder which could have lost the battle.

Equally indefensible is the French failure to make best use of their fighting components throughout the day. Cavalry was of little use against structures like Hougoumont and La Haye Sainte but artillery could and should have been brought to bear far earlier in proceedings, particularly against La Haye Sainte where the terrain presented no tangible problems for the deployment and employment of guns. Had some of 'Napoleon's daughters', as his heavy field guns were known, been used to batter the walls and gates of La Haye Sainte sometime after 2 p.m. during the first attack, it is implausible to suggest, given the resources allocated to its defence, that the structure would not have fallen at that time.[63] The consequences of losing such a pivotal mainstay so early in proceedings can only be speculated upon. While at Hougoumont, the ability to bring artillery to bear during the initial attacks was restricted to an extent by the woods. Lieutenant Colonel Lord Saltoun recorded that 'we suffered very little from artillery on the post' although he concedes that it was artillery that set fire to the house and farmyard.[64] Conversely, Wellington's use of artillery in defence of the structure demonstrated a far greater understanding of the need to weave the fighting components on the field of battle.

Such was Hougoumont – a decidedly important point in the Field of Battle, from its prominent position in the immediate front Right of the British line; and rendered ever memorable by the truly heroic and successful stand maintained throughout the day by the troops allocated for its defence.[65]

Siborne's description of Hougoumont is accurate in every sense. It was without doubt a 'decidedly important point' but it was not a pivotal bastion in the same way as La Haye Sainte. However, it was turned into a pivotal bastion by a failure, ultimately by Napoleon himself, to control Jérôme's obsession of turning a feint into a major effort. Hougoumont should never have become 'a battle within a battle'. Napoleon needed a bold stroke to achieve spectacular results and his decision to conduct a wedge-shaped thrust against the ridge at Mont Saint Jean was certainly not a mistake, and came close to succeeding, but Napoleonic tactics required space. The failure to mask Hougoumont and concentrate on capturing La Haye Sainte denied the French Army that space and funnelled their attacks into what General Foy described as 'a hail of death'. Adkin sums it up well: 'unlike Hougoumont whose possession was not critical to either side, La Haie Saint was vital to both'.[66]

The closing of the gates thereby thwarting *Sous-Lieutenant* Legros and his brave French infantrymen. Wellington was moved to write sometime later that the success of the entire battle had turned on the closing of the north gate by Lieutenant Colonel James Macdonell and his Coldstream guardsmen. (© National Museums Scotland)

CHAPTER 7

THE CAVALRY CHARGES

Ian Fletcher

The Battle of Waterloo is not only one of the most written about battles in history but is also one of the most painted, with scores of artists taking to their brushes and pens to produce some truly famous paintings depicting various incidents during the battle and the whole campaign. These range from Napoleon's return from exile on Elba to the Allies' entry into Paris. But perhaps the most enduring and iconic images of the Battle of Waterloo relate directly to two phases of the battle involving the charge by the British heavy cavalry early on the afternoon of 18 June 1815 and that by the massed squadrons of Napoleon's cavalry a few hours later. There are few students of the campaign, for example, who have not set eyes upon Lady Elizabeth Butler's depiction of the charge of the Scots Greys, or Denis Dighton's painting of Charles Ewart capturing the eagle of the French 45th Regiment. Nor can they have failed to see any one of numerous paintings depicting squares of Allied infantry, standing solid and defiant in the face of waves of charging French cavalry, a 'boiling surf' as one eyewitness put it.[1]

These two particular episodes continue to be not only the most painted of the various phases of the battle but also the subject of much controversy and dispute, largely around their command and control but also around their effectiveness. Indeed, both the charge by the British heavy cavalry and that by the French cavalry afterwards are usually considered to have been little short of disastrous for both commanders. However, whilst one of the charges was indeed an unmitigated disaster the other was largely successful, although this is usually dismissed by historians who have misinterpreted the casualty figures upon which they based their verdict.

BRITISH CAVALRY UNITS AT WATERLOO

The British cavalry at Waterloo – and this chapter refers specifically to British cavalry and not Allied cavalry – was very much a pale shadow of the cavalry which had done so much good work in the Iberian Peninsula and southern France between 1808 and 1814. Naturally, it had its off days – Vimeiro, Talavera and Maguilla spring instantly to mind – but there had been many more good days, beginning with Benavente, Sahagún and Mayorga, through Campo Maior, Fuentes de Oñoro, Villagarcia, Usagre and Los Santos, and continuing with Salamanca and Morales de Toro, to name just a few. Unfortunately, mud sticks, as they say, and having seen two examples of 'break failure'[2] in his first two major battles, Vimeiro and Talavera, Wellington seems to have taken a very dim view of his cavalry; consequently he was loathe to use it unless circumstances were decidedly in its favour. After receiving news of General 'Black Jack' Slade's misadventure at Maguilla in June 1812 Wellington accused Slade's cavalry of 'galloping at everything', an unfortunate tag that has largely stuck ever since, although recent efforts to rehabilitate his cavalry have, I am glad to say, appeared to have succeeded.[3]

But despite the improvement in the performance of the British cavalry in the Peninsula between 1811 and 1814 Wellington went into the Waterloo campaign still harbouring fears of a repetition of Vimeiro and Talavera, fears that were heightened by the regiments of British heavy cavalry that were sent to join his army in the Low Countries in the early spring of 1815. For whilst the regiments of British light cavalry in Wellington's Anglo-Dutch Army were almost all veterans of the Peninsular War – the 11th, 12th, 13th and 16th Light Dragoons, and even the 7th, 10th, 15th and 18th Hussars – the regiments of British heavy cavalry were, for the most part, untried. Gone were the magnificent veterans of the 3rd and 4th Dragoons and the 3rd, 4th and 5th Dragoon Guards. In their place were the 1st (King's) Dragoon Guards, the 2nd (Royal North British) Dragoons, otherwise known as the Scots Greys, and the 6th (Inniskilling) Dragoons. True, the arm was bolstered by the Household regiments, such as the 1st and 2nd Life Guards and the Royal Horse Guards, but even these regiments had seen only limited service towards the end of the Peninsular War where the unsuitable nature of the ground dictated they were not to play any sort of important role in the fighting. Only the 1st (Royal) Dragoons could be considered to have been real veterans, the regiment having done magnificent work in the Peninsula. Indeed, it is ironic that by far the most iconic regiment of British heavy cavalry at Waterloo, and a regiment that has featured in more paintings than any other, namely the Scots Greys, had not seen any overseas service whatsoever since 1795.[4] The King's Dragoon Guards was a regiment that had likewise seen no active service overseas for many years.

In his bid to capture the French Imperial Eagle at Waterloo, Sergeant Charles Ewart of the Scots Greys cut down the four escorts accompanying the eagle bearer and rode away with the standard. He received a commission as a reward for his gallantry. (Courtesy of René Chartrand)

The regiments that were destined to make the great charge on 18 June were brigaded thus; the 1st British Brigade, under Lord Edward Somerset, consisted of the 1st Life Guards, the 2nd Life Guards, the Royal Horse Guards and the King's Dragoon Guards, a total strength of around 1,226. The 2nd British Brigade, under Major General Sir William Ponsonby, numbered slightly fewer, at 1,181, and consisted of the 1st (Royal) Dragoons, the Scots Greys and the 6th (Inniskilling) Dragoons. Because of the nationalities of Ponsonby's three regiments, English, Irish and Scottish, the brigade became known as the Union Brigade, with Somerset's Brigade attracting the unofficial title of the Household Brigade, largely because of the presence of the Life Guards and Horse Guards.

The regiments of the Household Brigade and the Union Brigade had arrived in the Low Countries between April and May 1815 and spent the next few weeks idling away in camp until hostilities began in mid-June, whereupon they were ordered to march south, arriving too late to join in the fighting at Quatre Bras on 16 June. The following day, 17 June, however, saw the two brigades in action to a greater and lesser degree, covering Wellington's Army as it retired north to its position at Mont Saint Jean astride the main road to Brussels. It is worth noting how well the two brigades of heavy cavalry performed that day; fending off enemy advances whilst the infantry retired, the men of the

British cavalry in action in the Peninsula in 1814. Contrary to popular belief, Wellington's cavalry were far from being brainless gallopers. Indeed, they bettered their French counterparts on numerous occasions, with only a couple of very high profile misadventures, such as Vimeiro and Talavera, blotting their copybook. (Anne S. K. Brown)

ROYAL HORSE GUARDS,
BLUES.

Union Brigade, in particular, proving more than adept at operating in the style of light cavalry, skirmishing and exchanging carbine fire with the more numerous French cavalry force at Genappe, keeping them at arms length but never allowing themselves to become sucked into a more general action. Indeed, the Union Brigade and, to a lesser degree, the Household Brigade, performed magnificently during the retreat from Quatre Bras, never being compromised but turning in a thoroughly professional performance, something that frequently goes overlooked in the annals of the Waterloo campaign. The commander of the British cavalry, the Earl of Uxbridge, recalling the events of 17 June, was moved to write, 'thus terminated the prettiest field day I ever witnessed.'[5]

But despite their fine showing during the retreat from Quatre Bras on 17 June, the Union Brigade and Household Brigade will be forever judged on their performance on 18 June itself. Like almost everybody else on the battlefield of Waterloo on the morning of Sunday 18 June, the men of the two brigades of heavy cavalry had struggled to find decent shelter during a night of torrential rain that only petered out during the early hours of the morning. Thus, they presented a miserable, soggy sight as they took up their stations on that momentous Sunday morning, with both brigades forming up just south of the junction of the Nivelle road with the main road to Brussels, the Union Brigade to the east of the main road to Brussels and the Household Brigade to the west of it. Somerset formed his regiments with the 2nd Life Guards on the left, the King's Dragoon Guards in the centre and the 1st Life Guards on the right. The Horse Guards were in reserve behind them. Ponsonby, meanwhile, formed the Union Brigade with the 1st Royals on the right and the Inniskillings on the left. The Scots Greys formed up in rear of the first line as a reserve.

LEFT
A sketch of a British dragoon in 1815. Of the three regiments of British heavy dragoons at Waterloo only one, the 1st (Royals), had any experience of battle during the Napoleonic Wars. (Anne S. K. Brown)

MIDDLE
Royal Horse Guard in 1812 pattern uniform. The regiment played only a minor part towards the latter stages of the Peninsular War but performed well at Waterloo. (Courtesy of the Council of the National Army Museum)

RIGHT
A fine art illustration of the uniforms of the 16th, 13th and 14th Light Dragoons in 1815. (Anne S. K. Brown)

At some time around 11.30 a.m. (times vary considerably), Napoleon launched his attack beginning with an assault on the Chateau of Hougoumont which anchored Wellington's right flank. This had been in progress for some time before the French switched their attention to Wellington's left and the sector held by the infantry of General Sir Thomas Picton. The great French infantry attack by General Jean-Baptiste Drouet, Count d'Erlon's Corps, was the second great phase of the battle and was preceded by a heavy bombardment of Wellington's ridge by almost 80 guns that had been hauled forward onto a low ridge running roughly east to west across the Brussels road at a range of about 600 yards south of the crest behind which the Allied infantry was sheltering. The French gunners, in fact, had performed a prodigious feat in getting their guns so far forward considering the muddy state of the ground and although it had dried out somewhat it was still in an extremely bad state. Nevertheless, the Grand Battery, as it became known, was finally ready and at about 11.50 a.m. the 80 guns exploded into action sending a series of solid iron balls into the dense ranks of Allied infantry deployed on the slopes to the north of the Ohain road.

It is interesting to note that the four divisions of d'Erlon's Corps – commanded by Generals Quiot, Donzelot, Marcognet and Durutte – numbered almost 18,000 men, mostly veterans, with d'Erlon a veteran himself. When we compare this with the single largest attack of the Peninsular War, by Generals Girard and Gazan at Albuera, which numbered around 8,000 infantry, we may well imagine the strength of d'Erlon's attack and the power carried with it. Indeed, it needed something special to stop it. Also, d'Erlon had deployed his four attacking columns in columns of battalions, each with a width of between 180 and 200 men. His decision to use this more expansive formation of the columns at Waterloo was intended to compensate for the disadvantage the French had laboured under in the Peninsula, where French infantry columns had frequently come to grief at the hands of Wellington's Anglo-Portuguese infantry, who were drawn up in line. Rather belatedly, the French were changing their formation and it almost paid dividends.

The attacking French columns endured an uncomfortable advance, struggling across the muddy fields in the teeth of an increasingly heavy fire of Allied musketry and artillery, not to mention the withering fire being poured into them by the green-clad riflemen of the 95th that occupied the sandpit just to the east of La Haye Sainte. But, gradually, the French columns began to close on the crest of Wellington's ridge to the east of the Brussels road. Once at the crest the columns were immediately engaged by Picton's infantry who opened up a devastating rolling fire along the entire length of the line. However, it was at this point that something unusual happened; the French started to get the upper hand. Of course, there was nothing unusual whatsoever in French infantry getting the better of their opponents in Europe but it had rarely happened in the Peninsula in six years of fighting. But here at Waterloo, during the first major French attack of the day, they were doing just that. All along the crest at the Ohain road the attacking French troops had begun to cross the road and were actually passing through the hedge which partially ran along it. For those who had fought in the Peninsula it must have made a change to have got this far for, apart from at Sorauren, attacking French units rarely got within smelling distance of the British line before being driven back. However, on the field at Waterloo they had actually begun to drive the long, red lines back and for a few minutes were actually established on 'the plateau'. It was the first major French attack of the battle and for a while it looked as if it might succeed. Indeed, the French were on the brink of achieving a major breakthrough but any French thoughts of victory were soon to be quickly and ruthlessly dispelled when they suddenly became the unwilling victims of one of the most famous cavalry charges in history.

Lord Uxbridge, returning from behind Hougoumont where he had been supervising the positioning of some of his cavalry, looked towards La Haye Sainte and saw the dark masses of French infantry passing the farm to both its left and right. Quick to appreciate the situation he immediately galloped over to Somerset and ordered the Household Brigade, sitting at the foot of the reverse slope, to form line and prepare to charge, with the Life Guards and King's Dragoon Guards in the first line with the Horse Guards in support. He then galloped across to the east of the road where he found Ponsonby, patiently waiting whilst Major General Sir Denis Pack's infantry struggled to hold back the French at the crest above him. Uxbridge told Ponsonby to wheel the Union Brigade into line also, the 1st (Royals) and Inniskillings in the first line and the Scots Greys in support. He then returned to join Somerset before, in his own words, he 'put the whole in motion.'[6] Having issued his orders for the charge, Uxbridge took up a position just to the west of the main Brussels road and just in front of the left-hand squadron of the Household Brigade, that of the 1st Life Guards. Somerset's field trumpeter, the 16-year-old John Edwards,[7] then sounded the charge and the Household Brigade trotted forward.

The Household Brigade quickly gained the top of the ridge and charged down the slope to meet General Jacques-Charles Dubois' cuirassiers who were just to the west of La Haye Sainte. The 1st Life Guards were on the right of the line with the King's Dragoon Guards in the centre. On the left came the 2nd Life Guards with the Horse Guards in reserve. The heavy British cavalry came thundering down the slope and crashed into the ranks of Dubois' men,

A quite preposterous depiction of the 1st Life Guards charging French infantry in the midst of battle. Virtually every single thing about this picture is incorrect, particularly the fur caps, save for the fact that the French are on foot and the Life Guards are mounted. However, it gives a wonderful insight into the sheer amount of illustrated material that appeared during the years following the battle. (Anne S. K. Brown)

apparently sending them flying in all directions. Lieutenant Waymouth, of the 2nd Life Guards, who was taken prisoner during the charge, wrote that the Household Brigade and the cuirassiers, 'came to the shock like two walls, in the most perfect manner', and added, 'Having once penetrated their line, we rode over everything opposed to us.'[8] It was indeed an almighty crash as these two bodies of heavy cavalry collided with each other. The Household Brigade sent the French fleeing in all directions, the majority of them having to cut their way out and escape south along the main road as far as a cutting a few hundred yards south of La Haye Sainte where, through sheer weight of numbers, they became jammed and found themselves at the mercy of the Life Guards and King's Dragoon Guards who set about their business with a deadly efficiency, cutting

and hacking in all directions. The British themselves did not get off lightly, however, as a regiment of French chasseurs came to the top of the cutting and fired down into their tightly packed ranks, killing and wounding scores of them.[9] Elsewhere, the 2nd Life Guards and the left-hand squadron of the King's Dragoon Guards crossed to the east of the main road, north of La Haye Sainte, in pursuit of other cuirassiers and in doing so found themselves in amongst the Union Brigade.

Ponsonby's Union Brigade had charged shortly after the Household Brigade. The brigade formed with the 1st (Royals) on the right and the Inniskillings on the left with the Scots Greys in support, although some eyewitnesses claim that all three regiments were in line together at the moment the charge was made. On the extreme French right, Durutte's Division made good progress towards the main Allied line to the west of Papelotte, La Haye and Smohain, whilst on their left Marcognet and Donzelot headed straight for that part of the line held by Pack's Brigade and Major General Willem Frederik Bylandt's Dutch-

This picture is to be compared with the previous illustration of the Life Guards to give a far more realistic impression of what the 2nd Life Guards wore at Waterloo. (Anne S. K. Brown)

A fine depiction of the campaign dress worn by the 23rd Light Dragoons during the Waterloo campaign. The regiment had come to grief at Talavera in 1809 as a result of which they returned home to recover and played no further part in the Peninsular War. Waterloo was the regiment's first campaign since then.
(Anne S. K. Brown)

RIGHT
A Hamilton-Smith engraving of an officer of the 14th Light Dragoons in parade dress.
(Anne S. K. Brown)

Belgians. It is clear from eyewitness accounts that the attacking French troops had passed through the hedge lining the Ohain road and that the 92nd Highlanders were both 'recoiling' and 'in confusion.'[10] In fact, Ponsonby's men charged at the precise moment that the French infantry had gained the crest and as they went up the slope towards it the Union Brigade met the infantry of Pack's and Major General Sir James Kempt's Brigades wheeling back to let them through.[11] Judging by the eyewitness account of Captain Clark-Kennedy, of the Royals, the crucial intervention by the Union Brigade could not have been better timed:

The heads of the French columns, which appeared to me to be nearly close together, had no appearance of having been repulsed or seriously checked. On the contrary … they had forced their way through our line – the heads of the columns were on the Brussels side of the double hedge. There was no British infantry in the immediate front that I saw, and the line that had been, I presume, behind the hedges was wheeled

by sections or divisions to the left, and was firing on the left flank of the left column as it advanced. In fact, the crest of the height had been gained, and the charge of cavalry at the critical moment recovered it. Had the charge been delayed two or three minutes, I feel satisfied it would probably have failed.[12]

The signal for the Union Brigade to charge was given by Major George de Lacy Evans, Ponsonby's aide de camp, who waved his hat in the air to set the brigade moving. In fact, the Scots Greys had already begun to move slowly forward, for their commanding officer, Colonel Hamilton, observing the 92nd in difficulty, ordered them to do so. This is possibly how the Greys became level with both the Inniskillings and Royals who had originally been in front of them, although it is also possible that they moved forward, and a little to their left, in order to avoid the round shot which was continually bounding over the crest. All three heavy cavalry regiments then charged up the muddy slope towards the crest where the French were by now having thoughts of victory.

Thousands of French infantrymen were piling up against the crest of the Ohain road when the 1,100 men of the Union Brigade crashed into them. There was little an infantryman could do to combat the power of the charge once the cavalry got in amongst the massed infantry. The British cavalrymen were big men mounted on big horses and one officer of the 92nd, Lieutenant Winchester, actually described the Greys as having 'walked over' the French column.[13] Indeed, it is easy to imagine the huge grey horses simply knocking down all those who were unfortunate enough to find themselves in the way of the charge. Those who did manage to offer resistance were easily cut down or taken prisoner.

Away to the right of the Scots Greys the other two regiments of the Union Brigade had swept forward also, riding down both Marcognet's and Donzelot's men before charging across the Ohain road and down the slope beyond. Once again, the French could offer little resistance to the charge. Colonel Joseph Muter, commanding the Inniskillings, wrote:

The Inniskillings came in contact with the French columns of infantry almost immediately after clearing the hedge and (I should call it) *chemin creux*. We all agree in thinking that the French columns had nearly gained the crest, perhaps twenty to thirty yards down the slope. We think there were three French columns. The French column did not attempt to form square, nor was it, so far as we could judge, well prepared to repel an attack of cavalry. Our impression is that, from the formation of the ground, the cavalry was not aware what they were to attack, nor the infantry aware of what was coming upon them.[14]

It is interesting to note that Muter thought the French had not gained the crest, a view not shared by Clark-Kennedy of the Royals who, as we have already read, claimed that the French had passed the hedge and had reached the crest. This simply bears out the fact that two men, even though within a few hundred yards of each other, often saw, or thought they saw, totally different events unfolding before them. This perhaps illustrates just how difficult it was, given the smoke and confusion of battle, for participants to actually see what was really happening around them.

Meanwhile, on the right of the Inniskillings the 1st (Royals) had charged into Donzelot's Division and we may well imagine the Royals 'pressing' the French back down the slope in much the same way that a police horse controls a mob of demonstrators, or a large crowd. Here at Waterloo the French infantry, particularly those at the front who were hemmed in by those behind, were unable to offer any resistance whatsoever in their tightly packed crowd and were simply ridden or cut down. After the first few volleys it is almost certain that no French infantryman would have had enough room to go through the process of loading and firing his musket. Only those towards the rear probably had the time and, more importantly, the space to fire back at their assailants. The first phase of the charge of the Union and Household Brigades can be said to have come to a dramatic and very successful conclusion with the repulse of d'Erlon's infantry. Between them the two brigades, numbering no more than 2,300 sabres, had scattered approximately 15,000 French infantry, inflicting severe casualties, the precise number of which is unknown, and taking around 3,000 prisoners, with scores more apparently escaping in the turmoil afterwards. Two eagles were also taken, by Clark-Kennedy of the Royals and by Sergeant Charles Ewart of

TOP LEFT
Major General Sir William Ponsonby, commander of the Union Cavalry Brigade at Waterloo. He died during the great cavalry charge on the afternoon of 18 June. (Courtesy of the Council of the National Army Museum)

TOP RIGHT
Lieutenant General Henry William Paget, 2nd Earl of Uxbridge, lost a leg at Waterloo. There was a frosty relationship between Uxbridge and Wellington, as a result of him eloping with Wellington's sister-in-law. When asked how he felt about Uxbridge's appointment (the two men had not served together in the Peninsula) Wellington replied, 'Damn it, I don't care, provided he don't run off with me!' (Courtesy of the Council of the National Army Museum)

BOTTOM LEFT
Major General Lord Edward Somerset, commander of the 1st British Brigade, otherwise known as the Household Brigade. (© English Heritage)

BOTTOM RIGHT
Sir James Kempt served as a major general on Wellington's staff during the campaigns in Spain and France, and during Waterloo he took over the 5th Division when Picton was killed during the battle. (Courtesy of the Council of the National Army Museum)

the Greys. It was, in other words, a quite devastating attack and the French would not try any other serious infantry attack on Wellington's left centre for the rest of the day. However, it was now that Uxbridge's cavalry needed to show restraint. They had reached the bottom of the muddy valley floor and, having overthrown d'Erlon's column, set about securing prisoners who were escorted back to the Allied lines and then on to Brussels by both British infantry and cavalry. Indeed, the Inniskillings, who had a strength of only 396, having been so reduced during the charge, were further reduced in numbers when a squadron was sent to the rear in charge of French prisoners. But, not content with the success of the initial charge, the two brigades now demonstrated that the old failings of the British cavalry, first revealed at Vimeiro and Talavera, were still latent in 1815.

Many regimental officers had been either killed or wounded during the charge, whilst Uxbrige himself – by his own admission – was in no position to control his cavalry having gone forward with the Household Brigade. With the Union Brigade pouring down the slope on the east of the Brussels road, along with the 2nd Life Guards and the left-hand squadron of the King's Dragoon Guards, and with the Household Brigade galloping in pursuit of Dubois' beaten cuirassiers, all order became lost. The moment that every fighting cavalryman dreamt of – and every good cavalry officer dreaded – had arrived.

The British heavy cavalrymen's blood was well and truly up and having inflicted so much slaughter on the hapless French infantry, who fled across the valley like a flock of sheep, they were not about to stop now. After all, sitting about 300 metres or so further on, on a ridge just south of La Haye Sainte, was Napoleon's Grand Battery of over 80 guns. The two heavy cavalry brigades were now formed in a very rough line with the Scots Greys on the far left, with the Inniskillings on their right and the 1st (Royals) beyond these. The 2nd Life Guards and the left-hand squadron of the King's Dragoon Guards completed the 'line' to the east of the Brussels road. To the west of the road were, from left to right, looking south, the two remaining squadrons of the King's Dragoon Guards and the two squadrons of the 1st Life Guards. These were supported by the two squadrons of Horse Guards. Both brigades now pressed on up the muddy slopes to the Grand Battery where they began slaughtering the gunners and drivers. Away to the east, the Scots Greys rallied before attacking the guns.

Uxbridge himself thought that as many as 40 guns were put out of action, having been informed of the fact by a French artillery officer whom he later met in Paris. However, they could not be brought off because of the counter-attack by Napoleon's cavalry. The British cavalry rode in and out of the guns for quite some time within just 300 metres or so of La Belle Alliance, from where Napoleon watched with horror. Meanwhile, thousands of retreating French infantry who had been overtaken by the cavalry now came up and passed through the guns, apparently oblivious to the slaughtering going on there. Meanwhile Uxbridge tried desperately to get his men to heed the trumpets sounding the recall, but to little avail. The heavy cavalry continued to enjoy themselves until, exhausted by these efforts, they finally turned and looked back across the valley towards their own lines. It was at this point that they fully appreciated the extremely dangerous position they had got themselves into for, as they gazed back across the valley, and over the carnage they had left in their wake, they saw hundreds of enemy cavalrymen riding in from both left and right, cavalry they would now have to fight if they were going to make it back to their own lines.

What the two brigades of cavalry now had to do was to run the gauntlet of both infantry and cavalry in order to fight their way home. Scores would not succeed. The enemy cavalry approaching were Brigade General Martin-Charles Gobrecht's Brigade from General Charles-Claude Jaquinot's Division, being the 3rd and 4th Lancers, whilst from the direction of La Belle Alliance came two regiments of cuirassiers, the 5th and 10th. The men of the British cavalry regiments gathered themselves together for the return journey but had not gone far when the enemy cavalry struck. Scores of isolated British cavalrymen were cut down or speared by enemy lancers who now took their revenge for the devastation the British had wrought earlier. The two British brigades were scattered in isolated little groups who were easy prey for the French. The lancers were by no means invincible but they had the very distinct advantage of having a 2.75-metre-long lance with which to inflict their suffering on their adversaries who would, generally, have not been able to get within striking distance of them. It was a formidable weapon, demonstrated with terrible efficiency upon Colonel Sir John Colborne's Brigade at Albuera some four years earlier, and the lancers went to work with equal venom at Waterloo. Scores of wounded British cavalrymen were killed by the lancers, who showed no mercy; the Greys, for example, suffered more dead than wounded, which is rather unusual. The situation of the two heavy brigades was desperate. Ponsonby, leading the Union Brigade, was killed by enemy lancers, as was the commanding officer of the Scots Greys. In fact, only eight out of 23 officers of the Scots Greys were unwounded. The commanding officers of the King's Dragoon Guards and the 1st Life Guards were also killed. It was during this phase of the charge that the majority of the British heavy cavalry casualties probably occurred, which is backed up by de Lacy Evans who subsequently wrote, 'It was at this part of the transaction that almost the whole of the loss of the

Captain William Tyrwhitt Drake, Royal Hose Guards, *c*.1815. Tyrwhitt Drake was among the 20 officers and 255 men from the unit who fought with Somerset's Household Cavalry Brigade at Waterloo. (Courtesy of the Council of the National Army Museum)

The 1st King's Dragoon Guards, *c.*1813/15. The regiment was another of those which had not seen active service for many years but performed well at Waterloo. (Anne S.K. Brown)

Brigade took place.'[15] There was no support for the Union Brigade as the Greys, who should have been in the second line, were up front in the thick of the fight. To the west of the Brussels road, however, the Horse Guards had maintained some semblance of order and were able to support and bring off the Household Brigade without too much damage to themselves. Nevertheless, on the whole, the fight for survival for the two British heavy cavalry brigades was not a particularly successful one.

To the west of the main road things were only just showing signs of improvement. The Royal Horse Guards, dressed in their blue tunics, had gone into action numbering just over 200 sabres, but this small number of troops was enough to be able to help bring off the remains of the Household Brigade. Of the seven regiments of heavy cavalry which took part in Uxbridge's charge, only the Royal Horse Guards managed to maintain some semblance of order. They had formed the reserve of the Household Brigade and although they suffered just under 50 per cent casualties for the day, the majority of which almost certainly occurred during the charge, they stuck to their task and were able to protect the survivors of the charge to the west of the main road as they made their way back to the Allied lines. In fact, theirs was a timely intervention because, like the Union Brigade, the regiments of the Household Brigade had been enjoying themselves at the Grand Battery, cutting down the gunners and generally doing much mischief. However, these too quickly became exhausted by their efforts and when Brigade General Étienne-Jacques Travers' cuirassiers counter-attacked they were in no condition to offer serious resistance. The Household Brigade also suffered heavy losses from the fire of Lieutenant General Honoré Reille's divisions which lined the track from Hougoumont to La Belle Alliance, just beyond the Grand Battery.

Uxbridge himself, having led the Household Brigade, was in no position to control affairs, and found himself in a similar position to Brigadier General Robert Ballard Long at Campo Maior four years earlier. Despite attempts to call his men to order Uxbridge found he had lost all control of his brigade:

After the overthrow of the cuirassiers, I had in vain attempted to stop my people by sounding the Rally, but neither voice nor trumpet availed; so I went back to seek the support of the 2nd line, which unhappily had not followed the movements of the heavy cavalry. Had I, when I sounded the Rally, found only four well-formed squadrons coming steadily along at an easy trot, I feel certain that the loss the first line suffered when they were finally forced back would have been avoided,

A fine depiction of an officer of the Royal Scots Greys at Waterloo, although on the actual day his appearance would have been a great deal sorrier than this, following two days of campaigning in very bad weather. (Anne S. K. Brown)

and most of these guns might have been secured, for it was obvious the effect of that charge had been prodigious, and for the rest of the day, although the cuirassiers frequently attempted to break into our lines, they always did it *mollement* and as if they expected something more behind the curtain.[16]

It is curious that Uxbridge says that the second line, presuming this to be the Royal Horse Guards, 'unhappily had not followed the movements of the heavy cavalry'. The implication is that they should have been close on the heels on the first line, whereas surely by remaining a good distance to the rear they were able to maintain some order and be there to come to their comrades' aid when required. The Greys, to the east of the main road, had followed the movements of the Union Brigade but had been so close, probably in the first line, that they could not hold back once the charge got underway. Furthermore, from the casualties sustained by the Royal Horse Guards, it would appear that they had, after all, followed their comrades, or perhaps they were simply brought up afterwards and suffered their casualties in covering the retreat. The heavy cavalry also received assistance from the infantry during the retreat when Kempt advanced some of his infantry down the slope to the east of La Haye Sainte, partly to secure the many French prisoners and partly to cover the retreat of the remnants of the Union Brigade.

But the most effective support for the beleaguered heavy brigades, and in particularly the Union Brigade, came in the shape of Major General John Vandeleur's Brigade which had sat, along with Major General Hussey Vivian's Brigade, on the ridge above Papelotte. Vandeleur ordered his brigade, consisting of three squadrons each of the 11th, 12th and 16th Light Dragoons, to move in support of the Union Brigade, the remains of which were floundering in the mud away to his right. The brigade was positioned directly north of Papelotte, close to the Papelotte–Verd–Cocu road, more of a track which ran north down across the eastern end of the reverse and north to the latter hamlet. However, the ground in his immediate front presented him with two problems. First, a deep sunken lane, leading down to the east of the farm of La Haye, barred his way. Second, any move to his right and slightly to the south in order to cross the Wavre road at an easier point would bring him within range of Durutte's skirmishers, who at the time were attacking Papelotte. Therefore, he had his brigade wheel to the right and move along the reverse slope before turning to their left and passing through the Hanoverians of Colonel Best and Colonel von Vincke. Finally, the brigade crossed the Wavre road and, presumably, the Ohain road, before charging Jacquinot's lancers and the units of d'Erlon's Corps still remaining in front of the Allied position and in the valley.

The charge by Vandeleur's Brigade had the desired effect of extricating the Union Brigade from the confusion at the bottom of the valley and beyond. That it was carried out with complete success is open to debate, however, as the 12th Light Dragoons demonstrated the same tendency to lose any sense of an ordered attack and, as a consequence, suffered heavy casualties during the charge. Indeed, the regiment almost found itself on the verge of requiring rescue themselves. The 16th Light Dragoons, on the other hand, adopted a far more professional approach and the regiment's officers managed to hold their men in check and prevent them from getting out of hand. Significantly, the 11th Light Dragoons remained at the top of the ridge as a reserve and thus avoided becoming embroiled in the fight. In spite of the 12th charging further than they should have done, Vandeleur's three veteran Peninsular regiments performed their job well in supporting the Union Brigade at the moment of the latter's greatest danger. Losses within the ranks of the 12th Light Dragoons were fairly severe but the entire losses for Vandeleur's Brigade as a whole throughout the day totalled less than any of the individual regiments of the Union Brigade, which is, perhaps, a reflection of the difference in experience between the two brigades and in the way in which they were handled.

Casualties in the Union and Household Brigades were certainly severe, but were perhaps not as severe as generations of historians would have us believe, as we shall shortly see. The Union Brigade lost 525 killed, wounded and missing, a large proportion of the latter being amongst the dead. This was out of a total strength of 1,181, which represents a loss of just below 44.5 per cent. It is also

The 1st King's Dragoon Guards charging the Cuirassiers at Waterloo, a spirited painting by Harry Payne. (Soldiers of Gloucestershire Museum www.glosters.org.uk)

The 6th Inniskilling Dragoons charging at Waterloo. Along with the Scots Greys and the 1st (Royal) Dragoons, the Inniskillings provided the Irish element to the so-called 'Union' Brigade. The regiment claimed to have captured a French Eagle at Waterloo but lost it again during the fighting. The commanding officer later appealed for the regiment to be allowed to wear the eagle as its cap badge. (Anne S. K. Brown)

interesting to note regimental casualty figures. For example, the figures quoted in Siborne's *History of the Waterloo Campaign* (first published in 1844) show that the Scots Greys suffered more dead than wounded, 102 against 97, which probably reflects the ferocity of the attack by Jacquinot's lancers, who apparently thought little of finishing off any wounded enemy cavalrymen. The 1st (Royal) Dragoons showed a similarly high ratio of dead to wounded, 89 against 97, whilst the Inniskillings returned 73 dead against 116 wounded. It is very unusual to note also that the Scots Greys posted not a single officer or private as missing. In fact, the entire Union Brigade returned just 38 men missing, which again is probably accounted for by the merciless conduct shown towards wounded and dismounted cavalrymen by some of the French cavalry. The Household Brigade, which showed a strength of 1,226 at the beginning of the day, suffered 533 casualties, of which 250 were missing. The casualty rate of about 43.5 per cent is about the same as the Union Brigade and is still very high.

It is these high casualty figures that have been used by generations of historians to try to illustrate the indiscipline and even the failure of Uxbridge's charge. However, and this is where I lay the case for the defence, it is difficult to establish just how many of the 525 casualties in the Union Brigade and of the 533 casualties in the Household Brigade were sustained during the charge itself, for it should be remembered that although the brigade was in no fit state to repeat the exercise it did, nevertheless, remain on the battlefield for the remainder of the day, during which time it would have taken further casualties. Although it is a fairly safe bet that the majority of the brigades' casualties occurred during

The Scots Greys get stuck into the French at Waterloo. Although the Union Brigade was severely handled by the French cavalry after its initial charge, the brigade inflicted considerable damage to d'Erlon's infantry and, more significantly, to Napoleon's Grand Battery. (Anne S. K. Brown)

the charge against d'Erlon's Corps and the Grand Battery afterwards, we can be quite certain that not all of them were. The Union Brigade suffered casualties from the Grand Battery even before it had set off on its charge, whilst Clark-Kennedy of the Royals later wrote that the Union Brigade suffered severely during the afternoon when it was moved to the west of the Brussels road to support the infantry line that was buckling under intense pressure from the French. We can never be certain how many men were killed and wounded during the afternoon but if we believe what Clark-Kennedy wrote we can be sure casualties were not light.

Only a fool would suggest that the respective casualty figures for the Union and Household Brigades at Waterloo were purely as a result of Uxbridge's charge. After all, it would mean that neither brigade suffered a single casualty throughout the rest of the battle, which lasted for a further six hours or so after the charge had ended. To assume this was the case is simply absurd.

THE FRENCH CAVALRY AT WATERLOO

The controversy surrounding the famous charge by the British heavy cavalry at Waterloo is equalled, if not surpassed, by that which surrounds the massed charges of the French cavalry during the afternoon of 18 June 1815. Indeed, it is not possible to pick up a book about the battle without reading yet another explanation accounting for Marshal Michel Ney's behaviour on that fateful afternoon.

Wellington's infantry behind the ridge to the west of the Brussels road had been taking a fearful pounding from Napoleon's artillery, and from incursions by French infantry, throughout the afternoon. In fact, from accounts left to us it would appear that this 'unremitting shower of death', as one British soldier put it, had brought Wellington's line almost to breaking point. Almost three hours of constant shelling by French artillery had wrought havoc amongst the densely packed ranks of Allied infantry. Wounded soldiers steamed away from the front line, carried by unwounded comrades or escorted by many whose will to fight had simply vanished.

It is not clear whether Marshal Ney mistook this as a sign of an Allied retreat. We cannot be certain. After all, the view from the French positions allowed no sight of what was happening on the other side of Wellington's ridge, and unless Ney possessed X-ray vision he could not have seen what was happening there. What is certain, however, is that *something* happened on the Allied ridge which led him to believe that Wellington's line was on the brink of collapse and encouraged him to launch Napoleon's cavalry in wave after wave against

An incident depicting the French cavalry charges on the afternoon of 18 June. It very ably demonstrates the folly of cavalry charging four ranks of infantry in square, with each face bristling with steel. Unless supported by artillery or infantry such attacks were doomed to fail, unless some huge slice of good fortune befell them, such as a dead horse smashing into the ranks.
(Anne S. K. Brown)

Wellington's line in the hope that the Allied line would be finally pushed over the edge into ignominious defeat.

It was around 4 p.m. when Ney began to draw up the massed squadrons of Napoleon's cavalry, and it is doubtful whether the world had ever seen such a fabulous array on a battlefield. It is certainly the case that Wellington's British infantry had never seen such a display. In the Iberian Peninsula they had grown used to seeing French dragoons, chasseurs and the odd hussar regiment but they had never come across cuirassiers, carabineers, horse grenadiers, Dutch lancers and the like. It was all quite spectacular. And it was a relief also, for no sooner had Ney formed his massed squadrons for the attack than the French guns ceased playing upon the Allied line for fear of hitting their own side. Thus, when the French cavalry went pounding up the muddy slopes to attack Wellington's line it may have looked as if the end was nigh but it was, in fact, a blessed relief for the hard-pressed infantry waiting on the reverse slope.

When Napoleon's cavalry assembled between La Haye Sainte and the orchard to the east of Hougoumont the emperor himself was apparently absent from the field, allegedly feeling unwell. And so it was that command of the army at this vital period of the battle devolved upon Ney, who is said to have been suffering from a kind of 'shell shock' or battle fatigue following the campaigns in Russia and Germany. It certainly revealed a flaw in the French system of command. Indeed, Wellington has often been accused of being what we would probably today call a 'control freak', a man who was loath to delegate any responsibility to anyone other than his most trusted lieutenants, and only then on rare occasions. Napoleon, on the other hand, was more than comfortable allowing his marshals and generals to accept responsibility on the field of battle. The problem was, however, that by allowing Ney to take the reins at this most important time, Napoleon was effectively handing command of his army to a man who was evidently not suited to command on the day. It was something that Wellington would never have done. In fact, Wellington has provided us with a great 'barometer' at Waterloo as he always appeared to be at the right place at the right time. He was simply unwilling to allow anyone else to display initiative, and although this had long-term consequences for the British Army it certainly paid dividends on 18 June 1815.

The story of the French cavalry charges is simple enough. Once Ney had decided to launch his massed cavalry against Wellington's line he formed them in their regiments and for the next two hours or so led them in a series of charges which effectively achieved nothing whatsoever, other than becoming one of the most memorable episodes on any battlefield in history. It is estimated that there were 12 charges, each charge consisting of several waves of cavalry that swept up to the crest before disappearing out of sight of the main French Army behind the reverse slope. Here the cavalry came face to face with numerous Allied infantry squares, formed in a rough checkerboard formation,

A famous but somewhat inaccurate painting showing the French cavalry charges at their height. The cavalry are coming on way too fast. As Captain Mercer famously said afterwards in his journal, 'There was none of your furious galloping'. After the initial waves the ground would have been churned up to such an extent that it would have been impossible for cavalry to come on at anything other than a canter, particularly as they were going uphill and, presumably, after already having executed at least a couple of charges previously. (akg-images)

each supporting its neighbour with musketry. Each infantry square was formed of four ranks, bristling with bayonets, which proved an impenetrable barrier against Ney's cavalry. As long as the men inside each square held their nerve there would be no way through for the French cavalry who swarmed around the squares, thrashing away with their swords or lances, or firing their pistols or carbines into the squares at close range. Hundreds of French cavalrymen were lost on the bayonets of the infantry, or through their musketry. Then, realising the hopelessness of their situation the French rode on, passing between the squares before being dispatched by the waiting squadrons of Allied cavalry. Ney's men then turned to the west and passed to the north of Hougoumont before swinging left and heading south back to their starting positions in order to form for the next charge. The distance covered by each survivor in each charge, therefore, was about 4 kilometres from start to finish.

Naturally, each charge became more difficult than the previous one. The slope up which Ney's squadrons charged became littered with an increasing number of dead and wounded horses and men, whilst the already muddy ground was churned into a boggy morass as each wave went up the slope. The horses' exhaustion can easily be imagined. Indeed, it is little wonder that Captain Alexander Cavalié Mercer, commanding his troop of horse artillery on the crest, was moved to comment, 'there was none of your furious galloping', a reference, no doubt, to the popular image of cavalry charging full tilt at their opponents. And so it went on, with the French cavalry, frustrated and growing ever more desperate, struggling to

Major General William Ponsonby meets a sticky end during the charge of the Union Brigade at Waterloo. His horse was blown and got bogged down in a muddy field, leaving Ponsonby as easy prey for the vicious French lancers. A recent controversial theory, however, suggests that Ponsonby was taken prisoner but was only killed when a group of Scots Greys attempted to rescue him. (Courtesy of the Council of the National Army Museum)

pass the morass of mud, men and horses, to get to grips with an enemy that, with the passing of each charge, was growing ever more confident.

Much criticism has been levelled at Ney for forming so vast an array of cavalry on such a relatively narrow front, barely 900 metres between La Haye Sainte and the orchard at Hougoumont. But the greater criticism was, and always will be, Ney's failure to support the cavalry with infantry and artillery and, perhaps more perplexing, the complete failure by the French cavalry to spike the Allied guns.

When Ney's massed squadrons set off towards Wellington's ridge the Allied infantry commanders quickly ordered their battalions to form squares, the traditional and most effective way of dealing with cavalry. Once in these formations, however, the infantry were easy meat for infantry and artillery. And yet, for over two hours between 4 p.m. and 6 p.m. on the afternoon of 18 June 1815, barely a single infantryman advanced in support of the cavalry nor was a single gun brought forward to wreak havoc amongst the static and vulnerable – to infantry and artillery at least – squares. Of course, as the afternoon progressed the ground was churned over to such an extent that it would have been extremely difficult to get guns forward, though not impossible. And as for the infantry, perhaps they thought better of straying into the path of thousands of charging horses. But it is inconceivable that Napoleon's infantry officers failed to appreciate the opportunity afforded to them once the cavalry had forced Wellington's infantry into squares. So why did they not advance? It is a mystery. Whatever it was – an oversight, a lack of command, bad ground, fear – it allowed a golden opportunity to slip away.

As each wave of French cavalry swept over the Allied ridge Wellington's gun crews abandoned their guns for the relative safety of the infantry squares, leaving their pieces at the mercy of the French. And yet, for some unfathomable reason, none of the guns were spiked. It was a fairly simple process. Each cavalryman would have carried a pouch with headless nails and it would have been the easiest thing in the world for a trooper to dismount, take out one of the nails and drive it into the touch hole of the gun, rendering it completely useless. In effect, the gun would have been turned into a piece of scrap metal. For an infantryman the job would have been done by driving a bayonet into the gun and breaking it off. Again, an incredibly simple process. So why was this not done? Surely it would have occurred to these experienced French cavalrymen that by spiking the guns it would have left Wellington bereft of most of his guns to the west of the Brussels road. Various explanations have been put forward. John Keegan, in his classic *Face of Battle* (London, 1976), even suggests that a French cavalryman, with his assumed superior social standing, would never dismount in front of socially inferior enemy infantry. It seems unlikely but plausible. But perhaps the reason was far simpler.

An officer of the Inniskilling Dragoons fallen from his horse and trapped beneath the wheels of a gun at Waterloo. One would not give much for his chances unless one of his comrades arrived swiftly to spirit him away to safety. (Anne S. K. Brown)

Quite possibly, in the heat of battle and with musket balls flying around as thick as hail, the French cavalrymen simply didn't relish the idea of dismounting and going about the business of driving the nails into the guns. After all, it was a simple process but it was not a particularly quick one, and it may have been easy – albeit extremely risky – for an infantryman, or indeed a gunner, to run out of his square and deal with the cavalryman. There was obviously something up there on the bloody ridge at Waterloo that prevented Napoleon's cavalrymen, all experienced soldiers who had spent years campaigning throughout Europe and fighting on many a bloody battlefield, from dismounting and spiking the guns. But whatever it was we will never know.

CONCLUSIONS

One final point concerning the French cavalry charges: it is worth pointing out that the verdict upon the British heavy cavalry charge at Waterloo has usually been based upon the casualty figures, something which I have sought to address and dispel in this chapter. It is curious that in the many accounts of the Battle of Waterloo none have ever claimed that the casualty figures for Napoleon's cavalry on 18 June were as a result of the series of charges made by them between 4 p.m. and 6 p.m., the correct conclusion being that the casualty figures were for the entire day as a whole. Why is it, therefore, that the casualty figures for the Union and Household Brigades are almost universally attributed solely to the charge and not the day as a whole, even though they played a part in the rest of the battle following the charge?

So, having looked at the end result in terms of casualties of the British heavy cavalry charge, what did it actually achieve? Well, I believe it achieved a great deal. At a cost of just over 1,000 casualties Uxbridge's cavalry had completely destroyed the first great attack by Napoleon's infantry at Waterloo.[17] In fact, such was the effect of the charge that the French would not attack in any great strength to the east of the main Brussels road for the rest of the day. This left Wellington free to concentrate on the assaults on his right and centre. The struggle here was so intense that one cannot believe that Wellington would have been able to hang on had the French been able to launch further attacks against his left. True, the Prussian intervention occupied Napoleon's right flank during the late afternoon, but any further French attacks on the scale of d'Erlon's before the Prussian arrival would probably have tested even Wellington's resolve.

As for the conduct of the charge, it almost certainly gave Wellington a sense of *déjà vu*, as he harked back, no doubt, to Vimeiro and Talavera. In fact, he is reputed to have turned to Uxbridge and said, somewhat sarcastically, 'Well, Paget, I hope you are satisfied with your cavalry now.'[18] Much has been written about Uxbridge's absence from the Peninsula and there is little doubt that he was indeed sorely missed. However, when it came to the final test at Waterloo even he was found wanting. His command of the rearguard during the retreat from Quatre Bras was exemplary but on 18 June he allowed the heavy cavalry to charge too far, primarily because he had taken up a position from where he was unable to control the charge, as he himself pointed out later. 'I committed a great mistake in having myself led the attack. The carrière once begun, the leader is no better than any other man; whereas, if I had placed myself at the head of the 2nd line, there is no saying what great advantages might not have accrued from it.'[19]

It is also worth considering whether Uxbridge or indeed Wellington underestimated the French infantry or perhaps even overestimated their own. Had they become complacent after years of success in the Peninsula? After all, Wellington had grown used to seeing the French driven off countless battlefields in Portugal and Spain, which Uxbridge

The French eagle belonging to the French 105th *Régiment d'Infanterie*. Arguments raged afterwards as to who captured the eagle. There is little doubt that Captain Clark-Kennedy of the 1st Dragoons was responsible for killing the officer carrying the prized bird but it fell across the neck of the horse belonging to Corporal Styles of the same regiment. Styles grabbed the eagle and immediately carried it from the field in triumph, much to the chagrin of Clark-Kennedy. (Courtesy of the Council of the National Army Museum)

The Union Brigade on the early afternoon of 18 June, doing what all good cavalry were trained to do at such moments; spiking the enemy's guns. Every cavalryman carried a pouch with headless nails and the simple driving of one of these into the touch hole of an artillery piece effectively turned it into a piece of scrap metal. It remains a mystery why not a single Allied gun, overrun by the French cavalry on the afternoon of 18 June, was not similarly spiked. A French officer later admitted that as many as 40 French guns were put out of action by the British heavy cavalry during their charge on 18 June. (Courtesy of René Chartrand)

would have been well aware of, and perhaps they thought the outcome of d'Erlon's attack a forgone conclusion. Did the relative initial success of the French assault take Uxbridge and Wellington by surprise, forcing them to make rather hasty preparations for the heavy cavalry charge? There is certainly evidence to support this, with Uxbridge making a hurried dash from one side of the main road to the other, leaving some with the impression that the Scots Greys were to act as a reserve whilst others obviously thought otherwise. Then, without a moment to lose, the charge was launched, with the ensuing result examined above. I would suggest that, with more time and due care and attention, more precise preparations could have been made, with the individual brigade and regimental commanders being made aware of just exactly what their role would be in the coming charge. At Waterloo split-second timing was required and, as we have already seen, at least one British officer thought that the charge would have failed had it been delayed by just two or three minutes.[20] Ultimately, Uxbridge blamed himself for the error in not adequately organising a reserve and in his biography of his illustrious ancestor the Marquess of Anglesey wrote that Uxbridge 'was haunted by this error' for the rest of his life.[21] However, this is to detract from the more significant and wider achievement of the Union and Household Brigades at Waterloo, which Anglesey quite perfectly summed up:

> Whatever blame must attach to Uxbridge for leading the charge himself, it cannot be denied that by choosing exactly the right moment to launch it he had so completely smashed an infantry corps and a large portion of its artillery that it was virtually out of action until late in the day and then so reduced in numbers and enthusiasm as to have no major effect on the battle.[22]

Despite the criticism levelled at Uxbridge and the British heavy cavalry at Waterloo it must be admitted that, when we analyse the casualties suffered by the Union and Household Brigades and the damage inflicted upon d'Erlon's infantry in return, the British cavalry charge was a successful one.

However, when we examine the massed charges by Napoleon's cavalry between 4 p.m. and 6 p.m. it is difficult to make any case whatsoever for them being anything other than a complete and utter disaster. Indeed, there were three main results of the charges, all of which were to the benefit of the Allies. First, it gave the hard-pressed Allied infantry some much-needed relief, albeit temporary, from the French artillery barrage, the French guns being unable to fire whilst the charges were in progress. Secondly, the charges failed to break any of the Allied squares but resulted in thousands of casualties amongst the French cavalry; and, thirdly, and perhaps most importantly, it bought Wellington two hours of valuable time. After all, Wellington's strategy on 18 June was based on receiving assistance from the Prussians who were still some way off when the battle began. The time that Napoleon frittered away in needless cavalry charges effectively handed the Allies two hours, during which time the Prussians were able to reach the battlefield to make their telling contribution to the day's victory. We can only imagine what might have happened had Napoleon launched his Guard two hours earlier. But that, as they say, is history. As the old adage goes, 'time once lost is rarely regained'.

A nice Simkin depiction of a clash between British Horse Guards and French cuirassiers. Whether two formed bodies of cavalry would go head-to-head at this speed and in this manner is open to debate. It is a subject nicely dealt with by John Keegan in his classic *Face of Battle*. Much depended on consent, and on whether the two bodies were willing to open out their ranks to allow the enemy through in order to engage in close quarter combat. Eyewitness accounts would suggest that formed bodies of cavalry did indeed clash 'like two walls coming together', although whether it happened in the manner depicted by Simkin is unlikely. (Anne S. K. Brown)

CHAPTER 8

THE PRUSSIAN ARMY AT WATERLOO

CHARLES ESDAILE

In all the many years that historians have been writing about the Battle of Waterloo, few issues have proved as contentious as that of the role played by the Prussian Army. In brief, at one end of the spectrum there are those who regard the battle as a largely British affair in which the Prussians played but a minor role, while at the other there are those who rather claim that the battle was in reality a Prussian victory.[1] For a good example of the former tendency – one which is, of course, to be found most commonly among British accounts of the battle – we might cite David Howarth, whose work *A Near Run Thing: The Day of Waterloo* (London, 1968) over 40 years on remains one of the most attractive and accessible introductions to the subject that has ever been published. Thus, Howarth bases his account of the fight on the personal experiences of 14 participants in the battle, but of these not one is Prussian, while the general picture that we have of the Prussian role in the battle is neither very full nor very complimentary. Throughout the book there are scarcely half a dozen references to the forces of Field Marshal Gebhard Leberecht von Blücher, and those that do exist paint a picture that is barely more positive than it is negative. Blücher, true, is given full credit for promising to send help to Wellington in the aftermath of the severe defeat of Ligny, and, in the course of the morning of 18 June, doing everything he could to hasten the march of his troops from Wavre to the fringes of the Waterloo battlefield, while his character is painted in terms that are reasonably friendly. On the other hand Howarth repeats the distinctly dubious story that, to paraphrase Wellington, not only did Blücher pick the fattest man in his army to ride to him with the news that Napoleon had crossed the border at the completely unexpected spot of Charleroi, but that said officer had taken 30 hours to travel 48 kilometres. And, once the Prussians finally get into the action, Howarth rather spoils the effect by alleging that Blücher misjudged the place at which he should make his major effort and implying that the troops closest to Wellington's left wing were dispatched in the wrong direction. Thus:

> Now, at the time when the help of the Prussians was needed most urgently, they were marching not towards the ridge, but away. The duke knew that Blücher was attacking Napoleon's flank down in the village of Plancenoit. But this was not even in sight from the middle of the ridge: the spire of the village church could be seen from the left-hand end of the line, but that was all. He did not know how heavy the attack was or how successful. At best it was only an indirect help which would occupy some of Napoleon's forces. What he needed was direct help, a few thousand men who were not yet battle weary, to stop the gaps in the line, or to join it on the left so that he could move some of his own men towards

the centre. He had been sending aides all the afternoon along the ridge and beyond it to report on the Prussians' progress or to try to hurry them. Now he sent another, a colonel named Fremantle, to tell the nearest Prussian commander that the situation was desperate and to ask for help at once. Fremantle found the commander of the leading Prussian corps, General von Zieten. Von Zieten promised to come as soon as the whole of his corps was assembled, but he was reluctant to commit it bit by bit, which was a sound enough conventional decision. Freemantle, fretting with respectful impatience, said he could not go back to the Duke with an answer like that. But Von Zieten kept him waiting while he sent one of his own officers forward to reconnoitre. And that officer … saw the crowds of wounded, deserters and prisoners making for the forest, and came back to report that Wellington was in full retreat. Freemantle could not contradict him: by then, so far as he knew, it might have happened. And Von Zieten turned his troops and marched away to the south to support the rest of the Prussians at Plancenoit.[2]

As can be seen from the quotation, as the Prussian general most closely involved in the decision not to give direct support to Wellington's left, Lieutenant General Hans von Zieten is absolved from the charge of having acted out of wilfulness or anti-British feeling, but even so a few pages on the accusation is repeated that he was, to quote Howarth, 'marching away from the battle'. General Carl von Müffling – the same staff officer who had supposedly taken so long to reach Brussels from Charleroi on 15 June – is admittedly given the credit for galloping after Zieten's Corps and bringing it back to the ridge, but we hear little of what the Prussians actually did there, while the desperate fight at Plancenoit is dealt with in no more than a line or two. Thus: 'The fight against the Prussians at Plancenoit was still undecided. The main road back to France … was threatened by their advance; already their cannon fire was falling not far short of it.'[3] How the Prussians got this far, Howarth does not say, but at all events it appears that the threat which they posed could not have been that great, for very soon we learn that 'two battalions of the Garde … attacked at Plancenoit and turned the Prussians out of the village, and so removed the immediate threat to the flank and rear of [Napoleon's] army'.[4] Nor, meanwhile, do things get better as Napoleon's Army collapses in rout. We hear of the Prussians pursuing the French, certainly, but the very fact that they were in a fit state to pursue the enemy is used as ammunition against them. To quote Howarth yet again:

[Wellington's] army was exhausted. It had fought for nine hours. A few of the Prussians, at Plancenoit, had been in action for four hours, but Von Zieten's corps had not been in it for much longer than an hour, and more units were constantly arriving too late to take part at all.[5]

In the event, though, it transpires that the Prussians do not pursue very far – by the time that the fleeing French reached the village of Genappe some 6.5 kilometres from the main French position at the inn of La Belle Alliance, 'there were very few Prussians in pursuit; their infantry had halted, and perhaps 4,000 horsemen were pursuing 40,000 French'.[6] As a crowning image of the Prussian role in the battle, then, one is left not with a moment of glory, but rather with a moment of farce in the form of the famous incident in which the Royal Horse Artillery battery commanded by Captain Cavalié Mercer is shot to pieces by some stray Prussian gunners (complete with comic-book German officer: 'Ah! Mein Gott! Mein Gott! Vat is it you dos, sare! Dat is your friends de Proossiens, an you kills dem! Ah, mein Gott, mein Gott, vill you no stop, sare!').[7]

The line taken by Howarth is not an isolated one. On the contrary, indeed, it is one with a long history. In 1840, Edward Cotton, a veteran of the battle who had fought in the ranks of the 7th Hussars, published an account of the campaign entitled *A Voice from Waterloo* in which he took firm issue with what he perceived as a growing tendency to exaggerate the role of the Prussians. For example:

> It is doubtful whether Napoleon could have driven the British from the ground even if the Prussians had not arrived. The English troops had maintained their position for eight hours against the most experienced army and the ablest general ever France sent into the field: not a British regiment was broken, nor the Allied Army in a panic, nor, at any time, in serious danger of being penetrated. Further, even if the Prussians had not arrived, we are inclined to think that Napoleon could not, in the exhausted and dispirited condition of his troops, and the lateness of the hour, have driven the British from their ground. The junction of the Prussians was a part of Wellington's combinations for the battle. Their flank movement at Waterloo was similar to Desaix's from Novi to Marengo with this no small difference: that upon Bülow's troops joining, they found the Allied Army firm and unbroken and rather in advance of their position of the morning... We are not astonished that the French should employ this argument as a balm to their disappointment, but it comes with a peculiarly bad grace from the Prussians. Surely in thus taking the lion's share in this glorious victory, they do not think to cover their defeat at Ligny, or their unaccountable delay in arriving on the field of Waterloo... And, if true, as the Prussian official report represents, that Blücher had such a large force on the field to act, previous to, or during, Napoleon's last attack upon us, why did not Blücher ... roll up the French Army as Pakenham's division did at Salamanca.[8]

There is, then, a deeply Anglo-centric view of Waterloo that in its most extreme form suggests that the Prussians played, at best, a secondary role in the Allied victory: in brief, Napoleon's Army was already beaten when Blücher finally turned up very late in the day; still worse, meanwhile, the new arrivals, who had already failed Wellington by coming to grips with the French far later than they had initially promised, did not exert themselves nearly as much as they should have. If we are to believe the staunchly pro-Prussian Peter Hofschröer, indeed, in the years after the war repeated attempts were made to crush all those who sought to challenge an establishment view that allowed the Prussians just so much of the glory but no more.[9] Yet even in the lifetime of the duke it was easy enough to find views that were more balanced. An obvious place to begin here is the highly influential history of Revolutionary and Napoleonic Europe published by Sir Archibald Alison in 1860. Thus, though clearly written with a great degree of national pride, this makes it very plain that, in his eyes at least, Cotton had gone too far:

RIGHT
A Landwehr cavalryman of the sort that took part in Bülow's attack at Waterloo.
(Anne S. K. Brown)

LEFT
A typical Prussian infantry officer, c.1815. (Anne S. K. Brown)

In considering the comparative shares which the British and Prussian armies had in the achievement of this glorious victory, an impartial judgement must award the best share to the British troops. When it is recollected that the British soldiers and King's German Legion in the field did not exceed 37,000 and that, including the Hanoverians, the whole troops on whom reliance can be placed were only 52,000, and that they were assailed, for above five hours, by continual attacks from 74,000 veteran French under Napoleon's direction before even Bülow's Prussians arrived in the field at four o'clock, it must be admitted that this day must ever be reckoned as the proudest of the many proud days of English glory. On the other hand, it is equally clear that the arrival of Bülow's corps at that hour, which compelled Napoleon to detach the two divisions of Lobau's corps, and, at last, eleven battalions of his Young and Old Guard, to maintain Plancenoit against them, went far to ... bring nearer to an equality the military forces of the contending armies. Had they not appeared in force in the field, as they did at half-past seven at night, it is doubtful the French army would have been repulsed... The victory, at best, would have been dreadfully hard won, and probably little more than a sterile triumph like that of Talavera... It was unquestionably the arrival of the Prussians which rendered the success complete, and converted a bloody repulse into a total overthrow.[10]

To argue, then, that the British historiography of Waterloo was marked by excessive Anglo-centrism is a little unfair. Certainly, there were many factors pushing it in that direction, including, not least, the plethora of prints and paintings celebrating such episodes as the defence of Hougoumont, the charge of the Union Brigade and the repulse of the French cavalry, not to mention the constant desire to rehearse the triumphs of the Duke of Wellington, but the picture that emerges is far less uniform than is sometimes alleged. As a good example of the modern state of the historiography, we might cite David Chandler's *Waterloo: The Hundred Days* (Oxford, 1980), if only because its author was for many years the veritable doyen of Napoleonic campaign history. In this work the Prussians are described as entering the battle for the first time at about 4 p.m. – incidentally, a time rather earlier than that given in some other British accounts – and thereafter occupying more and more of Napoleon's attention, and, with it, his troops. Indeed, the account that we have is both relatively detailed and inclined to give full credit to the Prussians:

Now, however, Napoleon faced a real crisis. Domon's cavalry and Lobau's VI Corps were forming a new line at right angles to the main front ... and the French attacked before Bülow could deploy all his 30,000 men, but soon expended their energy. Bülow gave a little before the French, but then shifted his line of attack towards the village of Plancenoit, threatening to turn Lobau's right flank. The French could only

Ludwig Elsholtz's 1843 painting depicting the Battle of Plancenoit. (Public domain)

fall back, and by 5 p.m. the village was in danger as the Prussians swept towards it from three sides at once, for now Pirch's II Corps was coming into action to the south of Bülow… To stop the rot a division of the Young Guard was sent off … to recapture the lost parts of Plancenoit and ease the pressure on Lobau's tiring troops, thus enabling them to occupy a better position north-east of the village. The Young Guard managed to become masters of Plancenoit, but only briefly, for they were repulsed again by a new surge of Prussian attackers. There was nothing for it but to send in two battalions of the Old Guard… The Young Guard then regarrisoned the village, but the victors pressed a little too far beyond in pursuit of the discomforted Prussians and were tellingly forced to withdraw. Nevertheless, within an hour the situation on Napoleon's right flank had been stabilised.[11]

This passage is, perhaps, slightly more guarded than it appears at first sight – in the end, the Prussians are checked and Napoleon thereby afforded the opportunity to throw in the Guard in one last attempt to break Wellington's Army – whilst Chandler also later suggests that the pursuit was 'at first mainly a British affair'.[12] Yet the inclusion of a detailed account of the Prussian defence of Wavre against the attacks of Marshal Emmanuel de Grouchy takes the sting out of this issue, whilst Chandler ends on a note that is generous indeed. As he says, 'There can be little doubt that Waterloo would not have been won had not the Prussians arrived. This has sometimes been questioned by British historians, but the Prussian contribution was vital.'[13]

German historians, then, have little to complain about, whilst it might further be pointed out that it was a British initiative that produced *Waterloo: Battle of Three Armies* (London, 1979), this last being a unique attempt to tell the story of the battle through simultaneous exposition of the three competing national perspectives, and one which reaches a conclusion with which even the most die-hard Prussian cannot take issue. To quote the book's editor, Lord Chalfont:

> It is in the matter of the Prussian role in the battle that a little reassessment of historical viewpoints might legitimately be called for. Blücher's army ... played a

THE SITUATION AT PLANCENOIT AT 6 P. M., 18 JUNE 1815

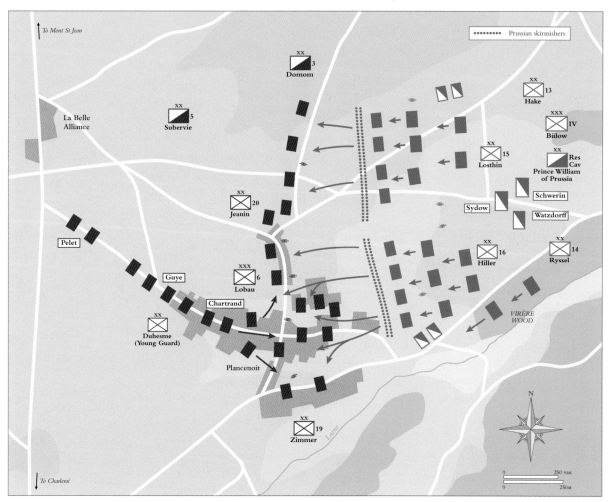

Prussian cavalry pursuing
Napoleon's broken forces towards
Genappe in the wake of the
French collapse.
(Anne S. K. Brown)

part in the Waterloo campaign, not least in the final battle, which has been
consistently underestimated by British historians… It was not only that the
Prussian attacks … forced Napoleon to detach precious reserves to safeguard his
flanks… The advancing Prussian forces were a constant factor in the battle
throughout the day – a persistent threat in the mind of Napoleon, who could not
give his entire attention to Wellington, and a reassurance to Wellington who could
concentrate on repelling the initial French attacks in the knowledge that, sooner
or later, the arrival of Blücher would decisively change the balance of forces.
Indeed, it is arguable that some of Napoleon's apparent errors of judgement were
brought about by the knowledge that, if he could not crush Wellington before
Blücher arrived, the day was lost.[14]

The point, then, is well made. Not all modern British writers are quite so
generous: both Jeremy Black and Andrew Roberts have in recent years
published studies that lean more towards Howarth than they do towards
Chalfont.[15] Yet sweeping allegations to the effect that 'most British historians'
have regarded 'the Duke of Wellington … as the sole or even the prime victor
of Waterloo' are, at the very least, wildly exaggerated.[16] That said, it does have
to be admitted that, for all the conscientious efforts of historians such as
Chandler, the British reader interested in Waterloo is far more likely to be
aware of the exploits of, say, the Royal Scots Greys or the Inniskillings than
they are of the 2nd Silesian Hussars or the 1st Pomeranian Landwehr. In this
bicentennial publication, then, it is fitting that some attempt should be made to

give a detailed account of the battle as it was experienced and fought by Blücher's forces. This story, of course, begins on the evening of 16 June in the wake of the Battle of Ligny. Dealt with elsewhere in the current volume, this action need not detain us here for very long, but it is worth considering the circumstances of the moment. The Prussian Army had not been routed, certainly, but its situation was nonetheless more than somewhat parlous. Many units had suffered terrible casualties; stragglers were scattered broadcast across the countryside; the troops were utterly exhausted; the army had all but been split in two by the last French attack; the whereabouts of the reserve ammunition was unknown; and, to cap it all, Blücher himself was missing and, for all his staff knew, dead. As for Wellington's forces, meanwhile, the one thing that was certain was that, notwithstanding a series of assurances on the part of their commander, they were not likely to arrive in the vicinity any time soon and could, in fact, be assumed to be retreating. In the circumstances, the Prussian chief of staff, Lieutenant General August von Gneisenau, would have been well within his rights to order his surviving troops to pull back eastwards towards Liège and thereby fall back on their line of communications, a direction in which he was further pulled, first, by deep dislike of the English and, second, by the conviction that the Prussian Army should never have been sent to Belgium in the first place. Yet, in what was perhaps the most vital decision of the whole campaign, Gneisenau ordered his forces to retreat northwards in parallel with what was assumed to be the intent of the Duke of Wellington and head for the town of Wavre. Needless to say, Prussian historians and those who sympathise with them have insisted that Gneisenau acted out of recognition that, above all, he needed to keep in touch with Wellington. Well, perhaps. But there were also circumstantial forces in play in that many Prussian troops were already moving northwards while it was clear that a move on Liège would leave Friedrich Wilhelm Count von Bülow's IV Corps, which, due to a combination of poorly written orders and the stubbornness of its commander, had failed to reach the area of Ligny on 16 June and was believed to be somewhere to the north, open to destruction. To claim, as Eberhard Kaulbach does, that 'the necessity of remaining in effective contact with [Wellington] must have been the decisive consideration for Gneisenau in making up his … mind' therefore seems a little foolhardy.[17]

Yet, in the end, even the fairest of caveats do not matter. Taken the decision was, whilst it was vigorously confirmed by a somewhat bruised and dishevelled Marshal Blücher, who was restored to his Headquarters a few hours later after the adventures on the battlefield that are detailed elsewhere, and the consequence was that by the evening of 17 June the whole of the Prussian Army was moving

into bivouacs in the area of Wavre. In the course of the day the disorder of the night before had been remedied, whilst the columns carrying the ammunition reserve had turned up safely during the afternoon and allowed the resupply of the I, II and III Corps, but the extent of the damage inflicted at Ligny had become all too apparent. In all, casualties had amounted to a minimum of 20,000 men, of which at least 8,000 were deserters, while the French had taken 22 guns. In terms of manpower, then, the army had lost fully a quarter of its strength, while the gaps in some infantry brigades – the worst hit were those of Zieten's I Corps – reached as many as 50 per cent. At the same time, the troops were very tired. However, according to Prussian sources at least, the combination of the absence of any French pursuit with the sterling efforts of Blücher, who had spent much of the day in the saddle encouraging his men, had restored the troops' morale, whilst communications had been restored with Wellington's Army, and a plan established for the morrow, it having been decided that Wavre would be held by a rearguard composed of roughly half the army while the rest of the troops moved to support the Anglo-Dutch. Here, then, are the orders that were issued to Bülow at midnight on 17 June:

> According to information just received from the Duke of Wellington, he has positioned himself as follows: his right wing extends to Braine l'Alleud; the centre is at Mont Saint Jean; [the] left wing at La Haye. The enemy is facing him and the Duke is expecting the attack and has asked us for our co-operation. Your Excellency will, therefore, with IV Corps under your command, move off … at daybreak, march through Wavre and move towards Chapelle Saint Lambert, where, if the enemy is not heavily engaged with Wellington, you will take up positions under

LEFT
The Prussian chief of staff, Lieutenant General August Neithardt von Gneisenau. (Anne S. K. Brown)

MIDDLE
Lieutenant General Johann von Thielmann, painted in the uniform of a Saxon Hussar officer. (akg-images)

RIGHT
Count von Bülow, Prussian IV Corps commander at Waterloo. (akg-images)

cover. Otherwise you are to throw yourself at the right flank of the enemy with the utmost vigour. II Corps will follow immediately to the rear of Your Excellency to lend support. I and III Corps will likewise hold themselves in readiness to follow in support should the need arise.[18]

It will be noted that at this point the movement that actually took place on 18 June had not yet fully been decided on. However, this is not surprising. In brief, at this point Blücher and Gneisenau had no idea how many troops had been sent to follow them, and the latter – a man who was by nature much more cautious than his commander – was therefore able to prevail upon the field marshal to stay his hand for the time being. But, if Gneisenau had felt any repugnance about supporting Wellington, this was now long gone: at least in principle, the chief of staff was determined to fight. Whatever his motives, he was not able to prevail for very long. At about 9.30 a.m. on 18 June, Blücher sent a message to the chief Prussian liaison officer at Wellington's Headquarters, Baron von Müffling, in which, without saying so in quite so many words, he announced that he was marching on Napoleon's right flank with not just one or two corps, but the bulk of his forces. Quite clearly, he saw an opportunity for a pitched battle in which the tables would be firmly turned against Napoleon, and thereby remedy the blow that had been dealt to his reputation

Blücher encourages his army in their march to Wellington's relief. (Print after R. Eichstädt)

at Ligny. The professional, then, was mixed with the personal, whilst it is impossible not to speculate that the chance was rendered all the sweeter by the fact that accomplishing Blücher's aim would enable him to pull off the feat that had so completely evaded Wellington on 16 June. However, in the end none of this matters: whatever the reason Blücher elected on the course that he did, it was the right decision, and one that firmly tipped the scales against Napoleon.[19]

For at least some men in the Prussian Army, these doings at the level of Headquarters made little difference: ordered to move the night before, IV Corps was already on the road at daybreak (4 a.m.). Why this force was chosen for the task of heading the Prussian advance was clear enough in that it was the only one of Blücher's corps that was still intact after the fighting of 16 June. That said, its situation was extremely unfortunate in that it was also the Prussian corps that was furthest from the Waterloo battlefield; for, whereas their fellows had spent the night camped in and around Wavre, Bülow's men had rather passed it at the little village of Dion le Monte a mile or so east of the town. Still worse, to reach the road that they needed to take to reach Napoleon's right flank, they had to pass through the bivouac of II Corps, cross the Dyle at Wavre by means of just one narrow bridge, and then negotiate the narrow streets of the town, which was already clogged up by the wagons, carriages and general impedimenta consequent upon the town being Blücher's Headquarters. All this meant that the corps' initial movement was attended by considerable delay: thus, it took two hours just to get the advanced guard through Wavre, matters then being made still worse by the outbreak of a serious fire in the heart of the town (so catastrophic was the site of this fire in terms of the movement of the army that it might almost be thought that it was started deliberately, but there is no evidence that this was the case, the reality being that it was probably the fruit of mere carelessness on the part of the soldiers billeted in the mill in which the blaze started). At all events, the whole affair is a prime example of what the famous military commentator, Carl von Clausewitz – a man who was very much an eyewitness to the events in question – later called 'friction', whilst, whatever the cause of the fire, the end result was that the last troops of IV Corps did not even leave their encampment until 10 a.m. Nor was this an end to the problem. Once through the town Bülow's men had to negotiate a single-track country road leading through undulating terrain to the village of Chapelle Saint Lambert and from there descend a narrow sunken lane to the little River Lasne before scrambling up again to the wooded plateau that closed off the north-eastern fringes of the Waterloo battlefield. With the tracks deep in mud due to the heavy rain of the night before, the going could not but be very slow, and that despite the decision that was taken to send the corps'

The Prussians were heavily
involved in the fighting at
Plancenoit, where, as depicted
here by Adolf Northern, they
stormed the cemetery.
(akg-images)

baggage train off to the safety of Louvain rather than attempt to drag it along in the wake of the troops. Meanwhile, the troops were very tired and the distance considerable: having marched many kilometres over the previous two days, some of the soldiers had not lain down until midnight the night before, and then been roused at 4 a.m.; as for the distance, it was a good 24 kilometres to the outskirts of the battlefield at Frischermont alone, the final objective of Plancenoit being perhaps 5 kilometres further on beyond that.[20]

As even the firmly pro-Prussian Peter Hofschröer is forced to admit, all this put the Prussian advance seriously out of kilter, a march that might in ordinary circumstances have taken IV Corps six hours actually costing it nearer 11, whilst even then Bülow did not take his men straight into action but rather paused in the woods north-east of Frischermont to send out a reconnaissance. And it was not just Bülow who ended up wildly delayed: ordered to follow IV Corps, II Corps did not get moving until midday, while, bivouacked as it was at Bierges, a little village on the Dyle a mile south-west of Wavre, I Corps had to wait for a further two hours before it could move more than a few hundred yards, the basic problem being that it could not reach the equally bad road that would take it to the position on Wellington's left flank which it had been decided should be

Schlacht bei Waterloo am 18 Juni 1815; a watercolour by Philip Heinrich Duncker showing the advance of Prussian infantry against French troops at Waterloo. Two eagles can be seen among the French, who are presumed to be foot chasseurs of the Imperial Guard. (Anne S. K. Brown)

OPPOSITE
A mounted Prussian general of the Waterloo period.
(Anne S. K. Brown)

its post in the battle to come. In the face of these difficulties, the Prussian commander was scarcely idle: he rode forth from his Headquarters at 11 a.m. and has been pictured as galloping up and down the lines of toiling troops shouting, 'Forward boys! Some, I hear, say it can not be done. But it must be done! I have promised my brother, Wellington! You would not make me a perjurer?'[21] To these exhortations, the troops seem to have responded with a will, but, in the end, mud is mud, and one may therefore be thankful that Napoleon delayed any movement on his own part until 11.30 a.m.: had he moved even an hour sooner, the day might very well have gone the other way. And, even as it was, Waterloo, as Wellington famously later said, was a 'near-run thing'. Not for nothing, then, was he at one point heard to murmur, 'Either night or the Prussians must come.'

The changing face of Prussian troops throughout the Napoleonic period. (Center) A bugler c.1792, (left) a private c.1806 and (right) a fusilier infantry NCO, c.1814–15. (Adam Hook © Osprey Publishing)

At last, however, the Prussians did come. Had Bülow had his way, IV Corps would not have entered the battle until he had concentrated all his troops, something that would probably have taken till at least 5.30 p.m., and, though now fully aware of the pressure which Wellington's Army was having to withstand – the battlefield could, after all, now be glimpsed from his advanced positions – he even sent Blücher a note to this effect.[22] As the Prussian commander realised, however, such a delay might prove fatal, and Bülow therefore received a tart note to the effect that he should go in with what he had even if the force available to him was no more than a single brigade. At about 4.30 p.m. IV Corps finally went forward. In the lead was a screen of two fusilier battalions, whilst behind them came the first two of its four brigades – 15th Brigade, commanded by Major General Michael von Losthin, and 16th

Prussian light infantry of the Volunteer Jaeger companies. The figures on the left and right are dated 1815, while the one in the middle is 1813. (Bryan Fosten © Osprey Publishing)

Prussian soldiers of 1813. This artwork illustrates the uniforms of the period that would have been seen at Waterloo. (Topfoto)

Brigade, commanded by Johann von Hiller – each of the two formations being composed of one three-battalion regiment of line infantry and two three-battalion regiments of *Landwehr*, together with a single eight-gun battery of field artillery. In support, meanwhile, rode a few advanced units of cavalry, though most of Bülow's mounted troops were back in the woods. Linking up with some troops from the Duchy of Nassau who had been holding the hamlets of La Haye and Papelotte, the right wing of Bülow's troops ejected the French from neighbouring Frischermont to the accompaniment of a brief cavalry mêlée, and moved steadily forward in the face of a thickening line of French skirmishers. Beyond Frischermont, however, the Prussians ran into serious problems in that they found the rising ground south of the village held by a strong force of French troops. Initially, the only enemy troops in a position to reinforce the Frischermont sector had been a single brigade of light cavalry, but as early as 1.30 p.m. Napoleon, who was by now well aware that the Prussians were coming, had responded to the danger by ordering General Georges Mouton's VI Corps to adopt a holding position south of the village.[23] According to some accounts, Mouton responded to the appearance of Bülow's men with a furious charge in an attempt to drive them back, but this seems unlikely: though many skirmishers certainly went forward, VI Corps seems rather to have stood entirely on the defensive. For a French perspective we might cite a French officer named Tromelin. Thus:

> The Prussian attack started towards 4.30 p.m. Our cavalry sabred the enemy squadrons. Then we formed in square by brigade and remained under fire of forty Prussian guns that caused us much damage… At 5.30 p.m., the enemy was reinforced by infantry and cavalry; the artillery fire became terrible. Maintaining a brave front, but suffering under the weight of shot, the four squares of the corps … retired slowly in the direction of Plancenoit where we finally established ourselves, already outflanked by Prussian cavalry. The debris of my three battalions occupied the gardens and orchards.[24]

Based on a painting by Georg Bleibtreu, this woodcut shows the Prussian advance under Blücher. (akg-images)

Broadly speaking, then, what happened appears to be this. Having started off bravely enough, Bülow's weary troops were brought to a halt by Mouton's men, and were unable to move forward again until the second echelon of XIV Corps came forward in its turn and thickened the line. Nor is this surprising: according to Kaulbach, both von Losthin and von Hiller were very concerned about their flanks and therefore kept up to one third of their infantry in reserve.[25] With Mouton's men now formed more or less on a north–south axis on a line stretching from the vicinity of Papelotte to Plancenoit – Bülow having apparently been ordered by Blücher constantly to edge to his left, the net effect had been to force back Mouton's right and therefore to cause the entire corps to pivot on its left flank – the latter village was now in the front line. Always a key Prussian objective, it now came under direct attack. At about 6 p.m., then, von Hiller launched a determined assault with two battalions of the 15th Line Regiment and two battalions of the 1st Silesian Landwehr. Pressing into the village from two sides, the Prussians overran most of the built-up area and captured three guns as well as several hundred prisoners, but in the centre of the village the church and its attendant graveyard formed a natural redoubt, while the elements of Mouton's Corps which held it refused to yield. To make matters worse, at the last minute reinforcements arrived in the shape of General

Prussian line infantry, 1811: an NCO, privates and an officer in parade dress. (Print after Theumen)

Guillaume Duhesme's Division of the Young Guard, and the Prussians were hurled back in disorder having suffered heavy losses. However, even as it was the situation was bad enough. Emplaced on the high ground beyond Plancenoit, the guns of IV Corps could now pound not just the high road but also the waiting French reserves. Waiting with the grenadiers of the Old Guard was Sergeant Hippolyte de Mauduit:

> For some time we did not have a single gun to reply to these uncomfortable neighbours… The emperor was immediately informed and a twelve-pounder battery of the Guard Reserve was … deployed a hundred paces above us… Its fire, well-directed, quickly reduced the effectiveness of the Prussian fire, which, nevertheless … caused us about fifty casualties. The shells … caused us the most damage. Three grenadiers of our company … were killed by one of them which exploded two paces from us… Each discharge thus knocked down several grenadiers, but our post was there, and neither the balls nor the shells would force us to abandon it.[26]

Grizzled veteran as he was, Mauduit goes on to claim that he and his fellows were unperturbed by this experience, but plenty of French troops displayed less

Foot Guards Regiment, 1812: an officer in undress, officer in full dress and NCs in parade dress. (Print after Theumen)

This reproduction of Carl Roechling's painting of the Battle of Gross Goerschen on 2 May 1813 shows that Prussian skirmishers and attack columns were used during this period, and is a good example of battlefield tactics in action.

nonchalance. They had been repeatedly told that Grouchy was on his way and yet were now confronted by fresh enemies. Not surprisingly, then, there were many troops who began openly to doubt the possibility of victory and even to start to slip away to the rear, while the growing sense of demoralisation was increased by the decision of the emperor's personal staff to start packing up his baggage so as to be ready to move in an instant. As one senior officer of the Guard put it, 'From then on, no one thought any longer of going to Brussels.'[27]

The Prussians, then, scarcely needed to take Plancenoit to have a dramatic effect on the fighting, and all the more so as it was about this time that the first representatives of I Corps began to emerge onto the ridge of Mont Saint Jean, thereby enabling a greatly relieved Wellington to start calling in troops from his left wing to plug the growing weakness in his centre, where La Haye Sainte had just fallen to the French.[28] Just because their guns could bombard the French reserves, however, the Prussians did not cease their efforts. On the contrary, Plancenoit now became the centre of a bitter battle in which at least two Prussian assaults were thrown back with heavy losses. Yet the weary IV Corps was now supported by the first troops to arrive from II Corps, and a further attack carried not just the same buildings that had been occupied before, but also the church, whilst the commander of the defending Young Guards, General Duhesme, was shot in the head and had to be carried from the field. In over-running the village, however, the attackers, who, it should be remembered, were mostly militia and had been on the march continuously for many days, had lost all order, and were therefore vulnerable to a counter-attack. Realising that all was lost unless he acted immediately, Napoleon ordered up the only reserves that he could spare in the form of the two battalions of the Old Guard, including one of chasseurs and the other of grenadiers. Instructed, by the emperor himself, not to fire a shot, but rather to press home their advance with the bayonet, the troops managed to get into the village and re-occupy the church, where they were joined by some survivors of the Young Guard, but the Prussians had only been driven back: very soon then, they were pressing around the village once more.[29]

With the situation at Plancenoit temporarily stabilised, Napoleon was free to throw his last reserves into battle at Mont Saint Jean in the form of four battalions of the Old Guard and six battalions of the Middle Guard. The fate of this attack is well known and need not concern us here. More to the point, however, is the sequence of events which surrounded it. According to the traditional British view, the repulse of the Guard from the ridge between Hougoumont and La Haye Sainte triggered a general collapse of morale that soon had the entire French Army fleeing from the field, whereas the Prussian version of events is that, just as the Guard breasted the ridge, Zieten ordered a general assault that broke the French line at Papelotte and La Haye, which had both fallen into the hands of the French a short time earlier, and precipitated the collapse for which the British have so often assumed responsibility. Here, for example, is the version of events later retailed by Gneisenau:

> It was half past seven, and the issue of the battle was still uncertain. The whole of the Fourth Corps and a part of the Second under [Major] General Pirch had successively come up. The French fought with a desperate fury, [but] some uncertainty was perceived in their movements and it was observed that some pieces of cannon were retreating. At this moment the first column of General von Ziethen [sic] arrived … near the village of Smohain on the enemy's right flank and

Following the battle, Blücher is given the captured medals, hat and rapier of Napoleon in Genappe. (akg-images)

instantly charged. This movement decided the defeat of the enemy. His right wing was broken in three places; he abandoned his positions. The troops rushed forwards at the *pas de charge* and attacked him on all sides, while, at the same time, the whole English line advanced. Circumstances were entirely favourable to the attack formed by the Prussian army: the ground rose in an amphitheatre, so that their artillery could freely open fire from the summit of several heights which rose gradually above each other, and in the intervals of which the troops descended into the plain, formed into brigades in the most perfect order, while fresh corps continually unfolded themselves, issuing from the forest on the height behind. The enemy, however, still preserved means to retreat till the village of Plancenoit … was, after several bloody attacks, taken by storm.[30]

Well, perhaps. It is certainly true that Zieten's troops launched a general advance about this time, and, further, that as the French Army collapsed, so the Prussians finally got into Plancenoit, which was by now ablaze from end to end.[31] Meanwhile, there are French accounts that are marked by a chronology that seems to coincide with that offered by Gneisenau. Here, for example, is Louis de Pontécoulant, an aristocratic officer serving in the Guard artillery:

Our line … was suddenly broken. The Prussian cavalry hurled itself into this breach and soon flooded the battlefield, sabring isolated soldiers and making it impossible for us to rally. The news, spread by malevolence or fear, that the Guard, the rock of

The climax of Waterloo – Blücher and Wellington meet at La Belle Alliance at the end of the battle. (Anne S. K. Brown)

the army, had been obliged to retire and was partly destroyed, augmented the disorder and the precipitation of the retreat.[32]

Yet Gneisenau is not wholly to be trusted. We know, for example, that he was decidedly hostile to the British, while in other places the account that he gives of the battle is, at the very least, grossly over-simplified. Here, for example, is his account of the entrance onto the battlefield of IV Corps: 'General Count Bülow … with two brigades and a corps of cavalry, advanced rapidly along the rear of the enemy's right wing.'[33] If this is taken to mean Bülow's circumvention of the Frischermont position, fair enough, but, especially if the reader knows the outline of the battle, the effect is to suggest that the troops proceeded all the way to Plancenoit, which is obviously very far from the truth. On top of this, meanwhile, it is simply not the case that Zieten launched his attack at the very moment of entering the battlefield: rather, I Corps clearly spent some time getting into position and skirmishing with the French in the course of which time an unfortunate incident took place in which some green-uniformed soldiers from the Grand Duchy of Nassau were fired upon. As the chief of staff of the I Corps, Lieutenant Colonel Ludwig von Reiche, later wrote:

> As the Nassauers were dressed in the French style of that time, our men took
> them to be the enemy and fired at them. Their commander, Prince Bernhard of
> Saxe-Weimar, rushed up to General Zeiten to clarify the misunderstanding,

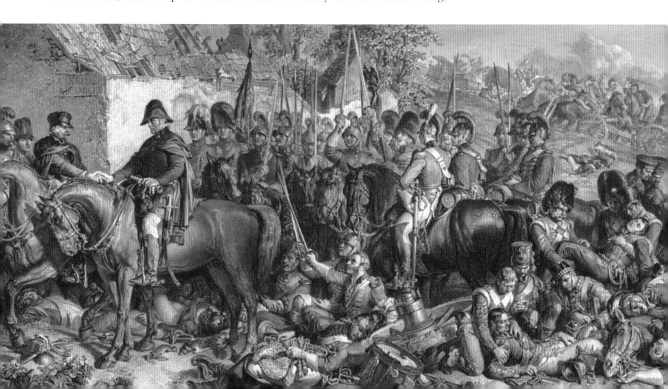

which he did in no uncertain terms. The general, not knowing the prince, made no excuses and calmly replied, 'My friend, it is not my fault that your men look like the French.'[34]

In all probability, then, what happened was a coincidence in that Zieten happened to advance virtually at the very moment the Guard was defeated. Both sides, then, are in the right, just as both sides have a similar share in the defeat of Napoleon. At all events the two armies now moved forwards in the great converging movement that formed the climax of the day. Sometime in the next hour or so, the two commanders encountered one another and shook hands, to the accompaniment of Blücher's famous comment 'Quelle affaire!' Near them, meanwhile, were strewn many of the 7,000 Prussians who had fallen in the battle. Yet even about this much-painted tableau there is controversy. Most sources suggest that it took place outside the inn of La Belle Alliance at about eight o'clock, but, mindful perhaps that the name 'Belle Alliance' – the name, incidentally, that Blücher wanted to give the battle and, indeed, used in its respect in private conversation for the rest of his life – was suggestive of a debt to the Prussians that he did not especially relish, Wellington himself suggested that the meeting took place somewhat later near the village of Genappe, a detail that also conveyed a neat hint that Blücher had come upon the scene very late indeed.[35]

To conclude, then, where are we? First of all, as we have seen, it is impossible to say that Wellington did not receive the support that he was promised from his Prussian allies. Despite terrible logistical difficulties, the serious effects of the Battle of Ligny and the dislike that was entertained of the British by many of his subordinates, Blücher managed to get most of his troops to the field at a time when they could still have a significant impact on the course of the battle, and, what is more, to deploy them in a manner that was highly effective. Secondly, once they reached the field the Prussian forces fought extremely well despite coming up against opposition of the highest quality – setting aside the Imperial Guard, even Mouton's troops were for the most part hardened veterans – and themselves being in large part composed of second-class troops who arrived on the field in a piece-meal fashion after a long and difficult approach march. Thirdly, Blücher kept close control of his troops throughout, and, despite the occasional error – most notably, the order that almost pulled I Corps away from its designated position on Wellington's left flank – directed them extremely well and refused to be diverted from the defeat of the emperor that was the central aim; particularly notable here is the manner in which at about 6 p.m. he rejected a desperate plea for help from

Lieutenant General Johann von Thielmann, whose III Corps was defending Wavre in the face of increasingly desperate French assaults with the tart remark that he would not give him so much as a horse's tail.[36] And, finally, the Prussian intervention on the battlefield tied down many thousands of French troops and spread serious demoralisation amongst Napoleon's forces, even if it did not actually save Wellington from complete disaster. In short, whilst we will never know for certain what would have happened had the Prussians not arrived on the battle field when they did, to pretend that they did not play an important role in the defeat of Napoleon at Waterloo is unwarranted. Whatever the battle is called, as generations of British historians have always recognised, it was indeed a *belle alliance*.

The Prussian Army returns home victorious after Napoleon's defeat at the hands of the Allies. (Anne S. K. Brown)

CHAPTER 9

LA GARDE RECULE!

Napoleon's Last Throw of the Dice

ANDREW FIELD

La Haye Sainte, the farmhouse that covered the very centre of Wellington's line, fell to the French at about 6 p.m. The implications of this were serious as Captain James Shaw Kennedy, a British staff captain, explains:

> The possession of La Haye Sainte by the French was a very dangerous incident. It uncovered the very centre of the Anglo-Allied army, and established the enemy within 60 yards of that centre. The French lost no time in taking advantage of this, by pushing forward infantry supported by guns, which enabled them to maintain a most destructive fire upon Alten's left and Kempt's right, and to drive off Kempt's light troops that occupied the knoll in his front. By this fire they wasted most seriously the ranks of the left of Alten's and the right of Kempt's divisions; so much so that Ompteda's brigade having been previously nearly destroyed, and Kielmansegge's much weakened, they were now not sufficiently strong to occupy the front which was originally assigned to them.[1]

It wasn't just Lieutenant General Charles Alten's Division that was suffering; Lieutenant Gawler, of the British 52nd Light Infantry, described Major General Peregrine Maitland's Brigade of Guards as reduced to the strength of 'a weak battalion', and General Sir Colin Halkett's Brigade to 'a few companies'.[2] In other British units, companies were being commanded by sergeants.[3] Much of the Allied cavalry in the centre was also at the end of its tether.

A hole was developing in the centre of the Allied line and young Shaw Kennedy, who later rose to become a general, claims the credit for realising it:

> We have already seen that La Haye Sainte was in the hands of the enemy; also the knoll on the opposite side of the road; also the garden and ground on the Anglo-Allied side of it;-that Ompteda's brigade was nearly annihilated and Kielmansegge's so thinned that those two brigades could not hold their position. That part of the field of battle between Halkett's left and Kempt's right was thus unprotected; and being the very centre of the Duke's line of battle, was consequently that point, above all others, which the enemy wished to gain. The danger was imminent; and at no other time of the action was the result so precarious as at this moment. Most fortunately, Napoleon did not support the advantage his troops had gained at this point, by bringing forward his reserve... I therefore, as the staff-officer present, galloped direct to the Duke, and informed him that his line was open for the whole space between Halkett's and Kempt's brigades... They [the French] had gained La Haye Sainte and its enclosures; held advantageous ground on its right and front; and were thus most advantageously placed for breaking through the Allied centre by a powerful effort of their reserves upon that point, supported by a general attack upon the whole line.[4]

The situation was serious, and if Napoleon had been able to launch a final, desperate attack, then there is no doubt that Wellington could well have faced defeat. But one important fact prevented the French emperor from seizing his chance: the Prussian advance on his right rear. Whilst Marshal Michel Ney had been fighting the battle against Wellington, Napoleon had been concentrating on what the Prussians were doing. He realised that until his right flank was secure he would be unable to organise and deliver the decisive blow against the Anglo–Netherlands Army.

The situation on the French right was critical; Georges Mouton Count Lobau's weak VI Corps had been pushed back by growing Prussian numbers to the edge of the village of Plancenoit and at 6 p.m., the time that La Haye Sainte eventually fell, the Prussians were on the point of launching an attack on that village. Lobau's tired troops could not hold and the village was lost. It was only after Napoleon had deployed the division of the Young Guard, and then two battalions of the precious Old Guard, into the village that his flank was temporarily secure.

Now, finally, the emperor could turn his attention to breaking the centre of Wellington's position. It was some time after 7 p.m.; Napoleon still had two hours of daylight to snatch a victory.

Napoleon and the Old Guard on the morning of the Battle of Waterloo. (akg-images)

PREPARATIONS

Napoleon may well have thought that the window of opportunity was still open. La Haye Sainte was in his hands, and the shattered remains of General Jean-Baptiste Drouet, Count d'Erlon's I Corps, although exhausted after their earlier abortive attack, were now putting increasing pressure on the centre of an equally exhausted Allied line. The farm of Hougoumont, which covered the right of the Allied line, had not been taken, but Wellington had been compelled to advance two brigades to ensure its security. General Gilbert Bachelu and General Maximilien Foy's Divisions, which had launched their abortive attack during the last flickering cavalry assaults between Hougoumont and La Haye Sainte, had had sufficient time to reform along with the remains of the cavalry and might be depended on to deliver one more effort. Despite the failure of the earlier assaults, the Allied line appeared shaken and devoid of any fresh reserves.

Although the whole of the Young Guard had been deployed to Plancenoit, the majority of the Middle and Old Guards were still fresh and uncommitted: two of Napoleon's eight Old Guard battalions had also been sent to Plancenoit, but the other six remained available to him. All of the six battalions of the Middle Guard were also available, giving him 12 battalions for a total of about 5,500 men.

Count Lobau, the French commander of VI Corps. (Anne S. K. Brown)

Napoleon musters his Guard. (Jean Auge, courtesy of Andrew Field)

However, he could not commit all these troops; the two battalions of the senior regiment, the 1st Regiment of Foot Grenadiers, supported by six 8-pounders and the *sapeurs* and *marins* of the Guard, were deployed to cover the junction of the road from Plancenoit with the main road. Given the Prussian threat from this latter village, they could not be spared for the assault. Furthermore, Major Duuring, commanding officer of the 1st Battalion of the 1st Foot Chasseur Regiment had been ordered to remain at Le Caillou to protect the

The Foot Grenadiers of the Old Guard were the senior regiment of the Imperial Guard. They did not wear their famous parade uniforms at Waterloo, but this plainer, more practical, but no less distinctive, uniform. (Courtesy of Patrice Courcelle)

Headquarters and the emperor's baggage. Thus, only three battalions of the Old Guard and six of the Middle Guard could be thrown into a final, desperate assault. However, although these represented relatively few troops with which to deliver it, they belonged to the superlative Imperial Guard, which had never failed to accomplish a mission given to them by the emperor. Napoleon gave the order for the available battalions to be moved to the north of La Belle Alliance.

On the ridgeline, Wellington, having been informed of the critical state of his centre right, took steps to reinforce it. To replace General Alten's battered division and the unsteady Nassauers, the duke called forward a brigade of Brunswickers. To their right stood the sad remains of General Sir Colin Halkett's Brigade consisting of the 30th, 33rd, 69th and 73rd Regiments. All had suffered at Quatre Bras two days earlier and after the hard fighting they had already been involved in the whole brigade now counted little more than a few companies. To their right was General Maitland's much-depleted brigade of foot guards; but next to them was General Adam's relatively fresh brigade, consisting of the 2nd Battalion and two companies of the 3rd Battalion of the 95th Rifles; and the 52nd and 71st Light Infantry. During the French cavalry charges Wellington had already had General Chassé's 3rd Netherlands Division called over from Braine-l'Alleud as the French had shown no inclination to sweep around his western flank. These were posted behind these weakened, but still defiant, British brigades.

The Allied cavalry in the centre was also much thinned and exhausted; the entire Union Brigade now counted only two weak squadrons. With the Prussians appearing in increasing numbers on his eastern flank, Wellington was able to draw to his centre the British light cavalry brigades of Major General John Vandeleur and Major General Hussey Vivian that had previously been posted there. These two brigades, consisting of three regiments of light dragoons and hussars respectively, had been deployed there to support the Nassau regiments in Papelotte, La Haye and Smohain on the Allied left and remained comparatively fresh.

Thanks to the Prussians, the duke had been given sufficient time to make the necessary preparations to meet the coming storm. Had the fleeting opportunity that the fall of La Haye Sainte offered Napoleon for the *coup de grâce* passed?

General Foy, who was well known and respected among his British contemporaries. (Courtesy of Andrew Field)

Napoleon had no intention of delivering his final, desperate attack with just the relatively few battalions of the Guard that were available to him. Orders were sent to both d'Erlon and Lieutenant General Honoré Reille to make a final effort with their exhausted men to second the Guard's assault by applying pressure onto the whole of the Allied line and attempts were made to put together a cavalry force still capable of concerted effort. Needless to say, the Grand Battery maintained its fire, and some guns had been dragged forward and were doing considerable execution to the crumbling Allied line.

General Lallemand led the French *Chasseurs à Cheval* of the Guard at Waterloo. Their involvement during the great cavalry charges meant they were unable to support the attack of the foot guard at the climax of the battle. (akg-images)

To re-invigorate his shattered and exhausted troops, Napoleon, perhaps genuinely encouraged by the sound of distant gunfire in the direction of Wavre where Marshal Emmanuel de Grouchy's troops were engaged with the Prussian rearguard, now resorted to a risky stratagem. Aware that his own troops would be discouraged if they knew the full extent of the Prussian attack on their right rear, he appears to have decided to turn the sound of gunfire to his own advantage by portraying it as the arrival of Marshal Grouchy's 30,000 men in their support. One of Marshal Ney's aides de camp wrote:

Despite being in the privileged Guard, not all the Middle Guard had received their new uniforms when the campaign began. Many had to wear the uniforms of their previous regiments or a combination of the two. Few wore the famous tall bearskin caps of the Guard. (Courtesy of Patrice Courcelle)

At 6pm, General Dejean [one of Napoleon's aides de camp] arrived close to Marshal Ney, '*Monsieur le maréchal*' he said to him, '*vive l'Empereur! Here is Grouchy!*' The Marshal immediately ordered me to ride along the whole line and announce Grouchy's arrival. Breaking into a gallop, raising my hat on the tip of my sabre and passing along the front of the line; '*Vive l'Empereur!*' I shouted to the soldiers, '*Here is Grouchy!*' This sudden cry was repeated by a thousand voices; the excitement of the soldiers was indescribable, they all cried, '*En avant! En Avant! Vive l'Empereur!*'[5]

Although Napoleon may have believed that Grouchy had arrived, this is unlikely; he had sent cavalry patrols in that direction and would surely have heard if 30,000 Frenchmen were entering the fight. It was, at best, a desperate hope and it was indeed a time for desperate measures. Spreading false news such as this risked disheartening the troops when they found out that it was not true, but if he could encourage them to one final effort it might just secure him victory.

General Antoine Drouot, commander of the Imperial Guard at Waterloo. (Anne S. K. Brown)

THE ADVANCE

Nine battalions of the Guard were available for the final attack, and Napoleon broke them down into two echelons. The first was to consist of the six battalions of the Middle Guard (the 1st/3rd and 2nd/3rd Grenadiers, the 1st/3rd and 2nd/3rd Chasseurs, and the single battalions of the 4th Grenadiers and 4th Chasseurs – the 4th Regiment of Chasseurs had combined its two weak battalions, weakened by the casualties suffered at the Battle of Ligny, into a single strong battalion, while the 4th Regiment of Grenadiers had entered the campaign with only one battalion due to recruiting problems). The second echelon consisted of the available battalions of the Old Guard (the 2nd/1st Chasseurs, the 1st/2nd Grenadiers and the 2nd/2nd Chasseurs).

Ney led many heroic actions, especially his command of the rearguard of the French Army during the retreat from Russia. However, he did not perform well during the Waterloo campaign and Napoleon lay much of the blame for his defeat on Ney's shoulders. (Courtesy of Andrew Field)

Once the Guard had assembled in the vicinity of La Belle Alliance, the six battalions of the Middle Guard were led forward in square by Napoleon himself into the bottom of the shallow valley that separated the two armies. Here they could not be seen by the Allied guns on top of the ridge.

After the disastrous commitment of the Guard cavalry during the afternoon, it appears that only a small, *ad hoc*, force of cuirassiers was available to support the attack. The only French cavalry that was fresh and uncommitted was that of General Piré (belonging to General Reille's II Corps), which was deployed on the extreme French left. But no effort seems to have been made to redeploy this still formidable force and the assault went forward without the support of fresh cavalry. However, some reserve artillery was available and a section of two guns from the Guard Horse Artillery was deployed between each square to give intimate support.

Instead of handing command of all six battalions over to Marshal Ney for the final assault, Napoleon took one of them (the 2nd/3rd Grenadiers) towards Hougoumont. Although this battalion might have been more usefully employed in the assault that was about to be launched it seems it was placed here to provide some protection in the direction of the large farm complex where several Allied brigades would find themselves on the flank of the assault.

As a result of the departure of the 2nd/3rd Grenadiers, five squares advanced behind Marshal Ney. General Petit, commander of the 1st Regiment of Grenadiers, reported:

> It was about 7pm: … the 3rd and 4th Chasseurs and [3rd and 4th] Grenadiers marched forward. They crossed to the left of the road where they were formed into battalion squares with the exception of the 4th Regiments that, because of their weakness of numbers, formed only one square each.[6]

By the accepted tactical principles of the day, the square was not considered an assault formation, and its use as such was very rare throughout the Napoleonic Wars. The reason for this is simple: it had been designed primarily as a defence against cavalry. In the assault, it was very difficult to keep it in good order marching over difficult ground and under fire and it could generate only a small amount of firepower to the front. In the large, unwieldy columns that his corps had used on the initial assault on the centre left of Wellington's line, General d'Erlon had tried to compromise between firepower and mass and yet got it disastrously wrong. However, the lesson had clearly been learnt and the Guard were not going to suffer the same fate. The superb discipline and experience of the Guard allowed their commanders to accept the risk of attacking in this formation. Furthermore, whilst many assault columns did not even try to deploy into line to engage in a firefight, again, the discipline of the Guard allowed them this option.

Another noteworthy tactical aspect of this attack was that the Guard were not preceded by a cloud of skirmishers: a standard French practice and one that was generally accepted as a vital part of any assault. Although the Guard were quite capable of acting as skirmishers, no reason is given for this significant omission. Whatever the explanation, Captain Prax, the adjutant major of the 3rd Chasseurs, was later to complain:

> I can't help thinking that if we had engaged the enemy first with some skirmishers which could have caused some disorder in his ranks, and that if we had marched behind them quickly and with the bayonet, our attack would have succeeded.[7]

The order of the battalions, in keeping with Guard seniority, was as follows: the 1st/3rd Grenadiers on the right, followed to the left and rear by the single square of the 4th Grenadiers, the 1st/3rd Chasseurs, the 2nd/3rd Chasseurs and then the large, single square of the 4th Chasseurs. This latter was over 800 strong on account of the joining of the two battalions. The single battalion squares averaged about 550 men. We can assume that each side of the square was three men deep giving a frontage of about 45 men: only about 35 metres.

Generals Friant and Poret de Morvan led the 1st/3rd Grenadiers, General Harlet the 4th. General Michel marched at the head of the 1st/3rd Chasseurs; Colonel Mallet, who had returned from Elba with his emperor, the 2nd Battalion, and finally, General Henrion with the 4th. Thus each square of the Guard had a general marching at their head, with a Marshal of France (Michel Ney) leading the whole.

From the shelter of the bottom of the valley, Ney led the advance to the left, away from the main road, skirting La Haye Sainte and heading towards the centre right of the Allied line. General Petit described the move:

> Formed in square in echelon, they moved forward, General Friant at the head of the 1/3rd Grenadiers, marching parallel to the road, the others following in the best order, conserving their distances as far as La Haye Sainte which they by-passed pursuing the enemy at the *pas de charge*, despite the losses from heavy artillery fire and musketry.[8]

Some historians have criticised the route taken by the Guard because of the difficulty of the ground after the great cavalry attacks. However, an eyewitness suggests this was not the case; 'The slope that led to the plateau was neither steep nor of difficult access…'[9]

Despite their rather motley appearance, the Middle Guard advanced with an admirable steadiness and discipline that was commented on by their British opponents. (Courtesy of Patrice Courcelle)

And so these confident and well-disciplined battalions marched forward in immaculate order with the drums beating the *pas de charge* and to repeated cries of '*Vive l'empereur!*' Although many accounts describe the advance coming under heavy artillery and musket fire it is probable that this is rather exaggerated; we know that most of the Allied infantry line remained on the reverse slope of the ridge and by this time of the battle the Allied skirmish line was thin and short of ammunition. Even the almost continuous line of artillery that had crowned the heights had suffered considerably and was no longer as formidable as it once had been. Indeed, one British eyewitness to the attack later claimed:

THE ATTACK OF THE MIDDLE GUARD

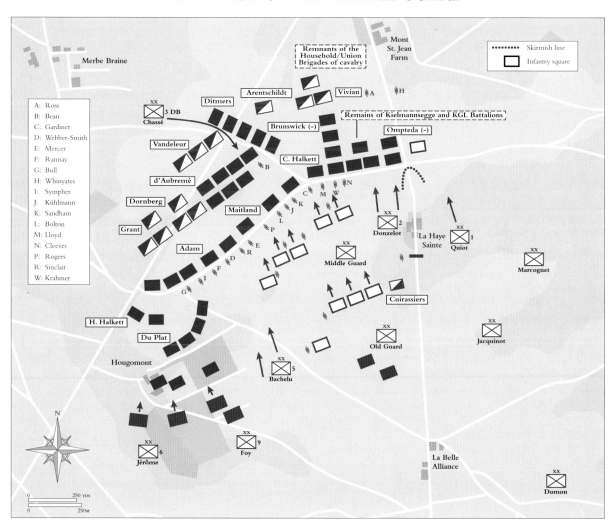

319

The attack of the Middle Guard. (Jean Auge, courtesy of Andrew Field)

I assert with no fear of contradiction, that in front of Halkett's brigade no single gun or skirmisher was in advance of or on the ridge to interfere with it [the attack of the Guard]… To my thinking, no body of the French army could have passed over to our front so little molested as the Imperial Guard. When they passed, where were the well-served batteries that had thundered on, or the lively skirmishers that had pelted their gallant predecessors?… In both cases silent. The French column that came to us, passed the ridge, as they say, *comme à la manoeuvre* [as on an exercise], without a skirmisher to cover it, and I cannot from my soul suppose why it should not.[10]

British accounts are unanimous in their respect for the order of this advance. Ensign Dirom of the 1st Guards, recalled:

The Imperial Guards advanced in close column with ported arms, the officers of the leading divisions in front waving their swords. The French columns showed no appearance of having suffered on their advance, but seemed as regularly formed as if at a field day.[11]

Macready of the 30th Regiment simply recalled, 'They … came over the hill in beautiful order.'[12]

THE ASSAULT

As Marshal Ney led the square of the 1st/3rd Grenadiers to the crest of the Allied ridge, his fifth horse of the day was killed beneath him. Freeing himself from the fallen animal, he continued to lead the attack on foot; bareheaded and with sword in hand.

The advance of the 1st/3rd Grenadiers had certainly impressed those waiting to receive them. A lieutenant of the British 30th Regiment remembered:

> This column came over the hill as if marching on a parade. I saw an officer a pace or two in front, as if regulating the time. I distinctly saw them carry arms as they halted, and then pour in their fire.[13]

Ensign Macready of the same regiment recalled:

> As they rose step by step before us, with their red epaulettes and cross belts put on over their blue great coats, and topped by their high hairy caps, keeping time, and their officers looking to their alignment, they loomed most formidably, and when I thought of their character, and saw their noble bearing, I certainly thought we were in for very slashing work…[14]

Before the 1st/3rd Grenadiers lay a ragged line of British and Brunswick infantry that opened fire on their square. Returning fire they saw the Brunswick battalions start to fall back and they were able to turn their attention on the British infantry, which continued to hold its position. The battalion commander, Major Guillemin reported:

> Arriving on the plateau that dominated the battlefield … we opened fire in two ranks. We remained in this position for some time, always losing many men… A battery of the Guard was a little ahead and to the left of this square. A little time afterwards, the battery was dismounted, the horses and the gunners killed or put *hors de combat*.[15]

Ensign Macready described the initial engagement:

> Arrived within about eighty paces of us (on the following morning I measured the distance which separated our dead from theirs), they halted, and, for a moment, stood as if amazed at our effrontery in offering opposition to their onward movement; then, saluting us, they commenced that work of death so often narrated, when our thinned ranks told but too well with what precision their fire was given.[16]

The Prince of Orange leads a gallant, but futile counter-attack against the advance of the French Guard. He was wounded in the shoulder and the counter-attack thrown back. (Anne S. K. Brown)

The same officer later wrote:

> … the fire thickened tremendously, and the cries from the men struck down, as well as from the numerous wounded on all sides of us, who thought themselves abandoned, were terrible. An extraordinary number of men and officers of both regiments went down in no time … at this instant we found ourselves commingled with the 33rd and 69th Regiments; all order was lost, and the column (now a mere mob), passed the hedge at an accelerated pace …
>
> The exertions of the officers, added to the glorious struggling of lots of the men to halt and face about, were rendered of no avail by the irresistible pressure, and as many cursing and crying with rage and shame, seized individuals to halt them, they were themselves jammed up against them and hurried on with the current, literally for many yards not touching the ground … I cannot conceive what the enemy was about during our confusion. Fifty cuirassiers would have annihilated our brigade …[17]

Spectators of this action from the second line, some of the British cavalry, also thought things were going badly: Lieutenant Luard, of the 16th Light Dragoons, later wrote:

> The fire became every moment hotter, and from the rapid way in which it approached us, appeared as if the enemy was carrying the hill by which we were partially covered, and I confess I thought at that moment the day was going hard with us, that the infantry were beaten, and that we (the cavalry), by desperate charges, were to recover what they had lost.
>
> The foreign troops in our front appeared to think so also, but they had not resolved to recover the day, for they began to give way rapidly. We closed our squadron intervals, and would not let them pass through …[18]

To the left of the 1st/3rd Grenadiers, the square of the 4th Grenadiers now came up parallel and started to exchange fire with the British battalions before it.

As the senior commander of the Guards Grenadiers at Waterloo, General Friant marched at the head of the attack before being wounded and forced to retire. (Topfoto)

As we have heard, the British troops nearest the 1st/3rd were now beginning to fall back in confusion and a hesitant infantry counter-attack (in fact led by the Prince of Orange) from the Allied second line was thrown back and the prince himself wounded.

At this moment, General Friant, the senior commander of the Guard Grenadiers, who was marching at the head of the attack, was wounded in the hand and forced to retire. In his memoirs, Napoleon wrote:

> General Friant, who had been wounded, and was passing by at this moment, said that everything was going well, that the enemy appeared to be forming up his rear-guard to support his retreat, but that he would be completely broken, as soon as the rest of the guard deployed.[19]

There was now a real danger of the Allied centre breaking completely. The 1st/3rd Grenadiers must have thought that, despite the heavy casualties they had suffered, they were now on the point of victory. However, at that very moment, through the dense smoke, they came under a most devastating fire of case shot from almost point-blank range which staggered them and brought down many men.

General Chassé, a Dutch officer who had fought in the French Army for many years but who now commanded the 3rd Netherlands Division, reported:

> At the same time I saw the *Garde Impériale* advancing, while the English troops were leaving the plateau *en masse* and moving in the direction of Waterloo; the battle seemed lost.
>
> Seeing at the same moment that the French Guard was moving forward to attack … I did not hesitate an instant to order the advance of our artillery, commanded by Major Van der Smissen, onto the height, who immediately opened a violent fire.[20]

Again, Macready described the scene:

> I can never forget the fearful slaughter which then took place in the ranks of the 33rd and 69th Regiments… But at that critical instant, Major Van der Smissen arrived with his light Belgian brigade of guns, and, taking up a position on our right, between us and the 33rd and 69th regiments, now warmly engaged, literally cut lanes through the column in our front …
>
> As they hesitated, another salvo of case shot smashed into their thinning ranks and then through the smoke came a column in overwhelming strength. Threatened

Napoleon, right, surveys the scene during the Battle of Waterloo. (akg-images)

with being crushed beneath its unstoppable momentum and with many of its officers already fallen, the square began to break up and suddenly disintegrated in flight.[21]

The appearance of this strong and fresh column of troops, Colonel Detmer's Brigade of Chassé's Division, was the last straw; having already suffered terrible casualties, lashed by the point-blank fire of the newly arrived, and hitherto uncommitted battery, and now threatened by a column of overwhelming strength, the morale and cohesion of the 1st/3rd Grenadiers broke and they disappeared from the ridge in a mob.

Major Guillemin, the commanding officer of the 1st/3rd Grenadiers, later wrote:

> … Marshal Ney came into my square and said to General de Morvan, 'General, it is necessary to die here!' We remained for some time, but the musketry and case shot vomited death from all sides and, in an instant, the square was no longer.[22]

To their left, the square of the 4th Grenadiers, although having had the satisfaction of seeing the British troops opposed to them breaking to the rear, had also suffered crippling casualties. Just as they saw their comrades break, and coming under close range artillery fire themselves, they realised they were in imminent danger of being outflanked and crushed by Detmer's column to their right. They had no option but to fall back also. Ensign Macready described their reluctant withdrawal:

There the 'Old Guard' stood, firm and undismayed, apparently doubtful how to act; no movement in advance, no movement to the rear. There they stood, with bold and manly front, when their comrades' disasters on their right shook that intrepidity and firmness of purpose which had hitherto marked their bearing… The cries of '*Vive l'Empereur*' '*Vive Napoleon!*' '*En avant!*' the roll of the drums, the devotion of the men, availed not. With an apathy and coolness unequalled as it was, on our part unexpected, the French Guards wheeled to the right-about and retreated from before us, retracing the steps which, with a mien indicating anything but an intention to retire, they had just before taken![23]

To the left of the two squares of grenadiers came the two squares of the 1st and 2nd Battalions of the 3rd Regiment of Guard Chasseurs. As they advanced the interval between them had closed and it appears they crossed the ridgeline marching almost parallel. On this flank of the assault, the squares had suffered rather more from artillery fire than the grenadiers. A lieutenant in the British artillery recalled:

The battery fired case shot from the moment they appeared on the crest of the hill (about 200 yards), and during the advance along the plateau, from which they suffered severely, the column waving, at each successive discharge, like standing corn blown by the wind.[24]

Dutch officer, General Chassé, who had previously fought with the French. (Rijksmuseum)

However, not all the Allied artillery was still in action as one of the chasseur officers, Captain Prax, noted: 'On our left was a numerous battery, unlimbered and abandoned by its gunners. These were not far away and their hesitation to return to their pieces was clear.'[25]

As the two squares of chasseurs arrived on the crest of the ridge, the same officer reported, 'We were astonished to find it almost abandoned and covered with dead!'[26]

Perhaps sensing victory the chasseurs moved forward. But hidden by the very summit of the ridge and crouching down in the rye lay two battalions of the imperturbable British guards (the 2nd and 3rd Battalions of the 1st Foot Guards), commanded by Major General Maitland. The order for the brigade to rise and engage the French was given by Wellington himself: 'Now Maitland! Now's your time!' Colonel Crabbé, who had just delivered a message to Marshal Ney and was making his way back to Headquarters, described what happened next:

Sabre in hand, I cleared myself a passage, when I suddenly found myself in the middle of the 3rd Regiment of Foot Chasseurs of the Guard, who were continuing to climb the slopes of Mont-Saint-Jean. At this very moment, a mass of English Guards suddenly appeared on the crest and released a terrible volley on us that caused heavy losses, and then charged us.[27]

The physical and morale effects of this volley, fired at the moment when the chasseurs felt they were on the point of victory, were terrible. Captain Prax reported that, 'All our heads of column were put *hors de combat*.'[28]

It was said that 300 men fell from the first volley alone and the effect of the fire seemed to force the head of the square bodily back. Colonel Mallet, commander of the 3rd Regiment of Chasseurs, and the commanding officers of both battalions, Major Cardinal of the 1st and Major Angelet of the 2nd, were all killed and General Michel, the second in command of all the regiments of chasseurs, also fell. The death of General Michel was described by his aide de camp, Captain Berthelot:

General Michel fell from his horse crying out, 'Ah, my god! I have broken my arm again!' I quickly dismounted and unbuttoned his coat to locate his wound. My general was dead; a ball had passed through his torso.[29]

Surprised by the sudden appearance of the wall of red soldiers, staggered and leaderless from the devastation caused by their volley, the two Guard battalions were unsure what to do and came to a halt about 20 metres from the Allied line.[30] Another British officer reported that:

The effect of our volley was evidently most deadly. The French columns appeared staggered, and, if I may use the expression, convulsed. Part seemed inclined to advance, part halted and fired, and others, more particularly towards the centre and rear of the columns, seemed to be turning round.[31]

Others reported that the two squares attempted to deploy into line so as to be better placed to return effective fire. However, what is clear is that there was hesitation and confusion in their movements and when the British line advanced with bayonets lowered the chasseurs were unable to meet the charge and before cold steel was crossed their morale broke and both squares disintegrated in flight.

Captain Powell of the British 1st Foot Guards recalled:

Immediately the brigade sprang forward. *La Garde* turned and gave us little opportunity to try the steel. We charged down the hill till we had passed the end of the orchard of Hougoumont, when our right flank became exposed to another heavy column (as we afterwards understood of the Chasseurs of the *Garde*) who were advancing in support of the former column. This circumstance, besides that our charge was isolated, obliged the brigade to retire towards their original position.[32]

The 'heavy column' that Captain Powell refers to was the final element of the assault, the square of the 4th Chasseurs. The rather disorganised British guards, in danger of being outflanked by this strong force, had no option but to withdraw. However, for whatever reason, the two battalions lost all cohesion and dashed back to the top of the ridge in something of a disorganised mob.

The 4th Chasseurs, no doubt heartened by this reaction to their advance, continued up the slope, 'with shouts, which rose above the noise of the firing'.[33] All that the chasseurs found in front of them was the battery of guns that had fired on their comrades with such telling effect. It was a most critical moment for the Allies, as Captain Millar of the 2nd Battalion of the 95th Rifles admitted:

The enemy [4th Chasseurs] advanced to the bend of the position, and forced back the left of my regiment, down the eastern slope of the ridge and the right of the one to the left [2nd/1st Guards], leaving an opening of between one and two hundred yards in the line. That appeared to me the most critical period of the battle; as there was only a line of Belgians behind, which would probably have made no great resistance, *all seemed lost* [his emphasis].[34]

However, off to the flank of the enemy square, but hidden by the ridgeline, lay the 52nd Light Infantry; a regiment with a fine reputation from the Peninsular War

PREVIOUS
Clad in a motley array of
headgear and uniforms, Imperial
Guardsmen in square formation
brace themselves for impact as
they prepare to repel enemy
cavalry. The regimental eagle,
of the pattern used in 1812–15,
is visible alongside a pair of
mounted senior officers in
bicornes. (akg-images)

and led by the famous Colonel Sir John Colborne. He had placed himself so that he could observe what was happening to his left and had seen the progress of the last square. Seeing it stop and open fire on the battery to his left, he sent his skirmishers forward against the flank of the square as he organised his attack.

When the square of the 4th Chasseurs stopped, the front face opened fire on the battery and soon swept away the remaining gunners; a British officer recalled, 'The brigade of guns in front of the 52nd right, which had fired incessantly during the first half hour, was now silenced by the intensity of the opposing musketry.'[35]

At much the same time, the left face of the square opened fire on the 52nd's skirmishers with telling effect. However, the skirmishers were suddenly replaced by the whole of the regiment, which delivered a crashing volley. Despite the square's strength, it could only oppose this assault with a single face, which was soon being smashed by the British fire. Although it appears that the chasseurs made some attempt to deploy into line to meet this threat, it was too little, too late.

For an eyewitness account of this action we must turn to a British officer of the 52nd:

> Our artillery ... had been playing upon the masses of the French Guard, but when we saw them there appeared to be no confusion amongst them; our advance put a stop to the fire of our artillery; it was not till the 52nd skirmishers fired into them that the Imperial Guard halted ... faced outwards and returned the fire; as the 52nd approached, our skirmishers fell back to the regiment, two of the three officers being severely wounded, and many of the men being either killed or wounded. The regiment opened fire upon the enemy without halting; the men fired, then partly halted to load, whilst those in the rear slipped round them in a sort of skirmishing order, though they maintained a compact line ... I consider that about 140 of our men were killed or wounded at this time, in the course of five or six minutes... As we closed towards the French Guard, they did not wait for our charge, but the leading column at first somewhat receded from us, and then broke and fled ...[36]

The attack of the Middle Guard had been defeated.

French accounts of the battle would have us believe that it was only at the defeat of the Middle Guard that Napoleon's subterfuge on the arrival of Marshal Grouchy was finally exposed. However, it is impossible to believe that most of the French Army was unaware of the Prussian appearance on the battlefield, given that they had started their attack at 4 p.m. By the time of the Guard's advance they were at Plancenoit in the rear of the army.

It is rather too convenient for some to claim that it was only now that the arrival of the Prussians became common knowledge, as *Chef de bataillon* Octave-René-Louis Levavasseur, aide de camp to Marsahl Ney, wrote:

> This news [that Grouchy had arrived] had hardly reached the end of our line when cannon fire was heard in our rear. The greatest silence, astonishment, anxiety followed the enthusiasm. The plain was covered with our wagons and a multitude of non-combatants who always followed the army; the cannonade continued and got closer. Officers and soldiers got muddled up, mixed with the non-combatants. Appalled, I closed up to the Marshal, who ordered me to go to find out the cause of this panic. I met up with General — who said to me, 'See, these are the Prussians!' I returned to find the Marshal, but could not. Our army then only presented an unformed mass, with all the regiments mixed up. At this fatal moment, command had broken down, everyone was taken aback in the presence of a danger they could not define.[37]

THE ROUT BEGINS

What is almost certainly true is that the repulse of the Guard coincided with the telling intervention of a second Prussian corps; that of Lieutenant General Hans von Zieten. General Friedrich Wilhelm Count von Bülow's IV Corps had already been fighting for some time at Plancenoit on the French right-rear. Zieten's men approached via the Allied left flank, and although there was an understandable delay as they orientated themselves, once they launched their assault on the apex of the French right, around Papelotte, the effect on the French troops fighting in this sector was catastrophic.

Wellington orders the advance after the repulse of the French Guard. The hussar officer in front of Wellington is the Earl of Uxbridge, his second in command and commander of the Allied cavalry. (Anne S. K. Brown)

The arrival of Zieten's men soon tipped the balance as the French were now considerably outnumbered and, having committed the guard, had no reserves left. On the French right there was only a single, tired brigade, General Brue's of the I Corps, to oppose the whole of Zieten's Corps. At first they put up a strong fight and General Charles-Claude Jacquinot, who commanded the cavalry division attached to the I Corps, even made some successful charges against the first tentative Prussian moves. However, as more and more of the Prussian troops came up the extent of their intervention became apparent and the French right flank started an increasingly disordered withdrawal.

It is certain that the final rout of the French Army started in the area of Papelotte as Zieten's men began to flood the battlefield. Having established his infantry beyond the difficult ground surrounding the hamlets on this part of the battlefield, his cavalry were then able to take up the advance. Lieutenant Pontécoulant of the Guard artillery reported:

> Our line, that until then had gloriously held against all the forces of a superior enemy, was suddenly broken. The Prussian cavalry hurled itself into this breach and soon flooded the battlefield, sabring isolated soldiers and making it impossible for us to rally. The news, spread by malevolence or fear, that the Guard, the rock of the army, had been obliged to retire and was partly destroyed, augmented the disorder and the precipitation of the retreat. The crowd became terrified; no description can do it justice …[38]

Sir John Colborne commanded the 52nd Light Infantry at Waterloo, and his actions, along with those of his skirmishers, ensured the regiment retained its fine reputation as they defeated the final echelon of the Middle Guard. (Topfoto)

The panic that had seized General Durutte's 4th Infantry Division, which was the right-hand division of the I Corps, began to communicate itself down the French line. It seems to have reached the centre of the line, around La Haye Sainte, just as the French troops there saw the unprecedented sight of the Guard retiring in chaos. It was the last straw; La Haye Sainte was given up without a fight and the troops in the area, threatened by the Prussians on their right and the British to their front and left, dissolved in panic.

As the debris of the Middle Guard attempted to rally on the valley floor a long line of red-coated infantry came over the ridge before them. Still in disorder and having suffered such heavy casualties in their assault, all hope for them was lost and they fled. After the repulse of the Guard, Wellington had waved his hat in the air, a sign that had been taken for a general advance. The move forward was led by Adam's Brigade who had continued their initial advance into the bottom of the valley in pursuit of the defeated Guard battalions. Some battalions, exhausted and low on ammunition, felt incapable of following and had slumped to the ground on the ridge; others, still resolute but equally exhausted, made a tentative advance but got no further than the floor of the valley. Colonel Hew Halkett's 3rd Hanoverian Brigade seconded that of Adam.

In the dead ground near to La Haye Sainte, lay the three battalions of the Old Guard: the 1st/2nd Grenadiers, the 2nd/1st Chasseurs and 2nd/2nd Chasseurs, and the 2nd/3rd Grenadiers that Napoleon had deployed to the left at the beginning of the attack. The emperor had originally planned to support the attack of the Middle Guard with these battalions but the situation had already changed dramatically and with the whole French Army slowly disintegrating around him, he had no option but to use them to form a screen behind which to try and rally the army before total disaster struck.

These four battalions were formed in square, 'in perfectly undisturbed steadiness',[39] and ran in a line between the main road towards Hougoumont. They had the sad remains of some cuirassier regiments in support and the French artillery was still firing over their heads. General Cambronne, commander of the 1st Regiment of Chasseurs was there, as was General Roguet, *colonel-en-second* of the Grenadiers.

THE SACRIFICE OF THE OLD GUARD

Meanwhile the 52nd, supported by the rest of its brigade, reached the floor of the valley, where they were confronted by the steady squares of the Old Guard. Here they hesitated, but were soon joined by Wellington himself who said, 'They won't stand, better attack them.'[40] The advance continued and the Guard battalions started their retreat.

The advance of the British line after the last desperate effort of the Imperial Guard had been frustrated by the steady and determined conduct of the Allied Army. (Anne S. K. Brown)

Closest to Hougoumont, the 2nd/3rd Grenadiers, commanded by Lieutenant Colonel Belcourt, were somewhat isolated from the other three battalions and thus rather vulnerable. In fact the advance of the Allied infantry had cut across their front to their right, towards the three battalions of the Old Guard. Standing alone therefore, they became the target of the Allied artillery and in such a dense formation they were soon suffering serious casualties. Sergeant Mauduit wrote:

> The balls, shells, and a little later, the caseshot, inflicted terrible losses. Nevertheless, it [the battalion of the 2nd/3rd Grenadiers] did not abandon its post; it only re-dressed its ranks as each salvo opened a gap, firing at hardly a quarter range, and soon 150 grenadiers out of 550 were struck down …[41]

The advance of the Allied infantry was closely followed by Vivien's and Vendeleur's brigades of fresh British cavalry. Vivien's troopers swept down on this isolated French battalion, but, secure in their square, the cavalry were repulsed. Seeing that the square maintained its discipline and cohesion, the cavalry quickly moved on to seek easier prey. Vivian's Brigade continued along the line of the main road, pressing the squares of the Old Guard in their retreat, whilst Vandeleur's Brigade pushed further to the west, turning the retreat of Reille's II Corps into a rout.

Given the helplessness of their position, Lieutenant Colonel Belcourt decided to withdraw. Continuing casualties forced them into a triangular formation as they had insufficient troops to remain in square. Later the triangle was attacked by Brunswick lancers, but again the cavalry was repulsed. However, it continued to suffer severely from the case shot being fired by horse artillery pieces that followed up their withdrawal. Eventually, the surviving guardsmen could take no more and the square broke up. Only 100 guardsmen, from the original 550, joined the 1st Regiment of Grenadiers near Rosomme.

The three remaining battalions of the Old Guard did not wait to encounter the advancing red line. An officer of the British 52nd Light Infantry recalled:

> The squares of the Old Guard made no attempt to deploy; but, after opening a heavy fire from their front and flanks, as soon as the opposing line came too near, with great steadiness ceased firing, faced to the rear, and commenced their retreat by word of command, the two right squares directly to the rear on the right side of the *chaussée*, pursued by the 71st and skirmishers of the 95th. The left square, accompanied at first by the cuirassiers, passing obliquely to the left, crossed the *chaussée* (which was crowded with fugitives) below La Belle Alliance, and then hastened towards Rosomme, along the left side of the road, followed closely by the

52nd Regiment, the two British regiments still in lines four deep. On crossing the *chaussée*, the cuirassiers fronted as if to charge; but their opponents pressed towards them, presenting their bayonets, unwilling to lose time either by firing or forming square, and the cuirassiers declined the contest.[42]

Major Guillemin, who had commanded the 1st/3rd Grenadiers during the assault on the ridge, wrote:

> We retired, the Marshal [Ney], the General [de Morvan] and I, to the square of the old grenadiers commanded by General Cambronne. Passing close to the farm [presumably La Belle Alliance], we were struck by a discharge of caseshot from an enemy battery placed on the road and by the volleys of several battalions. The Emperor, who was next to this square, seeing the battle lost, gave the orders for it to retire.[43]

General Cambronne later became famous for being the officer who, in response to a summons to surrender, is supposed to have replied, '*La Garde muert et ne se rend pas!*' ('The Guard dies, but does not surrender!') However, Cambronne himself is later quoted as saying, 'I did not say what is attributed to me, I replied with something else.'[44] Soon afterwards, wounded and trapped by his fallen horse, Cambronne was captured by Colonel Hew Halkett.

General Cambronne, commander of 1st Regiment of Chasseurs, who was famously reported to have said '*La Garde meurt et ne se rend pas!*' ('the Guard dies, but does not surrender'). (Anne S. K. Brown)

The 2nd/2nd Chasseurs formed the centre square of the three. Having received the order to retire, the commanding officer of this battalion, Major Mompez, directed it along the right of the main road. As it moved back it was in almost constant contact with Allied cavalry and infantry. A steady trickle of casualties and stragglers soon reduced the square to a mere handful of men. Further on they met the bloody remains of their sister battalion, the 1st/2nd Chasseurs, who had evacuated Plancenoit with the Eagle of the Chasseurs. However, despite this reinforcement the square could not maintain its order and it broke up, the men joining the flood of fugitives.

The third square, on the right of the line of three, was that of the 1st/2nd Grenadiers, commanded by Major Golzio. To its right were some weak regiments of cuirassiers and a regiment of *chasseurs à cheval*. Some French histories accuse this cavalry of deserting the grenadiers without orders and before they were seriously attacked. But the truth is, however willing they may have been, the debris of the French heavy cavalry was incapable of any further cohesive action. Colonel Ordener, who was commanding a brigade of cuirassiers, summed up the situation:

At this sight [the charges of Vivian and Vandeleur], the commotion penetrated our ranks; the devotion of our cavalrymen was finished, the sense of self-preservation overwhelmed it. In vain did we make our final efforts to keep them in line; they went down the slopes in disorder, swirled around the squares of the Guard and dispersed under a hail of musket balls.[45]

A British account illustrates the failure of the French cavalry to intervene:

… there are, however, described by others of the 52nd as having been three squares, with a body of cavalry on their right; they had three guns on their left, which fired a round or two of grape at us. The 52nd did not return the fire of these troops of the Old Guard. On our advancing, the French retired in good order. The cavalry on their right faced about to cover the retreat of their squares, but, on pressing on our pursuit, they prudently refused the encounter with our compact four deep line.[46]

The same officer went on to say:

Only one of their squares retreated by our left of La Belle Alliance and the Charleroi road; and this square the 52nd kept in view for nearly a mile further, until they lost sight of it about a quarter of a mile before it reached the farm house of Rosomme, where we brought up for the night.[47]

The square followed by the 52nd, to the left of La Belle Alliance, was that of the 2nd/2nd Grenadiers. Having out-marched their pursuers, their eventual fate is described by the commander of the 2nd Regiment of Grenadiers, General Christiani: 'The English skirmishers appeared and opened fire. Then I began my own retreat with my battalion in square; several balls fell amongst us that caused some confusion in the ranks.'[48]

General Cambronne is taken prisoner by Colonel Halkett, having been wounded and trapped by his fallen horse. (Rijksmuseum)

These four Guard battalions, three of them of the Old Guard, had achieved little and were ultimately lost; so few troops, even of such high calibre, had no chance of stalling the general advance of the Allied Army, and the increasing flood of Prussians.

Despite the helplessness of their situation, all British accounts agree that these battalions put up a heroic resistance. A lieutenant in the 52nd Light Infantry recalled:

Vivian's brigade of hussars came up rapidly in echelon of regiments to the assistance of the 71st. The cuirassiers, worn out as they were, and discouraged as they had reason to be, with much devotedness fronted in the line of La Belle Alliance, to protect the squares of the Old Guard, but a squadron of the 10th [Hussars] dashing at them, followed immediately by one of the 18th [Hussars], they were dispersed in hopeless confusion. The compact battalions of the Old Guard were not so soon routed: a part of the 10th having rallied after the charge on the cuirassiers, found itself under the fire of one of the squares; the men fell very fast, and there was no alternative but instantly to retreat or to charge.

The near approach of the 71st to another face of the same square, decided Sir Hussey Vivian to order the latter. The charge was very gallantly attempted; Major Howard, who conducted it, fell upon the bayonets; some of the grenadiers were cut down by men of the 10th, but even under such circumstances,-charged home by cavalry on two faces, (for the 18th immediately followed to the assistance of their comrades) and under heavy fire of infantry on the other,-the veterans knew too well their strength, and in what their safety consisted, to shrink from the contest: they closed well together, beat off the cavalry with a very destructive fire, and, in spite of the approaching infantry, made good their retreat.[49]

This artwork depicts the moment of the final stand of the Imperial Guard at Mont Saint Jean during the closing stages of the battle. (Anne S. K. Brown)

As the Old Guard squares struggled to resist the Allied advance, a large part of the rest of the army had become nothing more than a mob. The battlefield was now being flooded by Prussian cavalry to the east of the main road, and the two brigades of fresh British cavalry to the west. Against these, and their supporting infantry, the shattered and exhausted remains of the Guard could offer little serious resistance. Eventually, Napoleon had no option but to commit the only fresh cavalry left under his own hand: the Service Squadrons. These squadrons provided his own personal bodyguard and were drawn from each of the guard cavalry regiments to a total of about 400 men. Their gallant charge was quickly overwhelmed.

THE DISINTEGRATION OF THE FRENCH ARMY

Most French histories state that the French rout almost certainly started in Durutte's Division and that this, combined with the repulse of the Guard, rapidly communicated itself to the rest of d'Erlon's I Corps. Lieutenant Martin of the 45th Line Regiment recalled:

Everyone was fleeing as fast and far as possible. I did the same as everyone else.

The other Corps disbanded at the same time. Panic had seized the entire army. There was nothing more than a confused mass of infantry soldiers, cavalry and guns that rushed, all mixed together, across the plain like an unstoppable torrent, through the Prussian squadrons that charged them and the English battalions that descended from their plateau with cries of victory. Alone, several squares of the Guard, held back by Napoleon at the foot of La Belle Alliance, remained immobile as rocks in a raging sea. The crowds of fugitives passed between the squares and soon only the enemy surrounded them …[50]

Isolated from the immediate impact of the Prussian intervention, the situation on the French left was not yet so dire. The French II Corps did not break into

La Veille Garde a Waterloo 18 Juin 1815. (Anne S. K. Brown)

irremediable confusion on the defeat of the Guard, but attempted a more regular retreat. Reille himself reported that his corps retired in good order, but Captain Robinaux of the 2nd Line Regiment wrote:

> This [order] did not last long; we received several balls from behind us and the frightened soldiers, looking over their shoulders, saw our Polish lancers, whom they took for English cavalry [the French Guard lancers were dressed in red] and shouted, 'We are lost!' This call was repeated throughout the column and soon we were in complete disorder: each thought only of his own salvation. It is impossible to rally such lost soldiers.[51]

Marshal Ney is recognised for working hard to rally small bands of men and many French historians credit him with vain attempts to find death on the battlefield. The most common is his appeal to troops of Brue's Brigade of Durutte's Division. This account is based on a postscript to Durutte's own account of the battle in which he said:

> Chef de battalion Rulhières, who was with the 95th Line, and therefore part of the 2nd Brigade, told me in Paris a little time after the battle of Waterloo, that Marshal Ney, seeing the good order of Brue's brigade at the very moment that I left it to look for a route through the ravine, directed it onto the main road, taking it back several hundred paces. He appeared to want to stop the enemy at this point. He shouted to it with energy … 'I will show you how a marshal of France dies.'[52]

As the battle drew to a close, Napoleon fled the battlefield on horseback, his last throw of the dice having failed, and his army disintegrating around him. (Rijksmuseum)

Escorted by the exhausted and much depleted survivors of his Guard, Napoleon retreats from the battlefield. (akg-images)

Wellington too, in advancing close behind his lead troops, put himself in considerable danger. Close to La Belle Alliance, which had been Napoleon's observation post for much of the battle, he met Field Marshal Gebhard Leberecht von Blücher. Wellington later described the meeting: 'We were both on horseback; but he embraced me, exclaiming "*Mein lieber kamerad*" ["My dear friend" (in German)] and then "*Quelle affaire!*" ["What a business!"] which was pretty much all he knew of French.' Given the exhaustion of his troops, Wellington agreed that the Prussians should take on the responsibility for the pursuit; he gave orders for his own army to halt for the night. The 52nd Light Infantry had reached Rossomme; the cavalry of Vandeleur and Vivian only a little further.

For Wellington's Army the battle was over, but for the French the nightmare had much longer to run. The Prussians maintained a relentless pursuit and most Frenchmen were incapable of any further resistance; many were cut down unable to defend themselves. So complete was their disorganisation that the Prussians mounted a drummer boy on a stray horse and the sound of his drum was sufficient to keep the French on the run and prevent them from rallying.

Napoleon's last throw of the dice had resulted in failure and the total collapse of his army. Having ordered the three remaining battalions of the Guard near La Belle Alliance to withdraw, Napoleon had ridden back to the squares of the 1st Grenadiers at Rossomme. Showing some determination to stay with these squares and perhaps even seek his own death, he was bundled away by his closest staff. His hopes of rallying the army were hopeless in the darkness and chaos that surrounded him. His coaches, captured by the Prussians, were lost to him and he was forced to leave the battlefield on horseback; a weary path back to Paris, exile and ignominy.

CHAPTER 10

THE LEGACY OF WATERLOO

War and Politics in Europe in the 19th Century

HUW DAVIES

PREVIOUS
Wellington and Blücher meet
at the end of the battle, as
Napoleon's forces are finally
defeated. (Anne S. K. Brown)

'Quelle Affaire!' Field Marshal Gebhard Leberecht von Blücher's reputed exclamation to Wellington when they met at La Belle Alliance at around 9 p.m. on the evening of 18 June was an aptly chosen phrase to describe the momentous events that had occurred throughout that afternoon. Whilst most histories of the Battle of Waterloo conclude with this meeting, the military and political ramifications were only just beginning, and would have an impact on the course of European and global history for at least the next century. As Wellington and Blücher shook hands at La Belle Alliance, Napoleon was abandoning hope of rallying his troops at Genappe, and was preparing to retreat to Paris, where he hoped to orchestrate a defensive campaign.

Lieutenant General August Neithardt von Gneisenau, Blücher's chief of staff, continued to press Napoleon's retreating forces, eventually getting as far south as Frasnes, having captured 8,000 prisoners, 200 guns and over 1,000 supply wagons.[1] On top of this, the slaughter of French stragglers and wounded by the Prussian cavalry was brutal. 'That the French in their flight from Waterloo were unnecessarily butchered during many hours by the exasperated Prussians, is a fact,' wrote one British observer, 'which I can more easily explain than justify.'[2] This more than anything inhibited Napoleon's ability to defend Paris, but the Allied descent on the French capital was by no means clear cut.

Having failed to march to the sound of the guns on 18 June, Marshal Emmanuel de Grouchy managed to defeat the Prussian Lieutenant General Johann von Thielmann at the Battle of Wavre on the 19th. Thielmann had nevertheless achieved his objective of tying down 30,000 French soldiers and

The final retreat of the last two
squares at Waterloo by Henri-Paul
Motte. (Topfoto)

thus preventing Grouchy from marching to Napoleon's aid. There was nothing he could do, though, to prevent Grouchy, upon hearing of Napoleon's defeat, from retreating in good order back into France with his force intact.

In Paris by 21 June, Napoleon began to plan a defence based, as he had the previous year, around Laon. A scratch force of 55,000, composed of Grouchy's retreating corps, 15,000 National Guard in Paris and 17,000 volunteers was assembled. More generally, the military situation was comparable to the first half of 1813, and the impressive defence of Paris in 1814. Between them, Marshal Nicolas Soult and Marshal Louis-Nicolas Davout had 117,000 men, and 150,000 conscripts were already in the depots.[3] Elsewhere on the frontiers, the Austrians suffered a sharp defeat outside Strasbourg on 28 June, while small Napoleonic French forces kept the Allied armies busy in sieges and delaying actions along the Swiss border, in the Alps and at Toulon. Rebel forces in Provence and Brittany were also successfully repressed by 25 July, while irregular Napoleonic forces hampered the Allied advance throughout late June and July.

By then, of course, it was all too late. The politicians in Paris, having received news of Napoleon's defeat, now demanded his abdication. Force was briefly considered as a means of maintaining his grip on power, but was quickly discarded. Napoleon had based the legitimacy of his regime on his military success against France's European enemies, not against her own people.[4] 'I have not come back from Elba to have Paris run with blood.' Faced with declining political and popular support in Paris, Napoleon once again abdicated on 23 June, leaving for Malmaison, in the north-eastern Parisian suburbs.

The Anglo-Dutch and Prussian Armies commenced their advance toward Paris on the 19th. From his more advanced position, Blücher progressed rapidly, entering France and reaching Maubeuge by 23 June. Wellington's exhausted troops were unable to advance quite so rapidly, whilst Wellington also insisted on immaculate discipline: he did not want to excite the anger of the French population. Although British soldiers apparently behaved well, their Belgian counterparts caused serious concerns. By the same token, the Prussians were out to avenge the depredations of 1806.[5]

On 19 June, Wellington himself briefly returned to Brussels to oversee preparations for the reception of his wounded soldiers. Waterloo had been a devastating battle. 15,000 of Wellington's men lay dead or wounded on the field itself, along with a further 32,000 French and Prussian casualties. Some regiments had suffered particularly badly. The 1st Guards, for example, had lost 55 per cent dead and wounded.[6]

There is a sense from Wellington's private correspondence that he was a little disappointed at the way the battle had unfolded. 'Never did I see such a pounding

The Battle of Waterloo had been devastating for the armies involved, as well as the village. Here the destruction is clear to see, with the dead and wounded littering the battlefield while camp followers tended to them. (Anne S. K. Brown)

match,' he wrote to his old comrade, Marshal William Beresford. 'Both were what the boxers call gluttons. Napoleon did not manoeuvre at all. He just moved forward in the old style, in columns, and was driven off in the old style.' Still, the fact that the difference between defeat and victory balanced on a knife-edge did not escape Wellington. 'I had the infantry for some time in squares,' he continued, 'and we had the French cavalry walking about us as if they had been our own.' He concluded, 'I never saw the British infantry behave so well.'[7] Although it is difficult to estimate precisely what military lessons Wellington took from his experience at Waterloo, it is clear from the tone of letters such as this, that he had reservations about pursuing innovative military tactics and strategies. Revolutionary warfare had achieved so much, but in the end, when confronted by a strongly positioned and disciplined force, a battle had developed that bore greater similarity to 18th-century campaigns than those of Napoleon's heyday. Such thinking was to have important repercussions in British and European military development.

By 23 June, Wellington, further north than Blücher, had also entered France and was investing the fortress at Valenciennes, and storming the fortress at Cambrai. Three days later, Wellington was outside Péronne, but the town refused to surrender, and Wellington was compelled to send in Major General Sir Peregrine Maitland's 1st Guards Brigade. 'The troops took the hornwork which covers the suburb on the left of the Somme by storm, with but small loss,' Wellington wrote matter-of-factly to the Secretary of State for War,

The Duke of Wellington depicted as an old man surveying the battlefield of Waterloo, c.1840. (Courtesy of the Council of the National Army Museum)

Lord Bathurst. 'The town immediately afterwards surrendered, on condition that the garrison should lay down their arms, and be allowed to return to their homes.'[8]

Any sense that resistance was weakening and Paris would fall without a fight was dismissed on the following day when Grouchy attacked Blücher at Compiègne, checking the Prussian advance, and allowing Wellington to catch up. Grouchy attacked again on 28 June, before entering Paris on the 29th.[9] Wellington estimated – correctly – that the French had between 40 and 50,000 troops in Paris, whilst they had 'fortified the heights of Montmartre and the town of St Denis strongly', and 'the heights of Belleville are likewise strongly fortified'. Ever the pragmatist, Wellington concluded that the French 'have a strong position on this side of Paris',[10] and detailed his reservations to Blücher:

> It appears to me, that, with the force which you and I have under our command at present, the attack of Paris is a matter of great risk. I am convinced it cannot be made on this side with any hope of success ... and even ... if we should succeed the loss would be very severe.

Wellington understood that if an attack were necessary, 'we must incur a severe loss… But in this case it is not necessary.'[11] In a few days, the next of the Allied

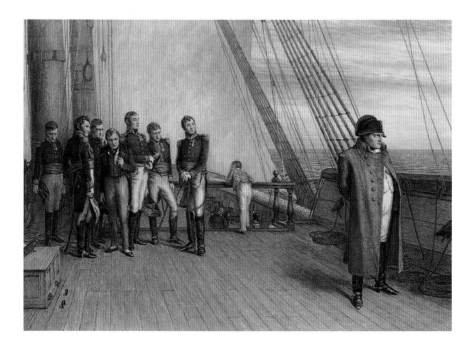

Following his surrender to the British on 15 July 1815, Napoleon was exiled to St Helena, over a thousand miles off the West African coast, and was carried there on the *Bellerophon*. (Anne S. K. Brown)

THE RACE FOR PARIS, JUNE 1815

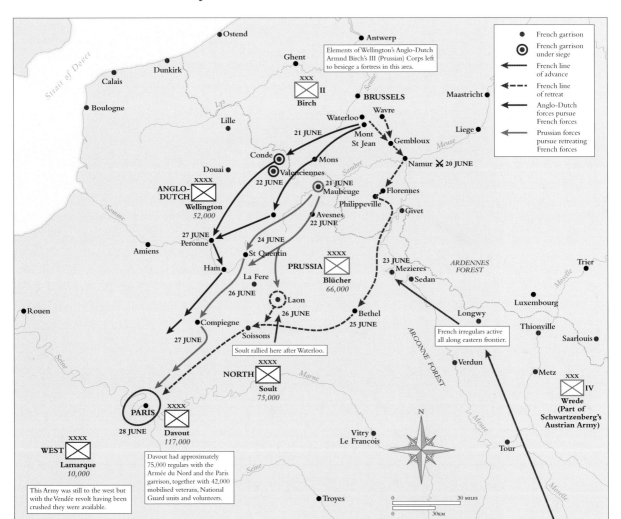

armies would arrive from the east, followed by the Allied sovereigns. Instead, Wellington proposed an armistice. In the event, in order to convince the French to accept the terms offered by the British and Prussians, Blücher moved his army to the south-west of Paris. With Paris surrounded on all sides, an armistice was signed, and the French Army retired south of the Loire, whilst the Prussians occupied the city.[12]

Napoleon meanwhile fled to Rochefort. As he fled, he reputedly wondered, 'What is to become of this poor France? I have done what I could for her.'[13] Wonder he might. France had indeed briefly been master of Europe under his leadership. But his insatiable quest for military glory, bound as it was to his deep-seated need for the approval of the French people, ultimately brought about French ruin. As he departed France, intelligence was received by Wellington that 'a great proportion of the 87 departments are ruined, or in a state of revolt.'[14]

Having briefly entertained the hope of crossing the Atlantic, he eventually surrendered to the British aboard HMS *Bellerophon*. The British pondered what to do with the fallen emperor. The prime minister, Lord Liverpool, initially favoured trial and execution as a rebel, but was persuaded out of this stance by his foreign secretary, Viscount Castlereagh. In response, the cabinet held 'strongly to the opinion that the best place of custody would be at a distance from Europe', and ultimately they decided to banish him to the tiny island of St Helena in the South Atlantic.[15] There Napoleon Bonaparte lived out the last of his days, reflecting sourly on his past successes, and providing copious explanations for his failures. He died in 1821, most likely of a form of stomach cancer, although several conspiracy theories exist as to the actual cause of his death.

With Paris in Allied hands, and Napoleon entering permanent confinement, attention now turned to securing the peace that had been so painstakingly decided at Vienna the previous autumn. Unmistakeably, Prussia wanted revenge. Prussian diplomats, and by extension the wider political and military class, including Blücher, had felt hard done by in the peace negotiations at Vienna. There the shifting sands of European diplomacy had one moment seen Prussia promised the whole of Saxony as compensation for the costs of the long war with France; whilst the next moment, that promise was diminished to no more than a third of Saxon territory.[16]

It is vital to view Prussian actions in the wake of Waterloo within this context. At Vienna, the tensions between the Great Powers over Prussia's claim on Saxony, and Russia's claim on Poland, had nearly resulted in another European war. If these questions could not be resolved quickly, Castlereagh had written, 'it will not suit the exhausted finances of Prussia to remain long armed and inactive; nor can Russia expose herself indefinitely to the encumbrance of large armies remaining unemployed … on her own frontier.' France and Austria would quickly be drawn into a war in Germany, and with the newly established independence of the Low Countries once more in the balance, Britain too would find it 'difficult … to abstract herself from the contest.'[17]

In July 1815, the circumstances were little different. Prussia, with a decisive contribution to the final defeat of Napoleon, could now claim greater compensation at the expense of France. The immediate manifestation of this renewed belligerence came in the treatment of Paris by the occupying Prussian Army. They demanded a contribution from the city totalling 110 million francs, and even sought to blow up the Pont d'Jena. Wellington was desperately worried 'that we shall immediately set the whole country against us, and shall excite a national war, if the useless, and if it was not likely to be attended with such serious consequences, I should call it ridiculous, oppression practised upon the French people, is not put a stop to…'[18]

Wellington was at pains to persuade Blücher to postpone his actions at least until the arrival of the Allied sovereigns. He implied that by acting in haste now, Blücher would throw away long-term Prussian ambitions at the expense of the short-term appeasement of his men's desire for revenge. 'The destruction of the bridge of Jena is highly disagreeable to the King and to the people, and may occasion disturbance in the city,' the duke wrote to his Prussian counterpart. 'It is not merely a military measure, but is one likely to attach to the character of our operations, and is of political importance.'[19] Blücher, though, was uninterested in political reasoning, and there was little Wellington could do to contain Prussian violence until the arrival of the Allied sovereigns.

Blücher's obsession with vengeance gave Wellington and Castlereagh, who arrived in Paris on 6 July, the opportunity to lay the foundations for a stable and long-lasting peace. Perhaps the most important immediate objective was the question of who would replace Napoleon on the throne of France. Dissent amongst the Allies existed from the moment Napoleon so effortlessly deposed Louis XVIII upon his escape from Elba. Tsar Alexander favoured a pact with the Bonapartists to replace Napoleon with his son. Austria favoured the imposition of the Duke of Orleans, a line thought to be supported by Charles Maurice de Talleyrand-Périgord, the French foreign minister, who had been coldly rejected by Louis XVIII in favour of his émigré advisors. Partly out of the necessity of a legitimate aim in order to gain the support of Parliament for the prosecution of another European campaign, the British were alone in supporting the second restoration of Louis XVIII.

Castlereagh worked hard during the 'Hundred Days' to convince his Allies to support Louis' restoration: a process that proved to be a two-way street. In order to buy Talleyrand's support, Louis had to be convinced to drop his incompetent émigré advisors, and appoint Talleyrand first minister. This was a difficult decision for Louis to take, as he viewed Talleyrand as untrustworthy and corrupt. Castlereagh agreed, 'yet I know not on whom H.M. can better depend. He has not a chance in the hands of those now around him. The fact is, France is a den of thieves and brigands, and they can only be governed by criminals like themselves…'[20] Neither the Russians nor Austrians were convinced Louis was the right man for the job, and it was only Wellington's quick victory at Waterloo that enabled the swift restoration of Louis.

The armistice that saw the capitulation of Paris at the beginning of July also facilitated the 'quiet restoration of His Majesty to his throne'. This, Wellington argued, was 'that result of the war which all the Sovereigns of all of us have always considered the most beneficial for us all, and the most likely to lead to permanent peace in Europe.'[21] In making this statement to Blücher, Wellington was plainly lying, but he knew better than anyone that once restored, none of the Allied sovereigns would act to depose Louis XVIII.

That said, the restoration was not quite so clear-cut, and Wellington was forced to negotiate with the treacherous Joseph Fouché, Napoleon's one-time head of secret police. 'If I had not settled with Fouché when I did, the Duke of Orleans would have been proclaimed next day, and that would have been a new trouble.'[22] In the event, Louis XVIII was obliged to adopt constitutional government, and elections were held in September. Talleyrand and Fouché were deposed in favour of the ultra-Royalist, and ultra-competent Armand-Emmanuel de Vignerot du Plessis, Duke of Richelieu.[23] Initially, Louis was far from popular. Nicknamed 'the King of the Tuileries' because of his constant presence at the Tuileries Palace and his staged garden parties, Louis was toothless, unable to influence the progress of the new negotiations that would determine the fate of his kingdom.[24]

In this matter he would have to rely on Wellington and Castlereagh, who could now turn their attention to securing the balance of power in Europe.

A British review takes place in Paris, 1815. Following Napoleon's defeat at Waterloo, the Allies marched into Paris on 29 June 1815. (Duplessis-Bertaux collection, courtesy of René Chartrand)

'The martial achievements of Great Britain and her Allies' – Napoleon is depicted captured and contained in a bottle, a trophy of the victorious Allies. (Anne S. K. Brown)

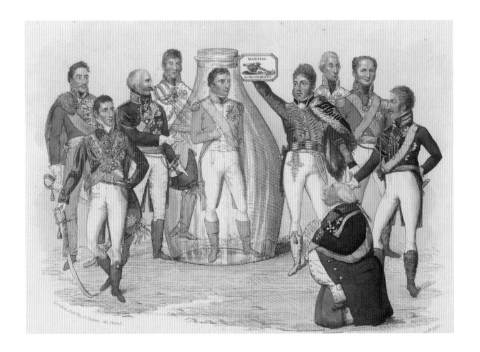

Charles Webster captured the severity of the situation the two Irishmen now faced. With hundreds of thousands of Allied troops streaming into France, they might have 'saved the dynasty, [now] they had the more difficult task of saving France.'[25] Wellington's new priority was the need to contain the worst excesses of his Allies.

During the preparations for the Waterloo campaign, Wellington had suggested the widespread use of commissaries, who would follow each of the armies and issue receipts to the population in anticipation of payment for the food and resources that they were compelled to provide the Allied armies. This system initially failed to protect anyone from the malevolence of the Prussian troops, who acquired supplies wherever they needed them with no concern for the property of the populations they took from, whether they be in Holland, Belgium or France. Wellington's system only found modest support amongst the cabinet in London. 'It is quite right to prevent plunder of every description,' wrote the prime minister, Lord Liverpool, 'but France must bear a part of the expenses of the war.'[26]

This state of affairs continued after Waterloo, until the arrival of Tsar Alexander. The emperor of Russia had, in the months since the Congress of Vienna, become a religious zealot. Gone were the excessive demands for the punishment of France, replaced by an uncharacteristic liberal attitude. The first manifestation of this transformation was his support for Wellington's commissary system in place of indiscriminate pillage. With the Russians now leading by example, it gradually became possible to restrain the collected German armies, although depredations continued.[27]

Castlereagh was left in no doubt of the danger to which the Allies had exposed themselves:

> If discipline and order are not upheld, King, Army, and People will forget their differences in one common feeling of resentment against foreign troops. The regeneration of France will be disappointed and the Allied armies will be involved in a protracted war and possibly compelled to retire from France without having effectuated their purpose of restoring it to peaceful habits.[28]

More generally, though, it would be more difficult to convince the Allies that France had to be maintained in a position of strength, rather than weakened so as to have no influence in the affairs of Europe. Indeed, it seems as though Castlereagh and Wellington were alone in holding these views. The British cabinet was, for the moment, decidedly hostile to restoring France to her pre-Revolutionary strength, and subscribed to populist sentiment that France should be severely punished. To do so, the prime minister himself argued, would 'be considered in no other light than as weakness, and not mercy… The prevailing idea … is, that we are fairly entitled to avail ourselves of the present moment to take back from France the principal conquests of Louis XIV.' He continued:

> France will never forgive the humiliation which she has already received – that she will take the first convenient opportunity of endeavouring to redeem her military glory – and that is our duty, therefore to take advantage of the present moment to prevent the evil consequences… It might have been not unwise last year to try the effect of a more magnanimous policy; but in the result of that we have been completely disappointed…[29]

Prussian long-term political ambitions matched the short-term depredations of her military. Whilst the chief Prussian negotiator, Karl August von

Joseph Fouché, Napoleon's one-time head of the secret police, with whom Wellington collaborated in order to ensure the restoration of the Bourbon monarchy and Louis XVIII. (akg-images)

Hardenberg, acknowledged there were difficulties restraining the Prussian Army, there was no disguising the 'spirit of vengeance against France' within Prussian policy, aimed specifically at augmenting their possessions.[30] In particular, Hardenberg wanted to separate Alsace and Lorraine from France, thereby augmenting the Netherlands and Bavaria, while Prussia would in turn annex Luxembourg and Mainz to her own territory.[31] Castlereagh and Wellington were decidedly opposed to such a scheme, and they broadly acquired the support of Russia and Austria, although the British cabinet remained cool on the issue. In mid-August, Wellington received intelligence that suggested that Prussia would act with or without the acquiescence of the Allies. 'The Prussians say out of doors,' reported the anonymous spy, '"Instead of negotiating about it, let us take possession, and hold fast."'[32] Moreover, the Prussians and the other minor German states wanted the French border fortresses in the north-east and east either ceded to the Allies, or razed, rendering the main route into France indefensible.

Castlereagh and Wellington, then, in attempting to secure the balance of power in Europe, faced an up-hill challenge. However, the main weight of political opinion in London, including that of the Prime Minister himself, reflected the British public mood, and was inclined to punish France by weakening her to such a degree that she would be unable to muster the strength to wage another war. Prussia was so too inclined, but saw the opportunity to expand her own territories as well. Castlereagh, though, saw that such exemplary punishment would, rather than reconcile France to her fate, merely encourage her to seek a means of regaining her territories at some later date. Far from securing the peace of Europe, it would light a fuse beneath it.

Wellington, also, was opposed to such a hard-line and unforgiving policy. In his view, any attempts to strip France of her territories and resources were to be firmly resisted. He had had bitter experience of a discontented France when he had served as British ambassador to Paris in 1814. 'The general topic of conversation,' then, he recalled in a formative dispatch on 11 August, 'was the recovery of the Left bank of the Rhine, and the unpopularity of the Government was attributed to its supposed disinclination to go to war to recover these possessions.'

Better to begin the process of restoring France to her pre-Revolutionary status, providing a clear objective to be aimed for, and to marginalise nationalistic voices. 'Revolutionary France is more likely to distress the world than France, however strong her frontier, under a regular government,' Wellington argued. 'That is the situation in which we ought to endeavour to place her.'[33] Wellington and his old friend Castlereagh found themselves making the same arguments: Wellington from the military point of view, Castlereagh from the political.[34]

Castlereagh recognised that the best way to convince both the other Great European Powers and his own cabinet was to reframe the discussion, as Wellington had in his 11 August dispatch. The Allies wanted to punish France, but France was not at fault, *Revolutionary* France was. In a series of principles upon which the negotiations were to be based, Castlereagh argued that 'the security to be required from France should be framed upon such principles, political and military, as shall afford to Europe an extraordinary and adequate protection against the *revolutionary* danger of France, so long as that particular danger may be presumed to exist.'[35] Castlereagh was overtly linking the expansionist ambitions of French power up to 1815 to the leadership of Napoleon Bonaparte, and the underlying conditions as set by the French Revolution. Forcing France to a position of economic destitution, with no means of recovery, would only recreate those conditions.

Karl August von Hardenberg, the chief Prussian negotiator who worked to create a long-lasting peace and put aside the Prussian desire for vengeance following the Napoleonic Wars. (akg-images)

Moreover, the cessions demanded of France by Prussia and the other minor German states would need to be guaranteed by the Allies. To Castlereagh, this seemed preposterous. He wrote angrily to Liverpool:

> The more I reflect upon it, the more I deprecate this system of scratching such a power. We may hold her down and pare her nails, so I hope we shall do this effectually, and subject to no other hazards of failure than must, more or less, attend all political or military arrangements, but this system of being pledged to a continental war for objects that France may any day reclaim from the particular States that hold them, without pushing her demands beyond what she would contend was due to her own honour, is I am sure a bad British policy.'[36]

Instead, surely it should be the responsibility of the states themselves to defend their new gains.

Nevertheless, 'strong reasons may no doubt be alleged to prove that the military power of France has long been too great for the peace and security of Europe,' Castlereagh contended, 'and that Europe owes itself now to repel the encroachments made by France upon its limits for a century past.' In such circumstances, 'it might be politic to incur the hazard of creating disunion amongst the Allies themselves by the difficulties to which these new distributions of territory would infallibly lead.' With characteristic understatement, Castlereagh observed that 'such a measure is at best problematical'.[37] Not only might Britain be drawn into a conflict between France and one or other of the states that had gained materially from France's loss, but she might also be drawn into conflict between those states over the spoils of war. Any territorial dismemberment of France would lead inexorably to further conflict.

Aware that these arguments alone were insufficient to placate those who believed that France represented a threat while she remained even as strong as she was in 1790, Castlereagh and Wellington suggested an army of occupation, totalling 100,000 troops, that would at French expense be garrisoned along the northern frontier, to the north-east and east of Paris. 'This position is both offensive and defensive in its character,' Castlereagh argued. 'It is too menacing to be passed, and it cannot be forced without a succession of sieges, whilst the army that occupied it is within ten marches of Paris, without an intervening fortress.' Moreover, 'the army that is to occupy it represents Europe. To menace or to attack that army is to declare war against Europe, the effects of which France will hereafter understand.'[38] The period of occupation initially proposed was five or seven years, whereupon, and only when the Allies were fully convinced that the flames of revolution in France had been extinguished forever, the fortresses would be returned to Louis XVIII, recognised by all as the representative of stability and security in France, weak and indecisive though he was.

The plans had Wellington's fingerprints all over them, and from a purely military perspective he argued coherently and persuasively. 'All persons appear to agree that the maintenance of the authority of the King is essential to the interests of the other powers of Europe; and, notwithstanding the difference of opinion regarding the extent of the force which ought to be maintained for a time in France,' Wellington wrote, 'it appears generally admitted that it is necessary to adopt it.' He continued:

Even despite Wellington's best efforts, King Louis XVIII was unable to fill Napoleon's shoes as a strong leader for France, leading others to direct him for their own purposes. (Anne S. K. Brown)

It is necessary to adopt it with different objects in view; first, to give security to the government of the King, and to afford him time to form a force of his own with which he can carry on his government, and take his fair share in the concerns of Europe; secondly, to give the Allies some security against a second revolutionary convulsion and reaction; and thirdly, to enable the Allies to enforce the payment of those contributions which they deem it just towards their own subject to lay on France in payment for the expenses of the war.[39]

The combination of these persuasive arguments, along with the forthright support of the tsar, convinced Whitehall and the Great Powers. 'In examining the confidential notes delivered in by the Russian, Austrian, and Prussian ministers, it appears that all are agreed' to the temporary military occupation of France, in order to stabilise the government of Louis XVIII, extinguish revolution and rebellion, and defend the position of the Great Powers in Europe.[40] Liverpool, meanwhile, expressed his approbation, in characteristic terms, as if he had been supportive all along, writing in October 1815:

With respect to those who think we ought not to have troubled ourselves about the internal situation of France, but have applied our exertions exclusively to the reduction of her power and the dismemberment of her territory, I have only to say that the policy of such a course of proceeding would have been at least doubtful … totally inconsistent with all the treaties, declarations, and manifestos which were formulated at the commencement of the contest.[41]

Louis XVIII signs the Second Treaty of Paris, 20 November 1815. (akg-images)

There remained some finer details to resolve: the precise division of the 600 million-franc indemnity; the restoration of artistic and culturally important works stolen by the French over the course of the war; the deployment and composition of the army of occupation; and the precise location of new fortresses designed to make the Belgian frontier truly impregnable. It took another six weeks to negotiate these issues, and the Second Treaty of Paris was finally signed on 20 November 1815.

On its own, this might have been Castlereagh's crowning achievement. He and Wellington had advocated a policy that sought to ensure the balance of power in Europe. It was a policy that the tsar had adopted and persuaded his fellow sovereigns to support. Wellington had won the war. Castlereagh now won the peace.

> The overthrow of the French army, the capture of Bonaparte, the continued union of Europe, and the protracted occupation of a military position in France, seem to provide adequately for the immediate danger, and at the same time to avoid the agitation of any new question which might disturb the settlement so happily effected at Vienna.[42]

Waterloo had been important because it had secured the peace so painstakingly negotiated in 1814.[43]

But this alone was only the tip of Castlereagh's ambition for peace in Europe. He wrote in a Memorandum at the end of August:

> Let the Allies then take this further chance of securing that repose which all the Powers of Europe so much require, with the assurance that if disappointed in their primary object by the military ambition of France, they will again take up arms, not only with commanding positions in their hands, but with that moral force which can alone keep such a confederacy together, and which has hitherto proved its greatest strength.[44]

Rather than a precarious balance of power in Europe, where peace was maintained by a combination of deterrence, coercion and, when necessary, violence, Castlereagh proposed a new idea. This idea had various names throughout the 19th century: some called it 'the European system'; others 'the confederacy', 'the great alliance' or simply 'the union'. By the end of the 19th century it had acquired a single name: the Concert of Europe.[45] Rather than a balance, Castlereagh proposed a concert of power in Europe, where problems

Viscount Castlereagh was the British foreign secretary. He represented British interests at the Vienna conference and worked closely with Wellington for a peace settlement, including the restoration of the Bourbon monarchy, as well as establishing a solid balance of power and peace in Europe. (akg-images)

and crises were resolved by discussion and compromise. To enforce this, the defensive elements of the Treaty of Chaumont, the alliance that had united the powers of Europe against Revolutionary and Napoleonic France, were to be re-affirmed. 'On the persuasiveness of which union,' wrote Castlereagh, 'it ought in wisdom to rely above every other measure of security for its future peace and preservation.' The European powers agreed 'to concert together and to take such measures as the security of Europe may require'.[46]

In so doing, Castlereagh had laid the foundations of international governance, a means by which dialogue resolved crises that otherwise might have required bullets and bayonets to determine. It is difficult to overstate the global significance of these decisions. The Concert of Europe helped maintain peace in Europe for the next century, and although destined to fail spectacularly in 1914, is arguably the blueprint upon which later attempts with the same aim were based.[47]

The Quadruple Alliance was signed at the same time as the Treaty of Paris, although its development ran in parallel with a bizarre but related 'Holy Alliance' proposed by the tsar that sought to unite the sovereigns and peoples of Europe in accordance with the principles of true Christianity.[48] Although Austria, Prussia and eventually Great Britain acquiesced in this arrangement through varying degrees of subservience and respect, Castlereagh's vision was much more realistic. The tsar appreciated this and supported it.

The sixth article was the only one that did not specifically pertain to France, and contracted the 'four Sovereigns for the happiness of the world' to 'renew their meetings at fixed periods … for the purpose of consulting upon their common interests, and for the consideration of the measures … considered the most salutary for the repose and prosperity of nations and for the maintenance of the peace of Europe'.[49]

Castlereagh envisaged regular meetings of Europe's leaders, to forestall looming crises and prevent future wars. All of this was guaranteed by a perpetual alliance of the Four Powers. Although the formal congress system broke down in 1822 because of fundamental disagreements between Britain and the continental powers, the Great Powers continued to reconvene on an *ad hoc* basis when new crises emerged. Webster counted 26 meetings in total between the first Congress at Aix-la-Chapelle in 1818 – which had seen the admission of Royalist France – and the final meeting in London in 1913. In that period, the Ottoman Empire was admitted in 1856, newly united Italy joined in 1867 and the German *Reich* replaced Prussia in 1871. The United States and Japan also began to participate towards the end of the century.

To suggest that the Concert of Europe was an unmitigated success would, of course, be misleading. No continent-wide conflict engulfed Europe between

Following the end of the
Napoleonic Wars, and well into
the 19th century, unrest broke out
across Europe, such as the Vienna
Uprising. Barricades sprung up
across European capitals as the
people challenged their
governments. The uprisings led to
reactionary authoritarianism,
increased nationalism and popular
politicisation. (akg-images)

1815 and 1914, but numerous wars between European states occurred, not least of which were the Italian *Risorgimento* (three wars of independence between 1848 and 1866), the Crimean War (1853–56), the Austro-Prussian War (1866) and the Franco-Prussian War (1870–71). The Concert framed these wars, and fed the development of European political ideas during the 19th century.

The Concert was not a formal structure or institution, had no written codes, charters or rules, and functioned entirely because of the submission of the Great Powers to its fundamental principles. Undoubtedly, the impact of Waterloo specifically, and of the Revolutionary and Napoleonic Wars more generally, helped frame this submission. In the period after 1815, European Great Powers were conservative-minded, sharing a determination to maintain the treaties that had ended the great war with France, preserve the new status quo so painstakingly negotiated at Vienna and resist revolutionary wars of aggression aimed at establishing new empires in Europe. This was a conscious reversal of the 18th-century dogmatic pursuit of the balance of power. Whilst Castlereagh and Wellington, Tsar Alexander, Klemens von Metternich (the Austrian foreign minister), Talleyrand and Hardenberg had all worked assiduously to produce a new balance, what they achieved was much more long lasting. As Paul Schroeder wittily puts it: 'European statesmen had learned that eighteenth-century poker led to Russian roulette, and decided to play contract bridge instead.'[50]

The Holy Alliance, agreed on 26 September 1815, between Russia, Prussia and Austria. Pictured here are the three monarchs. (akg-images)

In this atmosphere, the Concert of Europe was given the oxygen it required to breathe and to function. Although no formal written rules regulating the behaviour of states existed, historians have identified informal unwritten rules based on precedent. When great European questions emerged, only the five Great Powers could negotiate and decide a solution, whilst lesser powers could bring influence to bear on issues that directly affected them, but they had no veto. Similarly, no power could wage an aggressive war or foment revolution elsewhere in Europe. The Concert of Europe was likewise bound to deal with European concerns, and was unable to raise international issues of vital interest to another Great Power without its consent, except where that issue was of such significance that it affected more than one of the Great Powers. In such circumstances, no Great Power could prevent its discussion in Concert. The logical extension of this argument was that confrontations between Great Powers had to be avoided at any cost, and would be referred to the Concert if a resolution proved impossible. Most important was the unwritten rule that one power could not directly threaten, undermine or humiliate another.[51]

The system worked on moral rather than legal grounds, and any such system needed to demonstrate flexibility. The Concert proved inadequate at dealing with crises within (as opposed to between) Great Powers' sphere of interests. Thus, Great Britain acted with impunity in South Asia; Russia did so in Central Asia and the Far East; and latterly France and Britain did so in Africa. But in Europe, crises that in the 18th century might have produced regional conflicts that spiralled into general European war, were resolved within the framework of the Concert. Thus, the Greek Revolution between 1821 and 1832; the Belgian Revolution that began in 1830; and the Italian Revolution of 1848, were all settled without Great Power conflicts. This is not to say that blood was not shed, or that violence was ended as a result of Great Power intervention. The Great Powers acted so as to contain the violence and prevent the eruption of a general conflict. This was a step-change in European affairs.

Nor did the widespread European revolutions of 1848 destroy the Concert of Europe. While the social and political fabric of Europe was shaken to its core in 1848, the revolutions did not produce a general war, as the French Revolution had in 1789. The reasons for this happenstance are manifold, but what is clear is that foreign policy remained conservative, and there remained a desire to preserve peace and restrict the export of revolutionary ideals: the single greatest cause of conflict in 1789. Nevertheless, within six years a war between the Great Powers threatened the stability of Europe: the Crimean War.

Although the Crimean War did not erupt into a general conflict, it served critically to undermine the Concert of Europe. Why, then, in circumstances where the Great Powers had sought to avoid conflict at all costs, did the Crimean War break out? The answer is quite simple: the extra-European spheres of interest of two of the Great Powers began to collide, and no diplomatic mechanism within the Concert offered a solution to a problem born entirely outside the boundaries of Europe.

Ostensibly, the Crimean War erupted between Russia on one hand, and Austria, France, the Ottoman Empire and Great Britain on the other, because of Russian aggression against the slowly declining Ottoman Empire. The prospect of Russian control of Constantinople was too great a strategic threat to Austria, France and Great Britain. After all, the Eastern Question dominated Concert diplomacy from the 1820s, and was, in fact, the subject of the final meeting in 1913.[52] Yet, if this were the sole cause, a diplomatic solution would have been found through the mechanism of the Concert. The problem was that Russian encroachment into the Caucasus and Central Asia began directly to threaten British extra-European interests, namely those in South Asia.[53]

A diplomatic solution proved impossible in 1853–54, because Britain did not want a diplomatic solution: Britain wanted to threaten, undermine and humiliate Russia.[54] To understand why Britain behaved in such a way to destroy the diplomatic architecture that Castlereagh and Wellington had so painstakingly assembled in 1815, we have to understand why Britain wanted a Concert of Europe in the first place.

As Britain emerged as a global naval power in the 18th century, a choice between two grand strategies confronted her: the 'Blue Water', or the 'Continental' strategy.[55] Under Blue Water, British strategic aims were focused on colonial and imperial expansion, in order to expand her trading and commerce empire. By contrast, the Continental strategy saw British foreign policy focused on the stability of Europe, since only with an effective network of European alliances could Britain hope to expand her empire outside of Europe. In practice, of course, both were necessary and mutually dependent on one another.

Put overly simply, a balance of power in Europe was necessary to allow Britain to expand overseas; the empire was required to pay for the inevitable European conflicts that followed the repeated collapse of the balance of power. Historical precedent seemed to suggest the truth of this assertion. Britain had been successful in North America between 1758 and 1761 largely because her main enemy, France, suffered an attritional defeat in Europe at the hands of Britain's ally, Prussia. In the wake of victory in America, however, Britain abandoned her European alliances, and by 1781 had suffered her costliest colonial defeat at Yorktown that sealed the independence of the United States of America.[56]

Similar strategic decisions had governed British involvement in the French Revolutionary War, whilst Napoleon's overt interest in extra-European expansion throughout his reign ensured Britain's constant involvement in the war until his final defeat at Waterloo in 1815. 'I will find in Spain, the Pillars of Hercules, but not the limits of my powers,' Napoleon had written in 1808 as his forces struggled to conquer the Iberian Peninsula.[57] Such a comment clearly indicated Napoleon's interest in the Orient, whilst the secret terms of his alliance with Russia in 1807 also (perhaps absurdly) mentioned India.[58] This perfectly encapsulates why Britain had fought for so long against French hegemony in Europe.

It also explains the primary manifestation of British strategy during that war. It is no coincidence that Britain repeatedly acted to neutralise French naval power. Toulon, Den Helder, Boulogne, El Ferrol, Cadiz, Ostend, Copenhagen, Flushing and Antwerp were all attacked, sometimes more than once, and sometimes with mixed success, during the French Revolutionary and Napoleonic Wars. The primary aim of these assaults was not the capture of territory, but the destruction of French naval assets. The British Army was precision ammunition, and the Royal Navy was the gun that fired it.

The war had been devastatingly expensive, and had virtually neutralised the benefits of having an empire. Under the current system, building an empire would be pointless if the economic benefits were wasted on wars in Europe that were fought to enable Britain to build the empire. The Concert of Europe was therefore Britain's solution to this vicious circle. The basis of the Concert was to secure diplomatically what Britain had, in the past, fought for: the balance of power.

But by the early 1850s, Russia had emerged as a new France, a power that sought hegemonic power. The key difference was that Russia did not seek (at least for the time being) hegemonic power in Europe, but in Asia, and this directly threatened Britain's own imperial ambitions. Britain had already fought a costly war in Afghanistan between 1839 and 1842 over the perceived threat of Russian expansionism in Central Asia. Although an operational disaster, the war had nevertheless achieved its strategic objectives: a buffer zone to the north-west of British India that would, for the time being at least, prevent any Russian encroachment into Britain's sphere of interest.

The Crimean War was a turning point in the 19th century, threatening the stability of the peace which the Concert of Europe had sought to protect. Here, French infantry storm earthworks in the attack at the Battle of Malakoff, 7 September 1855. (Anne S. K. Brown)

In the Crimea, however, Britain perceived a different but related threat from Russia. The growth of Russian naval power in the Black Sea represented a clear threat to British grand strategy. The prospect that Russia might gain control of Constantinople, and therefore the eastern Mediterranean, and be within striking distance of Egypt, the Red Sea, and therefore India by a different route, was too much for Britain to stomach. True, Russian naval power was nowhere near so strong as to pose such a threat, but it would be easier to squash Russian naval plans when they were still embryonic. Britain did not want a diplomatic solution to the crisis in 1853–54, because a diplomatic solution would not see the neutralisation of Russian sea power. The war in the Crimea was designed to destroy Russian naval power.[59]

This, and this alone, was reason enough for the British to act to undermine the Concert of Europe, while the other Great Powers struggled to find diplomatic solutions. Throughout the crisis of 1853–54, Russia, Austria and France all proffered solutions that met Britain's demands. In reality, the demands that Britain put forward were irrelevant, since they were a front, and Britain, represented by another great foreign secretary, Lord Palmerston, simply changed the goalposts.[60]

Although Britain achieved her strategic objectives during the Crimean War, the war illustrated military developments of the first half of the 19th century, and the failure of the Great Powers to keep pace with these developments. In part, this was the result of the Battle of Waterloo as well. There, line had defeated column, and square had defeated cavalry. Britain had fought at least eight large-scale colonial conflicts between 1815 and 1854. During those conflicts, none of the large-scale troop movements that determined Napoleon's success in Europe had been possible, because South Asia and the Far East lacked the industrial and agricultural infrastructure that had made them possible in Europe.[61] Moreover, the lessons learnt from fighting large formations of disciplined infantry on the subcontinent reinforced Frederickian thinking on the use of infantry; that is to say that 18th-century ideas of the use of armies pervaded well into the 19th century.[62] Therefore, the lessons learnt in Britain's colonial conflicts reinforced the lessons learnt at Waterloo.

This lends some context to the enduring relevance of Wellington's disappointment at Napoleon's inflexibility at Waterloo. 'Napoleon did not manoeuvre at all,' he had written in the days following the battle. 'He just moved forward in the old style, in columns, and was driven off in the old style.'[63] This has led many historians to conclude that the British Army rested on its laurels in the years succeeding Waterloo. In fact, as Hew Strachan has demonstrated, it was Wellington who held development back. Despite impressive localised reforms that illustrated progressive thinking on systems of discipline and professionalisation, Wellington prevented any attempts to render these peripheral developments in the centre. The army itself remained unreformed, whilst its regiments, away on colonial garrison duty across the globe, frequently in contact with unpredictable and culturally diverse enemies, adapted at varying speeds to the emergence of new ideas and thinking.[64]

Whilst operational, tactical and administrative thinking and reform occurred unevenly and sporadically, thinking and reform in these areas was at least happening. Perhaps more egregious than his failure to foster centralised tactical and administrative reform, was Wellington's failure to adequately ensure sufficient articulacy in the art and science of strategy. Considering that Wellington's success in the Peninsular War, and to some extent at Waterloo, was partly the result of his ability to link the political and military levels, his reluctance to engender a similar understanding in his subordinates and successors is particularly sad.[65]

This resulted in an army that at least had the ability to fight, but lacked the ability to convey in a convincing and authoritative manner to politicians when and where it should fight. Military thought occurred in Britain in the years after Waterloo, most of it focused on the process of fighting rather than strategy, and most of the thinking that was conducted was done so by middle-ranking officers

The reach of the British Empire is clear to see in this map. It was only by establishing a secure and long-lasting balance of power in Europe that Britain was able to build such an empire.
(Anne S. K. Brown)

at Waterloo who had gone on to greater success and recognition in the empire. They published their thinking in monthly or fortnightly publications such as the *United Service Journal* (founded in 1827), the *Naval and Military Gazette* and the *United Service Gazette* (both founded in 1833).[66]

Of the foreign military theorists, it was Baron Antoine de Jomini, avidly read and promoted by the Francophile William Napier, who dominated British military thinking in the first half of the 19th century, with his focus on getting military forces into action and achieving the desired effect.[67] Although Clausewitz gained traction in Germany by the 1830s, it was not until the 1840s that German-speaking English enthusiasts emerged, whilst the Prussian thinker's *Vom Krieg* was not translated into English until 1873.[68]

Whilst he remained the preserve of German-speaking English military officers, Clausewitz' important ideas on strategy failed to gain any substantial degree of understanding. Indeed, British interpretations of Clausewitzian principles were, at best, simplistic, at worst, dangerous. 'Even the greatest of the Continental battles lasted entire days,' wrote one, Lieutenant Colonel John Mitchell. 'They were fought for the possession of posts or villages on which the world's fate seemed to depend … one bold contest would have been worth all this strategy a hundred times over.'[69]

The Crimean War clearly indicated that new thinking was needed on the application of military power. It would take six decades and the slaughter of the First World War for the process of technological and military innovation started in Crimea to reach its conclusion. Here, the British 55th Infantry cross bayonets with the opposing Russians. (Anne S. K. Brown)

Mitchell's interpretations of Clausewitzian principles suggested that he believed the primary aim of an army should be to fight, and do so with all available resources. In essence, a decisive battle should be sought and joined as rapidly as possible. This was emphatically not what Clausewitz held to be the key to strategy. Mitchell, along with other thinkers and writers in the period, British, Prussian and French, overlooked Clausewitz' argument that policy, means and national character were intimately linked in the development of a national strategy. Mitchell, and the army at large, failed to recognise, as they failed to recognise throughout the French Revolutionary and Napoleonic Wars, that the British Army was, in essence, an expeditionary force; in the words of Admiral Lord John Fisher, 'a projectile to be fired by the navy'.[70]

Wellington had recognised this during the Peninsular War, when, despite repeated arguments with his naval counterparts, he acknowledged that he would have been unable to fight without the continued support of the Royal Navy.[71] This knowledge governed his actions in the days before Waterloo, as he sought to prevent an outflanking manoeuvre by Napoleon that would cut the British off from their lines of communication to the sea. When Napoleon attacked the central position between the British and Prussian forces, Wellington was hard pressed to bring his widely dispersed forces into action at Quatre Bras on 16 June 1815.

Wellington, then, understood it. And there is some evidence that others understood these principles in the years prior to the Crimean War. In an *Aide-Memoire to the Military Sciences*, an attempt was made to define a 'British way of war'. Strategists could either adopt a continentalist view, which 'leads to operations of immense armies and objects which menace the very existence of states', or adopt 'the insular position of the empire and local conditions which resulted from it… Principally defensive measures at home, assistance to an ally abroad, and offensive expeditions to distant countries; mainly depending on the superiority of the Royal Navy, and with land forces in no case amounting to more than 50,000 national troops.'[72] Here, then, was the closest approximation to an accurate view of the British way of war that was encapsulated before the Crimean War, but it was in a book written for sappers and engineers, and therefore unlikely ever to be read by anyone in command.

It certainly was not on the bookshelf of Wellington's military secretary, FitzRoy Somerset, who, as Lord Raglan, commanded the British expeditionary army during the Crimean War. British grand strategy during that war was primarily aimed at eliminating the Russian naval presence at Sevastopol, and with it Russian naval superiority in the Black Sea, and beyond. This accorded with the strategic vision Britain had followed for at least 100 years. What Raglan lacked was

Carl von Clausewitz. In the wake of Waterloo, the Prussian military officer would write *On War*, destined to become a definitive piece of military strategic thought. Clausewitz' ideas did not gain much traction in Britain, where 18th century Fredrickian thinking remained popular following the success of such tactics at Waterloo. (akg-images)

Wellington's most important ability: to communicate effectively the limitations of military power to the strategic decision-makers in London.

Had Raglan understood British grand strategy in the 18th and 19th centuries then he might have understood that he would be required to command an amphibious assault against Sevastopol, and then he might have been able to explain that in 1854 the British Army was not capable of attacking an un-reconnoitred, well-fortified and strongly held peninsula. He did not understand, he did not explain, and the British Army became committed to a costly, bloody and attritional series of battles and sieges.

A dispassionate assessment would arrive at the conclusion that this was ultimately strategically successful. Russia was defeated and her naval power in the Black Sea was crippled. But at what cost? Casualties were horrendous. Of the 200,000 Allied forces committed to the Crimea, well over half fell, most – 75,000 French and 16,000 British – dying from disease. Russian casualties were similar in number.[73] Britain, with her limited manpower resources, could not fight wars of such magnitude herself. She did so by paying others to do it for her. This had not been possible under the Concert system, as Britain had wanted to make a particular example of Russia for her own strategic ends.

The Concert was not destroyed by the events leading to the Crimean War, although it was perhaps mortally wounded, as international relations commenced their long deterioration until 1914. The Great Powers of Europe continued to meet to discuss their differences until the year before the outbreak of the World War I. But they did so in a period that saw the early rise of the World Great Powers – the United States and Japan. This dichotomy produced varying reactions in Europe. Britain, perhaps as a result of the miserable disasters encountered in Afghanistan, the Crimea and in India in 1857, fostered Victorian moralism, and renewed its support of the Concert system, adopting a progressive agenda that highlighted internationalism. Germany, by contrast, as the only European Great Power lacking a significant overseas empire, turned in the other direction. Initially supportive of the Concert system in the wake of Waterloo, post-Crimea, and more so post-unification in 1871, Germany became anti-European, espousing nationalistic ideals.[74] The course seemed set for the emergence of the rivalries and disagreements that would spiral out of control in 1914.

The shadow of Waterloo fell long into the 19th century. From the outset, the post-war tensions between the Allies were apparent. Britain acted with apparent altruism, but her actions were primarily intended to recreate a European system that mirrored the old but replaced violence with discussion. This would give Britain ever-greater flexibility in expanding her empire. Castlereagh's greatest contribution to the history of international governance was the foundations for massive imperial expansionism. Perfidious Albion was unmasked in the crisis of 1853–54, but her army had not learnt the lessons of the Napoleonic War or of Waterloo, and it wasted itself in the Crimea. For Prussia, Waterloo provided the opportunity to reclaim some of the prestige she had failed to reclaim in 1814, but she found her way blocked by Britain, and initial engagement with the European Concert turned slowly to a quest for unification, the seeds of which had been apparent at the end of the Napoleonic Wars. Europe, opined Castlereagh in 1814, 'need never dread a German league; it is in its nature inoffensive, and there is no reason to fear that the union between Austria and Prussia will be such as to endanger the liberties of other states'.[75] In 1814, he was right. It was the failure of the European Concert adequately to account for the imperialistic ambitions of the Great European Powers that made Prussia, and then Germany, anti-European. Austria and Russia gained much from Waterloo. Austria became undisputed master of Central Europe, only facing eclipse in the 1860s. Russia, her position in the east reinforced, could, like Britain, now turn to empire-building, a process that would eventually bring her into contest with Britain and the other European states. Perhaps the biggest winner from Waterloo was France. She might have expected to pay an enormous price for the brief re-awakening of her support for Napoleon in 1815, but Britain, Russia and then Austria, held the line, and French power was maintained. It was essential to the success of the Concert of Europe.

The Waterloo Banquet. Every year on 18 June, the Duke of Wellington hosted the famous Waterloo Banquet to which all serving field officers at the battle were invited, along with surviving politicians of the era. This famous painting by William Salter depicts the 1836 banquet, the last that King William IV attended before his death the following year. (© English Heritage)

NOTES

Introduction

1.   Low, E.S., *With Napoleon at Waterloo and Other Unpublished Documents of the Waterloo and Peninsula Campaigns*, ed. Mackenzie Macbride (London: Francis Griffiths, 1911), p. 123.

The Battles of Ligny and Quatre Bras

1.   *Correspondance de Napoleon 1er* (Paris, 1859).
2.   Marshal Berthier was Napoleon's chief of staff from 1797 until 1815. His administrative genius to turn the emperor's expressed wishes into clear concise orders was a major factor in the successes of those years. He remained loyal to his new Bourbon masters in 1815 and died in mysterious circumstances on 1 June.
3.   *Commentaires de Napoleon 1er*, Vol.V (1867).
4.   *Correspondance de Napoleon 1er*.
5.   *Journal du Capitaine Francois: 1793–1830* (Paris, 1903–04).
6.   Pertz and Delbruck, *Gneisenau* (Berlin, 1864–65).
7.   Heymes, *Documents Inedites du Duc d'Elchingen* (Paris, 1833).
8.   Ibid.
9.   *Notes of Conversations with the Duke of Wellington 1831–51* (London, 1888). See also H. Houssaye, *1815: Waterloo* (London, 1900).
10. Ropes, J., *The Campaign of Waterloo* (1910), *Commentaires*, Vol.V.
11. Mercer, Gen A. C., *Journal of the Waterloo Campaign*, two volumes (London, 1870).
12. Ibid.
13. Ibid.
14. Ibid.
15. *Commentaires de Napoleon 1er*, Vol.V.

The Commanders

1.   The date of Wellington's birth is disputed but he regarded 1 May as his birthday; see, for example, Guedalla, P., *The Duke* (London, 1937) (first published 1931), pp. 479–80.
2.   Seeley, Sir John, *A Short History of Napoleon the First* (London, 1895), p. 30.
3.   Stanhope, Philip Henry, 5th Earl, *Notes of Conversations with the Duke of Wellington, 1831–51* (London, 1888), p. 182.
4.   Maxwell, Sir Herbert, *The Life of Wellington* (London, 1899), Vol. II, pp. 138–39.

5. Las Cases, E. A. D. M. J., Comte de, *Memoirs of the Life, Exile and Conversations of the Emperor Napoleon* (London, 1836), Vol. IV, p. 176.

6. Ibid., Vol. III, p. 299.

7. This statement has been translated variously, for example 'like eating lunch'; 'like a picnic' might best convey the meaning. Houssaye, H., *1815*, trans. E. A. Mann (London, 1900), Vol. III, p. 178.

8. Ségur, P. de, *History of the Expedition to Russia Undertaken by the Emperor Napoleon in the Year 1812* (London, 1825), Vol. I, p. 320.

9. Caulaincourt, A. L. L., *Memoirs of General Caulaincourt, Duke of Vicenza*, ed. J. Hanoteau, trans. H. Miles & G. Libaire (London 1935–38), Vol. I, p. 93.

10. Las Cases, Vol. IV, pp. 160–61.

11. Stanhope, p. 9.

12. Ellesmere, Francis, 1st Earl, *Personal Reminiscences of the Duke of Wellington*, ed. Alice, Countess of Strafford (London, 1904), p. 100.

13. Ibid., p. 179.

14. From Gonesse, 2 July 1815; Wellington, Arthur Wellesley, *The Dispatches of Field Marshal the Duke of Wellington during his Various Campaigns in India, Denmark, Portugal, Spain, the Low Countries and France*, ed. Lt Col J. Gurwood (London 1834–38), Vol. XII p. 569 (quoted as 'WD' hereafter).

15. These following quotations are from the early English translation of de Coster's account, in Sir Walter Scott's *Paul's Letters to his Kinsfolk* (Edinburgh, 1816).

16. 'Buonaparte' was the original spelling of the family name and continued to be used in English sources; this is from an early translation.

17. To Henry Torrens, 22 January 1813; *WD* Vol. X, pp. 33–34.

18. Griffiths, A. J., *The Wellington Memorial* (London, 1897), p. 308.

19. To Lord Liverpool, 25 July 1813; *WD* Vol. X, p. 569.

20. Fraser, Sir William, Bt, *Words on Wellington: The Duke; Waterloo; the Ball* (London, 1899), p. 37.

21. Longford, Elizabeth Countess of, *Wellington: The Years of the Sword* (London, 1969), p. 421.

22. To Lord Stewart, 8 May 1815; *WD* Vol. XII, p. 358.

23. Wellington, Arthur, 1st Duke, *Supplementary Despatches and Memoranda of Field Marshal Arthur Duke of Wellington KG*, ed. 2nd Duke of Wellington (London 1858–72), Vol. X, p. 219.

24. William Fraser, p. 3.

25. Mackinnon, D., *Origin and Services of the Coldstream Guards* (London, 1833), Vol. II, p. 215.

26. Frazer, Sir Augustus, *Letters of Colonel Sir Augustus Simon Frazer KCB*, ed. Maj Gen E. Sabine (London, 1859), p. 550.

27. Stanhope, p. 18.

28. Pattison, F. H., *Personal Recollections of the Waterloo Campaign* (Glasgow, 1873), p. 26.

29. Wheeler, W., *The Letters of Private Wheeler 1809–1828*, ed. B. H. Liddell Hart (London, 1951), p. 161.

30. Kincaid, Sir John, *Adventures in the Rifle Brigade* (London, 1830), and *Random Shots from a Rifleman* (London, 1835; repr. in Maclaren's combined edition, London, 1908), pp. 36 37, 245–46.

31. Ross-Lewin, H., *With the Thirty-Second in the Peninsular and other Campaigns*, ed. J. Wardell (Dublin & London, 1904), pp. 280–81.

32. Kennedy, Gen Sir James Shaw, *Notes on the Battle of Waterloo* (London, 1865), pp. 128–29.

33.   Augustus Frazer, pp. 559–60.

34.   William Fraser, pp. 276–77.

35.   Scott, Sir Walter, *Paul's Letters to his Kinsfolk* (Edinburgh, 1816; published anonymously), pp. 171–72.

36.   Moore Smith, G. C., *The Life of John Colborne, Field-Marshal Lord Seaton* (London, 1903), p. 213.

37.   Stanhope, pp. 118–20.

38.   Müffling, P. F. C. F., *Passages from My Life, Together with Memoirs of the Campaign of 1813*, ed. P. J. Yorke (London, 1853), p. 225.

39.   Ibid. pp. 212–13.

40.   Ibid., pp. 215–17.

41.   General Carl Wilhelm Georg von Grolmann, Blücher's quartermaster general.

42.   Stanhope, p. 110.

43.   Ibid.

44.   *WD* Vol. X, p. 484.

45.   Simpson, J., *Paris after Waterloo* (Edinburgh & London, 1853), p. 230.

46.   William Fraser, p. 274.

47.   Gleig, Rev. G. R., *The Life of Arthur, Duke of Wellington* (London, 1865), p. 496.

The Battle

1.   Report of Captain F. Weiz, 1st/1st Nassau, *The Waterloo Archive*, Vol. II, p. 183 (Barnsley: Frontline Books).

2.   Captain Cleves, Hanoverian Horse Artillery, ibid., p. 56.

3.   Beamish, N. L., *History of the King's German Legion* quoted in Glover (ed.), *The Waterloo Archive*, Vol. II, p. 43 (London: Buckland and Brown, 1993).

Waterloo Eyewitnesses

The author of this chapter wishes to express all gratitude to Yves Martin for the loan of numerous books of recollections. The excellent work by Andrew W. Field, *Waterloo: The French Perspective,* was used for checking many translations from the French. The ranks of the diarists were verified in Philippe de Meulenaere, *Bibliographie analytique des témoignages oculaires imprimés sur la campagne de Waterloo en 1815* (Paris, 2004).

1.   Lemonnier-Delafosse quotes taken from Lemonnier-Delafosse, J.-B., *Souvenirs militaires du capitaine Jean-Baptiste Lemonnier-Delafosse* (Paris: Le Livre chez Vous, 2002).

2.   Lagneau quotes taken from Lagneau, L.-V., *Journal d'un chirurgien de la Grande Armée* (Paris: Le Livre chez Vous, 2003).

3.   Petiet quotes taken from Petiet, Gen A., *Mémoires du général Auguste Petiet, hussard de l'Empire* (Paris, 1996).

4.   Field, A., *Waterloo, The French Perspective* (Barnsley: Pen & Sword, 2012), p. 6.

5.   Mercer quotes taken from Mercer, Gen A. C., *Journal of the Waterloo Campaign*, two volumes (London, 1870), Vol. 1.

6.   Kellermann quotes taken from Kellermann, Lt Gen, *Observations sur la bataille de Waterloo*, SHD 1M 719.

7.   Larreguy de Civrieux quotes taken from Larreguy de Civrieux, Sgt Maj L.-M.-S.-P., *Souvenirs d'un cadet* (Paris, 1912).

8. Martin, Lt J.-F., *Souvenirs de guerre du lieutenant Martin, 1812–1815* (Paris: Tallandier, 2007).

9. Tomkinson quotes taken from Tomkinson, W., *With Wellington's Light Cavalry* (Leonaur, 2006).

10. Wylly, Col H. C., *The Military Memoirs of Lieutenant-General Sir Joseph Thackwell* (London, 1908).

11. Wheeler quotes taken from Wheeler, W., *The Letters of Private Wheeler, 1809–1828* (The Windrush Press, 1994).

12. Playford, T., *The Memoirs of Sergeant-Major Thomas Playford, 2nd Lifeguards, 1810–1830* (Ken Trotman Publishing, 2006).

13. Hope, J., *The Iberian and Waterloo Campaigns: The Letters of Lt James Hope* (N&M Press, 2000), pp. 240–41.

14. Vallance quotes taken from *At Waterloo with the Cameron Highlanders*, Napoleonic Archive.

15. Gavin quotes taken from Gavin, W., *The Diary of William Gavin, Ensign and Quarter-Master of the 71st Highland Regiment, 1806–1815* (Ken Trotman Publishing, 2013).

16. Trefcon quotes taken from Trefcon, Col, *Carnet de campagne (1793–1815)* (Paris: Librairie des Deux Empires, 2003).

17. Canler quotes taken from Canler, L., *Mémoires de Canler, ancien chef du service de Sûreté*, tome 1 (Paris, 1882).

18. Simmons quotes taken from Simmons, Lt, *Lieutenant Simmons of the 95th (Rifles): Recollections of the Peninsula, South of France & Waterloo Campaigns of the Napoleonic Wars* (Leonaur, 2007).

19. Douglas quotes taken from Douglas, J., *Douglas's Tale of the Peninsula & Waterloo, 1808–1815* (London, 1997).

20. Pontécoulant, P.-G. Le D., de, *Napoléon à Waterloo, 1815* (repr. Paris: Librairie des Deux Empires, 2004).

21. Sperling quotes taken from Sperling, J., *The Letters of First Lieutenant John Sperling, Royal Engineers* (Ken Trotman Publishing, 2012).

22. Martin, Lt J.-F., 'Waterloo: lettre d'un officier genevois du 45e', in *Carnet de la Sabretache* (1895).

23. Kincaid quotes taken from Kincaid, Capt J., *Adventures in the Rifle Brigade in the Peninsula, France and the Netherlands from 1809 to 1815* (London, 1830).

24. Martin, *Souvenirs de guerre*, op. cit.

25. Duthilt quotes taken from Duthilt, P.-C., *Mes campagnes et mes souvenirs* (Paris: Le Livre chez Vous, 2008).

26. Cotton, E., *A Voice from Waterloo* (London, 1849).

27. Anton quotes taken from Anton, J., *Royal Highlander* (Leonaur, 2007).

28. Fleuret quotes taken from Fleuret, *Description des passages de Dominique Fleuret* (Firmin-Didot & Cie, 1929).

29. Martin, *Souvenirs de guerre*, op. cit.

30. Hibbert quotes taken from Hibbert, J., *Waterloo Letters: The 1815 Letters of Lieutenant John Hibbert, 1st King's Dragoon Guards* (Ken Trotman Publishing, 2007).

31. Siborne, Maj Gen H. T. (ed.), *Waterloo Letters* (London: Greenhill Books, 1993).

32. Uxbridge quotes taken from Anglesey, Marquess of, *One-Leg, The Life and Letters of Henry William Paget, First Marquess of Anglesey* (London, 1962).

33. Ibid., p. 141.

34. Bro, Gen, *Mémoires du général Bro, 1796–1844* (Paris: Librairie des Deux Empires, 2001).

35. Naylor, Capt J., *The Waterloo Diary of Captain James Naylor, 1st (King's) Dragoon Guards, 1815–1816* (Ken Trotman Publishing, 2008).

36. Dupuy, V., *Souvenirs militaires, 1794–1816* (Paris: Librairie des Deux Empires, 2001).

37. Levavasseur quotes taken from Levavasseur, O., *Souvenirs militaires, 1800–1815* (Paris: Librairie des Deux Empires, 2001).

38. Chevalier quotes taken from Chevalier, Lt J.-M., *Souvenirs des guerres napoleoniennes* (Hachette, 1970).

39. Wheatley (ed. Hibbert, C.), *The Wheatley Diary* (London, 1964).

40. Siborne (ed.), *Waterloo Letters*, op. cit.

41. Chateaubriand, F.-R. de, *Memoires d'outre-tombe*, ILLe partie, 1re époque, livre VI, ch.16.

42. Lindau quotes taken from Lindau, F., *A Waterloo Hero – The Reminiscences of Friedrich Lindau* (Pen & Sword, 2009).

43. Anglesey, Marquess of, p. 143.

44. Gronow, Capt, *Reminiscences of Captain Gronow* (London, 1862).

45. Morris, T., *The Napoleonic Wars* (Longmans, 1967).

46. Stanhope quotes taken from Stanhope, J., *Eyewitness to the Peninsular War and the Battle of Waterloo: The Letters and Journals of Lieutenant Colonel the Honourable James Stanhope, 1803 to 1825* (Pen & Sword, 2010).

47. Lawrence, W., *A Dorset Soldier: The Autobiography of Sgt William Lawrence, 1790–1869* (Spellmount, 1993).

48. Guyot, Gen Comte, *Carnets de campagnes, 1792–1815* (Paris: Teissèdre, 1998).

49. SHD 1M 719: *Note sur la charge de la division Lhéritier, épisode de la bataille de Waterloo, sans nom d'auteur.* In the *Carnets de la Campagne*, this text is attributed to *Chef d'escadron* L'Étang, but the original document in the Vincennes archives is not signed and only classified as 'from General L'Étang's succession'.

50. Robinaux, Capt P., *Journal de route du capitaine Robinaux* (Paris: Librairie des Deux Empires, 2009).

51. Jolyet, J.-B., 'Souvenirs de 1815', in *La Revue de Paris* (September–October 1903).

52. Gibney quotes taken from Gibney, *Eighty Years Ago or the Recollections of an Old Army Doctor, by the Late Dr. Gibney* (London: Bellairs & Company, 1896).

53. Marbot quotes taken from Marbot, Baron, *The Memoirs of Baron de Marbot*, translated from the French by Arthur John Butler, Vol. II (Longmans, Green & Co, 1913).

54. Gomm, Field Marshal Sir W., *Letters and Journals of Field-Marshal Sir William Maynard Gomm: From 1799 to Waterloo 1815* (London, 1881).

55. Fraser, Alexander, Lt Col, *Waterloo Campaign Letters Written by Lieutenant-Colonel Alexander Fraser, Lord Saltoun, 1st Foot Guards, 1815* (Ken Trotman Publishing, 2010).

56. Jeremiah, T., *A Short Account of the Life and Adventures of Private Thomas Jeremiah, 23rd or Royal Welch Fusiliers, 1812–1837* (Ken Trotman Publishing, 2008).

57. Place of Carrousel in Paris, where the Guard paraded during the First Empire.

58. Mauduit, H. de, *Histoire des derniers jours de la Grande Armée* (Paris: Le Livre chez Vous, 2006). 'Perhaps the most compelling of French accounts' (Andrew W. Field).

Hougoumont and La Haye Sainte

1. Adkin, M., *The Waterloo Companion* (London, 2001), p. 118 and Barbero, A., *The Battle: A New History of the Battle of Waterloo*, trans Cullen, J. (London, 2006), p. 16, the former providing Fitzroy Somerset's notes written a year after the battle as the foundation.

2. Fortescue, J., *A History of the British Army 1645–1870*, 20 volumes (London, 1899–1930), Vol. X, p. 348, states that the position at Mont Saint Jean had been studied by the Royal Engineers and that they had drawn up plans prior to the start of the campaign; while Elizabeth Longford's extensive research supports that Wellington's thumbnail was quite precise in tracing the line immediately behind La Haye Sainte and Hougoumont.

3. Cotton, E., *A Voice from Waterloo* (Mont Saint Jean, 1900), p. 37.

4. Moore Smith, G. C., *The Life of John Colborne, Field Marshal Lord Seaton* (London, 1903), p. 218.

5. Field, A., *Waterloo, The French Perspective* (Barnsley, 2012), p. 33, citing Lemonnier-Delafosse, *Souvenirs militaires du Capitaine Jean-Baptiste Lemmonier-Delafosse*.

6. Jomini, A., *The Art of War* (London, 1992, from original published in 1838), pp. 183–84.

7. Wellington has received, from some quarters including Napoleon himself, criticism for leaving such a large force a few hours' march from the main field. I find such criticism entirely unfounded when considering all the factors.

8. Adkin, p. 121.

9. Bassford, C., D. Moran and G. W. Pedlow, *On Waterloo, Clausewitz, Wellington and the Campaign of 1815* (USA, self published, 2010), p. 139.

10. These two brigades were positioned on the ridge immediately behind (to the north) of Hougoumont. The 1st Brigade, commanded by Major General Sir Peregrine Maitland, consisted of the 2nd and 3rd Battalions of the 1st (Grenadier) Guards and the 2nd Brigade, commanded by Major General John Byng, consisted of the 2nd Battalion Coldstream Guards and the 2nd Battalion Third (Scots) Guards.

11. There is not universal agreement that these Hanoverians and Lunebergers arrived any earlier than the 1st/2nd Nassau.

12. Adkin, p. 407.

13. Cotton, p. 32.

14. Siborne, H. J., *The Waterloo Letters* (East Yorkshire, 2009 reprint), p. 389.

15. Ludlow Beamish, N., *History of the King's German Legion*, two volumes (London, 1832–37), Vol. II, p. 353.

16. Kincaid, Capt J., *Adventures in the Rifle Brigade in the Peninsula, France and the Netherlands from 1809 to 1815* (London, 1830), p. 164.

17. Frischermont Chateau was demolished in 1857 and should not be confused with the Convent of Frischermont built in 1929.

18. Adkin, p. 144.

19. Consisting of the two battalions of the Orange Nassau Regiment and the remaining two battalions (2nd and 3rd) of the 2nd Nassau Regiment – the 1st Battalion having been detached to Hougoumont.

20. Jomini, pp. 182–83.

21. Fortescue, Vol. X, p. 378.

22. Black, J., *Waterloo: The Battle that Brought Down Napoleon* (London, 2010), p. 126.

23. Field, p. 89.

24. Wotton, G., *Waterloo 1815* (Oxford, 1992), p. 10 and Roberts, A., *Waterloo, Napoleon's Last Gamble* (London, 2005), p. 54.

25. Chandler, D., *The Military Maxims of Napoleon* (London, 2002), p. 57.

26. Ibid., p. 64.

27. Ibid., p. 61.

28. Bassford, Moran and Pedlow, p. 140.

29. Ibid., p. 171.

30. Field, citing *Napoleon's Memoirs*, p. 51.

31. Keegan, J., *The Face of Battle* (London, 1976), pp. 139–40. Napoleon had disbanded the balloon observation troops in the late 1790s and suggestions that Napoleon had an observation tower on the Rossomme heights are unfounded.

32. Bassford, Moran and Pedlow, p. 140.

33. Field, citing *Napoleon's Memoirs*, p. 57.

34. Barbero, p. 96.

35. Ibid., p. 84.

36. Ibid., p. 85.

37. Barbero, pp. 96–99 provides a possible explanation.

38. As Keegan points out these phases are an administrative convenience and not perceived or conceived at the time by the combatants. Keegan, p. 128.

39. See Barbero, pp. 98–99 and Field, p. 62.

40. Fortescue, Vol. X, p. 357.

41. Roberts, p. 56.

42. Paget, J. and D. Saunders, *Hougoumont, The Key to Victory at Waterloo* (London, 1992), p. 11.

43. Field, pp. 262–63.

44. Thiers, M. A., *Histoire du Consulat et de L'Empire*, 20 volumes (Paris, 1862), Vol. XX, pp. 495–96.

45. Ibid., p. 497.

46. Field, p. 67.

47. Shrapnel Papers, Wood to Shrapnel dated 19 June from Waterloo.

48. Siborne, *The Waterloo Letters*, p. 188.

49. Field suggests that the southern gate was also penetrated as well as a small gate on the western wall.

50. Thiers, Vol. XX, p. 498.

51. Field, citing Robinaux, p. 70.

52. Field, p. 262.

53. Ibid., p. 262.

54. It is unclear exactly which brigade of Quiot's Division surrounded and attacked the farm.

55. Ludlow Beamish, Vol. II, p. 354.

56. Field, citing Charras, p. 92.

57. Glover, G. (ed.), *Letters from the Battle of Waterloo – Unpublished Correspondence by Allied Officers from the Siborne Papers* (London, 2004), p. 244.

58. Chandler, *The Campaigns of Napoleon* (London, 1966), p. 1,080.

59. Glover, p. 245.

60. Weller, J., *Wellington at Waterloo* (London, 1967), p. 119 f. 1. The exact time, like so many during the battle, is subject to considerable debate.

61. Keegan, p. 132.

62. Siborne, W., *The Waterloo Campaign*, third edition (London, 1848), p. 476 f. Only one cart of rifle ammunition was allocated for the two light battalions of the KGL and in the confusion of baggage being moved back on the Brussels road had been 'thrown in a ditch'.

63. Glover, p. 246 and Siborne, *The Waterloo Campaign*, p. 475 confirm that French artillery did cause damage to the walls during the third attack.

64. Siborne, *The Waterloo Letters*, pp. 241–42.

65. Siborne, *The Waterloo Campaign*, p. 342.

66. Adkin, p. 374.

THE CAVALRY CHARGES

1. Siborne, H. T., *Waterloo Letters* (London, 1891), p. 216.

2. I borrow this lovely quote from the late Peter Edwards, author of several books on the Peninsular War. Being a farmer, Peter knew all about horses and what they could and couldn't do. He and I had several discussions on the subject whilst in the Peninsula together.

3. See Fletcher, I., *Galloping at Everything: The British Cavalry in the Peninsular War and at Waterloo, 1808–1815* (Staplehurst, 1999).

4. This was a trend that was to continue into the Crimean War when the Scots Greys loomed large in virtually all of the illustrations in *The Illustrated London News* following the Battle of Balaclava of 25 October 1854, until the more accurate reports of the Charge of the Light Brigade began to arrive, whereupon they tended to feature Lord Cardigan's Light Brigade.

5. Siborne, p. 7.

6. Ibid., p. 8.

7. Mann, Rev. Michael, *And They Rode On* (London, 1984), p. 36.

8. Siborne, p. 44.

9. Ibid., p. 38. Waymouth, in Siborne p. 44, quotes Major Kelly, of the Life Guards, as claiming that the Life Guards, 'made great slaughter amongst the flying cuirassiers who had choked the hollow way … and that this road was quite blocked up by dead.'

10. Siborne, pp. 78, 81 and 198.

11. Ibid., p. 61. De Lacy Evans, who actually gave the signal for the attack to begin by waving his hat in the air, said that the Union Brigade waited for a few minutes at the foot of the reverse slope in order to let the infantry wheel back and pass around the flanks of their squadrons and also to ensure that the French were a little 'deranged' at having to pass both the hedge and the road.

12. Siborne, p. 72.

13. Ibid., p. 383.

14. Ibid., p. 85.

15. Ibid., p. 62.

16. Ibid., p. 9.

17. I do not include the French assaults on Hougoumont as these were, by definition, intended to be only diversionary attacks as a prelude to the great assault on Wellington's left and centre.

18. Anglesey, Marquess of, *One-Leg: Life and Letters of Henry William Paget, First Marquess of Anglesey* (London, 1961), p. 135.

19. Siborne, pp. 9–10.

20. Ibid., p. 72.

21. Anglesey, p. 141.

22. Ibid., p. 142.

THE PRUSSIAN ARMY AT WATERLOO

1. Amongst these last, the most prominent is none other than Napoleon himself. For example, 'The Anglo-Dutch army was saved twice during the day by the Prussians: the first time before three o'clock by the arrival of General Bülow with 30,000 men, and the second time by the arrival of Marshal Blücher with 31,000 men.' Cf. Bonaparte, N., *The Waterloo Campaign*, ed. S. de Chair (London, 1957), p. 158.

2. Howarth, D., *A Near Run Thing: The Day of Waterloo* (London, 1968), pp. 164–65.

3. Ibid., p. 169.

4. Ibid., p. 174.

5. Ibid., p. 193.

6. Ibid., p. 199.

7. For the full story, cf. Mercer, Gen A. C., *Journal of the Waterloo Campaign* (London, 1927), pp. 177–79.

8. Cotton, E., *A Voice from Waterloo: A History of the Battle on the 18th June 1815*, third edition (London, 1849), pp. 198–89.

9. For the episode which is seen as the centrepiece of this alleged conspiracy, cf. Hofschröer, P., *Wellington's Smallest Victory: The Duke, the Model-Maker and the Secret of Waterloo* (London, 2004).

10. Alison, A., *History of Europe from the Commencement of the French Revolution to the Restoration of the Bourbons in MDCCCXV* (London, 1860), Vol. XIV, pp. 63–64. What makes this passage particularly interesting is that, despite accusations that British writers have forgotten the substantial non-British contingent in Wellington's forces, the author not only does not claim that the troops commanded by Wellington were all British, but also makes it clear that he equates the quality of many of the German troops concerned to that of their 'red-coat' allies. In fairness, it has to be said that Alison is particularly generous in respect of the Prussians. Written in the same era, the account of the battle produced by Sir Edward Creasy in his ground-breaking anthology, recognises that the Prussians fought hard at Plancenoit, but the reader will find no passage specifically giving them a major share in the responsibility for Allied victory; cf. Creasy, E., *The Fifteen Decisive Battles of the World* (London, 1859), pp. 329–90. Yet, if Creasy is somewhat lukewarm in his tone, the same cannot be said for the equally contemporaneous military commentator, Charles Chesney, the latter's *Waterloo Lectures* being so lavish in their praise of the Prussians that, according to Peter Hofschröer, the author of the official history published in Berlin in 1904 paid it the tribute of describing it as 'the first impartial English account'; cf. Chesney, C., *Waterloo Lectures*, ed. P. Hofschröer (London, 1997), p. x.

11. Chandler, D., *Waterloo: The Hundred Days* (Botley, 1980), pp. 150–51.

12. Ibid., p. 165.

13. Ibid., p. 195. In fairness, Chandler does go on to make a further point. Thus: 'There is no foundation in the belief held in some German circles that Blücher's role was wholly the vital factor. The Prussians could no more have defeated Napoleon on their own than Wellington could have mastered the French with the Allied army alone.' Ibid. But this is a fair comment, a further point that is suggestive of the want of partisan spirit with which Chandler writes being the fact that he goes out of the way to point out that Prussian casualties on 18 June included not just the 7,000 men who fell at Waterloo – a figure something less than half the Allied total of 15,000 – but also the 2,500 who were lost at Wavre. Ibid., p. 171.

14. Chalfont, Lord (ed.), *Waterloo: Battle of the Three Armies* (London, 1979), p. 191. It could be argued that the author goes too far here – for example, it seems odd to

argue, in effect, that Napoleon displayed indecent haste in his conduct of the day when he notoriously delayed the start of the battle for several hours in order to let the ground dry out after the storm of the night before – but hostility to the Prussians there is none.

15. Cf. Black, J., *The Battle of Waterloo: A New History* (New York, 2010) and Roberts, A., *Napoleon's Last Gamble* (London, 2005).

16. For the exact remarks from which this paraphrase is drawn, cf. Hofschröer, P., *1815: The Waterloo Campaign* (London, 1998–99), Vol. II, p. 338.

17. Chalfont (ed.), p. 65; for a more cautious assessment, cf. Uffindell, A., *The Eagle's Last Triumph: Napoleon's Victory at Ligny, June 1815* (London, 1994), pp. 114–15.

18. Cited in Chalfont (ed.), pp. 69–70.

19. According to the German historian Kaulbach, Gneisenau's doubts were still not quite put to rest: whilst publically approving of the decision, he had Blücher's adjutant, Count von Nostitz, write a private letter to von Müffling asking for his assurance that Wellington really did intend to stand and fight. To the end, then, a degree of coolness remained in Gneisenau's attitude that the situation simply did not warrant: whilst the Anglo-Dutch army might not have been able to come to the aid of the Prussians at Ligny, this was not in any way the fruit of ill-will. A much fairer question, then, would have been whether Wellington could withstand a French attack, it being very much to Blücher's credit that he never once seems to have considered that this might not be the case. For all this, cf. Ibid., pp. 70–71.

20. For all this, cf. Hofschröer, *1815*, Vol. II, pp. 48–55.

21. Cited in Henderson, E. F., *Blücher and the Uprising of Prussia against Napoleon, 1806–1815* (New York, 1815), p. 301.

22. It has to be said that Bülow does not come out of the afternoon at all well. Thus, whilst it is understandable that he should have felt the need to send out reconnaissance patrols to discover the exact position of the French forces, and in general to have exercised a degree of caution, some of his troops halted for as much as three hours, and it is difficult to see why he did not keep them moving forward, albeit at a rather slower pace than might otherwise have been the case. Cf. Hofschröer, *1815*, Vol. II, p. 97.

23. Already, then, the Prussians were having an effect: had Mouton's men joined the great attack on Wellington's centre that was launched at about this time, it could well have broken through rather than being driven back in disorder.

24. Cited in Field, A., *Waterloo: The French Perspective* (Barnsley, 2012), p. 165.

25. That something of the sort was the case is accepted even by Peter Hofschröer, who not only admits that Bülow's later claims of constant progress were exaggerated, if not downright mendacious, but also speaks of the firefight being so prolonged that some units ran out of ammunition; cf. Hofschröer, *1815*, Vol. II, pp. 118–19; for the caution displayed by Losthin and Hiller, meanwhile, cf. Chalfont (ed.), p. 134.

26. Cited in Field, pp. 168–69.

27. Cited in ibid., p. 166.

28. One can here deal very briefly with the incident made so much of by Howarth in which Zieten's troops are deemed to have caused consternation by marching off in the wrong direction. In brief, what appears to have happened is that, just as the first troops reached the Anglo-Dutch positions, an urgent message arrived from Blücher's Headquarters to the effect that help was needed at Plancenoit, and that I Corps should therefore abandon its march to join Wellington, and march to support Bülow. This produced some confusion, not least because the leading units of the force had already passed by the turning that represented the quickest route to Plancenoit and therefore turned around and marched back the way they had

come. Within a matter of minutes, however, Zieten had determined on his own initiative to ignore Blücher's orders and continue on his original way. Meanwhile, it cannot be stressed too strongly that talk of the Prussians marching the wrong way is over-blown. Blücher's orders may have been unnecessarily panicky – clearly over-wrought about the situation at Plancenoit, at one point he was heard to mutter, 'If only we had the damned village' – but the caprice or simple error of which Howarth hints is therefore a figment of the latter's imagination. Cf. Chalfont (ed.), pp. 145–46.

29. For all this, cf. Hofschröer, *1815*, Vol. II, pp. 122–24; Field, pp. 176–83.

30. Gneisenau, A. Neithardt von, *The Life and Campaigns of Field-Marshal Prince Blücher* (London, 1815), pp. 416–17.

31. French accounts are very clear that the village was evacuated by its surviving defenders rather than being stormed. According to Tromelin, for example, 'Towards eight o'clock in the evening, decimated by the Prussian attacks that were constantly reinforced, outflanked on our right by Blücher's cavalry, whose squadrons our own cavalry were not able to contain, and to our left by the English cavalry launched in pursuit of the army, one sensed that our battalions were in danger of falling into disorder, and the order was received to abandon Plancenoit … and retire towards the main road.' Cited in Field, p. 212.

32. Cited in ibid., p. 206. Compare this account, however, with that given by Bülow in his official report: 'The left flank of Wellington's army … had gained a considerable amount of ground, but strong masses of the enemy with much artillery were seen around La Belle Alliance. Thus, a general wheel to the [right] was ordered and carried out in a most orderly fashion, with our right flank near La Belle Alliance linking up precisely with the left flank of Wellington's army.' Cited in Hofschröer, *1815*, Vol. II, p. 130. If this means anything, it is surely that Wellington reached the French position before the Prussians launched their final charge.

33. Gneisenau, p. 413.

34. Cited in Hofschröer, *1815*, Vol. II, p. 127. This was, perhaps, a somewhat unwise line to take: forcibly incorporated into the Prussian Army in 1814, the troops of the Grand Duchy of Berg, a German principality created for Joachim Murat in 1806, went into battle at Waterloo wearing their old white uniforms, these being at least as French in their style as anything affected by the Nassauers.

35. For all this, cf. Parkinson, R., *The Hussar General: The Life of Blücher, Man of Waterloo* (London, 1975), pp. 239–40. Parkinson, incidentally, is yet another example of a British historian who has been more partial to the Prussians than is usually allowed; more than that, indeed, he openly accuses Wellington of having given them far too little credit in the official dispatch that he wrote in the wake of the battle.

36. Cf. Ibid., p. 238.

LA GARDE RECULE!

1. Kennedy, Gen Sir J. Shaw, *Notes on the Battle of Waterloo* (London: John Murray, 1865), pp. 123–24.

2. Major G. Gawler's reply to General Vivian's response to his article 'The Crisis and Close of the Action at Waterloo by an Eye-witness' in the *United Service Journal* (September 1833), p. 3.

3. 'What the Gordons did at Waterloo, From the Forgotten Diary of Sergeant D. Robertson', in *With Napoleon at Waterloo and Other Unpublished Documents of the Waterloo and Peninsular Campaigns* (London: Mackensie Macbride, 1911), p. 162.

4. Kennedy, pp. 126–28.

5. Levavasseur, O., *Souvenirs Militaires d'Octave Levavasseur, officier d'artillerie aide de camp du maréchal Ney (1802–1815)* (Paris: Plon, 1914), p. 303.

6. Petit, Gen Baron J-M, in an account given in the *English Historical Review*, Vol. 18, April 1903, p. 325.

7. Account of Captain Prax, reproduced in Cahier No. 15, Association Belge Napoleonienne, p. 65. This magazine contains the accounts of the officers of the Imperial Guard that had originally been published in *Carnet de la Sabretache*, 1905. *Carnet de la Sabretache* was the French equivalent of the *United Service Journal*.

8. Petit, letter to Pelet, Bourges, 18 May 1835, reproduced in Cahier No. 15, Association Belge Napoleonienne, p. 55.

9. Prax, reproduced in Cahier No. 15, Association Belge Napoleonienne, p. 65.

10. 'On a part of Captain Siborne's History of the Waterloo Campaign, By an Officer of the British 5th Brigade', in the *United Service Journal* (March 1845), pp. 396–99.

11. Siborne, H. T. (ed.), *The Waterloo Letters* (London: Arms and Armour Press, 1983), Letter 111, p. 257.

12. Ibid., Letter 139, p. 330.

13. 'On a Part of Captain Siborne's History of the Waterloo Campaign', op. cit., p. 397.

14. Ibid., p. 396.

15. Letter written 10 June 1835 by Guillemin, reproduced in Cahier No. 15, Association Belge Napoleonienne, p. 61.

16. 'The Crisis of Waterloo, By a Soldier of the Fifth Brigade', in *Colburn's United Service Magazine* (formally *United Service Journal*) 1852, Part II, p. 51.

17. 'On a Part of Captain Siborne's History of the Waterloo Campaign', op cit., pp. 400–01.

18. Siborne, Letter 61, p. 121.

19. Napoleon, *Napoleon's Memoirs*, ed. Somerset de Chair (London: Soho Books, 1986), p. 535.

20. General Chassé's letter dated 27 April 1836 to Colonel Nepveu, reproduced in Franklin, *Waterloo. Netherlands Correspondence* (Dorchester: Henry Ling, 2010), p. 116.

21. *The Crisis of Waterloo, By a Soldier of the Fifth Brigade*, p. 51.

22. Guillemin, letter written to General Haxo, 10 June 1835, reproduced in Cahier No. 15, Association Belge Napoleonienne, p. 61.

23. 'The Crisis of Waterloo, By a Soldier of the Fifth Brigade', p. 51.

24. Siborne, Letter 96, pp. 227–28.

25. Prax. Letter to Pelet, dated Cholet, 23 April 1835, reproduced in Cahier No. 15, Association Belge Napoleonienne, p. 65.

26. Ibid.

27. François, *Jean-Louis de Crabbé, Colonel d'Empire* (Nantes: Editions du Canonnier, 2006), p. 18.

28. Prax, Letter to Pelet, dated Cholet, 23 April 1835, reproduced in Cahier No. 15, Association Belge Napoleonienne, p. 66.

29. Berthelot, quoted in Le Boterf, *Le brave Général Cambronne* (Paris: Editions France Empire, 1984), p. 207.

30. Siborne, Letter 105, p. 244.

31. Ibid., Letter 111, pp. 257–58.

32. Ibid., Letter 109, p. 255.

33. Ibid., Letter 124, p. 293.

34. Glover, G. (ed.), *Letters from the Battle of Waterloo, Unpublished Correspondence by Allied Officers from the Siborne Papers* (London: Greenhill Books, 2004), Letter 128, p. 194.

35. Siborne, Letter 124, p. 292.

36. Leeke, *The History of Lord Seaton's Regiment at the Battle of Waterloo* (London: Hatchard and Co., 1866), pp. 45–47.

37. Levavasseur, pp. 303–04.

38. Pontécoulant, P.-G. Le D. de, *Napoléon à Waterloo 1815* (repr. Paris: Librairie des Deux Empires, 2004), p. 254.

39. Gawler's reply to General Vivian's response to his article, 'The Crisis and Close of the Action at Waterloo by an Eye-witness', in the *United Service Journal* (September 1833), p. 5.

40. Siborne, Letter 120, p. 277.

41. Mauduit, de, H., *Histoire des derniers jours de la Grande Armée* (Paris: Dion-Lambert, 1854), p. 446.

42. Gawler, 'The Crisis and Close of the Action at Waterloo by an Eye-witness', in the *United Service Journal* (July 1833), p. 305.

43. Guillemin, letter written to General Haxo, 10 June 1835, reproduced in Cahier No. 15, Association Belge Napoleonienne, p. 61.

44. For these words and a thorough and fascinating investigation into this famous episode of the battle, see Houssaye, *La Garde meurt et ne se rend pas, Histoire d'un mot historique* (Paris: Perrin, 1907).

45. Lot, *Les Deux Généraux Ordener* (Paris: Roger et Chernoviz, 1910), p. 95.

46. Leeke, p. 58.

47. Ibid.

48. Letter from General Christiani to Pelet, reproduced in Cahier No. 15, Association Belge Napoleonienne, p. 59.

49. Gawler, 'The Crisis and Close of the Action at Waterloo by an Eye-witness', p. 305.

50. Martin, Lt J.-F., *Souvenirs d'un ex-officier, 1812–1815* (Paris & Geneva: J. Cherbuliez, 1867), pp. 296–97.

51. Robinaux, Capt P., *Journal de Route du Capitaine Robinaux* (Paris: 1908), p. 209.

52. Reproduced in Coppens-Courcelle, *Waterloo 1815. Les Carnets de la Campagne* (Brussels: Tondeur Diffusion, 1999–2011), No. 4, p. 46.

The Legacy of Waterloo

1. Chandler, D., *Waterloo: The Hundred Days* (London: Osprey, 1980), p. 166.

2. Cotton, E., *A Voice from Waterloo: A History of the Battle Fought on the 18th June 1815* (London: Forgotten Books, 2009), p. 138.

3. Chandler, p. 179.

4. For more on this argument, see Esdaile, C., *Napoleon's Wars: An International History* (London: Allen Lane, 2008).

5. Fortescue, J., *A History of the British Army* (London, 1920), Vol. X, pp. 400–01.

6. Ibid., Vol. X, p. 396. The 1st Guards had suffered 1,100 casualties out of a complement of 2,000.

7. Gurwood, J. (ed.), *The Dispatches of Field Marshal the Duke of Wellington During His Various Campaigns in India, Denmark, Portugal, Spain, the Low Countries and France*, 13 volumes (London, 1852) (quoted as '*WD*' hereafter), Vol. XII, Wellington to Beresford, Gonesse, 2 July 1815, p. 529.

8. *WD*, Vol. XII, Wellington to Bathurst, Orville, 28 June 1815, p. 517.

9.   Fortescue, Vol. X, p. 399.

10.   *WD*, Vol. XII, Wellington to Bathurst, Gonesse, 2 July 1815, p. 532.

11.   *WD*, Vol. XII, Wellington to Blücher, Gonesse, 2 July 1815, p. 526.

12.   Fortescue, Vol. X, p. 400.

13.   Chandler quoting Napoleon Bonaparte, Paris, 23 June 1815.

14.   Wellesley, A., 2nd Duke of Wellington (ed.), *Supplementary Despatches and Memoranda of Field Marshal Arthur the Duke of Wellington, 1797–1818*, 14 volumes (London, 1858) (quoted as 'WSD' hereafter), Vol. XI, Private Intelligence, Paris, 7 August 1815, pp. 107–10.

15.   Stewart, Robert, 2nd Marquess of Londonderry, *The Memoranda and Correspondence of Robert Stewart, Viscount Castlereagh*, 12 volumes (London, 1848–54) (quoted as 'CC' hereafter), Vol. X, Liverpool to Castlereagh, Fife House, 15 July 1815, p. 430.

16.   Davies, H. J., *Wellington's Wars: The Making of a Military Genius* (London: Yale University Press, 2012), pp. 218–19.

17.   *WSD*, Vol. IX, Castlereagh to Liverpool, Vienna, 5 December 1814, p. 462.

18.   *WD*, Vol. XII, Wellington to Castlereagh, Paris, 14 July 1815, p. 558.

19.   *WD*, Vol. XII, Wellington to Blücher, Paris, 9 July 1815, pp. 552–53.

20.   Quoted in Webster, C., *The Foreign Policy of Castlereagh, 1812–1815: Britain and the Reconstruction of Europe* (London: G. Bell, 1950), p. 49.

21.   *WD*, Vol. XII, Wellington to Blücher, Gonesse, 2 July 1815, p. 527.

22.   Quoted in Webster, *Castlereagh*, p. 456.

23.   Webster, *Castlereagh*, p. 460.

24.   *WSD*, Vol. XI, Private Intelligence, Paris, 7 August 1815, pp. 107–10.

25.   Webster, *Castlereagh*, p. 456.

26.   *CC*, Vol. X, Liverpool to Castlereagh, Fife House, 10 July 1815, p. 423.

27.   Webster, *Castlereagh*, p. 462.

28.   Ibid., p. 463.

29.   *CC*, Vol. X, Liverpool to Castlereagh, Fife House, 15 July 1815, p. 431.

30.   *WSD*, Vol. XI, Castlereagh to Liverpool, Paris, 24 August 1815, pp. 137–38.

31.   Webster, *Castlereagh*, p. 466.

32.   *WSD*, Vol. XI, Private Intelligence, Paris, 7 August 1815, pp. 107–10.

33.   *WD*, Vol. XII, Wellington to Castlereagh, Paris, 11 August, 1815, p. 596.

34.   Webster, *Castlereagh*, p. 437. See also J. Bew, *Castlereagh* (London: Quercus, 2011).

35.   *WSD*, Vol. XI, Castlereagh to Liverpool, Paris, 24 August 1815, pp. 139–40 [my emphasis].

36.   Webster, C. K. (ed.), *British Diplomacy, 1813–1815* (London, 1921), Castlereagh to Liverpool, Paris, 4 September 1815, pp. 375–76.

37.   *WSD*, Vol. XI, Castlereagh to Liverpool, Paris, 31 August 1815, pp. 147–49.

38.   *WSD*, Vol. XI, Castlereagh to Liverpool, Paris, 24 August 1815, pp. 139–40.

39.   *WD*, Vol. XII, Wellington to Castlereagh, Paris, 31 August 1815, pp. 622–25.

40.   *WSD*, Vol. XI, Castlereagh to Liverpool, Paris, 31 August 1815, pp. 147–49.

41.   Quoted in Webster, *Castlereagh*, p. 477.

42.   *WSD*, Vol. XI, Castlereagh to Liverpool, Paris, 31 August 1815, pp. 147–49.

43.   Schroeder, P. W., *The Transformation of European Politics, 1763–1848* (Oxford: Oxford University Press, 1994), p. 567.

44.   *WSD*, Vol. XI, Castlereagh to Liverpool, Paris, 31 August 1815, pp. 147–49.

45. Holbraad, C., *The Concert of Europe: A Study in German and British International Theory, 1815–1914* (London: Barnes & Noble, 1970), p. 4.

46. *WSD*, Vol. XI, Castlereagh to Liverpool, Paris, 24 August 1815, pp. 139–40.

47. Mazower, M., *Governing the World: The History of an Idea* (London: Allen Lane, 2012), pp. 3–12.

48. Webster, *Castlereagh*, p. 481.

49. Holbraad, p. 1.

50. Schroeder, P. W., *Austria, Great Britain, and the Crimean War: The Destruction of the European Concert* (London: Cornell University Press, 1972), p. 404.

51. Ibid., p. 405.

52. Holbraad, p. 2.

53. See Yapp, M., *Strategies of British India: Britain, Iran and Afghanistan, 1798–1850* (Oxford: Oxford University Press, 1981).

54. Schroeder, *Destruction of the European Concert*, p. 409.

55. See, for example, Baugh, D., 'Great Britain's Blue-Water Policy, 1689–1815,' in *International History Review*, 10 (February 1988), pp. 33–58.

56. See Simms, B., *Three Victories and a Defeat: The Rise and Fall of the First British Empire, 1714–1783* (London: Allen Lane, 2008).

57. Bonaparte, N., *The Confidential Correspondence of Napoleon Bonaparte with his Brother Joseph, Sometime King of Spain*, two volumes (New York, 1856), p. 135.

58. Munch-Petersen, T., *Defying Napoleon: How Britain Bombarded Copenhagen and Seized the Danish Fleet in 1807* (London: The History Press, 2007), p. 249.

59. See Lambert, A., *The Crimean War: British Grand Strategy Against Russia, 1853–56* (Manchester: Manchester University Press, 1990).

60. Schroeder, *Destruction of the European Concert*, pp. 409–15.

61. Strachan, H., *From Waterloo to Balaclava: Tactics, Technology, and the British Army, 1815–1854* (Cambridge: Cambridge University Press, 1985), pp. 1–2.

62. Ibid., pp. 12–15.

63. *WD*, Vol. XII, p. 529, Wellington to Beresford, Gonesse, 2 July 1815.

64. Strachan, *Waterloo to Balaclava*, pp. vii–viii.

65. See Davies for in-depth analysis of Wellington's strategising during the Peninsular War.

66. Strachan, H., *Wellington's Legacy: The Reform of the British Army 1830–54* (Manchester: Manchester University Press, 1984), pp. 109–45.

67. Strachan, *Waterloo to Balaclava*, p. 2.

68. Ibid., p. 8.

69. Mitchell, John, *Thoughts on Tactics* (London, 1838), p. 120. Quoted in Ibid., p. 9.

70. Lambert, Andrew, 'Seapower, Strategy and the Scheldt: British Strategy, 1793–1914', unpublished paper presented at 'Waterloo: The Battle that Forged a Century', Conference, London, September 2013.

71. See Hall, C., *Wellington's Navy: Seapower and the Peninsular War, 1807–1814* (London: Chatham Publishing, 2004); and more generally, Knight, R., *Britain Against Napoleon: The Organisation of Victory, 1793–1815* (London: Allen Lane, 2013).

72. *Aide-Memoire to the Military Sciences*, three volumes (London, 1848–52), i, p. 2. Quoted in Strachan, *Waterloo to Balaclava*, p. 15.

73. Sweetman, J., *Crimean War* (Oxford: Osprey, 2001), p. 89.

74. Holbraad, pp. 112–13.

75. *WSD*, Vol. IX, Castlereagh to Wellington, Vienna, 25 October 1814, p. 372.

ORDERS OF BATTLE

FRENCH ARMY ORDER OF BATTLE

Grand Armée du Nord under the supreme command of Emperor Napoleon I.
Major Général (Chief of Staff): Marshal Soult, Duke of Dalmatia.
Commander of artillery: General of Division Charles-Étienne-François Ruty.
Field commanders under the direct command of Emperor Napoleon:

Marshal Ney, Prince of the Moskova:

On 16 June 1815, at the Battle of Quatre Bras, in command of the Left Wing: I Corps, II Corps (minus the Girard Division, present at the Battle of Ligny), III Cavalry Corps (minus the L'Héritier Division, present at the Battle of Ligny) and Imperial Guard light cavalry division.

On 18 June 1815, at the Battle of Waterloo, effective field commander of all the French forces present, minus those engaged at Plancenoit (VI Corps and elements of the Guard).

Marshal de Grouchy:

On 16 June 1815, at the Battle of Ligny, in command of the French Cavalry Reserve: I Cavalry Corps, II Cavalry Corps, the L'Héritier Division (detached from III Cavalry Corps) and IV Cavalry Corps.

Between 17 and 19 June 1815, in command of the Right Wing: III Corps (minus the Domon (cavalry) Division, present at the Battle of Waterloo), IV Corps, I Cavalry Corps (minus the Subervie Division present at the Battle of Waterloo, but with the Teste (infantry) Division attached to it) and II Cavalry Corps.

I CORPS

Unit	Commander	Complement
I Corps	Général Jean-Baptiste Drouet, Count d'Erlon	19,484 officers and men
1st Division	Général de Brigade Baron Joachim-Jérôme Quiot (commanding in the absence of Allix)	4,182
1st Brigade	Général de Brigade Baron Joachim-Jérôme Quiot	
2nd Brigade	Général de Brigade Baron Charles-François Bourgeois	
2nd Division	Général de Division Baron François Donzelot	5,317
1st Brigade	Général de Brigade Baron Nicolas Schmitz	
2nd Brigade	Général de Brigade Baron Aulard	
3rd Division	Général de Division Baron Pierre-Louis Binet de Marcognet	4,081
1st Brigade	Général de Brigade Antoine Noguès	
2nd Brigade	Général de Brigade Baron Jean-George Grenier	
4th Division	Général de Division Comte Pierre Durutte	4,034
1st Brigade	Général de Brigade Chevalier Pégot	
2nd Brigade	Général de Brigade Jena-Louis Brue	
1st Cavalry Division	Général de Division Baron Charles-Claude Jacquinot	1,661
1st Brigade	Général de Brigade Baron Adrien-François Bruno	
2nd Brigade	Général de Brigade Baron Martin-Chorles Gobrechet	
I Corps Artillery Reserve	Général de Brigade Jean-Charles De Salles	206
5 foot batteries		
1 horse battery		

II Corps

Unit	Commander	Complement
II Corps	Général Count Honoré Reille	25,000 men, 46 guns
5th Division	Général de Division Baron Gilbert Bachelu	4,290
1st Brigade	Général de Brigade Baron Pierre-Antoine Husson	
2nd Brigade	Général de Brigade Baron Toussant Campi	
6th Division	Prince Jérôme Bonaparte	8,019
1st Brigade	Maréchal de Camp Baron Pierre-François Bauduin	
2nd Brigade	Général de Brigade Jean-Louis Baron Soye	
7th Division	Général de Division Baron Jean Baptiste Girard	4,678
1st Brigade	Général de Brigade Vicomte Louis de Villiers	
2nd Brigade	Général de Brigade Baron Piat	
9th Division	Général de Division Comte Maximilien Sebastien Foy	5,493
1st Brigade	Général de Brigade Baron Jean-Joseph Gauthier	
2nd Brigade	Général de Brigade Baron Jean-Baptiste Jamin	
2nd Cavalry Division	Général de Division Baron Hippolyte Piré	2,025
1st Brigade	Général de Brigade Baron Hubert	
2nd Brigade	Général de Brigade Baron Wathiez	
II Corps Artillery Reserve	Général de Brigade Baron Jean Baptiste Pelletier	210
5 foot batteries		
1 horse battery		

III Corps

Unit	Commander	Complement
III Corps	Général de Division Dominique Vandamme	17,000 men, 38 guns
8th Division	Général de Division Baron Étienne-Nicolas Lefol	5,245
1st Brigade	Général de Brigade Baron Billiard	
2nd Brigade	Général de Brigade Baron Andre-Phillipe Corsin	
10th Division	Général de Division Baron Pierre-Joseph Habert	5,771
1st Brigade	Général de Brigade Baron Louis-Thomas Gengoult	
2nd Brigade	Général de Brigade Baron Rene-Joseph Dupeyroux	
11th Division	Général de Division Baron Pierre Berthézène	4,734
1st Brigade	Général de Brigade Baron François-Bertrand Dufour	
2nd Brigade	Général de Brigade Baron Lagarde	
3rd Cavalry Division	Général de Division Baron Jean-Simon Domon	1,197
1st Brigade	Général de Brigade Baron Jean-Baptiste Dommanget	
2nd Brigade	Général de Brigade Gilbert-Julien Baron Vinot	
III Corps Artillery Reserve	Général de Division Baron Jerome Dougereau	152
4 foot batteries		
1 horse battery		

IV CORPS

Unit	Commander	Complement
IV Corps	Général de Division Étienne Gerard	16,000 men, 38 guns
12th Division	Général de Division Baron Marc-Nicolas-Louis Pecheux	4,346
1st Brigade	Général de Brigade Chevalier Rome	
2nd Brigade	Général de Brigade Baron Schoeffer	
13th Division	Général de Division Baron Louis-Joseph Vichery	4,153
1st Brigade	Général de Brigade Baron le Capitaine	
2nd Brigade	Général de Brigade Comte Desprez	
14th Division	Général de Division Comte Louis Bourmont	4,570
1st Brigade	Général de Brigade Baron Hulot de Mazarny	
2nd Brigade	Général de Brigade Baron Toussaint	
7th Cavalry Division	Général de Division Baron Antoine Maurin	1,549
1st Brigade	Général de Brigade Baron Vallin	
2nd Brigade	Général de Brigade Chevalier Berruyer	
IV Corps Artillery Reserve	Général de Brigade Baltus de Pouilly	395
4 foot batteries		
1 horse battery		

VI CORPS

Unit	Commander	Complement
VI Corps	Général de Division Georges Mouton Count Lobau	10,300 men
19th Division	Général de Division Baron François-Martin-Valentin Simmer	4,151
1st Brigade	Général de Brigade Baron de Bellair	
2nd Brigade	Général de Brigade Chevalier Thevenet Jamin	
20th Division	Général de Division Baron Jean Baptiste Jeanin	3,311
1st Brigade	Général de Brigade Chevalier Bony	
2nd Brigade	Général de Brigade Comte de Tromelin	
21st Division	Général de Division Baron François-Antoine Teste	2,616
1st Brigade	Général de Brigade Baron Michel-Pascal Lafitte	
2nd Brigade	Général de Brigade Baron Raymond-Pierre Penne	
IV Corps Artillery Reserve	Général de Division Baron Henri-Marie Noury	214

I CAVALRY RESERVE CORPS

Unit	Commander	Complement
I Cavalry Corps	Général de Division Claude Pierre Pajol	3,100 men, 12 guns
4th Cavalry Division	Général de Division Baron Pierre-Benoit Soult	1,485
1st Brigade	Général de Brigade Houssin de St Laurent	
2nd Brigade	Général de Brigade Baron Ameil	
5th Cavalry Division	Général de Division Jacques Gervais, Baron Subervie	1,187
1st Brigade	Général de Brigade Comte Louis-Pierre-Alphonse de Colbert	
2nd Brigade	Général de Brigade Chevalier Antoine François Eugene Merlin de Douai	

Unit	Commander	Complement
Divisional Artillery	Capitaine Duchemin	
2 horse batteries		8 x 6lb guns, 4 x 5.5inch howitzers

II CAVALRY RESERVE CORPS

Unit	Commander	Complement
II Cavalry Corps	Général de Division Rémi Joseph Isidore Exelmann	3,300 men, 12 guns
9th Cavalry Division	Général de Division Baron Chevalier Jean-Baptiste Strolz	1,843
1st Brigade	Général de Brigade Baron Andre Burthe	
2nd Brigade	Général de Brigade Baron Vincent	
10th Cavalry Division	Général de Division Baron Louis Pierre Chastel	1,549
1st Brigade	Général de Brigade Baron Pierre Bonnemains	
2nd Brigade	Général de Brigade Jean-Baptiste Berton	
Artillery	Capitaine Bernard	
2 horse batteries		8 x 6lb guns, 4 x 5.5inch howitzers

III CAVALRY RESERVE CORPS

Unit	Commander	Complement
III Cavalry Corps	Général de Division François Étienne Kellermann	3,700 men, 12 guns
11th Cavalry Division	Général de Division Baron Samuel-François L'Heritier	2,062
1st Brigade	Général de Brigade Baron Cyrille Picquet	
2nd Brigade	Général de Brigade Baron Guiton	
12th Cavalry Division	Général de Division Baron Roussel D'Hurbal	1,794
1st Brigade	Général de Brigade Baron Amable Blanchard	
2nd Brigade	Général de Brigade Chevalier Donop	
Artillery	Capitaine Lebau	
2 horse batteries		8 x 6lb guns, 4 x 5.5inch howitzers

IV CAVALRY RESERVE CORPS

Unit	Commander	Complement
IV Cavalry Corps	Général de Division Comte Edouard Jean Baptiste Milhaud	3,000 men, 12 guns
13th Cavalry Division	Général de Division Wathier	1,376
1st Brigade	Général de Brigade Baron Jacques-Charles Dubois	
2nd Brigade	Général de Brigade Travers, Baron de Jever	
14th Cavalry Division	Général de Division Baron Jacques Antoine Adrien Delort	1,739
1st Brigade	Général de Brigade Baron Farine du Creux	
2nd Brigade	Général de Brigade Baron Vial	
Artillery	Capitaine Duchet	
2 horse batteries		8 x 6lb guns, 4 x 5.5inch howitzers

FRENCH IMPERIAL GUARD

Commander: Marshal Édouard Mortier (on sick leave, following a sudden attack of sciatica).

Unit	Commander	Complement
Grenadier Division	Général de Division Comte Friant	4,055
1er and 2e Bataillons, 1er Régiment de Grenadiers (Old Guard)	Général de Brigade Baron Petit	
1er and 2e Bataillons, 2e Régiment de Grenadiers (Old Guard)	Général de Brigade Baron Christiani	
1er and 2e Bataillons, 3e Régiment de Grenadiers (Middle Guard)	Général de Brigade Baron Poret de Morvan	
Major1er Bataillonm, 4e Régiment de Grenadiers (Middle Guard)	Général de Brigade Harlet	
Chasseur Division	Général de Division Morand	4,603
1er and 2e Bataillons, 1er Régiment de Chasseurs (Old Guard)	Général de Brigade Comte Cambronne	
1er and 2e Bataillons, 2e Régiment de Chasseurs (Old Guard)	Général de Brigade Baron Pelet-Clozeau	
1er and 2e Bataillons, 3e Régiment de Chasseurs (Middle Guard)	Colonel Mallet	
1er and 2e Bataillons, 4e Régiment de Chasseurs (Middle Guard)	Général de Brigade Henrion	
Young Guard	Général de Division Duhesme	4,283
1st Brigade	Général de Brigade Chevalier Chatrand	
1er and 2e Bataillons, 1er Régiment de Tirailleurs	Colonel Trappier de Malcolm	
1er and 2e Bataillons, 1er Régiment de Voltigeurs	Colonel Secrétan	
2nd Brigade	Maréchal de Camp Guye	
1er and 2e Bataillons, 3e Régiment de Tirailleurs	Colonel Pailhès	
1er and 2e Bataillons, 3e Régiment de Voltigeurs	Colonel Hurel	
Guard Heavy Cavalry Division	Général de Division Comte Guyot	1,718
Régiment de Vieille Garde Grenadiers à Cheval	Général de Brigade Jamin, Marquis de Bermuy	
Régiment de l'Impératrice Dragons	Général de Brigade Baron Letort (killed at Ligny), thereafter Major Hoffmayer	
Gendarmerie d'Elite	Capitaine Dyonnet	
Guard Light Cavalry Division	Général de Division Comte Lefebvre-Desnouëttes	2,557
1st Brigade	Général de Division Baron Lallemand	
Régiment de Vieille Garde Chasseurs à Cheval (French and Mameluke)	Général de Division Baron Lallemand	
2nd Brigade	Baron de Colbert-Chabanais	
1er Régiment de Chevau-Légère Garde Lanciers (French and Polish)	Colonels Schmitt and Jezmanowski	
2nd Régiment de Chevau-Légère Garde Lanciers (Dutch, French and Polish)	Colonel de Colbert	
Guard Artillery	Général de Division Baron Desvaux de Saint-Maurice	2,867 men, 126 artillery pieces
Old Guard artillery		
Foot Artillery	General Henri Dominique Lallemand	9 batteries, 72 pieces
Horse Artillery	General Duchand	4 batteries, 24 pieces
Artillery train squadron		
Auxiliary artillery		
Foot Artillery	Major Dubuard (called Marin)	3 batteries, 24 pieces

Unit	Commander	Complement
Horse Artillery	Capitaine Laurent	1 battery, 6 pieces
Artillery train squadron		
Guard Military engineers and Sailors	Général de Division Baron Haxo	519

ALLIED ARMY ORDER OF BATTLE

Combined British, Dutch and Hanoverian forces under the supreme command of Field Marshal Arthur Wellesley, 1st Duke of Wellington.

I CORPS

Unit	Commander	Complement
I Corps	Prince William of Orange	1,242 officers, 27,347 men, 56 guns
1st Division	Major General George Cooke	4,720
1st Brigade	Major General Sir Peregrine Maitland	
2nd Brigade	Major General Sir John Byng	
Artillery	Lieutenant Colonel Steven Adye	
Sandham's Field Brigade, Royal Artillery (R.A.)	Captain Charles Frederik Sandham	5 x 9lb guns, 1 x 5.5 inch howitzer
Kuhlmann's Horse Artillery Troop, King's German Legion	Captain Heinrich Kuhlmann	5 x 9lb guns 1x5.5 inch howitzer
3rd Division	Lieutenant General Sir Charles Alten K.C.B.	8,164
5th Brigade	General Sir Colin Halkett K.C.B.	
2nd Brigade, King's German Legion	Brevet Colonel Baron Christian von Ompteda	
1st Hanoverian Brigade	Colonel Friedrich, Count von Kielmansegge	
Artillery	Lieutenant Colonel John Samuel Williamson	
Lloyd's Field Brigade, R. A.	Major William Lloyd	5 x 9lb guns, 1 x5.5 inch howitzer
Cleeves' Field Brigade, King's German Legion	Captain Andreas Cleeves	5 x 9lb guns, 1x5.5 inch howitzer
2nd Netherlands Division	Luitenant-Generaal Hendrik de Perponcher Sedlnitsky	8,206
Artillery	Major Opstal	
1st Brigade	Generaal-Majoor Willem Frederik Bylandt	
Foot Artillery Battery	Kapitein A. Bijleveld	6 x 6-pdr gun, 2 x 24-pdr howitzer
Foot Artillery Battery	Kapitein E. J. Stevenart	6 x 6-pdr gun, 2 x 24-pdr howitzer
2nd Brigade	Kolonel Prins Bernhard von Sachsen-Weimar	147 officers, 4,272 men
2nd Nassau Infantry Regiment	Majoor Johann Sattler	
28th Regiment, Orange-Nassau	Kolonel Prins Bernhard von Sachsen-Weimar (subsequently promoted to brigade command mid-100 Days Campaign)	
3rd Netherlands Division	Luitenant-Generaal David Chassé	7,483
Artillery	Majoor van der Smissen	
1st Brigade	Kolonel Hendrik Detmer	
Horse Artillery Battery	Kapitein Carel Frederik Krahmer de Bichin	6 x 6-pdr gun & 2 x 24-pdr howitzer
2nd Brigade	Generaal-Majoor Alexander d'Aubremé	
Foot Artillery Battery	Kapitein Johannes Lux	6 x 6-pdr gun, 2 x 24-pdr howitzer

II CORPS

Unit	Commander	Complement
II Corps	Lieutenant General Rowland Hill, 1st Viscount Hill	27,000 men, 40 guns
2nd Division	Lieutenant General Sir Henry Clinton	6,833
3rd Brigade	General Frederick Adam	
1st Brigade, King's German Legion	Lieutenant Colonel George Charles Du Plat	
3rd Hanoverian Brigade	Lieutenant Colonel Hew Halkett	
Artillery	Lieutenant Colonel Charles Gold	
Sympher's Field Brigade, King's German Legion	Major Frederick Sympher	5 x 9lb guns, 1 x5.5 inch howitzer
Alm's Field Brigade	Captain Samuel Bolton	5 x 9lb guns, 1 x5.5 inch howitzer
4th Division	Major General Sir Charles Colville	7,212
4th Brigade	Lieutenant Colonel Hugh Mitchell	
6th Brigade	Major General George Johnstone	
6th Hanoverian Brigade	Major General Sir James Frederick Lyon	
Artillery	Lieutenant Colonel James Hawker	
Rettberg's Field Brigade Hanoverian	Major Charles von Rettberg	5 x 9lb guns, 1 x5.5 inch howitzer
Brome's Field Brigade	Major Joseph Brome	5 x 9lb guns, 1 x5.5 inch howitzer
1st Netherlands Division	Luitenant-Generaal J. A. Stedman	6,389
1st Brigade	Generaal-Majoor Ferdinand d'Hauw	
2nd Brigade	Generaal-Majoor Dominique J. de Eerens	
Foot Artillery Battery	Kapitein P. Wijnands	6 x 6-pdr gun, 2 x 24-pdr howitzer
Indies Brigade	Luitenant-Generaal Carl Anthing	
Foot Artillery Battery	Kapitein Riesz	6 x 6-pdr gun, 2x 24-pdr howitzer

CAVALRY CORPS

Unit	Commander	Complement
Anglo-Allied Army Cavalry Corps	Lieutenant General Henry William Paget, the Earl of Uxbridge	12,000 men, 30 guns
Household Brigade	Major General Lord Edward Somerset	
Union Brigade	Major General Sir William Ponsonby	
3rd British Brigade	Major General Sir Wilhelm von Dornberg	
4th British Brigade	Major General Sir John Vandeleur	
5th British Brigade	Major General Sir Colquhoun Grant	
6th Cavalry Brigade	Major General Sir Richard Hussey Vivian	
7th British Brigade	Brevet Colonel Sir Friedrich von Arentschildt	
Attached Artillery		
I Troop, Royal Horse Artillery (R.H.A.)	Major Robert Bull	6 x 5.5 inch howitzer
F Troop, R. H. A.	Lieutenant Colonel James Webber Smith	5 x 6-pdr gun, 1 x 5.5 inch howitzer
E Troop, R. H. A.	Lieutenant Colonel Sir Robert Gardiner	5 x 6-pdr gun 1 x 5.5 inch howitzer
Rocket Troop, R. H. A.	Captain Edward Whinyates	Rockets and 5 x 6-pdr gun 1 x 5.5 inch howitzer

Unit	Commander	Complement
H Troop, R. H. A.	Major William Ramsay	5 x 9-pdr gun, 1 x 5.5 inch howitzer
G Troop, R. H. A.	Captain Alexander Cavalié Mercer	5 x 9-pdr gun, 1 x 5.5 inch howitzer
1st Hanoverian Brigade	Colonel Baron von Estorff	
Netherlands Cavalry Division	Luitenant-Generaal Jean Antoine de Baron Collaert	3,634
1st Heavy Cavalry Brigade	Generaal-Majoor Albert van Zoudtlandt	
2nd Light Brigade	Generaal-Majoor Charles Étienne Baron Ghigny	
3rd Light Brigade	Generaal-Majoor J. B. Baron van Merlen	
Attached artillery and train		
Horse artillery half -battery	Kapitein A. Petter	3 x 6-pdr gun & 1 x 24-pdr howitzer
Horse artillery half -battery	Kapitein A. R. W. Geij van Pittius	3 x 6-pdr gun & 1 x 24-pdr howitzer
Cavalry of the Brunswick Corps	Major von Cramm	

RESERVES

The reserves, over 23,000 men and 56 guns, came under the direct command of Wellington during the Battle of Waterloo.

Unit	Commander	Complement
5th Division	General Sir Thomas Picton	7,158
8th Brigade	Major General Sir James Kempt	
9th Brigade	Major General Sir Dennis Pack	
5th Hanoverian Brigade	Colonel Ernst von Vincke	
Artillery	Major Heinrich Heise	
Rogers's Field Brigade	Captain Thomas Rogers	5 x 9lb guns, 1 x 5.5 inch howitzer
Braun's Field Brigade Hanoverian	Captain William Braun	5 x 9lb guns, 1 x 5.5 inch howitzer
6th Division	Lieutenant General Sir Galbraith Lowry Cole	5,149
10th Brigade	Major General Sir John Lambert	
4th Hanoverian Brigade	Colonel Charles Best	
Artillery	Major Heinrich Bruckmann	
Unett's Field Brigade	Major George W. Unett	5 x 9lb guns, 1 x 5.5 inch howitzer
Sinclair's Field Brigade	Captain James Sincalir	5 x 9lb guns, 1 x 5.5 inch howitzer
British Reserve Artillery	Major Percy Drummond	
A Troop, R. H. A.	Lieutenant Colonel Hew Ross	5 x 9-pdr gun, 1 x 5.5 inch howitzer
D Troop, R. H. A.	Major George Bean	5 x 9-pdr gun, 1 x 5.5 inch howitzer
Morrison's Battery, R. A.	Captain William Morrison	Formed Siege Artillery – not at battle
Hutchesson's Battery, R. A.	Captain Thomas Hutchesson	Formed Siege Artillery – not at battle
Ilbert's Battery, R. A.	Captain Courtenay Ilbert	Formed Siege Artillery – not at battle
Brunswick Corps	The Duke of Brunswick	5,376 men, 16 guns
Brunswick Advance Guard	Major von Rauschenplatt	
1st Brigade	Lieutenant Colonel Wilhelm Treunch von Butlar	
2nd Brigade	Lieutenant Colonel von Specht	
Artillery	Major Mahn	
Heinemann's Field Brigade	Captain von Heinemann	

Unit	Commander	Complement
Moll's Field Brigade	Major Moll	
Hanoverian Reserve Corps	Lieutenant General von der Decken	9,000
1st Brigade	Lieutenant Colonel von Bennigsen	
2nd Brigade	Lieutenant Colonel Beaulieu	
3rd Brigade	Lieutenant Colonel Bodecken	
4th Brigade	Lieutenant Colonel Wissel	
Nassau 1st Regiment	General Kruse	

PRUSSIAN ARMY ORDER OF BATTLE

The Prussian Army was led by Field Marshal Gebhard Leberecht von Blücher, Prince of Wahlstadt, and his chief of staff August von Gneisenau and remained independent from the Allied Anglo-Dutch-German Army during the course of the campaign.

I CORPS

Unit	Commander	Complement
I Corps	Generalleutnant Hans Graf von Zieten	32,500 men, 96 guns
1st Brigade	Generalmajor von Steinmetz	
2nd Brigade	Generalmajor Otto von Pirch (II)	
3rd Brigade	Generalmajor von Jagow	
4th Brigade	Generalmajor von Donnersmarck	
I Corps Cavalry	Generalmajor von Röder	*unknown*
1st Brigade	Generalmajor von Tresckow	
2nd Brigade	Oberstleutnant von Lützow	
I Corps Artillery	Oberstleutnant Lehmann	1,226
3 horse batteries (2nd, 7th and 10th)		
3 x 12-pdr field batteries (only 2nd and 6th present)		
5 x 6-pdr field batteries (1st, 3rd, 7th, 8th and 15th)		
1 Howitzer battery (1st)		

II CORPS

Unit	Commander	Complement
II Corps	Generalmajor Georg von Pirch (I)	33,000 men, 85 guns
5th Brigade	Generalmajor Tippelskirch	
6th Brigade	Generalmajor von Kraft	
7th Brigade	Generalmajor von Brause	
8th Brigade	Generalmajor van Bose	
II Corps Cavalry	Generalmajor Wahlen-Jürgass	4,468
1st Brigade	Generalmajor von Thumen	
2nd Brigade	Oberstleutnant von Sohr	
3rd Brigade	Oberst von der Schulenburg	1,382

Unit	Commander	Complement
II Corps Artillery	Oberst Rohl	
3 horse batteries (5th, 6th and 14th)		
2 x 12-pdr batteries (4th and 8th)		
5 x 6-pdr batteries (5th, 10th, 12th, 34th and 37th)		

III CORPS

Unit	Commander	Complement
III Corps	Generalleutnant Johann von Thielmann	25,000 men, 48 guns
9th Brigade	Generalmajor von Borcke	
10th Brigade	Oberst Kampfen	
11th Brigade	Oberst von Luck	
12th Brigade	Oberst von Stülpnagel	
III Corps Cavalry	Generalmajor von Hobe	3,424
1st Brigade	Oberst von der Marwitz	
2nd Brigade	Oberst von Lottum	
III Corps Artillery	Oberst Mohnhaupt	1,345
3 horse batteries (18th and 19th , 20th		
1 x 12-pdr battery (7th)		
2 x 6-pdr batteries (18th and 35th)		

IV CORPS

Unit	Commander	Complement
IV Corps	General der Infanterie Friedrich Wilhelm Count von Bülow	32,000 men, 132 guns
13th Brigade	Generalmajor von Hacke	
14th Brigade	Generalmajor Ryssel	
15th Brigade	Generalmajor von Losthin	
16th Brigade	Generalleutnant von Hiller	
IV Corps Cavalry	Prince William of Prussia	
1st Brigade	Oberst von Schwerin	
2nd Brigade	Oberstleutnant von Watzdorff	
3rd Brigade	Oberst von Sydow	
IV Corps Artillery	Oberst Braun	
3 horse batteries (1st, 11th, and 12th landwehr)		
3 x 12-pdr batteries (3rd, 5th and 13th)		
5 x 6-pdr batteries (2nd, 11th, 13th landwehr, 14th, and 21st landwehr)		

BIBLIOGRAPHY

INTRODUCTION

Hofshröer, P., *Wellington's Smallest Victory* (London: Faber and Faber, 2004).

Low, E.S., *With Napoleon at Waterloo and Other Unpublished Documents of the Waterloo and Peninsula Campaigns*, ed. Mackenzie Macbride (London: Francis Griffiths, 1911).

THE STRATEGIC BACKGROUND

Black, J., *The Battle of Waterloo: A New History* (New York: Random House, 2010).

Black, J., *From Louis XIV to Napoleon: The Fate of a Great Power* (Oxford: Routledge, 1999).

Black, J., *War in the Nineteenth Century: 1800–1914* (Oxford: Polity Press, 2009).

Rothenberg, G.E., *The Art of Warfare in the Age of Napoleon* (Indiana: Indiana University Press, 1978).

de Waresquiel, E., *Cent Jours: la tentation de l'impssible* (Paris: Fayard, 2008).

THE BATTLES OF LIGNY AND QUATRE BRAS

Brett-James, A., *The Hundred Days* (London, 1964).

Chandler, D., *The Campaigns of Napoleon* (London: Weidenfeld and Nicolson, 1966).

Chandler, D. (ed.), *Napoleon's Marshals* (London: Weidenfeld and Nicolson, 1987).

Dawson, A., P. Dawson and S. Summerfield, *Napoleonic Artillery* (Wiltshire: Crowford Press, 2007).

Esposito, V. J. and J. Elting, *A Military History and Atlas of the Napoleonic Wars* (New York: Arms and Armour Press, 1968).

Fuller, J. F. C., *The Decisive Battles of the Western World* (London: Eyre and Spottiswoode, 1955), Vol. II.

Glover, G. (ed.), *The Waterloo Archive* (London: Frontline Books, 2010), Vol. II.

Hamilton-Williams, D., *Waterloo – New Perspectives* (London: Arms and Armour Press, 1993).

Haythornthwaite, P., *Who Was Who in the Napoleonic Wars* (London: Arms and Armour Press, 1998).

Heymes, *Documents Inedites du Duc d'Elchingen* (Paris, 1833).

Hofschröer, P., *Waterloo – Quatre Bras and Ligny* (London: Arms and Armour Press, 2005).

Houssaye, H., *1815: Waterloo* (London, 1900).

Johnstone, R. M. (ed.), *In the Words of Napoleon* (London: Greenhill Books, 2002).

Lawford, J., *Napoleon – The Last Campaigns* (London: Book Club Associates, 1977).

Longford, E., *Wellington – The Years of the Sword* (London: Weidenfeld and Nicolson, 1969).

Mercer, Gen A. C., *Journal of the Waterloo Campaign*, two volumes (London, 1870).

Nosworthy, B., *Battle Tactics of Napoleon and his Enemies* (London: Constable, 1995).

Parkinson, R., *Hussar General* (London: Purnell Book Services, 1975).

Pertz and Delbruck, *Gneisenau* (Berlin, 1864–65).

Roberts, A., *Napoleon and Wellington* (London: Phoenix, 2002).

Ropes, J., *The Campaign of Waterloo, Commentaires de Napoleon 1er* (1910), Vol. V.

Siborne, H. T. (ed.), *The Waterloo Letters* (London: Arms and Armour Press, 1983).

Weston, J., *Historic Doubts as to the Execution of Marshal Ney* (New York, 1895).

THE COMMANDERS

Aubry, O., *Napoleon* (London, 1964).

Barnett, C., *Bonaparte* (London, 1978).

Baily, J. T. H., *Napoleon* (London, 1908).

Becke, A. F., *Napoleon and Waterloo: The Emperor's Campaign with the Armee du Nord* (London, 1914).

Caulaincourt, A. L. L., *Memoirs of General Caulaincourt, Duke of Vicenza*, ed. J. Hanoteau, trans. H. Miles & G. Libaire, three volumes (London 1935–38), Vol. I.

Chandler, D. G., *The Campaigns of Napoleon* (London, 1967).

Collins, I., *Napoleon, First Consul and Emperor of the French* (London, 1986).

Cronin, V., *Napoleon* (London, 1971).

Delbrück, H., *Das Leben des G.F.M. Grafen von Gneisenau* (Berlin, 1894).

Ellesmere, Francis, 1st Earl, *Personal Reminiscences of the Duke of Wellington*, ed. Alice, Countess of Strafford (London, 1904).

Fraser, Sir William Bt, *Words on Wellington: The Duke; Waterloo; The Ball* (London, 1899).

Frazer, Sir Augustus, *Letters of Colonel Sir Augustus Simon Frazer KCB*, ed. Maj Gen E. Sabine (London, 1859)

Gleig, Rev. G. R., *The Life of Arthur, Duke of Wellington* (London, 1865).

Glover, M., *Wellington as Military Commander* (London, 1968).

Gneisnau, A. W. A., *The Life and Campaigns of Field-Marshal Prince Blücher, of Wahlstatt* [sic], trans. J. Marston (London, 1815).

Griffith, P. (ed.), *Wellington Commander: The Iron Duke's Generalship* (Chichester, 1985).

Griffiths, A. J., *The Wellington Memorial* (London, 1897).

Griffiths, Maj A., *Wellington and Waterloo* (London, 1898).

Guedalla, P., *The Duke* (London, 1937) (first published 1931).

Haythornthwaite, P. J., *Wellington: The Iron Duke* (Washington DC, 2007).

Hibbert, C., *Wellington: A Personal History* (London, 1997).

Holmes, R., *Wellington: The Iron Duke* (London, 1997).

Houssaye, H., *1815*, trans. E. A. Mann (London, 1900), Vol. III.

James, L., *The Iron Duke: A Military Biography of Wellington* (London, 1992).

Jones, P. P., *Napoleon: An Intimate Account of the Years of Supremacy 1800–1814* (San Francisco, 1992).

Kennedy, Gen Sir James Shaw, *Notes on the Battle of Waterloo* (London, 1865).

Kincaid, Sir John, *Adventures in the Rifle Brigade in the Peninsula, France and the Netherlands from 1809 to 1815* (London, 1830).

Kincaid, Sir John, *Random Shots from a Rifleman* (London, 1835; repr. in Maclaren's combined edition, London 1908).

Lachouque, H., *The Last Days of Napoleon's Empire*, trans. L. F. Edwards (London, 1966).

Las Cases, E. A. D. M. J., Comte de, *Memoirs of the Life, Exile and Conversations of the Emperor Napoleon* (London, 1836).

Longford, Elizabeth Countess of, *Wellington: The Years of the Sword* (London, 1969).

Mackinnon, D., *Origin and Services of the Coldstream Guards* (London, 1833), Vol. II.

Marshall-Cornwall, Sir James, *Napoleon as Military Commander* (London, 1967).

Maxwell, Sir Herbert, *The Life of Wellington* (London, 1899).

Moore Smith, G. C., *The Life of John Colborne, Field-Marshal Lord Seaton* (London, 1903).

Müffling, P. F. C. F., *Passages from My Life, Together with Memoirs of the Campaign of 1813*, ed. P. J. Yorke (London, 1853).

Pattison, F. H., *Personal Recollections of the Waterloo Campaign* (Glasgow, 1873).

Parkinson, R., *The Hussar General: The Life of Blücher, Man of Waterloo* (London, 1975).

Roberts, A., *Napoleon and Wellington* (London, 2001).

Rosebery, Lord, *Napoleon: The Last Phase* (London, 1900).

Ross-Lewin, H., *With the Thirty-Second in the Peninsular and other Campaigns*, ed. J. Wardell (Dublin & London, 1904).

Schom, A., *Napoleon Bonaparte: A Life* (London, 1997).

Scott, Sir Walter, *Paul's Letters to his Kinsfolk* (Edinburgh, 1816; published anonymously).

Ségur, P. de, *History of the Expedition to Russia Undertaken by the Emperor Napoleon in the Year 1812*, two volumes (London, 1825), Vol. I.

Seeley, Sir John, *A Short History of Napoleon the First* (London, 1895).

Simpson, J., *Paris after Waterloo* (Edinburgh & London, 1853).

Stanhope, Philip Henry, 1st Earl, *Notes of Conversations with the Duke of Wellington, 1831–51* (London, 1888).

Unger, W. von, *Blücher* (Berlin, 1907).

Ward, S. G. P., *Wellington* (London, 1963).

Weller, J., *Wellington at Waterloo* (London, 1967).

Wellington, Arthur, 1st Duke, *The Dispatches of Field Marshal the Duke of Wellington During his Various Campaigns in India, Denmark, Portugal, Spain, the Low Countries and France*, ed. Lt Col J. Gurwood (London, 1834–38).

Wellington, Arthur, 1st Duke, *Supplementary Despatches and Memoranda of Field Marshal Arthur Duke of Wellington KG*, ed. 2nd Duke of Wellington (London 1858–72).

Wheeler, W., *The Letters of Private Wheeler 1809–1828*, ed. B. H. Liddell Hart (London, 1951).

THE BATTLE

Adkin, M., *The Waterloo Companion* (London: Aurum, 2001).

Bowden, S., *Armies at Waterloo* (Arlington USA: Empire Games Press, 1983).

Coignet, Capt. J., *The Note-Books of Captain Coignet* (London: Greenhill Books, 1998).

Crumplin, M., *The Bloody Fields of Waterloo* (Huntingdon: Ken Trotman Publishing, 2013).

Glover, G. (ed.), *The Waterloo Archive* (Barnsley: Frontline Books, 2010), Vol. II.

Haythornthwaite, P., *The Waterloo Armies* (Barnsley: Pen & Sword, 2007).

Lachouque, H., *Waterloo* (London: Arms & Armour, 1972).

Mercer, Gen A. C., *Journal of the Waterloo Campaign* (Barnsley: Pen & Sword, 2012).

Nosworthy, B., *Battle Tactics of Napoleon and his Enemies* (London: Constable, 1995).

WATERLOO EYEWITNESSES

Anglesey, Marquess of, *One-Leg, The Life and Letters of Henry William Paget, First Marquess of Anglesey* (London, 1961).

Anton, J., *Royal Highlander* (Leonaur, 2007).

At Waterloo with the Cameron Highlanders, Napoleonic Archive.

Bro, L., Gen, *Mémoires du général Bro, 1796–1844* (Paris: Librairie des Deux Empires, 2001).

Canler, L., *Mémoires de Canler, ancien chef du service de Sûreté*, tome 1 (Paris, 1882).

Chateaubriand, F.-R. de, *Mémoires d'outre-tombe*, IIIe partie, 1re époque, livre VI, ch.16.

Chevalier, Lt J.-M., *Souvenirs des gueres napoleoniennes* (Paris: Hachette, 1970).

Cotton, E., *A Voice from Waterloo* (London, 1849).

Douglas, J., *Douglas's Tale of the Peninsula & Waterloo, 1808–1815* (London: Leo Cooper, 1997).

Dupuy, V., *Souvenirs militaires, 1794–1816* (Paris: Librairie des Deux Empires, 2001).

Duthilt, P.-C., *Mes campagnes et mes souvenirs* (Paris: Le Livre chez Vous, 2008).

Field, A., *Waterloo, The French Perspective* (Barnsley: Pen & Sword, 2012).

Fleuret, D., *Description des passages de Dominique Fleuret* (Firmin-Didot & Cie, 1929).

Fraser, Alexander, Lt Col, *Waterloo Campaign Letters written by Lieutenant-Colonel Alexander Fraser, Lord Saltoun, 1st Foot Guards, 1815* (Huntingdon: Ken Trotman Publishing, 2010).

Gavin, W., *The Diary of William Gavin, Ensign and Quarter-Master of the 71st Highland Regiment, 1806–1815* (Huntingdon: Ken Trotman Publishing, 2013).

Gibney, *Eighty Years Ago or the Recollections of an Old Army Doctor, by the Late Dr. Gibney* (London: Bellairs & Company, 1896).

Gomm, Field Marshal Sir W., *Letters and Journals of Field-Marshal Sir William Maynard Gomm: From 1799 to Waterloo 1815* (London, 1881).

Gronow, Capt, *Reminiscences of Captain Gronow* (London, 1862).

Guyot, Gen Comte, *Carnets de campagnes, 1792–1815* (Paris: Teissèdre, 1998).

Hibbert, J., *Waterloo Letters: The 1815 Letters of Lieutenant John Hibbert, 1st King's Dragoon Guards* (Huntingdon: Ken Trotman Publishing, 2007).

Hope, J., *The Iberian and Waterloo Campaigns: The Letters of Lt James Hope* (East Sussex: N&M Press, 2000).

Jeremiah, T., *A Short Account of the Life and Adventures of Private Thomas Jeremiah, 23rd or Royal Welch Fusiliers, 1812–1837* (Huntingdon: Ken Trotman Publishing, 2008).

Jolyet, J.-B., 'Souvenirs de 1815', in *La Revue de Paris* (September–October 1903).

Kellermann, F. C., Lt Gen, *Observations sur la bataille de Waterloo*, SHD 1M 719.

Kincaid, Capt J., *Adventures in the Rifle Brigade in the Peninsula, France and the Netherlands from 1809 to 1815* (London, 1830).

Lagneau, L.-V., *Journal d'un chirurgien de la Grande Armée* (Paris: Le Livre chez Vous, 2003).

Larreguy de Civrieux, Sgt Maj L.-M.-S.-P., *Souvenirs d'un cadet* (Paris, 1912).

Lawrence, W., *A Dorset Soldier: The Autobiography of Sgt William Lawrence, 1790–1869* (Stroud: Spellmount, 1993).

Lemonnier-Delafosse, J.-B., *Souvenirs militaires du capitaine Jean-Baptiste Lemonnier-Delafosse* (Paris: Le Livre chez Vous, 2002).

Levavasseur, O., *Souvenirs militaires, 1800–1815* (Paris: Librairie des Deux Empires, 2001).

Lindau, F., *A Waterloo Hero – The Reminiscences of Friedrich Lindau* (Barnsley: Pen & Sword, 2009).

Marbot, Baron, *The Memoirs of Baron de Marbot*, trans. Butler, A. J., Vol. II (Longmans, Green & Co, 1913).

Martin, Lt J.-F., *Souvenirs de guerre du lieutenant Martin, 1812–1815* (Paris: Tallandier, 2007).

Martin, Lt J.-F., 'Waterloo: lettre d'un officier genevois du 45e', in *Carnet de la Sabretache* (1895).

Mauduit, H. de, *Histoire des derniers jours de la Grande Armée* (Paris: Le Livre chez Vous, 2006).

Mercer, Gen A. C., *Journal of the Waterloo Campaign*, two volumes (London, 1870), Vol. 1.

Morris, T., *The Napoleonic Wars* (London: Longmans, 1967).

Naylor, Capt J., *The Waterloo Diary of Captain James Naylor, 1st (King's) Dragoon Guards, 1815–1816* (Huntingdon: Ken Trotman Publishing, 2008).

Petiet, Gen A., *Mémoires du général Auguste Petiet, hussard de l'Empire* (Paris, 1996).

Playford, T., *The Memoirs of Sergeant-Major Thomas Playford, 2nd Lifeguards, 1810–1830* (Huntingdon: Ken Trotman Publishing, 2006).

Pontécoulant, P.-G. Le D. de, *Napoléon à Waterloo, 1815* (repr. Paris: Librairie des Deux Empires, 2004).

Robinaux, Capt P., *Journal de route du capitaine Robinaux* (Paris: Librairie des Deux Empires, 2009).

SHD 1M 719: *Note sur la charge de la division Lhéritier, épisode de la bataille de Waterloo, sans nom d'auteur.*

Siborne, Maj Gen H. T. (ed.), *Waterloo Letters* (London: Greenhill Books, 1993).

Simmons, Lt, *Lieutenant Simmons of the 95th (Rifles): Recollections of the Peninsula, South of France & Waterloo Campaigns of the Napoleonic Wars* (Leonaur, 2007).

Sperling, J., *The Letters of First Lieutenant John Sperling, Royal Engineers* (Huntingdon: Ken Trotman Publishing, 2012).

Stanhope, J., *Eyewitness to the Peninsular War and the Battle of Waterloo: The Letters and Journals of Lieutenant Colonel the Honourable James Stanhope, 1803 to 1825* (Barnsley: Pen & Sword, 2010).

Tomkinson, W., *With Wellington's Light Cavalry* (Leonaur, 2006).

Trefcon, Col, *Carnet de campagne (1793–1815)* (Paris: Librairie des Deux Empires, 2003).

Wheatley, E., (ed. Hibbert, C.), *The Wheatley Diary* (London: Longmans, 1964).

Wheeler, W., *The Letters of Private Wheeler, 1809–1828* (The Windrush Press, 1994).

Wylly, Col H. C., *The Military Memoirs of Lieutenant-General Sir Joseph Thackwell* (London, 1908).

HOUGOUMONT AND LA HAYE SAINTE

Adkin, M., *The Waterloo Companion* (London, 2001).

Barbero, A., *The Battle: A New History of the Battle of Waterloo*, trans. Cullen, J. (London, 2006).

Bassford, C., D. Moran and G. W. Pedlow, *On Waterloo, Clausewitz, Wellington and the Campaign of 1815* (USA, self published, 2010).

Batty, R., *A Historical Sketch of the Campaign of 1815* (London, 1820).

Black, J., *Waterloo: The Battle that Brought Down Napoleon* (London, 2010).

Chandler, D., *The Campaigns of Napoleon* (London, 1966).

Chandler, D., *The Military Maxims of Napoleon* (London, 2002).

Cotton, E., *A Voice from Waterloo* (Mont Saint Jean, 1900).

Davies, H., *Wellington's Wars: The Making of a Military Genius* (London, 2012).

Field, A., *Waterloo: The French Perspective* (Barnsley, 2012).

Fletcher, I., *A Desperate Business: Wellington, the British Army and the Waterloo Campaign* (Stroud, 2001).

Fortescue, J., *A History of the British Army 1645–1870*, 20 volumes (London, 1899–1930).

Girod de l'Ain, M., *Vie Militaire de Général Foy* (Paris, 1900).

Glover, G. (ed.), *Letters from the Battle of Waterloo – Unpublished Correspondence by Allied Officers from the Siborne Papers* (London, 2004).

Howarth, D., *A Near Run Thing* (London, 1968).

Jomini, A., *The Art of War* (London, 1992, from original published in 1838).

Keegan, J., *The Face of Battle* (London, 1976).

Kennedy, Sir J. Shaw, *Notes on the Battle of Waterloo* (London, 1865).

Kincaid, Capt J., *Adventures in the Rifle Brigade in the Peninsula, France and the Netherlands from 1809 to 1815* (London, 1830).

Lipscombe, Col N. J., *Wellington's Guns* (Oxford, 2013).

Longford, E., *Wellington* (London, 1969).

Ludlow Beamish, N., *History of the King's German Legion*, two volumes (London, 1832–37).

Mercer, Gen A. C., *Journal of the Waterloo Campaign*, two volumes (London, 1870).

Moore Smith, G. C., *The Life of John Colborne, Field Marshal Lord Seaton* (London, 1903).

Nosworthy, B., *With Musket, Cannon and Sword: Battle Tactics of Napoleon and His Enemies* (New York, 1996).

Paget, J., and Saunders, D., *Hougoumont: The Key to Victory at Waterloo* (London, 1992).

Roberts, A., *Waterloo: Napoleon's Last Gamble* (London, 2005).

Sabine, E. (ed.), *Letters of Colonel Sir Augustus Simon Frazer, KCB, Commanding the Horse Artillery in the Army under the Duke of Wellington* (London, 1859).

Schwertfeger, B., *Geschichte Der Königlich Deutschen Legion, 1803–1816*, two volumes (Hannover and Leipzig, 1907).

Shrapnel, Maj Gen H., The Shrapnel Papers 1761–1842, MD 871.

Siborne, H. J., *The Waterloo Letters* (East Yorkshire, 2009 reprint).

Siborne, W., *The Waterloo Campaign*, third edition (London, 1848).

Thiers, M. A., *Histoire du Consulat et de L'Empire*, 20 volumes (Paris, 1862).

Weller, J., *Wellington at Waterloo* (London, 1967).

Wellington, Arthur Wellesley, *The Dispatches of Field Marshal the Duke of Wellington During His Various Campaigns in India, Denmark, Portugal, Spain, the Low Countries, and France*, ed. Lt Col J. Gurwood, eight volumes (London, 1844–47).

Wotton, G., *Waterloo 1815* (Oxford, 1992).

THE CAVALRY CHARGES

Anglesey, Marquess of, *One-Leg: The Life and Letters of Henry William Paget, First Marquess of Anglesey* (London: Jonathon Cape, 1961).

Fletcher, I., *Galloping at Everything: The British Cavalry in the Peninsular War and at Waterloo, 1808–1815* (Staplehurst: Spellmount Publishers, 1999).

Fletcher, I., *The Peninsular War – Wellington's Battlefields Revisited* (Barnsley: Pen and Sword, 2011).

Mann, Rev. Michael, *And They Rode On* (London: Michael Russell Publishing Ltd, 1984).

Siborne, H. T., *Waterloo Letters* (London: Cassel and Co., 1891).

The Prussian Army at Waterloo

Alison, A., *History of Europe from the Commencement of the French Revolution to the Restoration of the Bourbons in MDCCCXV*, 19 volumes (London, 1860) Vol. XIV.

Bassford, C., *et al* (eds), *On Waterloo: Clausewitz, Wellington and the Campaign of 1815* (New York, 2010).

Black, J., *The Battle of Waterloo: A New History* (New York, 2010).

Bonaparte, N., *The Waterloo Campaign*, ed. S. de Chair (London, 1957).

Chalfont, Lord (ed.), *Waterloo: Battle of the Three Armies* (London, 1979).

Chandler, D. G., *Waterloo: The Hundred Days* (Botley, 1980).

Chesney, C., *Waterloo Lectures*, ed. P. Hofschröer (London, 1997).

Cotton, E., *A Voice from Waterloo: A History of the Battle on the 18th June 1815*, third edition (London, 1849).

Creasy, E., *The Fifteen Decisive Battles of the World* (London, 1859).

Field, A., *Waterloo: The French Perspective* (Barnsley, 2012).

Gneisenau, A. Neithardt von, *The Life and Campaigns of Field-Marshal Prince Blücher* (London, 1815).

Henderson, E. F., *Blücher and the Uprising of Prussia against Napoleon, 1806–1815* (New York, 1815).

Hofschröer, P., *1815: The Waterloo Campaign – the Duke of Wellington, His German Allies and the Battles of Ligny and Quatre Bras* (London, 1998).

Hofschröer, P., *1815: The Waterloo Campaign – The German Victory* (London, 1999).

Hofschröer, P., *The Prussian Army of the Lower Rhine, 1815* (Oxford, 2014).

Hofschröer, P., *Prussian Napoleonic Tactics, 1792–1815* (Oxford, 2011).

Hofschröer, P., *Waterloo, 1815: Wavre, Plancenoit and the Race to Paris* (Barnsley, 2006).

Hofschröer, P., *Wellington's Smallest Victory: The Duke, the Model-Maker and the Secret of Waterloo* (London, 2004).

Howarth, D., *A Near Run Thing: the Day of Waterloo* (London, 1968).

Mercer, Gen A. C., *Journal of the Waterloo Campaign* (London, 1927).

Müffling, C. von, *Passages from My Life, Together with Memoirs of the Campaign of 1813 and 1814* (London, 1853).

Parkinson, R., *The Hussar General: The Life of Blücher, Man of Waterloo* (London, 1975).

Roberts, A., *Napoleon's Last Gamble* (London, 2005).

Schmidt, O., 'The Prussian Army' in Fremont-Barnes, G. (ed.), *Armies of the Napoleonic Wars* (Barnsley, 2011).

Shanahan, W., *Prussian Military Reforms, 1786–1813* (New York, 1945).

Uffindell, A., *The Eagle's Last Triumph: Napoleon's Victory at Ligny, June 1815* (London, 1994).

Uffindell, A., and Corum, M., *On the Fields of Glory: The Battlefields of the Waterloo Campaign* (London, 1996).

La Garde Recule!

Anon., 'On a part of Captain Siborne's History of the Waterloo Campaign, By an Officer of the British 5th Brigade', in the *United Service Journal* (March 1845).

Anon., 'The Crisis of Waterloo, By a Soldier of the Fifth Brigade', *Colburn's United Service Magazine* (formally *United Service Journal*) (1852), Part II.

Cahier No. 15, Association Belge Napoleonienne. This magazine contains the accounts of the officers of the Imperial Guard that had originally been published in *Carnet de la Sabretache*, 1905.

Coppens, B. and P. Courcelle, *Waterloo 1815. Les Carnets de la Campagne* (Brussels: Tondeur Diffusion, 1999–2011), No. 4.

François, Hue, *Jean-Louis de Crabbé, Colonel d'Empire* (Nantes: Editions du Canonnier, 2006).

Franklin, J., *Waterloo. Netherlands Correspondence* (Dorchester: Henry Ling, 2010).

Gawler, Maj G. in the *United Service Journal* (September 1833). This was Gawler's reply to General Vivian's response to his article 'The Crisis and Close of the Action at Waterloo by an Eye-witness'.

Gawler, Maj G., 'The Crisis and Close of the Action at Waterloo by an Eye-witness', in the *United Service Journal* (July 1833).

Glover, G. (ed.), *Letters from the Battle of Waterloo, Unpublished Correspondence by Allied Officers from the Siborne Papers* (London: Greenhill Books, 2004).

Houssaye, H., *La Garde meurt et ne se rend pas, Histoire d'un mot historique* (Paris: Perrin, 1907).

Kennedy, Gen Sir J. Shaw, *Notes on the Battle of Waterloo* (London: John Murray, 1865).

Le Boterf, H., *Le brave Général Cambronne* (Paris: Editions France Empire, 1984).

Leeke, W., *The History of Lord Seaton's Regiment at the Battle of Waterloo* (London: Hatchard and Co., 1866).

Levavasseur, O., *Souvenirs Militaires d'Octave Levavasseur, officier d'artillerie aide de camp du maréchal Ney (1802–1815)* (Paris: Plon, 1914).

Lot, H., *Les Deux Généraux Ordener* (Paris: Roger et Chernoviz, 1910).

Martin, Lt J.-F., *Souvenirs d'un ex-officier, 1812–1815* (Paris & Geneva: J. Cherbuliez, 1867).

Mauduit, de, H., *Histoire des derniers jours de la Grande Armée* (Paris: Dion-Lambert, 1854).

Napoleon, *Napoleon's Memoirs*, ed. Somerset de Chair (London: Soho Books, 1986).

Petit, Gen Baron J-M., *English Historical Review*, Vol. 18, April 1903.

Pontécoulant, P-G. Le D. de, *Napoléon à Waterloo 1815* (repr. Paris: Librairie des Deux Empires, 2004).

Robinaux, Capt P., *Journal de Route du Capitaine Robinaux* (Paris: 1908).

Siborne, H.T. (ed.), *The Waterloo Letters* (repr. London: Arms and Armour Press, 1983).

'What the Gordons did at Waterloo, From the Forgotten Diary of Sergeant D. Robertson', in *With Napoleon at Waterloo and Other Unpublished Documents of the Waterloo and Peninsular Campaigns* (London: Mackensie Macbride, 1911).

THE LEGACY OF WATERLOO

Baugh, D., 'Great Britain's Blue-Water Policy, 1689–1815,' in *International History Review*, 10 (February 1988), pp. 33–58.

Bew, J., *Castlereagh* (London: Quercus, 2011).

Bonaparte, N., *The Confidential Correspondence of Napoleon Bonaparte with his Brother Joseph, sometime king of Spain*, two volumes (New York, 1856).

Chandler, D., *Waterloo: The Hundred Days* (London: Osprey, 1980).

Cotton, E., *A Voice from Waterloo: A History of the Battle Fought on the 18th June 1815* (London: Forgotten Books, 2009).

Davies, H. J., *Wellington's Wars: The Making of a Military Genius* (London: Yale University Press, 2012).

Esdaile, C., *Napoleon's Wars: An International History* (London: Allen Lane, 2008).

Fortescue, J., *A History of the British Army* (London, 1920).

Gurwood J. (ed.), *The Dispatches of Field Marshal the Duke of Wellington During His Various Campaigns in India, Denmark, Portugal, Spain, the Low Countries and France*, 13 volumes (London, 1852).

Hall, C., *Wellington's Navy: Seapower and the Peninsular War, 1807–1814* (London: Chatham Publishing, 2004).

Holbraad, C., *The Concert of Europe: A Study in German and British International Theory, 1815–1914* (London: Barnes & Noble, 1970).

Knight, R., *Britain Against Napoleon: The Organisation of Victory, 1793–1815* (London: Allen Lane, 2013).

Lambert, A., *The Crimean War: British Grand Strategy Against Russia, 1853–56* (Manchester: Manchester University Press, 1990).

Lambert, Andrew, 'Seapower, Strategy and the Scheldt: British Strategy, 1793–1914', unpublished paper presented at 'Waterloo: The Battle that Forged a Century', Conference, London, September 2013.

Mazower, M., *Governing the World: The History of an Idea* (London: Allen Lane, 2012).

Munch-Petersen, T., *Defying Napoleon: How Britain Bombarded Copenhagen and Seized the Danish Fleet in 1807* (London: The History Press, 2007).

Schroeder, P. W., *Austria, Great Britain, and the Crimean War: The Destruction of the European Concert* (London: Cornell University Press, 1972).

Schroeder, P. W., *The Transformation of European Politics, 1763–1848* (Oxford: Oxford University Press, 1994).

Simms, B., *Three Victories and a Defeat: The Rise and Fall of the First British Empire, 1714–1783* (London: Allen Lane, 2008).

Stewart, Robert, 2nd Marquess of Londonderry, *The Memoranda and Correspondence of Robert Stewart, Viscount Castlereagh*, 12 volumes (London, 1848–54).

Strachan, H., *From Waterloo to Balaclava: Tactics, Technology, and the British Army, 1815–1854* (Cambridge: Cambridge University Press, 1985).

Strachan, H., *Wellington's Legacy: The Reform of the British Army 1830–54* (Manchester: Manchester University Press, 1984).

Sweetman, J., *Crimean War* (Oxford: Osprey, 2001).

Webster C. K. (ed.), *British Diplomacy, 1813–1815* (London, 1921).

Webster, C., *The Foreign Policy of Castlereagh, 1812–1815: Britain and the Reconstruction of Europe* (London: G. Bell, 1950).

Wellesley, A., 2nd Duke of Wellington (ed.), *Supplementary Despatches and Memoranda of Field Marshal Arthur the Duke of Wellington, 1797–1818*, 14 volumes (London, 1858).

Yapp, M., *Strategies of British India: Britain, Iran and Afghanistan, 1798–1850* (Oxford: Oxford University Press, 1981).

INDEX

In 1973 the Duke of Wellington founded The Waterloo Committee following a successful joint effort with Lord Anglesey to stop the building of a motorway across the battlefield in Belgium. Since then, the Waterloo Committee has continued to preserve and enhance the battlefield, encourage historical research and promote public education and appreciation of the history of the wars between Great Britain, her allies, and France. 'Waterloo 200' was established in 2005, under the Waterloo Committee umbrella, and supported by Her Majesty's Government to oversee the commemoration of the bicentenary of the Battle of Waterloo.

First published in Great Britain in 2014 by Osprey Publishing,
PO Box 883, Oxford, OX1 9PL, UK
PO Box 3985, New York, NY 10185-3985, USA
E-mail: info@ospreypublishing.com
Osprey Publishing is part of the Osprey Group

A CIP catalogue record for this book is available from the British Library

Mark Adkin, Jeremy Black, Huw Davies, Charles Esdaile, Andrew Field, Ian Fletcher, Philip Haythornthwaite, Natalia Griffon de Pleineville, Nick Lipscombe, Peter Snow and Julian Spilsbury have asserted their rights under the Copyright, Designs and Patents Act, 1988, to be identified as the Authors of this Work.

ISBN: 978 1 4728 0104 3
e-book ISBN: 978 1 4728 1047 2
PDF ISBN: 978 1 4728 1046 5

Page layouts by Myriam Bell Design, UK
Index by Sandra Shotter
Cartography by Boundford
Typeset in Bembo
Originated by PDQ Media, Bungay, UK
Printed in China through Worldprint Ltd.

14 15 16 17 18   10 9 8 7 6 5 4 3 2 1

Front cover: French cavalry charge a square during the Battle of Waterloo. (akg-images); Page 6: Napoleon in the midst of battle. (Anne S. K. Brown); Page 10: The Prince of Orange wounded in battle. (Anne S. K. Brown)

The following will help in converting measurements between metric and imperial:
1 mile = 1.6km
1 yard = 0.9m
1ft = 0.3m
1in = 15.4mm
1lb = 0.45kg

www.ospreypublishing.com

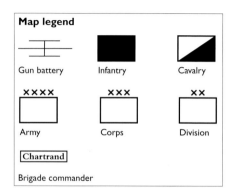

Map legend

Gun battery	Infantry	Cavalry
Army	Corps	Division

Chartrand

Brigade commander